THE MERTON ANNUAL

Studies in Culture, Spirituality, and Social Concerns

Volume 19   2006

Edited by

Victor A. Kramer

Merton
271.2
M575m
v. 19

Guest Editor for Selected 2005
International Thomas Merton Society Papers

David Belcastro

Book Reviews Coordinated by

Glenn Crider

The Continuing Tradition of Prayer and Continuing Social Awareness Sustain the Vision of Thomas Merton

Victor A. Kramer

I

We are pleased to include scholarly articles in this volume of *The Merton Annual* which have developed from presentations given at the San Diego General Meeting of the International Thomas Merton Society. Two pieces from that meeting are plenary addresses by priests who were clearly influenced by Merton. They establish a tone which rings well in our ears and hearts as we continue to assimilate the wisdom of the monastic tradition which reminds all of solitude, and paradoxically also calls us to testify as concerned for others throughout the world. We are one family.

The two addresses which were given by Dom John Eudes Bamberger, O.C.S.O. and by John Dear, S. J. might seem to stand at opposing poles of some theoretical range of possibilities. These men are quite different in age, background and presentation. Yet in fact, both overlapped in their definitions of concerns about the manifestation of the love of Christ for all. Both of their talks interpret Merton's sustained work as prophetic and in each we see clear examples of the continuing work of Thomas Merton infusing today's Christian consciousness. We are pleased to include these two addresses along with a short introductory commentary by Dewey W. Kramer, one of the founders of The International Thomas Merton Society. Her comments focus on the nature of the meeting in San Diego in 2005 and also clearly emphasize Merton's continuing importance. These talks set the tone for the San Diego Meeting. Other principal speakers, Sister Jose Hobday and Jim Wallis, along with Rabbi Michael Lerner, extended similar themes. All those speeches challenged us to see that Merton (as monk, as contemplative, and as writer) was no recluse. Both of the pieces by Abbot John Eudes Bamberger and John Dear wake us up. In her introductory note, Dewey Kramer places the two addresses by Bamberger and Dear in the context of the San Diego meeting with its emphasis upon our social awareness.

II

In the following section, including ten scholarly articles edited by Professor David Belcastro, we observe even more influence and usefulness. David Belcastro, as the subsection editor for the articles which have developed from oral presentations, provides a rationale for the selection and arrangement of these papers along with his focused comments. Truly we can see Merton's vision is being furthered. It is a vision both traditional and revolutionary. We see the same patterns in the remembrances written about John Wu who became Merton's good friend.

When I look at the many pieces which feed into this volume which have come out of the General Meeting of the International Thomas Merton Society in San Diego, it brings back both good memories of that meeting and of the many persons I met there—many of whom made presentations, submitted them as revised essays and then revised these papers for this book. Still others who have attended many of the ITMS meetings were there simply to learn and to celebrate.

The ten carefully expanded essays which have developed from the presentations at the ITMS San Diego Meeting open up many possibilities for renewed thinking about Merton. Being grounded in a "Spirit of Simplicity," as the essay by Dekar reminds us, led Merton rather naturally to the engagement of his Cold War Letters. Developing the habit of raising questions while still an undergraduate, this continuing mode of inquiry by Merton is affirmed in the two essays by Harford and Herron. Confronting how one is to be engaged in the contemporary world, yet remaining grounded in tradition, the essays by Hunter and Miller demonstrate that Merton's engagement always remained rooted in Truth. The good of society remains at the base of Merton's impulses, whether he is writing about peace and war or about non-violence. We are thankful to be able to include these essays which examine the myriad aspects of Merton's conscience as it is overflowing into our consciousness of the present moment. War, Hatred, Ecological Awareness, as examined in these essays, are subjects grounded in a continual seeking of God.

Similarly, in the interview which Glenn Crider has conducted with James Finley, we see still further immediate contemplative connections with Merton and contemporary society. I was privileged to meet Jim Finley first at a Conference about Merton as Contemplative held in Atlanta in 1980. That day, February 28, 1980, sparked many subsequent events—further conferences, papers, the establishment of two reading groups (one "Catholic" yet ecumenical, the other "Episcopalian" and socially engaged) as well as a meditation group. Also at that same conference of 1980, when Jim Finley spoke of his friendship with Merton, another one of the speakers was Fr. Tom Fidelis (Francis) Smith. Fr. Tom Francis, now the Retreat Master at Conyers Cistercian Monastery of the Holy Spirit, a daughter house of Gethsemani, has provided us with some commentary about a letter which Merton wrote to him in 1963 when Fr. Smith inquired about prayer. Smith's annotations, provided decades later, also stand as more proof of the continuing influence and usefulness of Merton. Somehow Merton cultivated a gift for suggesting connections both with the traditions of the past while prophetically suggesting how these very connections could lead into the future.

In 1980 Jim Finley spoke at the Atlanta conference which I had organized. That meeting was held at Georgia State University and called "Contemplation for Urban Man." Michael Mott, then a faculty member at Emory University, was there, along with Sister Elena Malits, C.S.C. of St. Mary's, Notre Dame. That conference has in its influences radiated outward to men, women, Catholics, Protestants and non-believers. We must assume that this has been the pattern over and over as more connections are made by scholars who recognize Merton's prescient abilities and it will continue to be the pattern.

Daniel Adams, another of this volume's contributors, spent a semester at Columbia [Presbyterian] Theological Seminary in Decatur, Georgia, but I was unable to meet him during that time. He is the author of a valuable Cistercian Publications book about Merton and the Protestant tradition. Now while I have still not met him, he is serving as a theology professor in Korea. Adams has provided us with a study of Merton and a Korean visionary who in terms of *Zeitgeist* see in similar ways. What we are again reminded of by Adams is that Merton will not be kept in conventional boxes of classification.

In the revised lecture included here by Robert Ellsberg, one of the Annual Thomas Merton Corpus Christi Memorial Lectures, at the church of Merton's Baptism, we see the direct influence which both Henri Nouwen and Merton have had upon the thinking of Mr. Ellsberg, a prominent Catholic Publishing House editor. He is someone who cherishes that influence. He also is someone who makes his daily work part of the tradition to which these two writers adhered.

Still other parts of this volume reflect Merton's importance world-wide in other ways. This is most apparent throughout all of the varied book reviews which we have included. His seeds so carefully planted truly make us aware that, as John Eudes Bamberger has written, Merton is a "prophet of renewal." In John Eudes Bamberger's recently published book about Merton and monastic renewal we see the distilled wisdom of Abbot John Eudes' wisdom of years of observation and prayer. Above all, in Bamberger's study we must be reminded that no monastic, no spiritual seeker, no prayerful person can ever function well abstractly.

John Eudes Bamberger's *Thomas Merton: Prophet of Renewal*[1] is a work of wisdom which delineates the articulation of the gifts of prophecy which Merton perfected in his sustained vocation, a life of prayer and writing. Bamberger is adamant about the importance of the breadth of Merton's study from Cassian and Augustine to Eastern writers like Chaung Tzu, whom he translated, along with the early Cistercians St. Bernard of Clairvaux and Aelred of Rievaulx, all of whom prepared Merton to articulate words for the significance of the contemplative essence not in the abstract, or as limited to the life of a cloistered monk, but rather as a fundamental ingredient already in all lives often so covered up by the multitudinous activities which so many individuals are compelled to take on within contemporary society.

Merton's study brought him to a simplicity of wonder, expressed in myriads of ways (in journal, poetry, essay, correspondence) which is both Catholic, rooted in the resurrection of Christ— the eschatology of his living presence, and a gift also mysteriously open to other ways of preparation (through Taoism or Buddhism). For the gift of wholeness which the Creator has already miraculously given is given to all.

When we see this fact, as Bamberger does so well, suddenly we see that Merton's powerful insights about our need to live in the knowledge of the love of the merciful Creator leaps into our consciousness and demands a turning toward compassion. Many persons who already subsist easily in God's mercy—individually or in corporate reactions—can forget their inherent appreciation of and need for the contemplative. They need this simple message. So many of the pages included here confirm such insights.

Always each of us deals with persons—and with persons in and of particular places. This is a key, the simplest key to the balance of life so frequently stressed within the Benedictine Tradition. This is also the key to the enduring success of the vision of Merton who building in the Benedictine manner of obedience and stability created a vision which goes beyond the cloister to embrace all open thinkers and seekers—Christian, secular, hopeful—all concerned about the world.

III

Once more I must thank all who have made this particular book a reality. David Belcastro is to be especially thanked for his steadfast contributions in helping select and edit the scholarly papers which make up The International Thomas Merton Society subsection. Many others have done considerable work to bring this ITMS-sponsored volume to fruition. We thank John Wu for his "vignettes" which fit so well within this context. Again, I am appreciative of the work which Glenn Crider as Production Manager has done consistently and well. He has this year also assumed responsibility not just for production, but also for doing the interview included here, as well as assuming the primary load of coordinating the book reviews.

We do not provide a stipend either for our contributors for their essays or to our book reviewers. These persons do what they do as a "labor of love." We especially thank them, as we also thank the Officers and Board Members of ITMS who have now officially endorsed the value of *The Merton Annual* and now support this publication as an ITMS project. I also thank Gray Matthews of the University of Memphis, Department of Communications, who has written this year's Bibliographic Survey. This job used to rotate among *The Merton Annual* editors. During the past years it has become the rotating responsibility of different ITMS members.

Our Board of editor members doing their work as referees; ITMS officers and Board Members; Patrick F. O'Connell (the editor of *The Merton Seasonal* assisting us with suggestions); and still others including the publisher Gray Henry, along with the continuing support of The Merton Legacy Trust, represented by Anne McCormick, have all contributed to the formation and success of this book. It is truly a community effort of *ora et labora*.

Notes

1. John Eudes Bamberger, *Thomas Merton: Prophet of Renewal* (Collegeville: Liturgical Press, 2005).

To Father Thomas Fidelis (Francis) Smith, O.C.S.O.*

Thomas Merton

June 29, 1963

Probably you are overdoing the Jesus Prayer a bit. I think it is all very well for a hard-headed nineteenth-century Russian monk to do that all day and all night, but it is not going to work for Americans today. And in any case, remember that you are adding this to an already rather heavy schedule. Our life as it stands is pretty overloaded with "means."

Personally I like the *Way of the Pilgrim* and it is a good stimulating book to read. The ideas are good, but we have to apply them to ourselves with due concern for our own situation. It seems to me that it is expecting too much to try to make our whole life center itself in the Jesus Prayer. And it is not necessary. I think that this repetition of the prayer is useful at certain times. I have recourse to it when I am plagued with distractions or half dead with sleep and can't do anything better. As for the breathing, I would get some idea of some good Yoga breathing, as described in a reliable book like Dechanet's *Christian Yoga*, and use that *sometimes*. But for the rest, the light of the Lord shines in our hearts always and all we need to do is to remind ourselves of it in the simplest possible way, and surrender to Him totally. If a simple ejaculation helps, well and good. Words do not always help. Just looking is often more helpful.

As to the inner warmth around the heart, as a result of pushing the prayer, don't fool with this. This is one of the misleading and risky aspects of Oriental prayer (see Simeon the New Theologian, who is off on this in many ways).

I think that reading some of the great Protestant O.T. theologians would help your prayer. Von Rad, for instance (without getting too stuck on his special axe-grinding), or Eichrodt. Any-

*Father Thomas Francis Smith is a monk of the Holy Spirit Monastery at Conyers, Georgia, who expressed an interest in the Jesus Prayer of the Eastern Church.

13

way, I'll send a paper I did based on some of this material and you can see what I mean, and evaluate it for yourself. I am no Scripture scholar.

It seems to me that the Bible is a much better source of light than the Jesus Prayer. But all sources fail, except God himself. And He is after all the most accessible. We get tired of means once in a while, and that is perhaps because we are nearer to the end than we realize.

It seems to me that we create obstacles for ourselves by setting up arbitrary division, "intellectual life" and "life of prayer." Each of us has to find the unity in which everything fits and takes its right place. For some, a certain amount of intellectual life is necessary for the life of prayer. Each must work out just what the right measure may be. And it varies, at different times of our life. The best thing is to acquire that discretion by which we can tell when to do what needs to be done, even though it does not seemingly fit in to some ideal plan of monastic spirituality. There are moments when all plans are useless. So while we cannot rely on them, we learn to rely more directly on God himself, Who cannot fail us …

The Context of Thomas Merton's Letter Concerning "The Jesus Prayer"*

Thomas Francis Smith

In the spring of 1963, with the first session of Vatican II completed, but not yet having sent shock waves through the Catholic Church regarding liturgy, morality, doctrine, and many other aspects of Church life, I myself was in a period of stagnation with regard to my spiritual life. At that time, Cistercian monks already had a full spiritual program. As a Trappist monk we had several hours a day of the Divine Office, all recited in Latin, while urged to supplement that with spiritual reading, meditation, the rosary and Stations of the Cross. I allowed myself to read J.D. Salinger's novel, *Franny and Zooey*, and while enjoying it very much, became introduced to this Russian form of prayer, called "The Jesus Prayer." The author mentions that it comes from the book, *The Way of the*

*Editor's Note:

June 29, 1963, Letter of Thomas Merton: Continuing Insight into Contemporary Spirituality.

Chosen for inclusion in Volume Three of Merton's Selected Letters, *The School of Charity*, this letter by Merton to Father Thomas Fidelis (Francis) Smith, O.C.S.O. is included as an "obscure" Merton publication for this volume. It is an answer to a specific inquiry about usage of the "Jesus Prayer" yet reveals Merton's wide-ranging interests in prayer.

Fr. Thomas, Retreat Master at Our Lady of the Holy Spirit in Conyers, GA, is an example of a fellow monk of Merton's generation who has both profited from exposure to Merton's writing and example and who also stands today as an excellent example of a Cistercian monk, like Merton, who has remained open to a wide variety of spiritual practices. Fr. Thomas already spoke about Centering Prayer and *lectio* at an Atlanta Merton Conference on February 28, 1980. He has long been an enthusiastic commentator on subjects as diverse as the contemporary Church, the importance of angels, Eastern religious practices, the Holy Trinity, as well as yoga as a spiritual discipline. His retrospective words place Merton's reply in context both to 1963 and as well in terms of the continuing evolution of spiritual practices in the contemporary world by a Cistercian monk.

Pilgrim. So after finishing the novel, I went to the library and signed out that book.

Immediately I became fascinated with this new method of prayer, and adopted it to my already overloaded schedule of vocal and liturgical prayer. This kind of prayer, however, grew on me, and so I started to decrease in the other areas and spent more time on the constant repetition of this prayer: "Lord, Jesus Christ, Son of God, have mercy on me the sinner," saying it several thousand times a day. I was even saying it unconsciously while listening to public readings and while milking cows! Eventually I got to feeling a warmth about my heart, and at night the prayer came on. I mentioned all of this to my confessor, and he suggested I write to Thomas Merton for his advice.

Since I was a bit scared of becoming either a mystic or maniac, I took his advice and wrote Fr. Louis (Merton). His reply came shortly afterwards, and I must admit, it was not what I was wanting to hear. I ignored his advice and continued in my imitation of the prayer of the Pilgrim. But within a few weeks, I felt the tension developing, and slowly cut back on the method and repetition, till after a few weeks, I dropped it completely.

I have never regretted this "Jesus Prayer" period because it was actually a prelude to a more contemplative type of prayer I soon learned from reading *The Cloud of Unknowing.* But I do suggest to persons who ask me about the "Jesus Prayer" to try the prayer as described by *The Way of the Pilgrim.* I do tell them, however, to be cautious within and repeat to them the sound advice about flexibility that Thomas Merton gave to me in his letter.

Thomas Francis Smith, O.C.S.O.

Complementary Approaches Illuminate Merton's Continuing Relevance for Today's Broken World

Dewey Weiss Kramer

The 2005 General Meeting of the International Thomas Merton Society in San Diego at the University of San Diego was excellently planned by President Erlinda Paguio and her Program Committee chaired by Jonathan Montaldo. The range of speakers, both for the plenary addresses and the invited contributions through proposals, was impressive. There were many stimulating addresses by prominent speakers including persons of other faiths, for example, Rabbi Michael Lerner and Editor Jim Wallis of *Sojourners*. These talks suggest the continuing importance of Merton's work for today's society.

The interaction of all the planned ingredients for this meeting which worked so well to make the program memorable seem, in retrospect, to be held in place by the two most prominent Catholic speakers who were invited to this meeting. Both of these speakers emphasized Merton's contributions to today's society as something always grounded in his consistent and prayerful contemplative stance. In the quite different addresses given by Fr. John Dear, S. J. and John Eudes Bamberger, O.C.S.O. we were reminded that no contemplative ever acts to avoid connections with society, but rather through a balance of prayer and action the contemplative always keeps the wider society's needs in a certain focus.

We were graced to have these two speakers help establish the tone for a meeting which has stimulated our thinking about the continuing contribution of Merton and his Cistercian charism. All this continues to be breathed into our society so full of a need to be grounded in the selflessness of the Holy Spirit.

Thomas Merton, Monk and Prophet of Peace: The Opening Address at the 2005 International Thomas Merton Society General Meeting

John Eudes Bamberger

My Brothers and Sisters,

If I have been invited to address you as we open this meeting it is due chiefly to the fact that I knew Thomas Merton the way a brother comes to know a brother by living the same way of life, sharing similar moral and spiritual values together in the same community. I have no other qualifying credentials or competence that might entitle me to speak to you on Peace and Non-violence in a world where, on the political level, the issues involved have become more intricate and so requiring a more ample information and insight than did the period of the cold war when Merton wrote. Accordingly, I offer these words as the limited contribution of one man's personal experience and reflections. They have been formed in good part under the influence of Merton's teaching and colored by memories of our shared experiences in the monastery during the last eighteen years of his life. Hopefully, they might usefully serve as a background for the subsequent discussions of a more technical nature.

I

Thomas Merton was a prophetic voice for his times. He spoke of God and of the spiritual life to large numbers of people with a fresh voice. In the words of Samuel Johnson, "he employed wit on the side of virtue and religion." At one point in the course of his writings on peace, he mentioned that he made no claim to be a prophet. Later, as he accepted the Pax Medal, he modestly commented that if he said beforehand what Pope John XXIII taught in his groundbreaking Encyclical *Pacem in Terris*, "that still does not make me terribly original, because these same things were said long ago by Popes and ... Fathers of the Church."[1]

However, from my first contact with Merton's writings, I viewed him as a prophetic voice for our times. In fact, I believe that Merton himself, already before he entered the monastery, was convinced he had a special gift to speak in God's name to his age. That is what accounts for his beginning to write an autobiography already at the age of twenty four, shortly after his conversion. This conviction led him to break with a tradition of centuries and to overcome the initial resistance of his superiors, by publishing a journal, *The Sign of Jonas*, about his day-to-day experiences and reflections as a Trappist monk not long after publication of his life story.

He continues to speak to us today in circumstances that, in many respects, are marked by the issues he identified half a century ago as crucial for the future of our world. His life and writings that have brought us together here in the cause of Christian faith and world peace are a living indication of his role as one who speaks in the name of the God of peace and justice. His concern for these issues was a fruit of the faith that grew out of his monastic life and contemplative prayer. Rightly to understand his approach to the issues of peace and non-violence, it is essential to advert to the fact that his chief, daily efforts were expended in what the monastic tradition calls "the work of the heart," that is, the prolonged struggle with the passions and contemplative assimilation of the truths of faith. Through this interior labor he became, as Gordan Zahn notes, a man "ahead of his time" because he was "in tune with his time."[2]

Merton viewed his times in the light of history. This perspective permitted him to observe with keen penetration that "somewhere in the last fifty years we have crossed a mysterious limit set by Providence and have entered a new era.... There has been a violent disruption of society and a radical overthrow of that modern world which goes back to Charlemagne."[3] Based on his contemplative experience he viewed the issues of war and violence in the broadest of contexts, as a crisis of the spirit as he stated in 1962:

> The present world crisis is not merely a political and economic conflict. It goes deeper than ideologies. It is a crisis of man's spirit. It is a great religious and moral upheaval of the human race, and we do not really know half the causes of this upheaval. We cannot pretend to have a full understanding of what

is going on in ourselves and in our society.... The moral evil in
the world is due to man's alienation from the deepest truth,
from the springs of spiritual life within himself.[4]

Anyone who reads some of the many books and articles written
about Merton the man and his thought, will soon realize that he
was uncommonly sensitive to the social forces at work in his world
and so was able to interpret its condition and spiritual needs with
an exactitude of insight. It will also be apparent that he was a many-
sided personality, richly complex, not always obviously consistent in his opinions. That he himself was aware of this is attested
to by the repeated revisions of his views and self-evaluations recorded in the twenty manuscript volumes of his diaries. The wide
variety of people who met him in person as well as those who
knew him only from his printed works, formed quite contrasting
conceptions of him and of his significance. He was at once more
simple and constant in his deepest purpose and more subtle in his
dealings and relations than most persons realized. Merton was
convinced that seeming inconsistency inevitably results from
growth and the process of transformation that is the Christian and
fully human life. He held quite deliberately the persuasion that in
the trajectory of life lived in a persevering search for the true self
as created by God, there is inevitable change, but under the surface there is a higher consistency at work.

Those of us who lived with him, especially we who were
formed as monks in large part by his teaching and counseling,
knew Fr. Louis (Merton's name in the monastery) as warm-hearted,
wise, fervent for monastic life, concerned for us as persons, personally accessible and, in a word, dedicated to our formation and
the good of the community. In his classes with us, it became apparent that he possessed an exceptional energy of intelligence together with an acuteness of insight and sensibility that spontaneously came to expression so that the genuine affection he inspired
was tempered by his restraint of respect.

Fr. Louis, it seems to me, was quite aware of his gifts and being sensitive to the vulnerability of his students, made it a point to
cultivate simplicity in his manner, giving free scope to his marked
sense of humor. He showed no reluctance, however, rather uncer-
emoniously to correct any of us who needed to be reminded of
some failure or called to account for inappropriate behavior. As
spiritual director Fr. Louis possessed an extraordinary fund of

empathy, rendered more sensitive and purified by his contemplative experience of God that was a source of ready understanding and deeply felt concern when one of us was undergoing a difficult trial of one kind or another.

Such then was our view as young monks of our Father Master. Nor did we have occasion as time went on to alter in any radical way this early impression. Our respect and affection, masked for the most part as is the rather casual manner of American men, persisted undiminished to the end, even as those of us who worked more closely with him became aware of his human weaknesses. Later I discovered that this fraternal affection was not always evident to Fr. Louis himself; at times of stress, especially after he moved into the hermitage, he too readily felt emotionally distanced. He misinterpreted as lack of concern the surface disengagement that resulted from the solitude he chose and which he had asked us to accept. The need for signs of the warmth of human appreciation and understanding remained in continuing tension with the equal attraction for solitude; this conflict persisted to the very end of his life and accounts for much of the seeming inconsistency in his life and writings. The various expressions of the resulting inner struggle have sometimes been misunderstood and wrongly interpreted by some biographers.

His affective sensitivity contributed greatly to his remarkable capacity to enter with feeling into the inner experience of others. This power of empathy in large measure accounts for a quality of his writings, of his teaching and counseling that enabled him effectively to communicate his views to a wide variety of persons. Many who read him feel he knew them and their struggles personally. That he was aware of the personal tonality this quality of empathy imparted to his writings appears in the preface he wrote to the Japanese translation of *The Seven Storey Mountain*:

Therefore, most honorable reader, it is not as an author that I would speak to you, not as a story-teller, not as a philosopher, not as a friend only: I seek to speak to you, in some way, as your own self. Who can tell what this may mean? I myself do not know. But if you listen, things will be said that are perhaps not written in this book. And this will be due not to me, but to One who lives and speaks in both![5]

In other words, Merton's writings are a continuation of his con-templative communion with God, conveying something of the life of the Spirit to those who, as he states, truly listen to the One who communicates with the reader as he does with the author.

II

If I have dwelt here on this personal character of Merton's work, it is because his writing on Peace, Social Justice and finally Non-violence remain vital and speak with pertinence to us today not only due to his insights and shrewd analyses, but no less because they are rooted in this personalizing and contemplative region of his soul. It was because Fr. Louis's sense of identity as a sinner, flawed, marginal, errant man, was as someone who was sought and found by the God of mercy. With the pathos of heartfelt experience he identifies himself with Jonas, the prophet of God's mercy. The Voice of God is heard in Paradise:

"What was vile has become precious. What is now precious was never vile. I have always known the vile as precious: for what is vile I know not at all. ... I have always overshadowed Jonas with my mercy.... Have you had sight of Me, Jonas My child? Mercy within mercy within mercy. I have forgiven the universe without end, because I have never known sin.... What was fragile has become powerful. I loved what was most frail...."[6]

It was awareness of receiving the mercy of God when he had strayed far that made him sensitive to the plight of the marginal and the weak who are the chief victims of violence and injustice. This profound sense of identity with the vulnerable stands at the root of his decision to involve himself in social issues that to many seemed outside the province of a cloistered monk. I submit that the contrary is true and is a major portion of his message to us. Monastic life and Christian life as such wherever it is lived, is a life of ongoing conversion. As we come to know something of the power, the holiness, the beauty and the loving goodness of God, revealed in Jesus our Savior, we become more aware of our need for mercy, and experience deeper empathy for others who have the same need. It is this profound sense of God's holiness and lov-ing mercy that, more than any other single factor, explains Tho-mas Merton's work for Justice, Peace and Non-violence.

Note: This is the text of the opening address of the International Thomas Merton Society, San Diego, California given on June 9, 2005. I leave it in the original form.

Notes

1. Thomas Merton, *The Nonviolent Alternative*, revised edition of *Thomas Merton on Peace*, ed., Gordon C. Zahn (New York: Farrar, Straus & Giroux, 1980), pp. 257-58.
2. *Nonviolent Alternative*, p. x.
3. Thomas Merton, *Passion for Peace: The Social Essays*, ed., William H. Shannon (New York: Crossroad, 1995), p. 134.
4. Thomas Merton, *Passion for Peace*, p. 83.
5. Thomas Merton, *"Honorable Reader": Reflections on My Work* (New York: Crossroad, 1989), p. 67.
6. Thomas Merton, *The Sign of Jonas* (New York: Harcourt Brace and Company, 1953), p. 362.

The God of Peace is Never Glorified by Human Violence: Keynote Address to the International Thomas Merton Society, June, 2005

John Dear

Thomas Merton has been one of my teachers, and it's a blessing to reflect on his exemplary life and astonishing witness. I'm 45, have been in the Jesuits almost twenty-five years now, went to college at Duke, decided one day that I really did believe in God and that I wanted to give my whole life to God, and the next thing you know, I was entering the Jesuits. I'm still trying to figure out how that happened. But before I entered the Jesuits, I decided I better go see where Jesus lived, so I decided to make a walking pilgrimage through Israel, to see the physical lay of the land, only the day I left for Israel in June 1982, Israel invaded Lebanon and I found myself walking through a war zone.

By the end of my two-month pilgrimage, I was camping around the Sea of Galilee, and visited the Church of the Beatitudes, where I read on the walls: "Blessed are the poor, the mournful, the meek, those who hunger and thirst for justice, the merciful, the pure in heart, the peacemakers, those persecuted for the sake of justice, and love your enemies." I was stunned. I walked out to the balcony, looking out over the Sea of Galilee, and asked out loud, "Are you trying to tell me something? Okay, I promise here and now to dedicate my life to the Sermon on the Mount, to promoting peace and justice, on one condition: if you give me a sign." Just then, several Israeli jets fell from the sky breaking the sound barrier, setting off a series of sonic booms, coming right toward me. After they flew over me, I look backed up at heaven, and pledged to live out the Sermon on the Mount and never ask for a sign again!

When I entered the Jesuits three weeks later, I was on fire with a desire to pursue the life of peace and justice. I started to study the writings of the great peacemakers, such as Gandhi, Dr. King, Dorothy Day, the Berrigans and from day one, Thomas Merton.

Like you, I've been reading Merton ever since. I think I've read everything he's published, and I'm amazed how he still speaks to me. In contrast to the culture, TV, the President, even the world, Merton remains a voice of sanity and reason and faith and clarity and hope, and I can't put him down. I don't know if you heard what the great theologian David Tracy recently said when he was asked what the future of theology in the U.S. would look like. He answered spontaneously, "For the next 200 years, we'll be trying to catch up with Merton."

In 1989, I visited the Abbey of Gethsemani for the first time, and became friends with Br. Patrick Hart. Later, when I was in prison for nearly a year for a Plowshares disarmament action, Brother Patrick wrote that Gethsemani wanted to support me, and he offered to let me stay for a while in Merton's hermitage, which was one of the great experiences of my life. I later published my journal from my retreat there called, *The Sound of Listening*. Later, again, I went back for another long stay. It was one of the greatest blessings of my life to live and pray in Merton's hermitage.

Over the years, Merton has helped me not only in my work for peace but in keeping me in religious life and the Church because whenever I get in trouble for working for peace and justice, or whenever I get discouraged about the Church or religious life, I recall how much trouble Merton was in for writing about war, racism, nuclear weapons and monasticism, how he stayed put, remained faithful, did what he could, said his prayers and carried on, so I take heart from Merton because he endured it all with love, with a good heart, and now we see how his life and sufferings and fidelity have born great fruit. I think we can all find new strength and courage from him to carry on and be faithful in our service to the God of peace.

When I think of Merton's "Revelation of Justice and Revolution of Love" and what Merton has taught me, I return once again to the wisdom of nonviolence. So I would like to share five simple callings that I have learned from Thomas Merton.

I

First, Merton invites us to become contemplatives, mystics, of nonviolence. Merton's whole life was based on prayer, contemplation and mysticism, but it was not so that we could go and hurt others, or bomb others, or dominate the world, but so that we could commune with the living God. I spent my first ten years as a Jesuit praying by telling God what to do, yelling at God for not making the world a better place, until finally, a wise spiritual director said, "John, that is not the way we speak to someone we love." A light went on in my mind: prayer is about a relationship with someone I love, with the God of love and peace, so my prayer changed to a silent listening, a being with God, which is what contemplative nonviolence is all about.

Merton knew that prayer, contemplation, meditation, adoration and communion mean entering into the presence of the God of peace, dwelling in the nonviolence of Jesus, that, in other words, the spiritual life begins with contemplative nonviolence, that every one of us is called to be a mystic of nonviolence.

So in prayer, we turn to the God of peace, we enter the presence of the One who loves us and who disarms our hearts of our inner violence and transforms us into people of Gospel nonviolence and then sends us on a mission of disarming love and creative nonviolence.

Through contemplative nonviolence, we learn to give God our inner violence and resentments, to grant clemency and forgiveness to everyone who hurts us; to move from anger and revenge and violence to compassion, mercy and nonviolence so that we radiate personally the peace we seek politically.

In the end, as Merton knew, peace is a gift from God. If we are addicted to violence, as the Twelve-Step model teaches, we need to turn to our Higher Power, confess our violence, support one another through communities of nonviolence, and become sober people of nonviolence. "The chief difference between nonviolence and violence," Merton writes, is that violence "depends entirely on its own calculations." Nonviolence "depends entirely on God and on [God's] word."[1]

When Jesus calls us to love our enemies, he said we should do so because God does so. God lets the sun shine on the just and the unjust, and the rain fall on the good and the bad. God is compassionate to everyone, and we should be too. This is the heart of contemplative nonviolence. Then we are able to see everyone as a human being, and to see God and become like God.

As we pursue contemplative peace like Merton, we learn, contrary to what the Pentagon tells us, that our God is not a god of war, but the God of peace; not a god of injustice, but the God of justice; not a god of vengeance and retaliation, but the God of compassion and mercy; not a god of violence, but the God of nonviolence; not a god of death, but the living God of life. We discover a new image of God. As we begin to imagine the peace and nonviolence of God, we learn to worship the God of peace and nonviolence, and in the process, become people of peace and nonviolence. "The great problem is this inner change," Merton writes. "We all have the great duty to realize the deep need for purity of soul that is to say, the deep need to be possessed by the Holy Spirit."

On his way to Asia, Merton told David Steindl-Rast that "the only way beyond the traps of Catholicism is Buddhism." In other words, every Catholic has to become a good Buddhist, to become as compassionate as possible, he said. "I am going to become the best Buddhist I can, so I can become a good Catholic."[2] That is the wisdom of Merton's contemplative life, to become like Buddhists, people of profound compassion, deep contemplative nonviolence. That is what he discovered with his experience in Polonnaruwa when he wrote: "Everything is emptiness and everything is compassion."[3]

This is what Merton meant when he wrote about Gandhi: "[Gandhi's] nonviolence was not simply a political tactic which was supremely useful and efficacious in liberating his people. ...On the contrary, the spirit of non-violence sprang from *an inner realization of spiritual unity in himself.* The whole Gandhian concept of non-violent action and *satyagraha* is incomprehensible if it is thought to be a means of achieving unity rather than as *the fruit of inner unity already achieved.*"[4]

So Merton calls us to be contemplatives and mystics of nonviolence, instruments of the God of peace.

II

Second, Merton teaches us to become students and teachers of nonviolence. Merton was not just a great teacher, but the eternal student. He was always studying, always learning, always searching for the truth. So when he started reading Gandhi in the 1950s and then meeting peacemakers like Daniel Berrigan and the folks from the Fellowship of Reconciliation and the Catholic Worker, he became a student and teacher of Gospel nonviolence, and I think that's what each one of us has to do—to study, learn, practice and teach the Holy Wisdom of nonviolence.

The lesson starts off with the basic truth: Violence doesn't work. War doesn't work. Violence in response to violence always leads to further violence. As Jesus said, "Those who live by the sword, will die by the sword. Those who live by the bomb, the gun, the nuclear weapon, will die by bombs, guns and nuclear weapons." You reap what you sow. The means are the ends. What goes around comes around. War cannot stop terrorism because war is terrorism. War only sows the seeds for future wars. War can never lead to lasting peace or true security or a better world or overcome evil or teach us how to be human or as Merton insists, deepen the spiritual life.

Underneath this culture of war and injustice is a sophisticated spirituality of violence, a spirituality of war, a spirituality of empire, a spirituality of injustice that has nothing to do with the living God or the Gospel of Jesus. In this false spirituality, we believe violence saves us, war brings peace, might makes right, nuclear weapons are our only security, God blesses wars, we seek not forgiveness and reconciliation but victory and domination, and the good news is not the love of enemies but the elimination of enemies. It's heresy, blasphemy and idolatry. The empire always tries to instruct the Church on sin and morality, telling us that certain personal behavior is sinful or immoral, while saying nothing about the murder of 130,000 Iraqis, in recent years, as if that were not sinful or immoral.

In a spirituality of violence, the Church rejects Jesus and the Sermon on the Mount as impractical, takes up the empire's just war theory, launches crusades and blesses Trident submarines and remains silent while Los Alamos churns out nuclear weapons and enjoys the comforts of the culture of war and injustice rather than taking up the cross of Gospel nonviolence. We have a private relationship with God, fulfill our obligations and go right along with the mass murder of our sisters and brothers around the world.

The empire wants the Church to be indifferent and passive; to be divided and fighting and silent, even to bless wars and injustice.

Unless we speak out and teach the wisdom of peace and nonviolence, the church will become like Hazel Motes' church in Flannery O'Connor's book *Wise Blood*, the "Church without Christ," where the lame don't walk, the blind don't see, the deaf don't hear, and the dead stay dead. That's what Merton learned.

The wisdom of nonviolence teaches that: War is not the will of God. War is never justified. War is never blessed by God. War is not endorsed by any religion. War is the very definition of mortal sin. War is demonic, evil, anti-human, anti-life, anti-God, anti-Christ. For Christians, war is not the way to follow Jesus. "The God of peace is never glorified by human violence," Merton wrote. In other words, peaceful means are the only way to a peaceful future and the God of peace. So like Merton, we have to study nonviolence, define it, talk about and think about how each one of us can become more nonviolent, and how we can create a church of nonviolence, even a new world of nonviolence. So Merton studies it and concludes: "What is important in nonviolence is the contemplative truth that is not seen. The radical truth of reality is that we are all one."[5]

Merton's nonviolence begins with the vision of a reconciled humanity, the truth that all life is sacred, that we are all equal sisters and brothers, all children of the God of peace, already reconciled, all already united, and so, we could never hurt or kill another human being, much less remain silent while our country wages war, builds nuclear weapons, and allows others to starve.

So nonviolence is much more than a tactic or a strategy; it is a way of life. We renounce violence and vow never to hurt anyone again. It is not passive but active love and truth that seeks justice and peace for the whole human race, and resists systemic evil, and persistently reconciles with everyone, and insists that there is no cause however noble for which we support the killing of any human being; and instead of killing others, we are willing to undergo being killed in the struggle for justice and peace; instead of inflicting violence on others, we accept and undergo suffering without even the desire to retaliate as we pursue justice and peace for all people.

Nonviolence is active, creative, provocative, and challenging. Through his study of Gandhi, Merton agreed that nonviolence is a life force more powerful than all the weapons of the world, that when harnessed, becomes contagious and disarms nations. So nonviolence begins in our hearts, where we renounce the violence within us, and then moves out with active nonviolence to our families, communities, churches, cities, our nation and the world. When organized on a large national or global level, active nonviolence can transform the world, as Gandhi demonstrated in India's revolution, or as Dr. King and the civil rights movement showed.

I worked for several years as executive director of the Fellowship of Reconciliation, which I think through John Heidbrink, helped to bring Merton and the Berrigans into the work for peace in 1960 and 1961. I learned like Merton through FOR that all the major religions are rooted in nonviolence. Islam means peace. Judaism upholds the magnificent vision of shalom, where people beat swords into plowshares and study war no more. Gandhi exemplified Hinduism as active nonviolence. Buddhism is all about compassion toward all living beings. Brace yourselves, Merton teaches, even Christianity is rooted in nonviolence.

The one thing we can say for sure about Jesus is that he practiced active, public, creative nonviolence. He called us to love our neighbors; to show compassion toward everyone; to seek justice for the poor; to forgive everyone; to put down the sword; to take up the cross in the struggle for justice and peace; to lay down our lives, to risk our lives if necessary, in love for all humanity, and most of all, to love our enemies. His last words to the community, to the Church, to us, as the soldiers dragged him away, could not be clearer or more to the point: "Put down the sword."

Now you might say this is the one moment where violence is justified. Peter was right to take up a sword, to kill to protect our guy, the Holy One. But Jesus issues a new commandment: "Put down the sword." That's it. We are not allowed to kill. That's why they run away; they realize he is serious about nonviolence, that we follow a martyr.

Jesus dies on the cross saying, "The violence stops here in my body, which is given for you. You are forgiven, but from now on, you are not allowed to kill." And God raises him from the dead, and he says, "Peace be with you." Then he sends us forth into the culture of violence on the mission of creative nonviolence.

I like how in one of his journals, in the early 1960s, Merton calls himself "a professor of nonviolence," determined to teach the church, even the world, the wisdom of nonviolence. We too need to teach nonviolence, and to call the Church to practice the nonviolence of Jesus, and to help it reject the just war theory and accept the risen Christ's gift of peace.

III

Third, Merton invites us to become apostles of nonviolence. We remember Merton's famous article for Dorothy Day and *The Catho-*

lic Worker, where he wrote: "The duty of the Christian in this crisis is to strive with all [our] power and intelligence, with [our] faith, hope in Christ, and love for God and [humanity], to do the one task which God has imposed upon us in the world today. That task is to work for the total abolition of war. *There can be no question that unless war is abolished the world will remain constantly in a state of madness and desperation in which, because of the immense destructive power of modern weapons, the danger of catastrophe will be imminent and probable at every moment everywhere.* [The Church] must lead the way on the road towards nonviolent settlement of difficulties and towards the gradual abolition of war as the way of settling international or civil disputes. Christians must become active in every possible way, mobilizing all their resources for the fight against war.... Peace is to be preached, nonviolence is to be explained [and practiced].... We may never succeed in this campaign but whether we succeed or not the duty is evident."[6]

Today there are 35 wars currently being fought with our country involved in every one of them. According to the United Nations, some 50,000 people die every day of starvation. Nearly two billion people suffer in poverty and misery. We live in the midst of structured, systemic institutionalization of violence which kills people through war and poverty.

From this global system comes a litany of violence—from executions, sexism, racism, violence against children, violence against women, guns, abortion, and the destruction of environment, including the ozone layer, the rain forests, and our oceans. Since 2003, we have killed over 135,000 Iraqis. But on August 6, 1945, we crossed the line in this addiction to violence and vaporized 130,000 people in Hiroshima and another 70,000 people, three days later in Nagasaki.

Today, we have some 25,000 nuclear weapons with no movement toward dismantling them; instead, we increase our budget for killing and send nuclear weapons and radioactive materials into outer space. We put missile shields around the planet, and plan even greater nukes.

I think we are called to be activists for peace like Thomas Merton. Jim Douglass told me that Merton, alone in his hermitage in the woods, did more for peace than most peace activists. I think that whatever we do, wherever we are, we have to be involved in the movements for peace and justice. None of us can do everything, but all of us can do something, like Merton, whether through our prayer vigils, marching, leafleting, protests or civil disobedience.

So I urge you to join Pax Christi, the international Catholic peace movement, or the Fellowship of Reconciliation; to be part of the ONE campaign working to lift the third-world debt; and the ongoing campaign to close the School of the Americas.

On August 6th, the 60th anniversary of the U.S. atomic bombing of Hiroshima, hundreds of us from Pax Christi will go to Los Alamos, New Mexico, the birthplace of the bomb, and in a spirit of prayerful, active nonviolence, we will put on sackcloth and ashes to repent of the sin of war and nuclear weapons and pray for the gift of nuclear disarmament. I hope you will join us, or you own local peace vigil.

On the first page of his book, *Peace in the Post Christian Era*, which was suppressed until its recent publication by Orbis Books, Merton writes: "[N]ever was opposition to war more urgent and more necessary than now. Never was religious protest so badly needed."[7]

IV

Fourth, Merton invites us to become visionaries of nonviolence. One of the many casualties of the culture of war is the imagination. People can no longer imagine a world without war or nuclear weapons or violence or poverty. They can't even imagine it, because the culture has robbed us of our imaginations.

We live in a time of terrible blindness, moral blindness, spiritual blindness, the blindness that will lead us over the brink of global destruction.

Our mission is to uphold the vision of nonviolence, like Merton, to point the way forward, the way out of our madness, to lift up the light, to lead us away from the brink.

We need to be the community of faith and conscience and nonviolence that lifts up the vision of peace, to help others imagine a world without war or nuclear weapons, the vision that teaches us to resist our country's wars and nuclear arsenal.

All my life, I've been trying to uphold a vision of a world without war, by serving the poor and homeless, visiting the war zones of the world, organizing protests and getting arrested 75 times, engaging in a Plowshares action, and working at the Fellowship of Reconciliation. Now I live way out in the desert of New Mexico where until recently I've been serving as the pastor of several churches among the very poor. It's like being a desert father on the margins. New Mexico is a land of great spirituality, but it's also the poorest state in the US, the birthplace of the bomb, and number one in nuclear weapons spending, and these days I'm in a lot of hot water for calling for the closing of Los Alamos. But I remember that Merton visited New Mexico twice before leaving for Asia and was impressed by its land and people and life on the margins. He knew that this was a special place with the potential of becoming a land of nonviolence.

You may have heard what happened to me recently. I had been living in a small desert town in northeastern New Mexico, serving five parishes, and speaking out against the war, when one morning, on November 20, 2003, the day after it was announced that the local unit of the National Guard was going to Iraq, at 6 a.m., 75 soldiers came marching down the street in front of my rectory and church, shouting battle slogans. They marched passed the church for an hour, then the shouting got real loud and I looked out the window and discovered that they were standing right in front of my house, filling up the street, shouting out, "Kill, kill, kill!" So I went out and gave them a speech, saying, "In the name of God, I order you to quit the military, not to go to Iraq, not to kill anyone or be killed, and to follow the nonviolence of Jesus because God does not support war, God does not bless war, God does not want you to wage war." They looked at me with their mouths hanging open, and then broke up laughing. So now, I'm totally notorious.

But I've been telling my peace movement friends that after you become completely notorious, I no longer have to go to demonstrations. From now on, the soldiers come to me!

Like Merton, we all need to become new abolitionists who imagine a world without war, poverty or nuclear weapons.

V

Fifth, Merton invites us to become prophets of nonviolence. Here is one of my favorite Merton quotes: "It is my intention to make my entire life a rejection of, a protest against the crimes and injustices of war and political tyranny which threaten to destroy the whole [human race] and the [whole world]. By my monastic life and vows I am saying NO to all the concentration camps, the aerial bombardments, the staged political trials, the judicial murders, the racial injustices," the violence and nuclear weapons. "If I say NO to all these secular forces, I also say YES to all that is good in the world and in [humanity]."[8]

I think that just as Merton learned to make his life a rejection of war by speaking out for peace, we must do the same thing and make our entire lives a rejection, a protest against the crimes and injustices and wars and nuclear weapons of our country and so become prophets of nonviolence to the culture of violence.

Merton teaches us to break through the culture of war and denounce the false spirituality of violence and speak the truth of peace and nonviolence. Remember how he wrote to Jean Leclercq, that the work of the monastery is "not survival but prophecy,"[9] in the biblical sense, to speak truth to power, to speak God's word of peace to the world of war, to speak of God's reign of nonviolence, to the anti-reign of violence. I think that's our task too—not survival, but prophecy.

Merton wrote to Daniel Berrigan in 1962, "If one reads the prophets with ears and eyes open then you cannot help recognizing our obligation to shout very loud about God's will, God's truth, and God's justice."

I'm sure Merton would have something to say about everything that is happening the world today, in this whole culture of war. So like Merton the prophet, our job is to call for an end to war, starvation, violence and nuclear weapons, to say, bring the troops home, end the U.S. occupation of Iraq, cut off all military aid to the Middle East and help the U.N. pursue nonviolent alternatives to this crisis.

In March 1999, I led an FOR delegation of Nobel peace prize winners to Baghdad. We met with religious leaders, like the Papal nuncio and Imans, United Nations' officials, non-governmental organizations, and even government representatives, but most importantly, we met with hundreds of dying children and saw with our own eyes the reality of suffering inflicted by the sanctions, because we have systematically destroyed Iraq's infrastructure by our bombs. Everywhere we went, the suffering people asked us right up front: Why are you trying to kill us?

Just as Merton condemned the Vietnam war and nuclear weapons and racism, I believe he would condemn the U.S. bombings, sanctions, and occupation of Iraq as a total disaster, a spiritual defeat. Iraq is not a liberated country. It is an occupied country, and we are the imperial, military occupiers. There is no representative democracy in Iraq, nor do we intend to create one, and if we are going to take the example and teachings of Merton seriously, then we have to do what he did and speak out against this horrific war. We're not cloistered monks or hermits, so we don't have any excuse.

The occupation of Iraq is not about September 11 or stopping their weapons of mass destruction, since they were destroyed. It's not about concern for democracy or disarmament or the Kurds or the Iraqi people. If we cared about democracy, we would have asked them how to bring democracy, as we did on our delegation. To a person, they said, "Don't bomb us Give us food and medicine, and fund nonviolent democratic movements." Instead, we responded militarily with sanctions and bombs.

If we cared about the possibility of Iraq having one part of a weapon of mass destruction, we would dismantle our 20,000 weapons of mass destruction. As I said in a recent protest in Santa Fe, if President Bush was looking for weapons of mass destruction, we found them: they're right here in our backyard. He does not need to bomb New Mexico; just dismantle our entire nuclear arsenal!

This war is all about Bush and Cheney's goal to control Iraq's oil fields, at any price, to gain financial control of the world economy. We bombed every single major building in Baghdad except for the Ministry of Oil. We have an imperial economy based entirely on oil and weapons, and to maintain this empire, we have to wage war and wars require the blood of children, the blood of Christ. You and I have to become, like Merton, the voice of the voiceless, the voice of sanity and peace.

"I am on the side of the people who are being burned, cut to pieces, tortured, held as hostages, gassed, ruined and destroyed," Merton wrote in the 1960s. "They are the victims of both sides. To take sides with massive power is to take sides against the innocent. The side I take is then the side of the people who are sick of war and want peace,"[10] who want to rebuild their lives and their countries and the world.

Like Merton, I think we too have to take sides. We have to side with the poor and the children, with the innocent, with our enemies, and be like Christ, who took sides when he said: "Whatever you do to the least of these, you do to me."

"It is absolutely necessary to take a serious and articulate stand on the question of nuclear war. And I mean against nuclear war," Merton wrote in the 1960s to his friend Etta Gullick. "The passivity, the apparent indifference, the incoherence of so many Christians on this issue, and worse still the active belligerency of some religious spokesmen, is rapidly becoming one of the most frightful scandals in the history of Christendom."[11]

If we are to be prophets of nonviolence like Merton, we have to speak out for an end to the occupation; call for the immediate return of our own troops; and call for the U.N. to resolve the crisis nonviolently and heal our Iraqi brothers and sisters.

We also need to call for an immediate end to all U.S. military aid to Israel and the occupation of the Palestinians, and instead fund nonviolent Israeli and Palestinian peacemakers, and say we're not anti-Semitic nor do we support suicide bombers, but that we want the Jewish vision of shalom. We support human rights for Palestinian children.

We must also demand that our country stop bombing and sending military aid to Colombia and the Philippines; close our own terrorist training camps, like the School of the Americas at Fort Benning, Georgia, as well as the CIA, NSA, and the Pentagon; and lift the entire third world debt.

We must demand that we cut our military budget; end the Star Wars missile shield program; dismantle every nuclear weapon and weapon of mass destruction, and undertake international treaties for nuclear disarmament; join the World Court and uphold international law; and then, redirect those billions of dollars toward the hard work for a lasting peace through international cooperation for nonviolent alternatives; to feed every starving child and refugee on the planet, end poverty, show compassion to everyone and protect the earth itself.

Merton teaches us, like Ezekiel and all the prophets, that whether we are heard or not, whether our message is accepted or not, our vocation is to speak the truth of peace, to become prophets of nonviolence, a prophetic people who speak for the God of peace.

Merton concludes his great essay, "Blessed are the Meek" on the roots of Christian nonviolence, by talking about hope, saying our work for peace and justice is not based on the hope for results or the delusions of violence or the false security of this world, but in Christ. Our hope is in the God of peace, in the resurrection.

Merton gives me hope, hope to become a contemplative and mystic of nonviolence and commune with the God of peace; hope to teach the wisdom of nonviolence to a culture of violence; hope to practice active nonviolence in a world of indifference; hope to speak out prophetically for peace in a world of war and nuclear weapons; hope to uphold the vision of peace, a world without war in a land of blindness and despair.

I looked up Merton's concluding advice to Daniel Berrigan in one of Merton's letters, and thought we could all take heart from Merton's encouragement: "You are going to do a great deal of good simply stating facts quietly and telling the truth," Merton wrote to Dan. "The real job is to lay the groundwork for a deep change of heart on the part of the whole nation so that one day it can really go through the metanoia we need for a peaceful world. So do not be discouraged. Do not let yourself get frustrated. The Holy Spirit is not asleep. Keep your chin up."

VI

So I urge you not to be discouraged, not to despair, not to be afraid, not to give in to apathy, not to give up, but instead, to become contemplatives, teachers, apostles, prophets, and visionaries of Gospel nonviolence, to take up where Merton left off, to go as deep as Merton did, to stand on Merton's shoulders, to transform the Church and the world into the community of Gospel nonviolence, so that we might do God's will, and announce like Merton, with Merton, the revelation of justice, the good news of the revolution of love. So let us pray:

God of peace, make us contemplatives of nonviolence, proph-ets of nonviolence, teachers of nonviolence, apostles of non-violence, and visionaries of peace like Thomas Merton. Help us to announce the Revelation of Justice and the Revolution of Love, that we may all welcome your reign of peace. Amen.

God of peace, give us courage and strength and faith to say NO, like Merton, to the evils of violence, war, greed, pov-erty, and nuclear weapons, and to say YES, like Merton, to Jesus' reign of nonviolence, love, justice and peace. Amen.

God of peace, we are blind. Give us the vision of peace to see every human being on the planet as our sister and brother, to love our neighbors and our enemies, to learn like Merton, that in the end, we are all one in you. Disarm our hearts and send us forth into a world of war and nuclear weapons, like Merton, like Dorothy Day, Martin Luther King Jr, and Mahatma Gandhi, that we too may be instruments of your peace. Amen.

Notes

1. Thomas Merton, "Blessed are the Meek" in *The Nonviolent Alternative* (New York: Farrar, Straus & Giroux, 1971), p. 216.

2. See David Steindl-Rast, "Man of Prayer," in *Thomas Merton, Monk: A Monastic Tribute*, ed., Patrick Hart (New York: Sheed and Ward, 1974), p. 88 [not a direct quotation].

3. Thomas Merton, *Asian Journal* (New York: New Directions, 1973), p. 235.

4. Thomas Merton, *Gandhi on Nonviolence* (New York: New Directions, 1965), p. 6.

5. Thomas Merton, "Blessed are the Meek" in *The Nonviolent Alternative.*

6. Thomas Merton, *Passion for Peace: The Social Essays* (Crossroad Classic, 1997), pp. 12-13.

7. Thomas Merton, *Peace in the Post Christian Era*, ed., Patricia A. Burton (Maryknoll, NY: Orbis Books, 2004), p. 3.

8. Thomas Merton, *Honorable Reader: Reflections on My Work* (New York: Crossroad, 1991), p. 66 [reprint].

9. Thomas Merton, *Survival or Prophecy? The Letters of Thomas Merton and Jean Leclerq*, eds., Patrick Hart and Jean Leclerq (New York: Farrar, Straus and Giroux, 2002), p. 175.

10. Thomas Merton, *Faith and Violence* (Notre Dame: Univ. of Notre Dame, 1968), pp. 109-110.

11. Thomas Merton, *The Hidden Ground of Love: The Letters of Thomas Merton on Religious Experience and Social Concerns* (New York: Farrar, Straus and Giroux, 1985), p. 349.

Thomas Merton's Revelation of Justice & Revolutions of Love: Perspectives from the San Diego Conference

David Belcastro

The Ninth General Meeting of the International Thomas Merton Society held in San Diego in June of 2005 focused attention on Merton's contribution to our understanding of the essential relation between spiritual formation and social action. In this volume of *The Merton Annual*, ten of the presenters have developed their papers into articles which continue the conversations initiated at that meeting. It has been rewarding to work as a guest editor with these writers whose academic disciplines and professional expertise contribute new insights into the life, work, and influence of Merton. The articles have been arranged in the following manner. Judith Hunter, Michael Sobocinski, and Fred Herron situate Merton's work within historical and intellectual contexts that inform our understanding of his monastic vocation of dissent, protest, and affirmation that challenged his contemporaries to rethink critical social issues confronting the world. Monica Weis, Lucien Miller, and John Collins direct our attention to places in Merton's life where revelations of the hidden wholeness of love became revolutions for justice and peace. Patrick F. O'Connell, James Harford, and Joseph Raab, exploring one of those places, open new inquiries into Merton's poetry, correspondence, and friendships with regard to his work on war and peace. And, finally, Paul Dekar draws our attention to Merton's spiritual formation and the monastic discipline of simplicity as a contributing factor to his social witness.

Judith Hunter's "No Solution in Withdrawal; No Solution in Conforming: Merton, Teilhard, Kung, and Curran" places Merton's dissent within the 1960's when notable Roman Catholics raised their voices in loyal opposition to the teachings of the Church. The author invites the reader to consider with her a perplexing question: "Why would these men express ideas that they knew would not be welcomed by Rome. All were ordered by Rome to stop expressing these ideas. All continued to love the church. None of them walked out. Why not?" This article compares and contrast ways in which these four men dissented and addressed the pressing issue of their days.

Michael Sobocinski's "The Psychology of Hatred & the Role of Early Relationships in Discovering Our True Self" illuminates our understanding of Merton's understanding of the self with insights from modern psychology on the interpersonal, multicultural, and constructivist perspectives self with regard to love and hate as epistemologies for justice. Love and hate define self and other. Love frees both self and other to realize the freedom that comes with full personhood, while hate restricts, confines, and ultimately imprisons us in our efforts at fleeing the anxious awareness of separation. Against this understanding of the self, Sobocinski demonstrates how questions of justice became radically transformed in Merton's writings.

Fred W. Herron in "The Bricoleur in the Monastery; Tactics in a Nothing Place" notes Merton's "continual ability to prompt, chide and even infuriate people who approach his work from a variety of perspectives" and "his ability to confirm the preconceived notions of so many of those who approach his work from such widely disparate and sometimes contradictory points of view." With this in mind, he turns to the French Jesuit historian, theologian and ethnologist Michel DeCerteau whose work on the *bricoleur* offers insights into ways in which Merton's complex and perplexing self might be understood as an authentic and creative process of disintegration of the social and cultural self and the reintegration of that self in Christ as a new creation.

Monica Weis's "Kindred Spirits in Revelation and Revolution: Carson & Merton" inquires into a moment in Merton's life where revelation moved to revolution; a moment initiated by a letter written by Merton in January of 1963 to Rachel Carson in response to her book, *Silent Spring*. Carson's book resonated with Merton's prophetic vocation and vision of creation as interconnected and interdependent. Monica Weis traces the movement in Merton's life from a contemplative appreciation of nature to a deepening sense of environmental justice from which would eventually emerge social protest against the destruction of nature by the modern world.

Lucien Miller's "Merton—John Wu Letters: The Lord as Postman" presents the correspondence between Merton and John Wu as "a hidden yet seminal movement among the religious encounters between East and West in the Twentieth century." Noting these two men were opposites in politics, brothers in spirit, and mourners over the loss of a woman, Lucien demonstrates how they inspired, taught and consoled each other through a correspondence that lasted six and one-half years. Perhaps more importantly, we are led to see how emerging from this correspondence was the growing awareness that Western Christianity needs the East, and that a reawakening to the Gospel can occur through an encounter with Asian traditions.

John P. Collins's "From 'Political Dance of Death' to 'General Dance.' An Insight into the Cold War Letters" traces the movement in Merton's thought on war and peace from the propensity for self-destruction, the political dance of death, to the general dance with God which offers the world an opportunity to discover the deeper reality of unity and harmony that alone is able to overcome disunity and separation that drives the military-industrial machines of nations to manufacture war.

Patrick F. O'Connell's "The Landscape of Disaster: The War Poems of Thomas Merton" draws our attention to poetry written during the period preceding Merton's entrance into the Abbey of Gethsemani in December of 1941 which provides an opportunity "both to observe Merton's struggles with the moral, political and spiritual issues of war at this critical point in his life, and to see him trying to articulate these struggles in poems that are aesthetically coherent and intellectually and emotionally effective." O'Connell presents an overview, in roughly chronological order, of Thomas Merton's premonastic war poems, highlighting the particular approach to the war taken in each poem.

James Harford's "Lax, Merton, and Rice on War and Peace" recalls Merton's lifelong friendship with Robert Lax and Edward Rice, their correspondence, and articles for *Jubilee*, the magazine that all three worked on for fifteen years. Harford shows how these letters and articles, as well as, writings in other publications, share their thoughts on the absurdity and cruelty of war, and of the importance of peace activism. His book length study of this same subject is also published this year.

Joseph Quinn Raab's "Comrades for Peace: Merton, the Dalai Lama and the Preferential Option for Nonviolence" recalls the encounter between Thomas Merton and the Dalai Lama, the two most prominent monks of modern times, and then seeks to clarify the religious sources of their common commitment to nonviolence with a special emphasis on its monastic character. Finally, Joseph Raab offers some reflections on the contribution of their legacy to the growing momentum of the nonviolent option in Christian theology and practice.

Paul R. Dekar's "The Spirit of Simplicity: Merton on Simplification of Life" considers an early and less-known book on the subject of simplicity in the Cistercian tradition. In addition to providing historical background and summary of its contents, Dekar shows how the insights developed in this early work continue to unfold in later works and why this revival of monastic values is of importance to the world today as it struggles against narcissism, depersonalization and totalitarian structures.

Together, these papers provide us with an opportunity to clarify and deepen our understanding of Merton as a monk who struggled with himself and the world in which he lived and in that struggle discovered his authentic self, a self grounded in God's love; a love that compelled him to participate in a community of dissenters and protestors who call us to join with them in the movement from revelation to revolution.

No Solution in Withdrawal—No Solution in Conforming: Merton, Teilhard, Kung and Curran

Judith Hunter

Thomas Merton, Pierre Teilhard de Chardin, Hans Kung, and Charles Curran strongly influenced American Catholic culture during the time period covered in this article.[1] All spoke clearly. Their words affected many minds and many hearts, including mine. All these priests expressed some ideas which they knew would not be welcome in Rome. Why? This investigation focuses on that question and suggests answers. All were ordered by Rome to stop expressing those ideas. All continued to love the Church. None of them walked out. Why not? The paper ends with a brief indication of how each person addressed that question.

The goal of this article is to tell these four stories as seen through the eyes of these four people by examining their perception of the issues, using their own words when possible. The term dissent, as used here, refers to public intellectual dissent that asserts a position differing from the position advocated by those in power. The study places Merton's dissent within the larger context of other Catholic dissent influencing American Catholics during the last decade of Merton's life (1958-68)—the years just prior to, during, and just after the Second Vatican Council (1962-65). It does so in three ways: 1) by characterizing the context and the manner of each person's dissent, 2) by relating Merton's strong responses to his reading of Teilhard and Kung, and 3) by comparing the way in which Merton dissented to the ways in which Teilhard, Kung and Curran dissented.

This article does not provide general information on background issues such as Vatican II, the anti-modernist movement,[2] or the intellectual history of the U.S. during the 1960s.[3] Nor does the paper evaluate the merits of Merton's position on nuclear war, Teilhard's position on the evolutionary process, Kung's position on structural reform of the Church, or Curran's position on birth control. Instead, the article focuses on each person's expressed motivation for dissent and on the institutional response the dissent evoked. Although the paper looks at dissent which affected the American Catholic public between 1958 and 1968, it will be necessary also to refer to the difficulties with Rome that Teilhard encountered in 1925, Kung in 1979, and Curran in 1986.

Of course this article reflects my own perceptions. I am a lawyer with a background in intellectual history and I bring that training to these events and to my reflections on them.

Pierre Teilhard de Chardin

Although this paper focuses primarily on Merton, it begins with Teilhard because Teilhard's dissent preceded and may even have influenced Merton's own.

Teilhard's ideas first became widely available to American Catholics with the publication in English of *The Phenomenon of Man* in 1959 and *The Divine Milieu* in 1960. Teilhard's thought spread rapidly and so did news of his difficulties with Rome. In order to understand the influence of Teilhard on American Catholics during the 1960s, we must examine the crisis Teilhard faced in 1925.

In 1925 Teilhard was a 44-year-old Jesuit paleontologist at the Institut Catholique in Paris.[4] Fossil evidence found in many parts of the world indicated that the human species had evolved over long periods of time. While Teilhard was visiting at a Jesuit seminary, a friend of his, a Jesuit professor of dogmatic theology, asked Teilhard to speak to the students and to put down on paper his ideas about how the biblical account of Adam and Eve and the theology of 'the fall' could be reconciled with the evolutionary account of human origins. Although he had only a few days before the visit ended, Teilhard did so, describing his "Note on Some Possible Historical Representations of Original Sin" as a tentative effort.[5] Without telling Teilhard or his friend, an unknown person sent a copy of that draft to the Holy Office in Rome. The practice of 'delation,' sending information to the Vatican in this manner, had long been standard practice.[6]

The Holy Office, through the head of the Jesuit order located in Rome, told Teilhard that he was never again to say or write anything "against the traditional position of the Church on the matter of original sin."[7] Consider the ramifications of that order. The traditional position was developed in total ignorance of the concept of evolution and of fossil evidence. Refusing to allow highly educated Catholic specialists to try to reconcile the traditional position with new knowledge leaves the question unanswered by those best able to answer it. That is a very high price for any organization to pay—a valuable opportunity lost. The evidence shows that from the 1904 beginning of the anti-modernist campaign[8] until the Second Vatican Council, the Holy Office did not perceive its role in terms of lost opportunity but in terms of preserving the existing tradition from significant change. Neither the incorporation of new knowledge nor the resolution of contemporary problems was deemed to be a priority. The greatest priority was to preserve intact explanations that had been developed in the past. Since Teilhard's essay offered novel approaches, he was deemed to be in error precisely because his explanation conflicted with the existing explanation. Teilhard was not asked to come up with a better explanation; he was ordered not to conflict in any way with the existing explanation.

Teilhard was also ordered to resign his teaching position, abandon the rich academic and social environment of Paris, and leave France. As a Jesuit and a professor, he had tried to reconcile the two roles he loved, that of priest and professor. He was given a forced choice between the two. In May he wrote to a fellow Jesuit: "Dear friend, help me a little. I have behaved properly; but what I feel inside is something like a death agony or a storm."[9]

While agonizing over the decision that faced him, Teilhard met with a group of French Jesuit professors who fully understood his position. They all advised him to obey.[10] Teilhard concluded that the most honorable thing he could do was to submit. In August he wrote to a close friend: "When I thought of the comfort I drew from the appreciation of all these minds, which were really reliable and devoted to the Church, I realized what enormous damage and scandal would have been caused by any act of indiscipline on my part . . ."[11] For the next thirty years, from 1925 until his death in 1955, Teilhard was never allowed to publish his religious writings and never permitted to return to France to live, despite his repeated requests.[12]

In the very same months that Teilhard dealt with his crisis, a man named Scopes was on trial in Tennessee for violation of a state statute prohibiting the teaching of evolution.[13] John H. Scopes received his full legal rights. Consider the rights Scopes had that Teilhard did not have: the right to a list of the specific charges against him, the right to testify in his own defense, the right to face and cross-examine his accuser, the right to counsel, the right

to go free if the prosecutor could not prove his guilt beyond a reasonable doubt, the right to appeal, etc. Teilhard got none of these.
These rights developed over centuries within the English common law to prevent the abuse of power. No comparable development occurred within the Vatican.

Note that the Tennessee legislature passed the statute prohibiting the teaching of evolution in order to preserve the existing,
traditional, explanation of the biblical account of Adam and Eve.
In other words, civil as well as Church authorities tend to favor
time-honored customs. The difference here is the treatment of the
accused. A person accused of violating the official position in Tennessee has rights that a person who is accused of violating the
official position in the Vatican does not have.

For the rest of his life, from age 45 to 75, Teilhard continued to
obey the order not to publish his religious writings. He accepted
the conditions imposed upon him. Exiled and often lonely, he
continued to work on a vision that incorporated both what he perceived as religious truth and what he perceived as scientific truth,
holding on to both, trying to reconcile them, developing his "synthesis of all things *in Jesu Christo.*"

In a famous letter to the head of the Jesuit order, dated October 12, 1951, he stated both sides of the coin. On the one side: "In
my awareness of this synthesis of all things in Jesu Christo, I have
found an extraordinary and inexhaustible source of clarity and
interior strength and an atmosphere outside of which it has become physically impossible for me to breathe, to adore, and to
believe."[14] On the other side:

> I fully recognize that Rome may have its reasons for believing
> that in its present form my vision of Christianity is premature
> or incomplete, and that as a consequence, it cannot presently
> be diffused without creating problems.
>
> It is on this important point of exterior fidelity and docility
> that I wish particularly to assure you (and this is the essential
> point of this letter) that, despite certain appearances, I am de-
> termined to remain "a child of obedience."[15]

What factors frame Teilhard's dissent?

1) In 1925, because an unknown person delated him to
Rome, he was caught unawares in a situation not of his own
choosing. He was presented with a choice between exile and

continuing to be a Jesuit or staying in France and leaving the order. Knowing full well that Rome knew almost nothing about the evolution of the human species and was unsympathetic to and ignorant of evolutionary findings, he nonetheless chose to accept the discipline that Rome had meted out.

2) He saw his choice as either subjecting the church to damage and scandal or protecting the Church; he chose to preserve the public image of the Church. He gave great weight to the example of his peers. He knew and admired French Jesuits who had been targeted by the Vatican's anti-modernist purges. He believed that he should obey as they had done.

3) Once he had taken his course, he never changed it. On the one hand he obeyed the order. On the other hand he was determined to develop his thought, hoping that the day would come when he could discuss his work publicly.[16] As the 1951 letter shows, he deferred to the judgment of Rome, on the stated grounds that Rome knew better than he what was in the best interests of the Church. He did not withdraw from the Church; nor did he agree with intellectual positions he saw as untenable. His actions indicate that he saw no solution in withdrawal; no solution in conforming.

Thomas Merton

In 1960, five years after Teilhard's death, Merton wrote a review of Teilhard's newly published *The Divine Milieu* and submitted that article to the censors. The superior of his order, headquartered in Rome, after consulting a professor in Rome, refused Merton permission to publish the book review. He told Merton that Rome admitted that particular book of Teilhard's was "harmless." "But one must not say anything in favor of T. de C. One must 'make the silence' regarding T. de C."[17] 'Making the silence' is a time-honored Roman practice of simply ignoring, erasing, dissenters. Rome had ostracized Teilhard during his life and had no intention of changing that treatment after his death.[18]

Merton followed the order not to publish the article on Teilhard but he did not like the way Teilhard was being treated: "I refuse to form part of an indignant chorus against him, and I refuse even to form part of a silently disapproving or hostile assembly of righteous critics. I refuse to draw back from him shaking my garments.

I have nothing but sympathy for his attempt to take a new view of things."[19]

In his journal the next day Merton complained about church authorities in general. He granted that they were "in good faith," but insisted that their presuppositions—"are wrong—the placid assumption that since 'the will of the superior is always the will of God,' . . . they are always infallible and sacrosanct. The subject has no appeal. His voice should not even be heard . . ."[20]

Merton saw that the premise that those in power always speak for God was a false premise. However, the Holy Office habitually operated on that premise and expected obedience based on that premise.

Two weeks later Merton wrote in his journal:

> Struggle in my heart all week. My own moral conflict never ceases. Knowing I *cannot* and *must not* simply submit to the standards imposed on me, and merely conform as "they" would like. This I am convinced is wrong – but the pressure never ceases. It takes every possible form. But it is not obedience. I will do what they tell me, but I will not and cannot think as they think. If I did I would be untrue to God, to myself and to all those who for some reason or other have a kind of confidence in me.[21]

Merton, like Teilhard, struggled against the pressure to conform. Like Teilhard, Merton was willing to do what he was told, but not willing to think as he was told. He saw the latter as morally wrong because it dissolves personal integrity.

An earlier entry in Merton's journal, November 15, 1957, contemplated a similar issue. Simultaneously full of joy at being at Gethsemani and full of anguish at certain mores, points of view, sets of values that were 'clearly printed between the lines' at Gethsemani, he struggled with the conflict.

> [I]t will always remain morally impossible for me simply to "conform" and to settle down and accept the official rationalization of what is going on here....
>
> But a great deal of the trouble comes from the fact that I look for a formula and expect to find a good one. If you want to find satisfactory formulas you had better deal with things that can be fitted into a formula. The vocation to seek God is not one of them. Nor is existence. Nor is the spirit of man...

There is no solution in withdrawal. No solution in conforming...[emphasis added]
[F]aith is infinitely more than blindly defending yourself with a few catchwords!
I do want Truth and will pay any price for it. And yet I know that I have found it already."[22]

Merton's 'resolution' of the conflict was to realize that he must continue to struggle. He explicitly rejected the option of conforming to the status quo; he explicitly rejected the option of walking out. Neither path would take him where he wanted to go. He stayed within the institution, for he found Truth there, but he continued to struggle for he also found falsehood within the 'official rationalizations.'

By 1961, Merton, at the age of 46, deeply concerned about the very real threat of nuclear war, was coming to believe that he had a duty to speak out.[23] In the early 1960s, the American public was in a state of extreme anxiety over the risk of nuclear war. People were talking about 'preemptive first strikes' against the Communists, using slogans like 'Better Dead than Red' and building bomb shelters in their backyards. The cold war was building up to the Cuban missile crisis. Neither the American Catholic hierarchy nor American Catholic theologians were opposing these currents.[24] In a struggle between the two dominant world powers, Catholics tended to see communism as the enemy and U.S. military power as the best way to 'protect the free world'. In October of 1961, Merton wrote in his journal:

I am perhaps at a turning point in my spiritual life: perhaps slowly coming to a point of maturation and the resolution of doubts—and the forgetting of fears. Walking into a known and definite battle. May God protect me in it... I am one of the few Catholic priests in the country who has come out unequivocally for a completely intransigent fight for the abolition of war....[25]

William Shannon, in *Passion for Peace*, emphasizes that Merton struggled before and after he reached this decision.

Yet despite his misgivings about himself and his message, despite his concern about the abdication of responsibility on the part of so many of his fellow-citizens, he knew that he had to continue, with whatever means at his disposal, to combat war and to work for the creation of a stable and lasting peace. Commenting on the prison writings of Father Delp, he says:

Christ our Lord did not come to bring peace as a kind of spiritual tranquilizer. He brought to his disciples a vocation and a task: to struggle in the world of violence to establish His peace not only in their own hearts but in society itself.[26]

Two months later, shortly before Christmas, Merton wrote: "More and more the conviction haunts me, that I shall sooner or later be silenced . . . Maybe the best is to say quickly and wisely and fully all that I have to say, all at once, and then let the blow fall."[27] Merton deliberately proceeded to publish as much and as fast as he could. In mid March, he wrote Ping Ferry that the American hierarchy was expressing displeasure with his writings on peace and that he might be silenced.[28] On April 26, 1962 he learned that the blow had fallen—the superior of the order had forbidden him to publish writings on the ethics of using atomic weapons.[29] Three days later, Merton revealed his thoughts in a letter to Jim Forest:

[I]n substance I am being silenced on the subject of war and peace... It reflects an astounding incomprehension of the seriousness of the present crisis in its religious aspect. It reflects an insensitivity to Christian and ecclesiastical values, and to the real sense of the monastic vocation. The reason given is that this is not the right kind of work for a monk, and that it "falsifies the monastic message." Imagine that: the thought that a monk might be deeply enough concerned with the issue of nuclear war to voice a protest against the arms race, is supposed to bring the monastic life into *disrepute*...

Now you will ask me: How do I reconcile obedience, true obedience (which is synonymous with love), with a situation like this? Shouldn't I just blast the whole thing wide open, or walk out, or tell them to jump in the lake?...

I am where I am. I have freely chosen this state, and have freely chosen to stay in it when the question of a possible change arose. If I am a disturbing element, that is all right. I am not making a point of being that, but simply of saying what my conscience dictates and doing so without seeking my own interest. This means accepting such limitations as may be placed on me by authority, not merely because it is placed on me by authority, and not because I may or may not agree with the ostensible reasons why the limitations are imposed, but out of love for God who is using these things to attain an end which I myself cannot at the moment see or comprehend…"[30]

What factors frame Merton's dissent?

1) He decided that the issue of nuclear war was so important that he would follow the course his conscience dictated and use his writing talents to do all he could short of violating a direct command.[31] He was aware that his stand would anger his superiors and many of his readers and was willing to pay that price.

2) He obeyed not because he agreed with the order or with the reasoning or the motives of his superiors, but on the stated ground that God wanted him to obey the order for reasons Merton could not understand.

3) He continued to work against war in ways that had not been forbidden. He published articles that did not come within the scope of the order, distributed the unpublished Cold War Letters to friends and friends of friends, and after the encyclical *Pacem in Terris* was issued, he immediately asked again for permission to publish, on the grounds that his writing was in agreement with the encyclical.[32]

A comparison of the dissent of Merton and Teilhard reveals significant similarities. Merton was convinced that the way in which the just war theory[33] was being interpreted was inadequate in the context of nuclear war, especially the bombing of cities. Teilhard was convinced that the traditional explication of Adam and Eve and original sin was inadequate as a factual explanation of human origins and of the presence of evil and death in the world. Each felt that the traditional response needed to be revised in the presence of new facts. Each tried to develop a better approach. Each was punished for his effort to integrate new knowledge with the old. The people in Rome whose job it was to protect the status quo correctly sensed a threat to the status quo and dealt with that threat by silencing the messenger. In Merton's case, the Holy Office was not involved; on his own authority, the head of the Cistercians silenced Merton on the topic of war. In Teilhard's case, the Holy Office made it clear to the head of the Jesuits that Teilhard should be silenced. Both Merton and Teilhard agonized over the conflict between the demands of Rome and their own convictions. Once Rome spoke, they obeyed, continued to agonize, and worked to develop and refine their positions in hopes of eventually persuading the authorities to let them speak. It caused them real pain to accept the fact that on issues they deemed absolutely central to what Christianity was all about, the authorities had suppressed their voices. Both expressed disillusionment with the institution but continued to identify with it. They obeyed because they thought they should obey, even though they were convinced that the orders had been issued in ignorance of the truth. They submitted without public protest.

Under no conditions would either Merton or Teilhard have held a press conference to openly challenge the Church.

Hans Kung and Charles Curran were much more willing to confront the Church publicly. Both had studied in Rome for many years. Kung was ordained in Rome in 1954, Curran in 1958. When they left Rome they were familiar with the way the Vatican Curia actually worked and the attitudes of the major players. They were also aware of the inhibitions that the Vatican's anti-modernist efforts had imposed on Catholic theology. The Second Vatican Council was called not long after their student days in Rome. Each was strongly influenced by the process of Vatican II and by the values it expressed.

Hans Kung

Kung's impact upon American Catholicism during the 1960s may be gauged from the themes in his 1961 book, from his 1963 lecture tour of the States, and from a 1968 declaration he drafted and 1,360 theologians signed. Each will be considered in enough detail to give some indication of the impression they made on American Catholics.

Hans Kung was 33 years old when he wrote *The Council, Reform and Reunion* in 1961.[34] His ambitious goal was to influence the agenda of the upcoming Vatican Council. His message was that the church should reform itself so that its own defects did not prevent reunion with the other Christian churches. Kung dissented from the prevalent view that the church was a perfect society. He named failings without minimizing or excusing them, thus breaking the taboo against open, public, direct criticism of the Catholic Church from within.

In the chapter titled "The Framework for Catholic Renewal" he stated: "The Pope intends that the Council, with the reunion of separated Christians in mind, shall undertake a true reform; in fact a genuine renewal."[35] Asking "What may we, as Christians, do?" Kung addressed four areas.

First, We Can Suffer . . . Anyone who has never, as a member of the Church, suffered on account of his Church, has never known her as she really is or never loved her. Genuine suffering on account of the Church springs from love of the Church: love for a Church who is too unlike her Lord.[36]

Second, We Can Pray. . . It is the Spirit who will form all things anew. The daily prayer of Christians in the Church, for the Church and not least for themselves, will be *Veni, Sancte Spiritus*:

What is filthy, do thou wash,
What is dry, do thou refresh,
What is wounded, do thou heal;
What is rigid, do thou bend,
What is frozen, do thou melt,
What is wandering, do thou rule.[37]

Third, "We Can Criticize. While we suffer and pray, we do not have to give our assent and amen to *everything* in the Church. Criticism, indeed loud criticism, can be a duty . . .

As a Church of *men*, sinful men, the Church, though of divine foundation, *needs* criticizing; as the Church of *God* she is, more than any other institution, *worth* criticizing. To show by criticism what has become humanly deformed in the Church is a necessary preliminary to any reform. How can failures and abuses be corrected if they cannot be spoken of and discussed?[38]

Fourth, We Can Act.[39]

[T]his is what we may, with God's grace, do: in the cause of renewal we can suffer, pray, criticize, and above all act; not for revolution, not for restoration, not for a mere change of heart nor a mere reform of abuses but for a creative reform of the state of the Church . . . The ancient basilica is not to be torn down and rebuilt . . . nor is it merely to be scrubbed down, patched up and dusted off; it is to be, in accordance with the ancient plan of its founder, but for the needs of this new age, *renewed*.[40]

Merton loved Kung's book. His journal noted: "If I wanted to start copying bits of it I would end by copying page after page, because I am so glad these things are at last said."[41] In his letters, Merton called Kung's book "splendid," "remarkable," "exciting," "a breath of new life," "awake and frank and not wild, but objectively Catholic in the finest sense."[42] Further, "It is one of the most forthright, direct and powerful statements of our actual condition and problem that I have ever seen."[43]

In March 1962 as Merton finished reading *The Council, Reform and Reunion* he pondered its message in his journals. (The ellipses below are in the original.)

> Whether it is easy to love the Church, the Church as she *is* [underlined twice] and not as she might be . . . To love the "poor" sinners, yes. For we count ourselves among the poor ones.
>
> But the great, complacent, obtuse, powerful and self-satisfied sinners who are aware only of their righteousness, who close the doors, who do not enter in and help others out, the Grand Inquisitors who build their own structure on top of God's structure and attach more importance to what they themselves have built than to what He builds . . . Yet they are in their own way patient and gentle. They too suffer. They too have a kind of humility. But they are *closed* [underlined twice]. There are human realities to which they absolutely refuse to be sensitive. For they have somehow come to believe that a certain kind of compassion is a weakness they cannot afford.[44]
>
> Finishing the Küng book on *The Council, Reform and Reunion.* Tremendous, clear, outspoken. Will his hopes be realized? He is sane about them, and realistic. A sobering discussion of possibilities which may never be realized. If they are not, it will be a disaster.[45]

Merton acknowledged that some churchmen had closed minds, righteous attitudes, lack of compassion, and inquisitorial habits. He did not condemn them as bad people: "Yet they are in their own way patient and gentle. They too suffer." Merton, recognizing that the goals outlined in Kung's book might not be realized, was also convinced that failure to achieve them would be disastrous for the Church.

In 1963, after the first session of the Second Vatican Council, Hans Kung arrived in the U.S. to begin an 8-week lecture tour.[46]

Two weeks before his arrival he read in the *Washington Post* of February 23, 1963 that the Catholic University of America had banned lectures on campus by Godfrey Diekmann, Hans Kung, John Courtney Murray and Gustav Weigel.[47] Joseph Fenton, who placed the ban, had long been the dean of the theology school at Catholic University and a close friend of Cardinal Ottaviani, the head of the Vatican Congregation for the Doctrine of the Faith. John Tracy Ellis, a historian of American Catholicism and for many years a faculty member of Catholic University, reported:

> The reason given by the administration was that since these four men… all represented the progressive school of thought, and since the institution belonged to the entire hierarchy of the United States, the university should not show partiality to any single aspect of theological thought while the ecumenical council was still debating certain controverted issues on which the four theologians were thought to hold a single point of view. The fact that in banning the representatives of this point of view an advantage was implicitly given to the opposing side in a way that jeopardized the neutrality which the administration was desirous of safeguarding seems to have been overlooked by the rector of the university and his associates.[48]

When Kung arrived in the U.S., Cardinal Cushing offered Kung his full support and escorted him to his first lecture at Boston College. Kung's goal, in his words, was to be "honest and direct without academic fussiness and clerical unctuousness."[49] He talked about the 'elephant in the living room'—freedom and the Church. His book *Freedom Today*[50] is based on the themes of that lecture tour. In Boston, Kung received his first standing ovation; 3,000 people were still clapping as he left the hall with Cardinal Cushing. He spoke to 5,000 at McCormick Place in Chicago; 6,500 at the University of San Francisco. At St. Louis University, in the presence of 8,500 people, Kung was granted an honorary degree.[51] Merton regretted that Kung had not come to Gethsemani while he was in the U.S. for his 1963 lecture tour.[52] Tentative plans for Kung to come had been made but did not materialize.

In 1968, only three years after the Second Vatican Council, Kung drafted a declaration entitled *For the Freedom of Theology*.[53] Yves Congar, Karl Rahner and Edward Schillebeeckx edited the declaration; 1,360 Catholic theologians, from 53 countries, signed it. The declaration began:

> In full loyalty and unequivocal fidelity to the Catholic Church we, the undersigned theologians, consider ourselves prompted and obliged to make the following point publicly and with great seriousness: The freedom won for theologians and theology by the Second Vatican Council for service to the Church must not be placed at risk again today.[54]

"Since the threat to free theological work now seems to be on the increase again," the theologians stressed the need for the personnel of the Congregation for the Doctrine of the Faith to represent the "legitimate multiplicity of today's theological schools," rather than presenting the appearance of partisan bias "for the sake of a certain theological party line."[55]   The theologians stated that in today's world, erroneous theological notions could not be stopped by compulsory measures. They could be corrected only through unimpeded, objective, scholarly discussion and research. The use of procedures derived from the Inquisition not only harmed the development of healthy theology, it also damaged the credibility of the entire Church. The theologians recommended specified procedural guidelines to be implemented for future investigations, including rights for the accused.[56]

The significance of this declaration lies not only in its content, but in its timing (only three years after the Council), in its leaders (Kung, Congar, Rahner and Schillebeeckx), in its signatories (1,360 Catholic theologians throughout the world), and in its hope (that the Vatican would revise its procedures). The declaration did not dissent from the Church envisioned by the Council. It was a straightforward statement that the Congregation was acting in a way that was contrary to the principles of Vatican II, an explanation of why that behavior was harmful to the Church, and a list of specific reforms that should be instituted. The very act of loyalty to the goals of the whole church as stated in Council documents was dissent from the attitudes, structures, and procedures of the Congregation.

During Merton's lifetime, what factors framed Kung's dissent?

1) Kung demonstrated direct, open, public discussion of structural problems within the Church. He spoke with clarity, erudition, and boldness. He did not mince words. Structural

problems included procedural practice which denied rights to those accused, as well as the standard practice of making decisions without input from those affected and doing so behind closed doors.

2) Kung struggled to protect freedom and diversity within the Church. He resisted the efforts by the Congregation for the Doctrine of the Faith to revert to the status quo before the Council by imposing its own view as the only legitimate view.

3) Kung worked with groups, building coalitions to express mutual concerns and to propose structural remedies. He was willing to be a standard bearer, as shown by his role in the declaration *For the Freedom of Theology.* He spoke not only to the academy and to the hierarchy but directly to the public, writing so that his theology was accessible to the lay reader.

One similarity between Kung and Merton is that both made it a point to write in a way that a general reader could understand. Both wrote with fluency and passion. One difference is that Kung spent a great deal of time working with groups on matters of common interest. Merton, in contrast, was hesitant about joining groups, concerned that they might do things he would not approve, aware that he could not participate effectively in the ongoing dynamics of groups outside the monastery. During the 1960s Merton resisted pressure to come out of the monastery to work for peace and justice, convinced that he could make his greatest contribution by continuing to live as a monk, nourishing both his self and his writing from the same source. Another difference between the two is that whereas Kung tried hard to change the institutional Church through structural reform, most of Merton's work was directed not toward revision of organizational structures, but toward internal change within individuals.

Kung could be iconoclastic and to my knowledge felt no need to apologize for it. Merton could also be iconoclastic but he did feel a need to apologize for it. He tried to write in a way that would avoid antagonizing others. His goal was to establish the common ground he shared with his readers and from that base persuade them to see the reasonableness of the position he was advocating. Under no conditions would Kung have perceived himself to be a 'guilty bystander'; he was professionally and fully in the fray. Sometimes Merton was similarly immersed, as he was with his anti-war writing, but more often he tried to stand outside it, to perceive it from a detached, monastic perspective. This stand-point, although removed, was not aloof. Merton's claim was that being an outsider was the best standpoint for him given all the givens, the place from which he could best be himself, understand what was really important, and do his best work.

The love that both Merton and Kung had for the Church forti-fied their determination not to withdraw. On the other hand, their shared view that the Church was "too unlike her Lord" enabled them to resist pressure to conform to attitudes and mores preva-lent within the culture of the Church.

Charles Curran

Two events brought Charles Curran to the attention of American Catholics in the late 1960s: first a tenure controversy at Catholic University in 1967 and second, the *Statement of Catholic Theologians* issued shortly after the release of the birth control encyclical in 1968.

In 1967, Charles Curran, 33 years old at the time, applied for tenure at the Catholic University of America.[57]   Six years earlier, Curran had earned a doctorate from the Gregorian University in Rome and a doctorate from the Academia Alfonsiana, the Redemptorist University in Rome. The topic of his first disserta-tion was the prevention of conception after rape, through which he learned about the biological, medical and theological aspects of the act of conception. His second dissertation focused on St. Alphonsus Ligouri's emphasis on the 'subjective' state of the per-son in contrast to the 'objective' legal norms the Jansenists were championing during Ligouri's lifetime. While in Rome, Curran had studied under Joseph Fuchs and Bernard Häring, both of whom were later members of the papal birth control commission.

John Tracy Ellis in *American Catholicism* described the cultural change that was occurring in many American Catholic colleges in the decade before Curran applied for tenure. Ellis noted that in the early part of the twentieth century, the norm was:

> well-nigh universal docile acceptance in Catholic circles not only of the teachings of the Church but also of the authoritar-ian regimes that governed the Church's colleges. To question an article of Catholic belief or to challenge a ruling by a presi-dent or a dean in a Catholic institution was almost unthink-able.

Some years before Vatican Council II, however, a more critical spirit and a greater eagerness for the democratic process began to pervade the leading Catholic centers of learning
. . . .

One of the first places where the conflict between the proponents of a broader and more genuine freedom for faculty and students and a highly conservative administration broke into the open was the Catholic University of America.[58]

Curran's application for tenure received the unanimous support of the faculty of the school of theology and the unanimous approval of the academic senate. There was no opposition from the administration, so the standard tenure process was successfully concluded.[59] In a "sudden and unexplained move," the trustees of Catholic University decided that Curran's contract would not be renewed for the following year.[60]   In effect, Curran was fired. The faculty of the School of Theology unanimously reaffirmed their confidence in Curran, noting that no charges had been made against him. The dean, Walter J. Schmitz, stated: "the academic freedom and the security of every professor of this University is jeopardized . . . . [The theology faculty] can not and will not function until Father Curran is reinstated."[61]

He concluded by inviting the other schools of the university to join the theologians' protest, an appeal that met with an immediate and overwhelming response from most of the other faculties, except that of the School of Education. Almost within a matter of hours the institution came to a standstill by a virtually total boycott of classes until such time as Father Curran would be restored to his post . . . [T]he trustees' procedure at Chicago, to which Paul J. Hallinan, Archbishop of Atlanta, had alone entered a negative vote, met with such instant, vigorous, and sustained opposition from both faculty and students that after a week of boycott the trustees capitulated completely and the chancellor announced that Father Curran had been reinstated and his promotion approved.[62]

In 1967 all the members of the board of trustees were members of the American hierarchy. Their action in firing Curran, like the university's 1963 action in banning the four theologians from speaking on campus, was an effort to ensure that only official positions would have a voice on campus.

Somewhat more than one year after the tenure controversy, on July 29, 1968, Vatican officials released the long awaited birth control encyclical, *Humanae Vitae*, at a press conference in Rome at 4:30 a.m. Washington time.[63] The American bishops released an English version of the encyclical at a press conference that Monday afternoon in Washington, D.C. At 5:00 p.m. that same day, a group of ten theology teachers, five from the Catholic University of America and five associated with other institutions, met to "read, analyze, discuss and evaluate" English language copies of the encyclical.[64] "Before and during the discussion, the members of the group had been in contact with other theologians throughout the country. It was finally agreed that a statement would be made and released to the press the next day."[65] One of the underlying reasons for their decision to do so is stated below:

The Statement of the Theologians was not the first public statement on the issue. On July 29 a number of American bishops made statements about the Encyclical. For example, the Archbishop of Washington said: 'I call upon all priests in their capacity as confessors, teachers, and preachers of God's word to follow without equivocation, ambiguity or simulation the teaching of the Church on this matter as enunciated clearly by Paul VI.'[66] Such a reaction on the part of American bishops was not wholly unexpected. In January, 1968, the American bishops had released their pastoral letter, *The Church in Our Day*, which did not adequately distinguish between the absolute assent of faith and the conditional religious assent which is due to noninfallible authoritative teachings. This letter failed even to mention the possibility of dissent from authoritative, noninfallible teaching.[67]

Two Catholic University professors (Hunt and Tracy) had pointed out this confusion to one of the bishops on the drafting committee of the pastoral, but no changes were made. Thus on the American scene it was obvious that many Catholics, including bishops, were not totally aware of what the Theologians' Statement referred to as the common teaching about the possibility of dissent from authoritative teaching. People who did not have this knowledge faced the false dilemma of either accepting the teaching of the Encyclical or thinking they had to reject their Roman Catholic faith commitment. Undoubtedly, one could propose many reasons to explain why this was not common knowledge in the Church in the United States, but the important matter remains the fact that a large number of Roman Catholics did not know the existence of the right to dissent from authoritative teachings when there is sufficient reason for such dissent.[68]

The *Statement by Catholic Theologians* was drafted that evening. Each of the ten theologians present then contacted other theologians by phone to read the statement to them and ask if they would be willing to sign the Statement. Curran called Bernard Haring, a noted theologian and member of the birth control commission, who added his name.[69] At a press conference the next morning, July 30, less than 24 hours after the bishops' press conference, about 10 of the signers were present and available to the press. Curran acted as the spokesperson for the group of 87 theologians who had endorsed the Statement by that time. The next day, July 31, letters and copies of the Statement were mailed to the approximately 1,200 members of the Catholic Theological Society of America and the College Theology Society. In the next few months, American Catholic theologians from 200 institutions added their signatures to the Statement, bringing the total number of signers to 600.[70]

At another press conference the following day, August 1, all the American lay members of the papal birth control commission "publicly agreed in substance, in accord with their respective competencies, with the Statement of the Theologians."[71] The spokespersons were commission members Andre Hellegers and Thomas Burch, from Georgetown University, and the special consultant to the commission on historical matters, John Noonan, from the University of California at Berkeley.[72]

Clearly, this entire sequence of events constituted organized, widespread, public dissent.[73]

The *Statement by Catholic Theologians* began by acknowledging a distinct role for the hierarchical *magisterium*; indicated that the Catholic tradition assigns to theologians the responsibility to evaluate and interpret pronouncements of the *magisterium* in the light of the whole tradition; noted that the encyclical was not an infallible teaching; and commented on the positive values concerning marriage expressed in the encyclical. It is significant that the next major point concerned not birth control but ecclesiology.

[W]e take exception to the ecclesiology implied and methodology used by Paul VI in the writing and promulgation of the
document: they are incompatible with the Church's self awareness as expressed in and suggested by the acts of the Second
Vatican Council itself. The Encyclical consistently assumes that
the Church is identical with the hierarchical office. No real
importance is afforded the witness of the life of the Church in
its totality, the special witness of many Catholic couples is neglected . . . .[74]

The encyclical rejected "the majority view presented by the Commission established to consider the question," and "the conclusions of a large part of the international Catholic theological community."[75] This part of the Statement voiced a sense of betrayal, a
perception that an encyclical issued in this manner was an explicit
rejection of the Vatican II understanding that the deliberations of
the papal birth control commission mattered, that the theological
community mattered, that the witness and testimony of Catholic
couples mattered.[76] The methodology of and result reached by
the encyclical inextricably bound together the issues of ecclesiology
and birth control.[77]

   After stating substantive reasons for their disagreement with
the theology underpinning the encyclical, the theologians stated:
"It is common teaching in the Church that Catholics may dissent
from authoritative, noninfallible teachings of the magisterium
when sufficient reasons for so doing exist."[78]

   The theologians ended with two final points.

Therefore, as Roman Catholic theologians, conscious of our
duty and our limitations, we conclude that spouses may responsibly decide according to their conscience that artificial
contraception in some circumstances is permissible and indeed
necessary to preserve and foster the values and sacredness of
marriage.

   It is our conviction also that true commitment to the mystery of Christ and the Church requires a candid statement of
mind at this time by all Catholic theologians."[79]

The first of the sentences immediately above addressed the issue
of birth control; the second was a direct challenge to all Catholic
theologians to openly, honestly, and publicly express their positions.

During Merton's lifetime, what factors framed Currans's dissent?

1) Curran chose and was chosen to be a spokesperson for a large group of Catholic theologians. At the time he was 34 years old and a vice president of the Catholic Theological Society of America. He wanted, as his peers did, to explain to those Catholics who felt that they must either conform to the encyclical or withdraw from the Church that that perception could be a false dilemma.

2) The theologians agreed that the laity should have information known to theologians that the hierarchy had not made available to the laity. The decision to publish that information was taken after efforts to incorporate such information into the bishops' pastoral had been rejected and after some bishops had demanded complete unquestioning compliance with the encyclical.

3) Curran cared deeply about academic freedom, a concept based on the premise that full and fair discussion is in the best interests of the group because it leads toward greater truth. He also was convinced that the biological and theological bases for the encyclical were unsound.

Although this article has focused on events that occurred during the last decade of Merton's life, it is necessary to state here that after Merton's death the Congregation acted against both Kung and Curran, declaring them to be 'neither suitable nor eligible' to function as professors of Catholic theology. The history of the Vatican's action against Kung in 1979 is fully documented in *Kung in Conflict* [80] and that of the Vatican's action against Curran in 1986 is fully documented in *Faithful Dissent*.[81]

This paper has reviewed Merton's comments on Teilhard and Kung. I searched, unsuccessfully, to find comments Merton made about Curran. The fact that I did not find any did not mean that none existed. I asked William Shannon who said that as far as he knew Merton never mentioned Curran. Given Shannon's extensive knowledge of the Merton corpus, I take that statement as conclusive.

Merton did make a few remarks in his journal about the birth control encyclical. On August 1, 1968, three days after the encyclical was issued and two days after the Statement, Merton discussed the encyclical, and probably the fact that the theologians had made a statement, with Father Raymond.

> [S]topped in at the hospital to talk to Fr. Raymond who was operated on last week . . . He was full of truculent opinions and satisfaction about the new birth control encyclical ('There will be a schism'). A curious thing, that encyclical! I wonder what will come of it![82]

Significantly, Merton said nothing about his own opinion of the encyclical. Merton's journal for August 5 recorded news he had received from Ping Ferry: "John Cogley in protest against Pope Paul's birth control encyclical, has given up his column in 25 diocesan papers."[83] Again, Merton says nothing about his own position. Merton had broad interests but he did not attempt to keep up on everything and birth control was not a subject he chose to engage, although in his letters he occasionally made a brief remark on the topic. At that time, the summer of 1968, Merton was preparing for his trip to Asia.

Comparing the style of Merton's dissent to that of Curran's highlights Merton's role as a non-expert with Curran's role as an expert. When Merton tried to convince his readers in the early 1960s that nuclear war was a moral evil and that Christians should act to prevent catastrophe, he was not an expert on the subject of nuclear war nor did he pretend to be. He had qualms about his role; he stepped in to do a job that he was convinced needed to be done and that other prominent American Catholics simply were not doing. In contrast, in 1968 Curran acted as a leader of a group composed of articulate, like-minded professionals analyzing a document they had been trained to analyze. Curran's views, as evaluated by his peers, were modulated and moderate. He spoke precisely from his expertise in the field of Catholic moral theology. Another difference was that Merton's habit was to express his opinion in his own idiosyncratic way, whereas Curran was comfortable with group statements and group action. It is very hard to imagine Merton as a member of a group of moral theologians, and almost impossible to imagine him participating in a press conference that many people saw as direct disobedience.[84] Curran was a participant and an activist in the situations described above. Merton did not want to join the fray; he preferred to be an observer—he fought efforts to pull him into an activist role. Merton deliberately chose to stay within the monastery, accepted his stance as a 'bystander' and to some extent did feel 'guilty' about it. But not guilty enough to change his basic stance. He chose to be a monk, to be a contemplative, and to write on topics important to him to the extent he could in the time remaining after he had met those prior commitments.

Having compared Merton's dissent to that of each of the other three, the article now considers two social factors that go far to explain how the dissent of Teilhard and Merton and their response to Vatican orders differed from that of Kung and Curran.

First, it would have been foreign to the cultural milieu in which Teilhard and Merton lived for them to protest publicly as Kung and Curran did. It was almost unthinkable. Prior to Vatican II, public criticism of the Church from within was deemed to be very close to sedition. The Church presented itself as a 'perfect society.' That image became much more complex when, from 1962 to 1965, Vatican II was often front page news. Thousands and thousands of articles appeared explaining to the general public, Catholic and non-Catholic alike, the differing goals and values of various groups within the Church. The American Catholic public became accustomed to open discussion of the struggles within the Church. The American Catholic hierarchy for multiple reasons, including their age and status, tended to think that public dissent was disloyal. Before, during and after Vatican II some groups within the Church saw dissent as legitimate and as urgent. Kung and Curran were in the latter group for multiple reasons, including their age and status. Their attitudes were formed at a time when many of their peers saw reform as an urgent need and open, public discussion as a necessary means to accomplish that reform. When Teilhard and Merton chose not to publicly criticize the Church the climate of the times was very different than it was when Kung and Curran chose to directly and publicly protest actions the church had taken.

Second, both Teilhard and Merton were individual thinkers. No one else was saying what they were saying. When ordered to be silent, each of them made an individual decision to be silent and that settled the matter. In contrast, Kung and Curran spoke not just as individuals but as members of a group. Granted, the 'group' was in many ways unorganized and amorphous; nonetheless in some way Kung and Curran were chosen leaders. In fact, it may well be that the reason they were singled out for censure was precisely their leadership role. Without doubt, their censure was intended to 'send a message' to persons in addition to the principals. The 'aloneness' characteristic of Teilhard and Merton contrasts to the 'togetherness' Kung and Curran shared with those who agreed with and rallied around them. One by-product of the communal aspect of the dissent of Kung and Curran is that they acted with the support of others, whereas Merton and Teilhard acted without it. Granted, Merton and Teilhard were in contact with some people who understood the issues and offered support. Granted also, no amount of support from others could remove the pain Kung and Curran personally suffered. It remains true that Merton and Teilhard were more alone and cut off from like-minded people than were Kung and Curran.

In some significant ways, Merton differed from all three of the others. First, Teilhard, Kung and Curran were 'cradle Catholics' who entered seminaries at a young age; Merton had much more experience of the world before he became a convert at age 23 and entered the monastery at age 26. Second, Teilhard, Kung and Curran obtained doctoral degrees, became acknowledged experts in their fields, and spoke out on the basis of that expertise. In contrast, Merton read widely in any subject matter area that interested him at the time and quickly grasped the main points well enough that he was ready and willing to comment on the subject. His goal was not to do scholarly research but to search for wisdom wherever he could find it, most often within the monastic tradition, and then to incorporate it into his life and writing. Third, Teilhard, Kung and Curran had difficulty with the entity that was called the Holy Office and later renamed the Congregation for the Doctrine of the Faith. The Vatican determined that aspects of the theological positions taken by Teilhard, Kung and Curran were unacceptable. In contrast, Merton's orthodoxy was not challenged. Merton was silenced by the head of his order on the ground that it was 'inappropriate' for a Trappist monk to be writing on the topic of nuclear war. It was deemed 'inopportune' for Merton to be taking such a strong stance against nuclear war at a time when most of his superiors and most of the American Catholic hierarchy saw the U.S. nuclear arsenal as a legitimate means of defense.

As stated in the beginning, the main purpose of this article is to tell four stories, whenever possible doing so from the viewpoint and in the words of the principal. The paper puts Merton's dissent into the larger context of other Catholic dissent also affecting the American Catholic public during the last decade of Merton's life

(1958-1968). As noted at the beginning of the paper, it will end by addressing the fact that each of these people continued to love the Church and chose to stay within the institution. Rome made deliberate efforts to restrict the influence of these four thinkers, to label their positions as 'beyond the pale,' to marginalize their voices. They felt the weight of the system when it was thrown against them. Yet they continued to identify themselves with and commit themselves to the institutional Church—warts and all. None of them chose to leave the priesthood or the Church. They did not withdraw. Nor did they conform.

The term love need not include infatuation, illusion, or refusal to admit the defects of the beloved. At times each of these people said harsh things about the Church. Each knew the truth of Kung's words:

> Anyone who has never, as a member of the Church, suffered on account of his Church, has never known her as she really is or never loved her. Genuine suffering on account of the Church springs from love of the Church: love for a Church who is too unlike her Lord.[85]

The rest of the article presents first, a statement by each person, second, a few remarks about the circumstances in which the statement was written and on its meaning, and third, a reflection on the statement in light of the following thought from David Tracy.

> [T]heologians, like all inquirers, would betray their vocation and indeed their own way of being religious, if they simply yielded to coercion. There is, after all, the reality of intellectual integrity. When that integrity is gone, all true inquiry ceases. When persuasion is abandoned, the vacuum is soon filled by the furies let loose by coercion. Along that way lies presumption for the few and despair for the many. But presumption and despair are theological vices whose only service is to clarify anew the need for hope as the central theological virtue of our period—a hope grounded in faith, intellectual integrity, and courage; a hope functioning as the love empowering all true persuasion in the community of hope.[86]

Statements made by Curran, Kung, Teilhard, and Merton will be considered in that order. The chronological order of the statements themselves is 1926, 1967, 1980 and 1986, but I have not followed that sequence. Out of the many things each of these people said, I have selected a few words I think relevant to why each of them chose to stay within the Church. The statements of Curran and Kung explicitly address that question; those by Teilhard and Merton do not explicitly address it, but I find the selected statements to be indicative of their answer to it.

Charles Curran

I am conscious of my own limitations and my own failures. I am aware of the consequences of what is involved. But I can only repeat what I wrote Cardinal Ratzinger in my final response of April 1, 1986: 'In conscience at the present time I cannot and do not change the theological positions I have taken.' In my own judgment and in the judgment of the majority of my peers I have been and am suitable and eligible to exercise the function of a Professor of Catholic Theology.

I remain convinced that the hierarchical teaching office in the Roman Catholic Church must allow dissent on these issues and ultimately should change its teaching. My conviction in this matter is supported by a number of factors. First, the overwhelming support of my theological colleagues has buoyed me personally and strengthened my own hope for the ultimate acceptance of these convictions. Second, the best and the mainstream of the Catholic theological tradition support my basic approaches. According to Catholic theological tradition, the word and work of Jesus must always be made present and meaningful in the contemporary historical and cultural circumstances. The Catholic tradition also insists on the transcendence of faith and the principle that faith and reason can never contradict one another. In addition, Catholic ethics has insisted on an intrinsic morality. Something is commanded because it is good and not the other way around. Authority must conform to the truth . . .

I remain a loyal and committed Roman Catholic. I pray daily that I might continue to love and serve the Church without bitterness and anger.

I will continue to work for the legitimacy of some theological and practical dissent, the need to change some official hierarchical church teachings, the importance of academic freedom for Catholic theology, and the need for just structures to deal with the inevitable tensions that from time to time will exist between theologians and pastors. I believe these are all for the good of the Roman Catholic Church—my Church.[87]

Curran's words are excerpted from his public statement issued August 20, 1986, two days after he was notified that the Vatican had determined that he would "no longer be suitable nor eligible to exercise the function of a Professor of Catholic Theology."[88] In his statement, Curran summarizes the reasons he cannot agree with the official position. He acknowledges that it is hard not to be bitter and angry when what he sees as his legitimate dissent is seen by the Vatican as intolerable. He prays to overcome his dejection. He promises to continue to work for a Church that will respect the intellectual integrity of its theologians and its members and will cease to rely on unjust structures to coerce submission. He states his conviction that these changes will make the Church to which he has committed himself a better Church. His tone, as usual, is composed and moderate.

Tracy recognized that for a theologian simply to yield to coercion, to change a carefully thought out position in order to avoid censure, would destroy the integrity of the theologian. Curran chose to retain his integrity rather than to conform to an official position that he could not perceive as in accord with truth. Following the Vatican's action, Curran continues to hope that eventually the church will change and commits himself to work toward that end. As I see it, his actions demonstrate, in Tracy's words, "hope grounded in faith, intellectual integrity, and courage."

Hans Kung

After an unjust and unfair procedure on the part of the highest ecclesiastical authorities, I was deprived by decree of the title of "Catholic theologian" and an attempt was made to drive me out of my faculty of Catholic theology after twenty years of teaching there and to thrust me—without being overscrupulous about methods—to the margin of my Catholic Church very shortly after I had completed twenty-five years as a priest....

Why then do I remain a Catholic? The answer will first of all be for me as for many other people: I do not wish to allow that to be taken away from me which throughout my life has become valuable and dear to me. In the first place, I was born into this Catholic Church: baptized it is true, into the much larger community of all those who believe in Jesus Christ – nevertheless, born at the same time into a Catholic family which is dear to me, a Swiss Catholic parish to which I am always glad to return: in a word, into a Catholic homeland which I do not want to lose, which I do not want to abandon . . .

The Catholic Church must not become confused simply with the Catholic hierarchy, still less with the Roman bureaucracy . . .

[F]or the sake of the freedom of theological science, I have had to resist throughout all the years an interrogation of an Inquisition according all rights to itself and practically none to the accused person. That much I owe to those also who have suffered—and, as it seems, will suffer in the future—under these inhumane and un-Christian measures....

I know that I am not alone in this controversy about true catholicity. I shall fight against any acquiescence together with the many people who have hitherto supported me. We must continue to work together for a truly Catholic Church that is bound by the Gospel. For this, it is worthwhile to remain a Catholic.[89]

After the Vatican's sudden and unexpected declaration, issued December 18, 1979,[90] that Kung was not eligible and not suitable to exercise the function of a professor of Catholic theology, many people asked Kung why he tolerated such treatment. In early January, 1980 Kung wrote a seven page essay titled "Why I Remain a Catholic." The selected words above, extracted from that essay, show his Catholic faith has deep and lasting value to him. He does not want to lose his bond with fellow Catholics or to abandon the ship in a storm. After the censure, as before, Kung sees the Church as broader and deeper than the Vatican and the hierarchy. He mentions what he has talked about at length elsewhere—the procedures of the Congregation, derived from those of the Inquisition, accord almost all rights to the Congregation and practically none to the accused person. Kung remains committed to the structural reforms he was advocating before the ban.

His tone, as usual, is forthright and plainspoken, calling it as he sees it, expressing his determination to 'fight against any acquiescence' to what he deems to be unjust or untrue. Considering

Kung's words in light of Tracy's statement, it is clear that Kung, by temperament, is not likely to yield to coercion. In no way does Kung compromise his intellectual integrity. He reasserts his determination to continue to work with others for structural reform, including freedom for theologians and rights for the accused. To do so requires hope. To do so right after Kung had suffered the Vatican attack upon his work required faith, hope, and love.

Pierre Teilhard de Chardin

I admit all the defects, but I tolerate them even as I react against them, because for now they are inseparable from what seems to be the only axis along which human activity can legitimately progress. Believe me when one has penetrated to this axis of the Christian attitude, the ritual, disciplinary and theological encrustations matter little more than musical or acoustical theories matter to the enjoyment of a beautiful piece of music. Truly, there is a Christian *note* which makes the whole World vibrate like an immense gong, in the divine Christ. This note is unique and universal and in it alone consists the Gospel. Only it is real (happily). And for this reason it is inevitable that, in trying to fix and hold its reality, men analyze it out of sight (as the physicist does with the most divine nuances of sound and color). This is what begets, under the very simple dogma, an unlimited complexity which is aggravated by theorists' presumption in substituting their constructs for reality. In any case, for you, as for everyone, there is only one road that can lead to God and this is the fidelity to remain constantly true to yourself, to what you feel is highest in you. Do not worry about the rest. The road will open before you as you go.[91]

Teilhard wrote the above words not in a statement intended for the public but in a private letter to a personal friend who was not a Catholic.[92] Teilhard seems to be responding, in a way he hopes a non-Catholic can understand, to a question the friend seems to have asked— why do you put up with the conditions imposed on you? Teilhard wrote on June 11, 1926, approximately a week after he had arrived in Tientsin, China, where he had gone following the command that he leave his teaching position in Paris and leave France.

Teilhard characterizes the Church's "ritual, disciplinary and theological encrustations" as a by-product of too much theorizing. In an effort to understand Christianity, 'men analyze it out of sight,' substituting 'an unlimited complexity which is aggravated by theorists' presumption in substituting their constructs for reality.' He advises his friend to set all that aside, concentrating instead upon the only road that can lead to God, 'the fidelity to remain constantly true to yourself, to what you feel is highest in you.' For himself, Teilhard chose to accept the Catholic Church, admitting its defects, reacting against them, but ultimately tolerating them, seeing them 'for now' as inseparable from the gospel of Christ.

Teilhard's tone is very much his own. It is unlike that of Curran and Kung. Analyzing is their job. Their role as theologians is to devote their energies to distinguishing 'the axis' of Catholicism from its 'encrustations' and to develop persuasive reasons to move past the 'encrustations,' while trying not to substitute their own constructs for reality. To the extent that theology is the analytic study of mental concepts, Teilhard was no theologian. Here he describes the Christian message as music; he wants to listen to and be absorbed in the music, not to compose acoustical theories. Elsewhere, Teilhard expressed his wish that he had had the talent to be a musician or a novelist instead of what he was. His decision to take himself as he was preceded the work product he gave the world.

Tracy said that 'theologians, like all inquirers, would betray their vocation and indeed their own way of being religious, if they simply yielded to coercion.' Teilhard was not an analytical theologian, but he certainly was an inquirer, a visionary, a synthesizer. Far from betraying 'his own way of being religious,' Teilhard was true to what was highest in him and he accomplished that within the Church. Although Teilhard suffered periodic bouts of severe depression, he avoided what Tracy calls the theological vice of despair, living instead in 'a hope grounded in faith, intellectual integrity, and courage.'

Thomas Merton

It remains to speak one word to the monks themselves; that is, to those who now, at this time, are persevering in monasteries and hermitages. That word is: *do not be impatient and do not be afraid.* Do not imagine that everything depends on some instant magic transformation of constitutions and of laws. You already have what you need right in your hands! You have the grace of your vocation and of your love. No earthly situation has ever been ideal. God does not need an ideal situation in order to carry out his work in our hearts. If we do what we can with the means and grace at our disposal, if we sincerely take advantage of our genuine opportunities, the Spirit will be there and his love will not fail us. Our liberation, our solitude, our vision, our understanding and our salvation do not depend on anything remote from us or beyond our reach. Grace has been given to us along with our good desires. What is needed is the faith to accept it and the energy to put our faith to work in situations that may not seem to us to be promising.[93]

Robert Coles, who wrote a forward for the revised edition of *Contemplation in a World of Action,* the volume from which the above words were taken, perceptively notes that here Merton is writing from "his manner of being."[94] Merton's words stem not from book learning, not from systematic analysis, but from the monastic tradition and hard life experience. The tone is both matter-of-fact and hopeful. Merton is speaking to his fellow monks and, by inference, to us.

Here is a "rough translation" of Merton's message. Don't wait impatiently for better days. Have no fear. Face today's facts. Life is and always will be imperfect. Make the best of it. Take advantage of the opportunities at hand. Don't put your hopes in future structural reform. Freedom, solitude, vision, understanding and salvation are close by, not far away. You have what you need. Use it. Do what you can with what you've got. Have enough faith to put your energies to work in situations that do not look promising. Grace has been given to you. God has the power to work in your heart. Allow that to happen. The love of the Spirit will not fail you. Trust that love.

How does the Tracy quote apply to Merton? Merton learned how to parse his sentences to satisfy his censors, including the censor in his head that genuinely did not want to further polarize the world. He tried to make himself understood to a broad audience, to build on what we have in common. When he got polemical, and sometimes he did, he criticized himself for that posture.

At the same time, Merton knew that to accept values that were 'clearly printed between the lines' at Gethsemani but alien to what he stood for would have been an act that was "untrue to God, to myself and to all those who for some reason or other have a kind of confidence in me."[95]   In Tracy's words, 'There is, after all, the reality of intellectual integrity. When that integrity is gone, all true inquiry ceases.' Merton's decision to obey the order not to publish his writings on nuclear war did not damage his intellectual integrity. All parties knew that he had not changed his position on the issue. There were times when Merton was close to despair, but he kept being pulled back to what Tracy called 'a hope grounded in faith, intellectual integrity, and courage; a hope functioning as the love empowering all true persuasion in the community of hope.'

Merton knew by November 15, 1957 that: "There is no solution in withdrawal. No solution in conforming."[96]   During the last decade of his life, day by day, at Gethsemani, Merton lived into his solution.

We discover our identity when we accept our place and our way in the midst of persons and things, in a historical situation, that we do not have to completely understand. We simply see that it is our own place and decide to live in it, for better or for worse. In the light of this simple and primordial acceptance, a natural consent, an obedience to reality that is already analogous to the obedience of faith, we can finally "be ourselves."[97]

Notes

1. Very briefly, Thomas Merton (1915-1968), American, was a writer and a Cistercian (Trappist) monk who spent 27 years at the Abbey of Gethsemani in Kentucky. Pierre Teilhard de Chardin (1881-1955), French, was a paleontologist and a Jesuit who spent thirty years outside France, most of that time in China, doing field work, research and writing. Hans Kung, born 1928, Swiss, is a theologian and a diocesan priest who argued in favor of structural reform of the Catholic Church and who has worked for many years on global ethics. Charles Curran, born 1934, American, is a theologian and a diocesan priest who acted as spokesperson for many theologians with respect to the 1968 birth control encyclical and who, since 1991, has taught ethics at Southern Methodist University.

2. Modernism in religion is described in *The Concise Columbia Ency-clopedia*, second edition (1989) as a "movement to reconcile developments of nineteenth- and twentieth-century science and philosophy with historical Christianity. It arose from the application of modern critical methods to the study of the Bible and the history of dogma and stressed the humanistic aspects of religion." More broadly, the term 'modernism' refers to a widespread cultural tendency to grant less deference to authority and to tradition and more weight to reason and empirical evidence. Even more broadly, the term refers to the social changes accompanying the rise of the middle classes as the power of aristocratic classes declined and to the rise of nations organized as political democracies as monarchies declined. Groups supporting such changes were referred to as modernists and groups opposing them as anti-modernists. See also note 8.

3. A few endnotes, such as the two above, have been inserted to explain items that may not be familiar to some readers.

4. Information about Teilhard in this section is taken from four sources. The first source is Robert Speaight, *Teilhard de Chardin – A Biography* (London: Collins, 1967), especially pp. 136-141. Within the context of this paper it is worth noting that Speaight also wrote book reviews of Merton's *The Sign of Jonas* and *The Secular Journal of Thomas Merton* published in the London Tablet in 1953 and 1959. See Marquita Breit, Patricia Burton, Paul Pearson, *'about Merton' – Secondary Sources 1945-2000 – A Bibliographic Workbook*, (Louisville, KY, The Thomas Merton Foundation, 2002), p. 107.

The second source is Mary Lukas and Ellen Lukas, *Teilhard* (Garden City, NY: Doubleday, 1977), especially pp. 71-75 and 84-96.

The third source is Ursula King, *Spirit of Fire – The Life and Vision of Teilhard de Chardin*, (Maryknoll, NY: Orbis, 1996), especially pp. 104-109. This biography is more recent than the others and makes available to the reader new research and much material from the archives of the Fondation Teilhard de Chardin and the Éditions de Seuil in Paris, and from the Georgetown University Library Archives in Washington, D.C.

The fourth source is the English translation of the first major biography of Teilhard, originally published in French in 1958, only three years after Teilhard's death, i.e., Claude Cuenot, *Teilhard de Chardin - A Biographical Study* (Baltimore, MD: Helicon, 1965). This biography glosses over Teilhard's problems with Rome, as shown in the following example: "It was decided – without any rancour, we note – that Teilhard was to confine himself to purely scientific publications, and that he was to leave Paris. Painful though this was to Teilhard, he was consoled by the sympathetic attitude of his superiors and of his friend [Edouard] Le Roy, and by his own realization that it was only through the Church and the

Society [of Jesus] that advance in the spiritual life could be found" (p. 61). With the possible exception of 'rancour,' that statement is true, but the tone and the brief treatment minimize the problem.

5. The text of "Note on Some Possible Historical Representations of Original Sin" is reproduced in Pierre Teilhard de Chardin, *Christianity and Evolution* (New York: Harcourt Brace Jovanovich, 1974), pp. 45-55.

6. When the Papal Secretary of State wrote Merton's abbot to urge a "diminution of contacts with Protestant ministers and scholars" Merton inferred that he had been delated to Rome for his ecumenical efforts in the early 1960s. Thomas Merton, *Turning Toward the World – The Pivotal Years*, ed., Victor A. Kramer (San Francisco: HarperCollins, 1996), p. 187 [December 22, 1961].

7. "[T]he article came to the eyes of Cardinal Merry del Val [the head of the Holy Office], who was as alert to the suspicion of heresy as a foxhound is alert to the scent. He made sharp representations to the General of the Jesuits, Father Ledochowski, who had already been warned from other sources. Ledochowski was no more qualified than Merry del Val to appreciate the difficulties apparent to Teilhard, as they were to so many others, and Teilhard was asked to promise that he would neither say nor write anything 'against the traditional position of the Church on the matter of original sin.'

"The demand was at once, he complained, 'too vague and too absolute.' . . . New censors were called in, and in spite of all the efforts in his favour made by Monseigneur Baudrillart, Rector of the Institut Catholique, and by his own immediate superiors, Rome was implacable." With reluctance, and on the advice of his friends, Teilhard signed the document Rome demanded. (Speaight, *Teilhard de Chardin – A Biography*, pp. 136-137; see also King, *Spirit of Fire*, pp. 106-107).

8. A basic description of modernism is given above in note 2. One of the popes who took a strongly anti-modernist position was Pope Pius X (1903-14) as illustrated by *Lamentabili*, a decree issued by the Holy Office in July of 1907, condemning 65 propositions ascribed to modernism, and by the encyclical *Pascendi*, issued in September 1907. The anti-modernist campaign was directed first against those Catholic intellectuals the Holy Office deemed to be modernists, and later became a general effort to prevent Catholics from being influenced by modernism. For example, clergy were required to take oaths against modernism and teachers accused of promoting modernism were summarily removed from their positions.

9. May 16, 1925 letter from Teilhard to Auguste Valensin, S. J. The letter continues: "I think I see that if I went off on my own or kicked over the traces in one way or another (and humanly speaking it would be so simple and 'easy') I should be unfaithful to my belief that every-

thing that happens is animated by our Lord; and to my belief in his worth, which is greater than all the elements that make up this world of ours. Furthermore I should compromise the religious value of my ideas. People would think I was straying from the Church; I should be accused of pride" (Speaight, *Teilhard de Chardin – A Biography*, p.138; see also King, *Spirit of Fire*, p. 108).

10. "The memory of the Modernist witch-hunt was too recent for Teilhard's Jesuit superiors – sympathetic as many of them were, and notably his own Provincial – to run unnecessary risks. It was ten years since Bergson had been put on the Index, and *Etudes* had taken the measure of a persecution which was still counting its victims" (Speaight, *Teilhard de Chardin – A Biography*, p. 138).

11. The passage continues: "nothing spiritual or divine can come to a Christian, or to one who has taken religious vows, except through the Church or his Order" (Speaight, *Teilhard de Chardin – A Biography*, p. 139: August 16, 1925 letter from Teilhard to Edouard Le Roy).

12. A chronology listing Teilhard's visits to France can be found in *The Letters of Teilhard de Chardin and Lucile Swan*, edited by Thomas M. King, S.J., and Mary Wood Gilbert, (Scranton, PA: University of Scranton Press, 2001. pp. 299-302). (The book was originally published by Georgetown University Press in 1993.) Teilhard received permission to visit France 6 times between 1926 and 1945, 8 times between 1946 and 1951 (he had a major heart attack in 1947), and once in 1954. With respect to Teilhard's efforts to publish his religious writings, he wrote both *The Divine Milieu* and *The Phenomenon of Man* in China, hoping they would pass the censors in Rome. In 1948 he went to Rome in hopes that he would obtain permission to publish and to request permission to accept a chair at the College de France but both requests were denied. "[T]he answer, when it came, was blandly and blankly negative; Teilhard must neither publish nor teach" (Speaight, *Teilhard de Chardin – A Biography*, p. 285).

13. The Scopes Trial began in July 1925. John H. Scopes, a teacher in a public school in Tennessee, was charged with violation of a state statute that prohibited the teaching in public schools of theories contrary to the popular conception of the biblical account of human creation. William Jennings Bryan was the lead lawyer for the prosecution; Clarence Darrow was the primary defense attorney.

14. Pierre Leroy, *Letters From My Friend Teilhard de Chardin 1948-1955* (New York: Paulist Press, 1980), p. 105. The original French version was published in 1976.

15. Leroy, *Letters From My Friend Teilhard de Chardin*, p. 106.

16. The purpose of the following note is to explain how Teilhard's work came to be published. In France, following the issuance of the

encyclical *Humani Generis* in 1950, there was a "large scale *integriste* (that is to say fundamentalist) offensive . . . The atmosphere in ecclesiastical circles was reminiscent of the worst years under Pius X. Five professors – men of great distinction – had been forced to leave the Lyon scholasticate . . ." (Speaight, *Teilhard de Chardin – A Biography*, p. 298). "The rightist religious paper, *France Catholique*, began a series about the types of religious deviation reproved by *Humani Generis*, and chose as the subject of the first of the articles Teilhard's philosophy" (Lukas, *Teilhard*, p. 293). Despite the fact that Teilhard was now 70 years old and had suffered a major heart attack, he and his superiors thought it best that he leave France. All parties realized that he might die abroad. Friends had urged him to leave the Jesuits and become a secular priest so that he would have control over his manuscripts. He refused. "'It would mean,' he said, 'cutting myself off from my 'divine milieu'; I should be breaking the thread that binds me to the will of God . . . .'" (Cuenot, *Teilhard de Chardin - A Biographical Study*, p. 307). A few days before Teilhard was scheduled to leave France, July 5, 1951, his friend, Raymond Jouve, the editor of Études, a French Jesuit periodical, told Teilhard that Jouve would never be able to publish Teilhard's work and urged him to secure the future of his writings. "Three days before Teilhard's proposed departure, therefore, he [Jouve] went to him to ask for a decision as to the disposition of his papers. He found Teilhard sitting in his room, surrounded by his baggage, seemingly paralyzed with indecision. Seeing he had no choice but to take the case in hand himself, he put Teilhard's moral quandary (as a purely hypothetical problem) to a [Jesuit] canon lawyer who happened to be visiting the house. As the canonist saw it, two possible courses of action were open to Teilhard: to consider the essays the property of the Society, or to follow what his conscience told him was his real vocation and make provision for the preservation of his papers after his death. Both decisions, said the canonist, were equally legitimate" (Lukas, *Teilhard*, pp. 296-297). Cuenot's account states that "his vow of poverty was no bar to his ownership of his own manuscripts, and, though canonists are not at all in agreement on this point, canon law does not formally prohibit their being disposed of by gift or testament" (Cuenot, *Teilhard de Chardin - A Biographical Study*, p. 307). Jouve conveyed the information from the canon lawyer to Teilhard and Jouve suggested Jeanne Mortier as a faithful and dependable lay person who could act as legatee (Lukas, *Teilhard*, p. 297). Mortier had "studied scholastic philosophy for ten years at the Institut Catholique without finding satisfaction. She was overwhelmed when she read a typed copy of *Le Milieu Divin* and then met Teilhard in January 1939" (*The Letters of Teilhard de Chardin and Lucile Swan*, p. 297). Shortly before he sailed, Mortier visited the Jesuit house where Teilhard was staying to say goodbye. Teilhard wrote out a short statement saying that in case of his death all rights over his non-scientific writings were to go to Mortier (King, *Spirit of Fire*, p. 207). Speaight concludes his account of this event with these words: "His cause would no longer be debated *in camera* and before a packed jury" (Speaight, *Teilhard de Chardin – A Biography*, p. 301).

17. Merton, *Turning Toward the World*, p. 64 [November 14, 1960]. Within the context of this paper it is worth noting that Teilhard may have been aware of *The Seven Storey Mountain*. There is an intriguing comment in his January 25, 1949 letter to a friend in New York City. Teilhard wrote: "Sorry for the Trappist monk. . . : but it becomes more and more evident every day that no religion will satisfy Man henceforth, unless it combines together both the faith in Heaven and in Earth." The ellipsis is in the version of the letter printed in Pierre Teilhard de Chardin, *Letters to Two Friends 1926-1952*, ed., Ruth Nanda Aschen (New York: New American Library, 1968) p. 194. *The Seven Storey Mountain* had been published in October of 1948 and it is possible the friend had written Teilhard about it. If Merton is the monk, Teilhard is presumably referring to the world-denying tone of *The Seven Storey Mountain*.

18. Within the context of this paper, a comment Hans Kung made about Teilhard is relevant here. Speaking of his own student years in Rome in 1951, Kung states: "[A]t that time there is much that I don't know or understand. For example, that as early as 1926 the Jesuit Pierre Teilhard de Chardin had lost his chair at the Institut Catholique and since then has been persecuted by the Roman Inquisition; that he is not allowed to see a single of his theological works printed during his lifetime; indeed that in the course of the purge following the 1951 encyclical *Humani generis* he is banished somewhere into the backwoods of New York State, where on Easter Day 1955 just one person will follow his coffin to the grave. As a visiting professor in New York in 1968, one day I will travel 160 kilometres along the Hudson to his burial place and will be distressed that the tomb of the great palaeontologist and theologian is not marked in any way, so that I have difficulty finding it. '"*Damnatio memoria* – obliterated from memory' – an old Roman custom!" Hans Kung, *My Struggle for Freedom – Memoirs* (Grand Rapids: Michigan, Eerdmans, 2003), p. 71. Sometime prior to the fiftieth anniversary of Teilhard's death, April 10, 2005, a marker like that of the other Jesuits buried in Poughkeepsie, New York was placed at the gravesite.

19. Merton, *Turning Toward the World*, p. 65 [November 14, 1960]. The fact that Merton disapproved of the way Teilhard had been treated does not mean that Merton liked what Teilhard had to say. Merton read *The Divine Milieu* and some of de Lubac's work on Teilhard but never seemed to see and value what many others found in Teilhard. Two 1967

essays "The Universe as Epiphany," and "Teilhard's Gamble," are in Thomas Merton, *Love and Living*, eds., Naomi Burton Stone and Patrick Hart (New York: Farrar, Straus & Giroux, 1985), pp. 171-191. Richard W. Kropf, "Crying with a Live Grief: The Mysticism of Merton & Teilhard Compared," is a well-researched and interesting article in *The Merton Annual*, volume 5, 1997, pp. 227-45.

20. Merton, *Turning Toward the World*, p. 67 [November 15, 1960].

21. Merton, *Turning Toward the World*, p. 70 [November 28, 1960].

22. Thomas Merton, *A Search for Solitude – Pursuing the Monk's True Life*, ed., Lawrence Cunningham (San Francisco: HarperCollins, 1996) pp. 138-139. The title of this paper comes from this passage. Each of these thinkers independently reached the conclusion that there was no solution in conforming to positions they found unwarranted and unacceptable. Each also decided that there was no solution in withdrawing, depriving themselves of a relationship with the Church, and leaving the field to those pronouncing such positions. They chose to stay and work within the institution.

23. A perceptive and thorough account of Merton's anti-war writing and the toll it exacted can be found in Thomas Merton, *Peace in the Post-Christian Era*, ed., Patricia A. Burton (Maryknoll, NY: Orbis, 2004), pages xxv-lv. Burton's introduction, titled "The Book That Never Was," is based on her close study of the text Merton had been forbidden to publish in 1962 and on her extensive knowledge of the Merton corpus. Burton contributed two items to volume 17 of *The Merton Annual*—an editorial note (pp. 14–15) and an article concerning the book that Merton had been forbidden to publish (pp. 27–57). It was through her efforts that the "book that never was" later came to be.

24. In the introduction to *Passion for Peace* Shannon states: "It is not easy for us to grasp the anguish that this struggle posed for Merton . . . We live at a time when it is not an uncommon thing for Roman Catholics to protest against war . . . . But in 1961 . . . no Catholic priest or bishop – at least none well known – had spoken out against war." Merton struggled over what he should do. "Merton faced it in 1961; I think it is safe to say he agonized over it throughout that year and the next and actually never set it aside. The struggle, simply stated, was this: Should I, a monk of Gethsemani vowed to silence and solitude, speak out against the terrible violence of war that threatens the very life of the planet, or should I keep a discreet silence as the appropriate stance for a monk?" (Thomas Merton, *Passion for Peace*, pp.1-2).

25. Merton, *Turning Toward the World*, p. 172 [October 23, 1961]. In the same entry, Merton referred to a current article in *America* in which a Jesuit "condoned – even apparently encouraged – the business of sitting in your fallout shelter with a machine gun to keep others out! That

is the best Catholic theology has had to offer in this country, so it appears" (Merton, *Turning Toward the World*, p. 173).

26. Merton, *Passion for Peace*, pp. 3-4.

27. Merton, *Turning Toward the World*, pp. 186-187 [December 22, 1961]. In the same entry, Merton referred to Fr. Ford S.J. who, although one of "the *minority* of U.S. Catholic moralists who are against the nuclear bombing of cities, assures me that I *cannot* deduce from the statements of Pius XII against nuclear war that the nuclear bombing of cities is 'condemned'" (p. 186).

28. "The top brass in the American hierarchy is getting wind of my articles and is expressing displeasure. An editorial in the Washington Catholic *Standard*, evidently by a bishop, takes very strong exception to the *Commonweal* article and I am strongly reproved for 'startling disregard of authoritative Catholic utterances and unwarranted charges about the intention of our government towards disarmament.'

"In actual fact the editorial twists and misquotes my own statements, trying to make me out an absolute pacifist and trying to make it appear that I said the Pope had taken a stand which was a condemnation of all war.

"So you see it is beginning. The whole line taken by this editorial is the official Pentagon line. Russia's attitude is the real obstacle to peace. It is implied that I am unjust to our government by my 'gross conclusions' which say that indiscriminate destruction is what is intended in the use of nuclear weapons . . .

"This is a straw in the wind and I guess in a little while there will be more than straws, there will be pine trees. Which may make it difficult or even impossible to bring out the book on peace I was hoping to do. . . . And of course there is no harm in my sharpening up my use of theological statements and trying to make them more foolproof. I wish I were more of a professional, for the sake of peace."

Thomas Merton, *Letters from Tom – A Selection of Letters From Father Thomas Merton, Monk of Gethsemani, to W.H.Ferry, 1961-1968*, chosen and edited by W. H. Ferry (Scarsdale, NY: Fort Hill Press, no date), pp. 26-27. The same text is found in Thomas Merton, *The Hidden Ground of Love: The Letters of Thomas Merton on Religious Experience and Social Concerns*, ed., William H. Shannon (New York: Farrar Straus & Giroux, 1985), p. 210.

29. Merton, *Turning Toward the World*, p. 216 [April 27, 1962]. See also Merton, *Peace in the Post-Christian Era*, Burton's introduction, pp. xxxiii-xxxv; Shannon, *Silent Lamp*, pp. 222-223; Forest, *Living with Wisdom*, p. 144; and Mott, *The Seven Mountains of Thomas Merton*, pp. 378-379.

30. Thomas Merton, *The Hidden Ground of Love*, pp. 266-268 [Letter to Jim Forest April 29, 1962]. The book Merton was forbidden to publish in 1962 was published in 2004. See note 23 above.

31. Merton felt a duty to do as much as he could. He considered a direct order from his superiors directing him to stop to be the limit beyond which he could not go. This attitude of Merton's is somewhat clarified by Ed Rice, a college friend of Merton's and editor of *Jubilee*, a Catholic publication in which Merton's book review of Teilhard's *The Divine Milieu* would have appeared but for the decision by the superior of the order that it should not published. Rice says that Merton wrote "in summary of an idea of Teilhard's, but one which was essentially his as well, "One of the most formal obligations of the Christian is to struggle against evil, whether it be moral or physical. The Christian can only resign himself passively to the acceptance of evil when it is quite clear that he is powerless to do anything about it. Hence it is an utterly false Christianity which preaches the supine acceptance of social injustice, ignorance, impossible working conditions, and war as though it were virtue to 'take' all this and 'offer it up' without even attempting to change anything." Edward Rice, *The Man in the Sycamore Tree: The Good Times and Hard Life of Thomas Merton* (Garden City, New York: Doubleday, 1972), p. 86. Merton went as far as he could go with his anti-war writing until he met with an absolute order that he was powerless to change. He then stopped doing what the order, narrowly interpreted, prohibited.

32. Merton told Jim Forest: "I wrote to the Abbot General and said it is a good thing Pope John didn't have to get his encyclical through our censors: and could I now start up again?" Letter to Jim Forest dated April 26, 1963 (*The Hidden Ground of Love*, p. 274). Shannon notes that *Pacem in Terris* came a year after Merton was silenced on the topic of war and made a number of points that Merton had made. "Merton promptly wrote to the abbot general, Dom Gabriel Sortais, expressing mock relief that Pope John had not been an American Cistercian. For the American censors would never have approved the Pope's peace encyclical" (Shannon, *Silent Lamp*, p. 223).

33. Augustine and others contributed to the development of the just war theory which maintained that war could be justified under certain conditions and that Christians could engage in just wars. Needless to say, that theory was developed long before the development of twentieth-century weapons of mass destruction. Some people tried to adapt the theory to the new conditions. Others maintained that the damage to citizens and the environment caused by nuclear war required a new analysis.

34. Hans Kung, *The Council, Reform and Reunion,* (New York: Sheed and Ward, 1961). In his memoir, *My Struggle for Freedom,* Kung discusses *The Council, Reform and Reunion* at pages 261-267.

35. Kung, *The Council, Reform and Reunion,* p. 38.

36. Kung, *The Council, Reform and Reunion,* pp. 38-39. Merton copied the last sentence into his journal on March 10, 1962. Merton, *Turning Toward the World,* p. 210.

37. Kung, *The Council, Reform and Reunion,* p. 41. Kung makes the point that prayers are especially needed for theologians who are working to clarify ideas and to clear away the debris of centuries of polemic. p. 43.

38. Kung, *The Council, Reform and Reunion,* p. 44.

39. Kung, *The Council, Reform and Reunion,* p. 50.

40. Kung, *The Council, Reform and Reunion,* pp. 59-60.

41. Merton, *Turning Toward the World,* p. 209 [March 10, 1962].

42. Thomas Merton, *Witness to Freedom: The Letters of Thomas Merton in Times of Crisis,* ed., William H. Shannon (New York: Farrar Straus & Giroux, 1994), pp. 45-46. Merton goes so far as to say in effect that Kung did for Merton what Merton did for many others, that is, clarified things that the reader had sensed but not yet articulated. "A book like this makes one realize many, many things. It enables one to judge and to accept many things that were felt heretofore in the conscience only as obscure and ambiguous gnawings. It is then quite true that we are right to feel so uncomfortable and so terribly beaten down by the old negative, falsely conservative, and authoritarian spirit that purely and simply clings to the status quo for its own sake" (p. 46).

Merton wrote in more measured tones to Thérèse Lentfoehr in Thomas Merton, *The Road to Joy – Letters to New and Old Friends,* ed., Robert Daggy (New York: Farrar, Straus & Giroux, 1989), p. 242.

43. In a March 10, 1962 letter to John Tracy Ellis, referred to later in this paper, Merton wrote: "You must by now have had a look at the new Hans Kung book, *The Council, Reform and Reunion.* If you have not, then do by all means get it as fast as ever you can. I think it is not out but I have a review copy. It will really gladden your heart. It is one of the most forthright, direct and powerful statements of our actual condition and problem that I have ever seen. It is a most remarkable book and it will have a terrific impact. What the results will be, no one can say, but it is in a lot of ways a portent . . ." (*Hidden Ground of Love,* p. 178).

44. Merton, *Turning Toward the World,* pp. 209-10 [March 10, 1962].

45. Merton, *Turning Toward the World,* pp. 213 [March 24, 1962].

46. In his memoir, *My Struggle for Freedom,* Kung discusses the 1963 lecture tour at pages 302-315.

47. Merton was aware of this ban. On February 19, 1963, he refers to it in a letter to Sr. Thérèse Lentfoehr. Merton, *The Road to Joy – Letters to New and Old Friends*, p. 243.

48. John Tracy Ellis, *American Catholicism*, (Chicago, University of Chicago Press, second edition, revised, 1969), pp. 211-212. The publicity and the resulting criticism of the ban caused Catholic University to revoke it. Kung, *My Struggle for Freedom*, p. 303. Kung did speak in Washington, D.C. during the summer of 1963 at both Catholic University and Georgetown.

49. Kung, *My Struggle for Freedom*, p. 304.

50. Hans Kung, *Freedom Today* (New York: Sheed and Ward, 1966). The book is dedicated to Boston College, the first U.S. university to extend Kung an invitation to speak, and to St. Louis University which gave him his first honorary doctorate.

51. Kung, *My Struggle for Freedom*, p. 304. Data about the size of the audience is provided on pages 305, 308, and 311.

52. Thomas Merton, *The School of Charity – The Letters of Thomas Merton on Religious Renewal and Spiritual Direction*, ed., Patrick Hart (New York: Farrar, Straus & Giroux, 1990), p. 188 [December 20, 1963 letter to Kilian McDonnell].

53. Hans Kung, *Reforming the Church Today* (New York: Crossroad, 1990), pp. 177-180. During the Council, Kung had served as a *peritus* (expert). He was familiar with the Vatican curia, especially the Holy Office, renamed the Congregation for the Doctrine of the Faith during the closing days of the Second Vatican Council. Cardinal Ottaviani, the Prefect of the Congregation, did not agree with the goals and values of the majority of the voting members of the Council.

54. Kung, *Reforming the Church Today*, p. 177.

55. Kung, *Reforming the Church Today*, p. 178.

56. Kung, *Reforming the Church Today*, p. 177-179. The declaration is one of the documents included in *Reforming the Church Today*, published in 1990. At that time, Kung added a postscript to the declaration stating that the Congregation for the Doctrine of the Faith issued a procedural ordinance "that accepts some of the desiderata put forth; but it ignored, and to this day still ignores, the most important ones." Kung, *Reforming the Church Today*, p. 179-80. A different translation of the document is reproduced in Hans Kung, *Kung in Conflict*, edited with translation and commentary by Leonard Swidler (New York: Doubleday, 1981), pp. 26-31.

57. Many of the facts concerning Curran in this paper are taken from one of four sources of information.

The first source is Charles Curran, Robert Hunt and the 'Subject Professors,' *Dissent In and For the Church – Theologians and Humanae Vi-*

tae, (New York, Sheed & Ward, 1969). It was written by professors from Catholic University who signed the *Statement by Catholic Theologians*. They explain what they did, why they did it, and provide theological support for their actions.

The second source is John Hunt and Terrence Connelly, *The Responsibility of Dissent: The Church and Academic Freedom* (New York: Sheed and Ward, 1969). It was written by the lawyers representing the theologians. It lays out the academic freedom issues and describes the legal proceedings of the academic panel set up to determine whether the subject professors had violated their contracts with the university. The faculty hearing committee vindicated the accused professors.

The third source is Charles Curran, *Faithful Dissent* (Kansas City, MO: Sheed & Ward, 1986). It was written by Curran in 1986 and covers some of the 1968 material as it relates to the Vatican's 1979-1986 investigation of Curran. See especially pp. 15-20 which covers the 1967-68 period.

The fourth source is William H. Shannon, *The Lively Debate – Response to Humanae Vitae* (New York: Sheed and Ward, 1970). It provides a contemporary examination of the birth control issue. The first half of the book begins with *Casti Connubii* and follows developments up to the time of the encyclical. The second half analyses the encyclical and then provides dozens of detailed accounts of the many responses by bishops, national conferences of bishops, theologians and laity. The final chapter addresses both the functioning of authority in the Church and the theology of dissent. The book does what this paper does not – it examines 'the big picture' of the birth control controversy, within which the *Statement by Catholic Theologians* arose. Shannon covers the *Statement by the Theologians* on pp. 148-150 and the response of the American lay members of the papal birth control commission on pp. 183-187.

At the time this paper was written, one excellent source was not yet available—Charles E. Curran, *Loyal Dissent: Memoir of a Catholic Theologian* (Washington D.C.: Georgetown University Press, 2006). Curran's mature reflections on his role in the 1960s and on the church today show his broad understanding, depth, and insight.

58. Ellis, *American Catholicism*, pp. 210-211.

59. This description of the 1967 tenure controversy is taken from Ellis, *American Catholicism*, pp. 216-19.

60. Ellis, *American Catholicism*, p. 216. "The reason for the punitive measure against Father Curran was never clearly stated, although it had been rumored that it had resulted from his teaching on birth control, a rumor that was stoutly denied by the university's chancellor, Archbishop Patrick A. O'Boyle."

61. Ellis, *American Catholicism*, p. 216. Ellis cites the students' weekly newspaper, *The Tower*, April 25, 1967, p. 4.

62. Further, "In both the Curran case and that of the banned theologians in 1963 informed persons realized that the progress of the university in these and other matters was hampered in no small measure by the prime weakness from which the institution suffered and which lay at the bottom of many of its difficulties. That weakness stemmed from what might be described as 'excessive ecclesiasticism' which periodically showed in various forms, especially in the use of the university as a steppingstone for careers in the Church and, second, in the interference from time to time in its academic affairs of high ecclesiastics whose knowledge and understanding of what a university was about left much to be desired." Ellis, *American Catholicism*, p. 216-217.

63. Curran, *Dissent In and For the Church*, p.5. Within the context of this paper it is worth noting that members of the press notified Curran that the encyclical was about to be released while he was working on his German language skills at St. Bonaventure, near Olean in upper New York state. Merton had taught at St. Bonaventure immediately before entering Gethsemani.

64. Curran, *Dissent In and For the Church*, p. 5.

65. Curran, *Dissent In and For the Church*, p. 5. The issues involved in the birth control controversy had been widely discussed for many years and these theologians had been studying the relevant theology for longer than that. When they focused on the encyclical, they were reviewing material with which they were already familiar. They said in the Statement: "In actual fact, the Encyclical demonstrates no development over the teaching of Pius XI's *Casti Connubii* whose conclusions have been called into question for grave and serious reasons. These reasons, given a muffled voice at Vatican II, have not been adequately handled by the mere repetition of past teaching" (Hunt, *The Responsibility of Dissent*, p. 204).

66. Curran, *Dissent In and For the Church*, p. 7. The text quoted in this paper contained a note. What appears here as note 66 appeared in the original text as note 1 and read as follows: "*Washington Evening Star*, July 30, 1968, p. A-4. The article referred to the fact that O'Boyle 'released his statement to newsmen by telephone from Pennsylvania.'" That note is found at Curran, *Dissent In and For the Church*, p. 26.

67. Curran, *Dissent In and For the Church*, p. 7. The text quoted in this paper contained a note. What appears here as note 67 appeared in the original text as note 2 and read as follows: "*The Church in Our Day* (Washington, D. C.: U.S.S.C., 1968), pp. 69-73." That note is found at Curran, *Dissent In and For the Church*, p. 26.

68. Curran, *Dissent In and For the Church*, pp. 7-8.

69. "The most noted theologian among the original eighty-seven signers of the Washington statement was Bernard Haring, the German theologian whose three-volume *Law of Christ* had already become a contemporary classic in Catholic moral theology. The evening before the meeting [July 30, 1968 press conference] at the Mayflower Hotel, Father Charles E. Curran who had studied under Father Haring in Rome, contacted his former teacher by telephone (Haring was lecturing at Santa Barbara, California at the time) and asked for his support. 'I almost fell off the chair when he said Yes,' Curran said. [Shannon cites the *National Catholic Reporter*, August 7, 1968 for the quotation.]

"Father Haring's decision to add his name to the list of dissenting theologians was significant, not only because of the worldwide respect he enjoys, but for two additional reasons. First, he had been secretary to Vatican II's subcommission on marriage and the family, and a member of the theological section of the papal birth control commission. Secondly, up to the time of the encyclical's publication, he had exercised great caution and had not really taken an unambiguous stand" (Shannon, *The Lively Debate – Response to Humanae Vitae* pp.166-167).

70. Curran, *Dissent In and For the Church*, pp. 6-7.

71. Curran, *Dissent In and For the Church*, p. 8.

72. Curran, *Dissent In and For the Church*, p. 8.

73. "This *immediate, organized, public dissent* by Roman Catholic scholars from a formal and authoritative papal teaching was unprecedented in Church history . . .

"The joint publication of the Statement of dissent from *Humanae Vitae*, was, of course, inconsistent with the view, not uncommon in some Catholic circles, that the role of the theological scholar in the Church was to offer his supporting services to the pronouncements of the hierarchical teaching office of the Church, or else to be silent. Moreover, those who held this view, which included many members of the American hierarchy, considered the Statement to be a scandalous, disloyal action. Such challenges raised a central question: can a Roman Catholic dissent from an authoritative papal teaching and still claim good standing with the Catholic Church? The Statement, of course, had insisted that such a right to dissent existed in the Church and was applicable to the birth control Encyclical. The Statement inherently also claimed that those who did so dissent had the right to make their views public.

"While these issues are essentially Catholic *intellectual* issues, they were joined in a practical context. The Statement, by communicating the right to dissent, told millions of troubled Catholics that their apparent choice between their own consciences and the papal teaching on contraception was a false dilemma: the theologians asserted that Catholics could dissent in practice on the issue *without* putting themselves outside the Church. Many troubled bishops, however, felt that the dissenting theologians were going beyond the bounds of their science and usurping a pastoral teaching function that properly belonged solely to the hierarchy. The *Statement by Catholic Theologians,* therefore, was not only a continuation of the birth control controversy but also a springboard to new questions on the right to dissent itself and on the role and relationship of bishops and theologians," (Hunt, *The Responsibility of Dissent,* pp. 5-6).

74. Hunt, *The Responsibility of Dissent,* p. 203.

75. Hunt, *The Responsibility of Dissent,* p. 204.

76. William Shannon in a section of *The Lively Debate* titled "The Theology of Dissent" lists a number of ways in which dissent may be useful to the church, including this one: "Responsible dissent freely allowed in the Church will protect the Church authority from being isolated. Father John J. O'Callaghan expressed the feeling of many about *Humanae Vitae,* when he said: 'The idea of Pope Paul, alone on the remote heights of teaching authority, agonizing over the [birth control] decision which only he must make, does not appeal to me,'" (p. 201, citing John J. O'Callaghan, Reflections on *Humanae Vitae, Theology Digest* 16 [Winter 1968], p. 325).

77. Some commentators have stated that the primary reason that *Humanae Vitae* prohibited birth control was that the Vatican was unwilling to change the position it had taken in *Casti Connubii.* For example: "Why did Paul VI ignore the more humane and personalistic teaching on responsible parenthood that his own birth control commission, following *Gaudium et spes,* had recommended? Why did he return to a rigoristic teaching based on a Stoic understanding of natural law? As Karl Rahner wrote: 'It becomes clear in the encyclical itself that the real and primary reason for adhering to this position is the need that is felt to hold firm to the traditional teaching of Pius XI and Pius XII'" (Philip S. Kaufman, *Why You Can Disagree and Remain a Faithful Catholic,* New York: Crossroad, 1991, pp. 51-52). The Rahner quote is cited as "On the Encyclical '*Humanae Vitae,'" Theological Investigations,* XI (New York: Seabury, 1982), p. 266.

78. Hunt, *The Responsibility of Dissent,* p. 204.

79. Hunt, *The Responsibility of Dissent,* pp. 204-05.

80. Hans Kung, *Kung in Conflict,* edited with translation and commentary by Leonard Swidler (New York: Doubleday, 1981). *Kung in Conflict* includes the correspondence among Kung, the Vatican and the German bishops concerning several of Kung's books; documents generated during the investigation of Kung's orthodoxy; and public state-

ments issued throughout the world by those dismayed by the Vatican's determination that Kung was 'neither suitable nor eligible' to exercise the function of a professor of Catholic theology.

81. Charles Curran, *Faithful Dissent* (Kansas City MO: Sheed and Ward, 1986). *Faithful Dissent* provides a narrative account beginning with Curran's student days in Rome in the 1950's and finishing shortly after the Vatican's 1986 decision that he was 'neither suitable nor eligible' to exercise the function of a professor of Catholic theology. It includes the correspondence between the Vatican and Curran during the entire investigation and statements made by the hierarchy and theologians during 1986.

82. Thomas Merton, *The Other Side of the Mountain – The End of the Journey*, ed., Patrick Hart (New York, HarperCollins, 1998), pp. 149-50.

83. Merton, *The Other Side of the Mountain*, p. 150. John Cogley, a prominent Catholic, an editor at *Commonweal* and religion editor at the *New York Times*, left the church in protest against the encyclical.

84. See note 73 above.

85. Kung, *The Council, Reform and Reunion*, p. 39.

86. David Tracy, "On Hope as a Theological Virtue in American Catholic Theology," in Hans Kung and Gerald Swidler, editors, *The Church in Anguish: Has the Vatican Betrayed the Council?* (New York: Harper and Row, 1987), p. 272.

87. Curran, *Faithful Dissent*, pp. 275-276.

88. Curran, *Faithful Dissent*, p. 271. The word 'nor' is in the original; it is not a typographical error.

89. Hans Kung et al (contributors to an issue of the *Journal of Ecumenical Studies*), *Consensus in Theology? A Dialogue with Hans Kung and Edward Schillebeeckx* (Philadelphia: Westminster Press, 1980), pp. 159-165.

90. The Vatican had objected over the years to a number of Kung's books, including *Infallible? An Inquiry* (1970). In its 1979 statement, the Vatican objected to Kung's book *The Church Maintained in Truth – A Theological Meditation* (1979) and to an introduction Kung wrote in 1979 for another person's book on the topic of infallibility. Kung, *Kung in Conflict*, pp. 384-388.

91. Teilhard de Chardin, *Letters to Two Friends* 1926-1952 (New York: New American Library, 1968), pp. 30-31.

92. The prologue to Teilhard's *Letters to Two Friends*, was written by Rene d'Ouince, S. J., a former religious superior of Teilhard. He cites a letter the friends wrote to him: "By eliminating all personal reference, each of us has tried, insofar as possible, to efface the personalities of the recipients. For if the publication of these letters is useful, it will be so

solely for what they reveal of the mind and thought of their author. It is for this reason that we have wished to remain anonymous." Teilhard de Chardin, *Letters to Two Friends*, p.4.

93. Thomas Merton, *Contemplation in a World of Action*, (Notre Dame, IN: University of Notre Dame Press, 1998), p. 26.

94. Merton, *Contemplation in a World of Action*, p. vii.

95. Merton, *Turning Toward the World*, p. 70 [November 28, 1960].

96. Merton, *A Search for Solitude* p. 139.

97. Merton, *Contemplation in a World of Action*, p. 52.

The Psychology of Hatred and the Role of Early Relationships in Discovering Our True Self

Michael Sobocinski

To see a World in a Grain of Sand
And a Heaven in a Wild Flower,
Hold Infinity in the palm of your hand
And Eternity in an hour.

William Blake, "Auguries of Innocence"[1]

Introduction: Justice and Difference

The search for justice and peace that informed the Ninth General Meeting of the International Thomas Merton Society "Revelation of Justice—Revolution of Love," is of the utmost concern to all. No matter where one turns, questions of justice are prominent, demanding our invested attention and care, challenging us to reach beyond the personal interests, geographical boundaries, and restrictive ideologies that delimit the range of our compassion. Natural disasters such as tsunamis, hurricanes, and earthquakes bring the ravages of drought and famine, which point out inequities in the distribution of scarce resources across lines of social and economic class, nationality, and race. Clean water, consistent food sources, basic sanitation, and adequate shelter are beyond the reach of millions. Technologies continually push back the frontiers of medicine, while many in the world go without the most basic health care, unable to afford treatment that is assumed by those with means. Genocide, terrorism, and the invasion of countries remind us that our political ideologies and religious beliefs threaten to obscure our shared humanity.

Numerous philosophers have explicated the concept of justice. As the medical ethicists Beauchamp and Childress point out, these various "accounts all interpret justice as fair, equitable, and appropriate treatment in light of what is due or owed to persons. A situation of justice is present whenever persons are due benefits or burdens because of their particular properties or circumstances."[2] The principle of formal justice, traditionally attributed to Aristotle, lays out a common, minimal requirement of all subsequent theories of justice. This principle tells us that equals must be treated equally, while unequals may be treated unequally according to relevant differences. However, the theory provides no real guidance in determining the criteria for judging whether two or more individuals are to be considered equals, nor does it state the "particular respects in which equals ought to be treated equally and provides no criteria for determining whether two or more individuals are in fact equals."[3] What the principle of formal justice does, however, is establish the requirement that only those differences that are pertinent to the issue at hand be considered in making decisions. Many instances of justice concern what is known as distributive justice, which "asks on what basis should the goods or services [of society] be proportioned, especially when there are competing demands, and on what basis should the burdens associated with society be distributed."[4] Thus, the decision to distribute scarce medical resources on the basis of irrelevant attributes, such as a patient's race or gender, would be judged unethical.

The Western ethical tradition is firmly grounded upon considerations of justice and respect for the autonomy of individuals to make decisions regarding their well-being. Together these principles exert a pervasive influence not only on the actual choices that are made in the interest of pursuing one's self-interest, but also on the recognition of ethical concerns in the first place. Common use of the concept of "autonomy," which refers both to an ethical principle as well as to a theory of developmental growth and maturation, promotes a sense of intellectual "fuzziness" that somehow equates personal well-being with independence and individualism. In contrast, autonomous choice in the ethical realm refers to the ability to make decisions regarding one's well-being that are free of controlling or coercive influences. Autonomy as a goal of personal development has been highly valued in the prevailing intellectual paradigm of the West, such that our understanding of what constitutes "well-being" and the "person" have both been shaped by an overemphasis upon the individual apart from the interactive, contextual nature of persons. And yet there is increasing evidence to suggest that our largely uncritical acceptance of the primacy of the autonomous, independent individual may be based upon fundamentally erroneous assumptions regarding the nature of reality. How we understand the very notion of *equals* may represent the misleading influence of our usual sensory perceptions, rather than reflection upon an underlying, substantial reality.

Interactive Reality and the Interdependent Self

I recall spending long summer evenings lying on the cool grass as a young child of eight or nine. My closest childhood friend and I would watch the green bottleflies and listen to the crickets and the wind rustling the leaves, discussing our hopes for the future, such as possible careers, where we would live, and various other topics called forth from the seemingly limitless potential of life. And we would gaze out into the infinity of forever. I clearly remember trying to wrap my mind around the concept of infinite space and a universe without boundaries, of timelessness without beginning or end. Besides ending up with that unique sort of headache that occurs when the two hemispheres of one's brain seem to slide past one another when confronted with the irreconcilable—and then don't quite re-align—I remember coming to the conclusion that either there had to be a Divine Being, or else we were the objects of the cruelest joke imaginable, in which case there was at least an omnipotent malevolent force in the universe. The sense of great potential cast against the backdrop of infinity was an overriding, almost palpable presence at those times. We both felt incredibly small, insignificant, and yet at the same time energized and enlivened with the possibilities that life presented.

I relate this personal story now not because it is unique, but rather because I believe that this experience delimits the parameters of much of what I hope to convey in this article. The awareness of our absolute contingent nature, the beginnings of our individual lives in the unknown past, our deaths in the unknowable future, and our essential aloneness are in fact intertwined and interpenetrating questions that are posed in each of us. The choices that we live out in response to them are our attempts to realize and to know our true nature and unique personal identities. Ultimately, these choices not only allow us to know ourselves, but to be known by others, in an unfolding dialectic of becoming.

As a psychologist specializing in treating children and youth who have suffered chronic, often severe relational trauma, what has become clear to me is that the very possibility of authoring a coherent response to the question of life arises out of our relationships. Purpose and meaning throughout the course of life is a matter of sustaining community with other invested persons, just as healing from trauma requires their responsive presence. It is the earliest attachments between children and their caregivers that serve in many ways as models for later relationships, guiding expectations that subtly shape our views of others as well as of ourselves. Luckily, parents are not required to be unerringly aware of and completely responsive to their child's needs in order to promote healthy growth and development. When those entrusted with a child's care are not overwhelmed by their own unmet needs or circumstances, these emotional ties provide a "good enough" interpersonal environment which fosters security, safety, comfort, and closeness, as well as the ability to tolerate and manage life's frustrations and disappointments. From such a relational foundation the growing child is empowered to explore the world and discover her own interests, abilities and successes.

Given this vantage point, which understands that the division between the "psychological" and the "social" is more apparent than substantial, I want to suggest that the promotion of peace and justice in our world lies in understanding and fostering the formative power of these critical early relationships. To overcome the external distractions and apparent differences that divide our world, we must appreciate the psychological, developmental, and spiritual significance of what Merton meant when he wrote that "The conditions of our world are simply an outward expression of our own thoughts and desires."[5] Or, again, as he reminds us, a "man who lives in division" and "is not a person but only an 'individual.' . . . The man who lives in division is living in death. He cannot find himself because he is lost; he has ceased to be a reality."[6] In a contextual, communal view of the self, one that seeks to integrate and indeed transcend both the inner and outer realities of experience, how might we understand this assertion? What types of thoughts and desires is Merton referring to here? How do they develop, and how might we seek to alter the conditions of our own lives, the lives of our families, friends, those we work alongside, and those we know only from afar? How do we take this insight and leverage it to achieve the ideal of peace and justice?

Developmental biology, neurochemistry, various fields within psychology, including feminist, constructivist, and multicultural thought, as well as the study of trauma, present a portrait of human growth which highlights our essential interdependence. This emerging understanding, following the course set by modern physics, challenges the notion of an independently existing self, of a reality that can be objectively grasped beyond the active, constructive efforts of the knower to bring meaning to phenomena. Gary Zukav, writing almost thirty years ago in *The Dancing Wu Li Masters* of the history of our understanding of the nature of light, explains this fundamental quality of reality as leading "to the conclusion that the world consists not of things, but of interactions. Properties belong to interactions, not to independently existing things, like 'light.'"[7] Since that time physics has consistently demonstrated that the interactive nature of phenomena points to a reality that frequently contradicts our usual sense perceptions, which conveniently simplify and separate the world into discrete objects and events.

Numerous investigations support the critical importance of the earliest interactions between infant and caregiver in forming the biological basis, the complex pathways of neurons in the developing brain, of the nascent sense of self. What we are learning is that these relationships influence "every aspect of . . . internal and external functioning throughout the lifespan."[8] The critical role assumed by others in facilitating the development of the capacity to regulate our feelings and behaviors, develop a basic trust in the world, and fashion a stable and coherent sense of self provides the psychological foundation for later developmental tasks. The dialectic relationship between the "conditions of our world" and the "thoughts and desires" to which Merton refers find their beginning in our attachment relationships, for it is here that inner and outer realities intermingle; it is here that our subjective experience of our selves, of others and of our place in the relational world first finds expression. If we are to fully appreciate their significance, we must realize that, as psychologist James Garbarino has so eloquently stated

there is no such thing as 'a baby;' there is only 'a baby in relation to someone else.' An infant cannot survive psychologically and spiritually on its own. To begin the process of human development, a child needs not so much stimulation as responsiveness; children need to make connection through entering into a relationship.[9]

From an Eastern spiritual and philosophical context, the Dalai Lama approaches this same phenomenal aspect of the self through reference to the Buddhist concept of dependent origination, or *ten del*, which suggests that "our habitual notion of self is in some sense a label for a complex web of interrelated phenomena."[10]

Love and Hate as Ways of Knowing

In order to realize justice, we must come to terms with one of the more disturbing aspects of our human nature. We must examine the psychology of hate. While hate is not always associated with aggression and violence, it plays a critical role in the continuing acts of inhumanity that mark our world. Without an adequate grasp of this basic phenomenon, our ability to understand and alter those conditions threatening the viability of society is necessarily limited.

Against the backdrop of our essential human aloneness, the fundamental question of life itself is uttered anew in each of us. Both love and hate are epistemologies, ways in which we seek to answer this question, and therefore know the nature of reality, including our own selves and other persons. This search for knowledge is the basic human response to the dilemma posed by existence. Erich Fromm expresses the essence of this challenge when he reminds us, "the question is: How can we overcome the suffering, the imprisonment, the shame which the experience of separateness creates; how can we find union within ourselves, with our fellowman, with nature."[11] According to Fromm, while the question which each of us must in some manner answer in living our lives is always thus reducible, there are only two basic answers:

One is to overcome separateness and to find unity by *regression* to the state of unity which existed before man was born. The other answer is to be *fully born*, to develop one's awareness, one's reason, one's capacity to love, to such a point that one transcends one's own egocentric involvement, and arrives at a new harmony, at a new oneness with the world.[12]

Merton, like Fromm, sees but two inherent possibilities to life's question. He writes in *New Seeds of Contemplation* that "There are two things which men can do about the pain of disunion with other men. They can love or they can hate."[13] The question of life affords no other choice. Through our encounters with the Divine that flow out of the call to love, we overcome "the prison of one's separateness"[14] and achieve a unity which transcends this aloneness. This response is one of a radical freedom arising out of personal responsibility for owning our response to the dilemma of separation, and which openly embraces the anxious contingency of life.

The awareness of separation, incompleteness, and aloneness also brings a hunger for transcendence, for becoming more than what we are when born. This transcendence, writes Erich Fromm, is

one of the most basic needs of man, rooted in the fact of his self-awareness, in the fact that he is not satisfied with the role of creature, that he cannot accept himself as dice thrown out of the cup. He needs to feel as the creator, as one transcending the passive role of being created.[15]

For Merton, this same innate tendency is captured in the following: "Our vocation is not simply to *be*, but to work together with God in the creation of our own life, our own identity, our own destiny."[16] Several paragraphs later he writes *"The seeds that are planted in my liberty at every moment, by God's will, are the seeds of my own identity, my own reality, my own happiness, my own sanctity."*[17] How do we nurture these seeds? What are the requisite conditions that will allow them to break forth from the earth following their long repose beneath winter's snow, finally to reach the warmth of the sun?

The other "answer"—that offered by hate—is in some respects both compelling and comforting in its simplicity, offering reassurance and distraction through a denial of the dependent nature of human beings. This response turns away from awareness of our existential aloneness, and instead seeks comfort and solace in a "craving for certainty,"[18] and an absolute control over life. In this quest the other is effectively excluded from the self, resulting in a greatly impoverished self. Hatred simplifies the world of the one who hates, reducing the rich ambiguity inherent within the diversity of human experience to simple, dichotomous categories, leaving no "psychological space" available for another's subjectivity. Hatred is blind to the essential truth that Garbarino speaks to in the words quoted above, namely that we are all called into being only "in relation to someone else." In the response of hate we abdicate personal responsibility for daring to reach beyond separateness to the recognition that we are all already one, and that it is only through the continual revelation of the Divine through creation that we *are* at all.

People often "nurse" their hatred, which in turn dominates and consumes the person who hates. The experience of carefully stoking one's hatred with the kindling of real and imagined injustices, together with fantasies of revenge upon one's perpetrators, is commonplace. Although promising comfort, solace, continuity, and organization of experience, the ultimate cost of hate is the forfeiture of genuine human freedom. Inevitably, as Alford points out, "In hatred one transforms interpersonal bonds into bondage and relationships into prisons."[19] The hated other, despised for representing, withholding, or threatening to take that which is needed or desired, for causing unjust pain and suffering, or for pointing out feared unworthiness and precipitating the experience of shame and humiliation, nonetheless provides the one who hates with an organizing sense of meaning and purpose.

Hatred is born of anxiety, fear, and vulnerability. It is dominated by a myopic, obsessive focus, as the person who hates locates within another that which they secretly believe they lack – an elusive gift that has somehow been denied them. Feelings of envy and the fear of being revealed as unworthy of love and acceptance compel the person to action, in the vain hope of overcoming perceived faults and insufficiencies. Such attempts to "win" a sense of adequacy through force of will and individual effort lead only to further feelings of lack and separation, as the feared alienation from others that initially gives rise to hate grows stronger. The person who hates is thus tightly bound to the hated one, at the enormous cost of the loss of personal freedom. Merton describes this bondage as

> hell . . . where no one has anything in common with anybody else except the fact that they all hate one another and cannot get away from one another and from themselves . . . . And the reason why they want to be free of one another is not so much that they hate what they see in others, as that they know others hate what they see in them: and all recognize in one another what they detest in themselves, selfishness, and impotence, agony, terror and despair.[20]

The recognition that we each struggle in our own manner with the feelings that Merton presents here removes hate from the realm of the exceptional or the abnormal, and emphasizes our ability to hate as well as to love one another. It is not only the mass murderer, rapist, or leader of a genocide who is capable of hate, but each of us.

C. Fred Alford, in a penetrating analysis of the dynamics of hate, points out that the experience of merger with another that characterizes hatred functions to calm, soothe, and reassure the one who hates that they are not alone; it seeks as well to appropriate the hated other, to "become what otherness knows—or is."[21] Hatred hides in the false security of a state of merger which seeks to obliterate those external differences which emphasize our apparent separation and disconnection. The experience of merger that defines hatred involves the temporary loss of personal boundaries and our usual self-other distinctions. It confuses possession and control with communion, and objectifies both the one who hates and the one who is hated. In Alford's view, hate is an avoidance and denial of life itself, masquerading as intimacy. In a primitive way, hatred, whether of a person or a group, by providing the experience of merger, is in some distorted way relational in nature. Alford's chapter, "Hate is the Imitation of Love," explores in depth this relational aspect, reminding the reader that a more accurate appreciation of hate understands it as a grotesque distortion or imitation of love, which ultimately "corrodes the ego, wearing away the self,"[22] leaving one "empty," and "depleted." Hate is not the opposite of love; instead "hatred comes frighteningly close to love."[23]

While hatred seeks knowledge of the other through control and possession, love seeks to know and to be known in return. This distinction is critical to understanding the relationship between hatred and love, as it is only through risking being genuinely and intimately known by another that we transcend the illusory sense of radical autonomy and aloneness provided by our ordinary sensory experiences. These common perceptions readily mislead us into viewing personal adequacy as dependent upon our individual efforts at meeting basic material, psychological, and spiritual needs. And the belief in the independent existence of objects—including persons—leads quite naturally to the fear that there is only a limited supply of the "good stuff" that we need in order to feel adequate and complete. Self-worth operates within a model of economic scarcity, where "market forces" determine our relative value.

In response to human needs for "a positive identity, the need for feelings of effectiveness and control over important events, the need for positive connection to other human beings, and the need for autonomy,"[24] the call to love is a call to transcendence. Only love recognizes the spurious nature of questions of personal adequacy, of our fears over having our basic needs met, of being worthy of attentive care. Love understands that what is needed for the realization of our true identities is already present within us as a human organism, as the communal Body of Christ here on earth. As Merton expresses this idea,

> because God's love is in me, it can come to you from a different and special direction that would be closed if He did not live in me, and because His love is in you, it can come to me from a quarter from which it would not otherwise come.[25]

In responding to the call to love, we find that it is through connection, through interaction with all of reality, that the true self emerges. Writing in *Disputed Questions*, Merton addresses love as the ultimate context and ground of our being, highlighting its ability to bridge the isolation and separateness so integrally tied to the human condition:

> By love man enters into contact first with his own deepest self, then with his brother, who is his other self, and finally with the wisdom and power of God, the ultimate Reality . . . . Because it is love it is able to bridge the gap between subject and object and *commune in the subjectivity of the one loved*."[26]

The Relational Nature of Hate

Just as love defies ready understanding, there is no single, commonly accepted definition of hate. A dictionary entry for of hate is "1. to dislike intensely or passionately; feel extreme aversion for or extreme hostility toward."[27] In common usage, people speak of hate in many ways: "I really hated her when she left me for another man." "I hate myself when I act like that." "I hate chicken liver." "I hate the way that the government treats the elderly, or the poor, or gays, or the homeless." "I hate people who gossip about others." "I hate the weather today." "I hate the Yankees." "I hate rap music."

The causes of human aggression and violence are multifaceted and interactive. Social, historical, economic, and political factors, various conflicting ideals, including those of technological progress, religious beliefs, and even personal interests such as the advancement of one's career, may all intersect in the genesis of violence. People may feel intense, even homicidal hatred for another and not engage in acts of violence. They may also engage in acts of violence without experiencing hatred.

My purpose here is not to survey all of the major conceptualizations of hate, nor to arrive at a consensus definition, but rather to explore the relational origins of hate, to understand how the earliest relationships with caregivers can plant the seeds of rage, aggression and hatred. Various usages of hate over the centuries have emphasized either intense negative feelings or an enduring attitude toward another who is the object of one's hatred. The behavioral component of hate has also been understood in several ways, with some authors speaking of withdrawal and others of attack as characteristic of hate. From a psychological perspective, Baumeister and Butz offer a representative definition of hate as "a stable emotional pattern marked by severely negative feelings toward some person or group."[28] As Royzman, McCauley and Rozin[29] explain hate can be seen as comprised of both anger and fear, where the object of one's hatred "not only is blamed for some past maltreatment of oneself or someone one cares about but is also recognized as a source of future threat."[30] The notion of threat is central to many theories of hate, speaking to a continuing vulnerability of the self in the face of a future that holds no certainty of attaining either continuity or coherence.

Robert Sternberg proposes a complex theory of seven different types of hate that draws upon various combinations of three main components: 1) the negation of intimacy or distancing from the object of one's hatred, which may be motivated by feelings of disgust or revulsion; 2) passion in hate, which is expressed as either intense fear or anger in response to a threat; 3) decision-commitment, which involves cognitions of devaluation and diminution through contempt.[31, 32] Sternberg's theory is relevant to understanding hate in both individuals and groups. The relational aspects of hate are prominent in Sternberg's theory, and like Alford, he proposes that hate is psychologically related to love, represent-ing neither the opposite nor the absence of love.[33]

The relational qualities of hate are important to keep in mind, especially in the current age. Technological developments provide highly efficient means of killing one another, often across great distances. We are able to witness death and devastation as it oc-curs, which adds to the seemingly impersonal nature of violence in our world, where videogames imitate life and life itself becomes increasingly surreal. As Merton comments, "Instead of understand-ing death, it would seem that our world simply multiplies it. Death becomes a huge, inscrutable *quantity*."[34] However, as Alford em-phasizes, even in such a situation, given both our proclivity for projecting disavowed aspects of ourselves onto others, as well as our ability for identifying with the suffering of others, "most vio-lence has the quality of attachment,"[35] meaning that it involves relationship of one form or another.

At its core hate incorporates an intensely negative view of the object of one's hatred, whether a person, group, or even a nation. It is grounded in the human tendency to differentiate between *us* and *them*, and further, to devalue *them*. Cognitively, humans are well adapted to noticing differences in the world around them, and assigning value to these differences according to their utility in making the countless decisions that life requires. Human con-sciousness—with its exquisite awareness of separation and differ-ence—can rather easily mislead us into equating the external dis-tractions of life, such as the pursuit of power, wealth, or status, with our basic adequacy and worth. Personal worth then becomes elusive and illusory, shifting with the changing fortunes in our life circumstances. In the extreme this desperate grasping after per-sonal worth can drive one to a violent "taking" of the other. Whether our differences are understood as proof of an essential alienation from others—thereby announcing the impossibility of union—or as ways in which we serve to complement and com-plete one another is of fundamental concern. Do we cherish our differences as a source of rich diversity, or do we feel threatened by them? How each of us responds to human difference may be profoundly influenced by the relationships we establish in the first years of life. Examining these may illuminate possible motivations for devaluing the other, as well as insight into the purpose that such devaluation serves.

Intense devaluation of the other, while not identical with hate, constitutes "an essential ground out of which hate can grow."[36] It is this extreme differentiation of self and other which ultimately serves as the prerequisite for the dehumanization and objectification that makes violence against self or other possible. And it is this imposition of an "alien-otherness" on other persons that makes them somehow so different from the one who hates that they

> can be seen as expendable, undeserving nonentities who are eligible targets of exploitation (e.g., illegal immigrants, animals), or they can be seen as evil enemies who are eligible targets of violence. Whether nonentities or enemies, those outside the scope of justice are morally excluded and seen as less than human.[37]

Once another person is removed from the realm of moral concern, the possibility of actions of an aggressive or violent nature is greatly increased. It is simply not possible for one human being to murder another person. In order to kill someone it is first necessary to objectify that person, to utterly ignore their indwelling Divinity so as to reduce them to the category of some thing that can then be annihilated. However, it is also true that the extent to which someone objectifies another person reflects the degree to which they themselves have become objects to themselves. The American psychiatrist Harry Stack Sullivan captured the foundation for this observation in a basic psychological principle:

> If there is a valid and real attitude toward the self, that attitude will manifest as valid and real toward others. It is not that as ye judge so shall ye be judged, but as you judge yourself so shall you judge others; strange but true so far as I know, and with no exceptions.[38]

The Call to Unity

In *New Seeds of Contemplation*, Merton draws his readers' attention to the possibilities for the co-creation of our identities contained within our deepest feelings of aloneness, unworthiness, and insufficiency: "There is in every weak, lost and isolated member of the human race an agony of hatred born of his own helplessness, his own isolation. Hatred is the sign and the expression of loneliness, of unworthiness, of insufficiency."[39] This "rankling, torment-

ing sense of unworthiness that lies at the root of all hate"[40] paradoxically contains within it the seeds of love and of our true identities. It is precisely here, in convincing us that our weaknesses
and wounds make us unworthy, that hatred pulls its sleight-of-
hand, substituting the illusion of self-sufficiency for a compassionate appreciation of how our woundedness serves to call forth that
which is vital, generative, and healing in other persons. Writing in
Love and Living, Merton poignantly expresses the corrective experience that allows us to see through the illusion of inadequacy and
separation:

> I cannot find myself in myself, but only in another. My true
> meaning and worth are shown to me not in my estimate of
> myself, but in the eyes of the one who loves me; and that one
> must love me as I am, with my faults and limitations, reveal-
> ing to me the truth that these faults and limitations cannot
> destroy my worth in *their* eyes; and that I am therefore valu-
> able as a person, in spite of my shortcomings, in spite of the
> imperfections of my exterior 'package.'[41]

Love, in contrast, is a letting go of control and order, which is something that the person who is consumed by hate cannot risk. While
hatred seeks to violently wrest away that which it craves from
another person, love understands, however obscurely, that such
attempts ultimately do violence to both self and other. Genuine
human existence requires the courage to realize the freedom that
is inherent in each unfolding moment. It embraces the discovery
of self that is found only in the affirmation of the essential oneness
of all persons. The courage to honestly confront the "now," without reliance upon the various diversions that we so often employ,
depends upon a deep sense of trust, and a faith that grasps that
the question of our worthiness is a non-question. It is this "faith
that one is loved by God although unworthy – or, rather, irrespec-
tive of one's worth"[42] that is the ground out of which our true
identity emerges.

The person who loves has learned the lesson of compassion,
that "my brother and I are one. That if I love my brother, then my
love benefits my own life as well, and if I hate my brother and
seek to destroy him, I destroy myself also."[43] Love sees beyond
the illusion of control, and realizes that it is through the renunciation of attempts to control others that we are freed from the prison

of our apparent separation. It grasps the truth that, so long as we draw arbitrary boundaries between self and other based upon our common sensory perceptions, we ignore our communal human existence, and turn our backs on that union with the Divine which is our birthright. This is the true "secret" of humanity, which Merton referenced in a discussion of Sufism during his Alaska visit of 1968:

> The secret of man is God's secret; therefore, it is in God. My secret is God's innermost knowledge of me, which He alone possesses. It is God's secret knowledge of myself in Him . . . . it is the secret of man in God himself.[44]

Merton goes on to speak of the unqualified "yes" that is the affirmation of our identity. "My destiny in life—my final integration—is to uncover this 'yes' so that my life is totally and completely a 'yes' to God, a complete assent to God."[45] This affirmation is an act of faith, and an opening of our own truest identity through a receptivity which acknowledges the interpenetration of God and each member of the human community.

Infant Attachment and the Genesis of Mind

As discussed above, the insidious sense of depletion, emptiness, insufficiency, and abandonment that characterizes the self that hates is a key to understanding both the origin and function of human hatred. These are many of the same descriptors used to describe infants and young children who have known chronic relational trauma, such as physical or sexual abuse and neglect. Interactions that are inconsistent, intrusive, punitive, neglectful, withdrawing, or withholding may all contribute to overwhelming the infant's fragile coping responses. Messages regarding the infant's essential worth and "knowability" are communicated through these interactions and incorporated into the early developing sense of self. The pull toward despair, helplessness and hopelessness may be strong in an infant who has experienced this profound lack of attunement. In extreme cases, where their increasingly more frantic efforts at eliciting caregiver attention consistently fail, infants have been observed to literally "give up" and surrender the will to live.

In an oft-quoted passage from *New Seeds of Contemplation*, Merton reminds us:

At the root of all war is fear: not so much the fear men have of one another as the fear they have of *everything*. It is not merely that they do not trust one another; they do not even trust themselves . . . . It is not only our hatred of others that is dangerous but also and above all our hatred of ourselves: particularly that hatred of ourselves which is too deep and too powerful to be consciously faced. For it is this which makes us see our own evil in others and unable to see it in ourselves.[46]

In these lines we see several of the developmental antecedents of hatred, qualities that arise in our earliest relationships. In particular, Merton references "our hatred of ourselves," an intensely personal experience of shame and humiliation often acquired at an age before readily accessible verbal memories are available, and which may be "too deep and too powerful to be consciously faced." The interactions that produce these intense feelings often involve inconsistent, rejecting or ridiculing primary caregiver responses to the young child, which lead to the development of the child's view of herself as unworthy of help and undeserving of comfort.[47] Such experiences may give rise to cognitive schema, or ways of organizing one's understanding of self in relation to others, that unconsciously lead to actions that produce the feared rejection and thereby reinforce the belief in the self as unworthy, flawed, or perhaps damaged.

The newborn infant is unable to regulate her internal affective state, and is almost completely dependent upon the ongoing physical presence and empathic responsiveness of the caregiver for these functions; she cannot calm or soothe herself when anxious, sad, or angry, nor can she restore her inner equilibrium when overly excited. She cannot stimulate herself when she is essentially "bored." As straightforward as it is challenging, "the essential task of the first year of human life is the creation of a secure attachment bond of emotional communication between the infant and primary caregiver,"[48] which serves as the foundation for later development. The accurate differentiation of internal and external experiences, the growth of a richer, more finely-nuanced subjective experience, the exploration of objects in the environment, the attainment of an ever-greater sense of personal autonomy and competence—all of these developmental tasks are contingent upon the physical and psychological availability of the caregiver.

It is the infant's inherent, unarticulated potentialities for meaning that the sensitive caregiver must accurately recognize in order to internalize a sense of her subjective experience as worthy of others' attentive care. From out of this dynamic rhythm of mutual emotional responsiveness and influence, the infant learns to trust in the predictability and safety of the world. Quite literally, we now understand that the caregiver is intimately involved from birth in the development of the child's brain structure and chemistry—the caregiving other is embedded in the self from the moment of birth. The genesis of mind is itself entirely dependent upon the provision of meaningful experience and occurs only within the context of relationships with other human minds. The very continuity and coherence of the self across time relies upon the consistent availability and responsiveness of this relationship, and therefore represents a life-and-death concern for the infant and young child. I believe that this is the same phenomenon that Merton was referring to when he wrote:

> the deep "I" of the spirit, of solitude and of love, cannot be "had," possessed, developed, perfected . . . . This inner "I," who is always alone, is always universal: for in this most inmost "I" my own solitude meets the solitude of every other man and the solitude of God. Hence it is beyond division, beyond limitation, beyond selfish affirmation.[49]

It is through sustaining caregiving relationships that we first learn about and discover ourselves—only through knowing and being accurately known by the caregiver do we know ourselves. This is a basic need for human beings, what Daniel Stern calls "an intersubjective need to be understood."[50] John Bowlby, who developed the attachment paradigm, referred to these dynamics as "reciprocal interchange."[51] Alan Schore writes of this relational phenomenon, emphasizing that the sensitive caregiver is "psychobiologically attuned not so much to the child's overt behavior as to the reflections of his/her internal state."[52] Out of these earliest interactions, the child also develops the ability to distinguish between internal emotional states and self from non-self; begins to integrate experiences across past and present, and into the future; evaluates subjective experience in ways that guide behavior; develops skills of social adjustment; learns control of mood, drive and responsibility; gains the capacity to cope with emotional stressors; and learns to understand the emotional states of other persons, which is the precursor of empathy.[53] This latter skill, the ability to take the perspective of another and understand their subjective experience *as it means for them*, is necessary for the attainment of mutuality or reciprocity in relationships, and thus opens up the very possibility of social life through the growth of the capacity for empathy. This interactive, dialectical process, in which caregiver and infant mutually influence one another in a joyful dance of becoming, is beautifully captured in Merton's words:

> Because God's love is in me, it can come to you from a different and special direction that would be closed if He did not live in me, and because His love is in you, it can come to me from a quarter from which it would not otherwise come.[54]

Love as the Way to Justice

Reflecting upon Merton's thoughts on the nature of love and hate, I have attempted to integrate a working sense of what Merton is saying from a spiritual perspective with what I have learned from the perspective of clinical and developmental psychology. Merton's discussion of hate calls us to empathically approach the rageful protest of a spirit that is faced with the threat of dissolution and fragmentation, and which is fighting against annihilation. When Merton speaks of "the rankling, tormenting sense of unworthiness that lies at the root of all hate,"[55] he is acknowledging our need for unconditional love and acceptance, as well as the spiritual reality that, left to our own, we are incapable of earning love. Love, properly understood, cannot be deserved, and in fact it is only because of our wounds, faults and failings that we are lovable at all. It is only our incompleteness that calls forth from others the fullness of their gifts and potentiality for being, which in turn complement and complete us.

Merton's reminder of the sense of unworthiness that torments each member of the human race points out the seductive nature of human hatred, which would have us believe the evidence of our senses and usual experience of self and other. Hatred convinces us that our shortcomings, brokenness and wounds are evidence of insufficiency rather than pointing beyond these superficial differences to our basic union with one another. In addition to this, he is directing our attention (perhaps unknowingly) to those earliest relationships with parents and other caregivers, who are blessed with the opportunity to participate in the co-creation of the child's developing sense of self. When Merton writes in the introduction to the Vietnamese edition of *No Man Is An Island* that, in order for peace to be possible in our world, it is imperative that we "recognize that our being itself is grounded in love: that is to say that we come into being because we are loved and because we are meant to love others,"[56] he is addressing not only the sustaining love of the Divine, but a core psychological truth as well. The realization of our potential as caring, productive human beings is dependent upon our ability (and, at times, the good fortune of circumstance) to enlist invested others who join our efforts at bringing coherence and meaning to experience. As Robert Kegan pointed out some twenty years ago

> Who comes into a person's life may be the single greatest factor of influence to what that life becomes. Who comes into a person's life is in part a matter of luck, in part a matter of one's power to recruit others, but in large part a matter of other people's ability to be recruited . . . . however much we learn about the effort to be of help, we can never protect ourselves from the risks of caring . . . In running these risks we preserve the connections between us. We enhance the life we share, or perhaps better put, we enhance the life that shares us.[57]

The larger interpersonal context in which we discover our true identities is defining of what it means to be human, and when we grasp this we are challenged to view the "other" in an inclusive, encompassing manner, considering their welfare as integrally connected with our own. Justice considerations become radically altered when the scope of our ethical concern is thus expanded. The obligation to treat equals as equals as the foundation of acting justly becomes transformed, as our usual distinctions between self and other lose their familiar boundaries. We are challenged to love both self and other, to embrace the division and conflict that divides us from one another. We must genuinely encounter the complexity, ambiguity, and interdependent nature of humanity, before finally grasping the spiritual reality that "we do not exist for ourselves alone, and it is only when we are fully convinced of this fact that we begin to love ourselves properly and thus also love others."[58]

The person whose village has been swept away by a tsunami, the earthquake victim facing the oncoming winter without adequate shelter, the person whose country is being torn apart by genocide, the starving child who may not see tomorrow, the person who continues to experience economic discrimination on the basis of gender or the color of her skin, the African victim of AIDS whose plight is ignored by those nations with the means to ease her suffering, and the Sunni Muslim who rages against the invasion of his country are all, "members of a race which is intended to be one organism and 'one body.'"[59]

Merton demonstrates throughout his works a deep belief in the role of the Divine and other persons in the working out of our true identity. While not trained formally as a psychologist, Merton develops a highly sophisticated understanding of the self that anticipated many current developments in psychology. His writings on spirituality and contemplation in particular contain within them lines of thought more recently found within the interpersonal, multicultural, and constructivist perspectives. Merton and these contemporary scholars of the self consistently challenge the notion of the independently existing, autonomous individual. While the language employed by Merton and others, such as Alan Schore, to describe the development of the self may show considerable variation, the description of the self that emerges is one that emphasizes the central importance of our relationships and the interdependence that informs our search for identity and meaning.

Both love and hate are in this respect a response to the question that life poses in each of us, just as each are epistemologies that embody a fundamental relational stance that defines self and other. One answer frees both self and other to realize the freedom that comes with full personhood, while the other restricts, confines, and ultimately imprisons us in our efforts at fleeing the anxious awareness of separation. In this regard Merton's words from *The Inner Experience* challenge us to consider as matters of ultimate concern the implications of these ways of knowing, as he reminds his reader that one's "inner self is, in fact, inseparable from Christ and hence it is in a mysterious and unique way inseparable from all the other 'I's' who live in Christ, so that they all form one 'Mystical Person' which is 'Christ.'"[60]

Against this understanding of the self, questions of justice become radically transformed. The original revolutionary and transcendent qualities of Christ's message of love calls forth from each of us the response of love and compassion. Our ethics is itself challenged and transformed. Rather than focusing intently on identifying distinct characteristics for determining relevant issues of who is to be considered an "equal" in any given situation, we are drawn instead to the unmistakable conclusion that we are all equals, and that "Every other man is a piece of myself, for I am a part and a member of mankind . . . . What I do is also done for them and with them and by them . . . . [M]y life represents my own allotment in the life of a whole supernatural organism to which I belong."[61]

Notes

1. William Blake, "Auguries of Innocence," in *British Literature: Volume II. 1800 to the Present*, ed. Hazelton Spencer, Walter E. Houghton, Herbert Barrows, David Ferry, and Beverly J. Layman (Lexington, MA: D.C. Heath and Company, 1974), p. 30.

2. Tom L.Beauchamp and James F. Childress, *Principles of Biomedical Ethics*, 5ᵗʰ ed. (Oxford: Oxford University Press, 1994), p. 327.

3. Beauchamp and Childress, *Principles of Biomedical Ethics*, p. 328.

4. Karen Strohm Kitchener, *Foundations of Ethical Practice, Research, and Teaching in Psychology* (Mahwah, New Jersey: Lawrence Erlbaum Associates, Inc., 2000), p. 186.

5. Thomas Merton, *"Honorable reader": Reflections on my work* (New York: Crossroad Publishing Company, 1991), p. 125.

6. Thomas Merton, *New Seeds of Contemplation* (New York: New Directions, 1961), p. 48.

7. Gary Zukav, (1980). *The Dancing Wu Li Masters: An Overview of the New Physics* (New York: Bantam New Age, 1980), p. 95.

8. Allan N. Schore, *Affect Regulation and the Repair of the Self* (New York: W.W.Norton & Company, Inc., 2003), p. 3.

9. James Garbarino, *Lost boys: Why Our Sons Turn Violent and How We Can Save Them* (New York: The Free Press, 1999), p. 38.

10. H.H. The Dalai Lama, *Ethics for the New Millenium* (New York: Riverhead Books, 1999), pp. 42-43.

11. Erich Fromm, D.T. Suzuki, and Richard DeMartino, *Zen Buddhism and Psychoanalysis.* (New York: Harper Colophon Books, 1960), p. 87, italics in original.

12. *Zen Buddhism and Psychoanalysis*, p. 87.

13. Merton, *New Seeds*, p. 72.

14. Erich Fromm, *The Art of Loving* (New York: Harper Perennial, 1989), p. 27.

15. *The Art of Loving*, p. 46.

16. Merton, *New Seeds*, p. 32.

17. *New Seeds*, p. 33.

18. Erich Fromm, *The Heart of Man: Its Genius For Good and Evil* (New York: Harper & Row, 1964), p. 42.

19. C. Fred Alford, "Hate is the Imitation of Love," in *The Psychology of Hate*, ed., Robert Sternberg (Washington, DC: American Psychological Association, 2005), p. 236.

20. Merton, *New Seeds*, p. 123.

21. Alford, "Hate Imitation of Love," p. 237.

22. "Hate Imitation of Love," p. 241.

23. "Hate Imitation of Love," p. 237.

24. Ervin Staub, "The Origins and Evolution of Hate, With Notes on Prevention," in *The Psychology of Hate*, ed., Robert Sternberg (Washington, DC: American Psychological Association, 2005), p. 55.

25. Merton, *New Seeds*, p. 67.

26. Thomas Merton, *Disputed Questions* (San Diego: Harcourt, Brace & Company, 1960), pp. 101-103.

27. Webster's New Universal Unabridged Dictionary (New York: Barnes & Noble Publishing, Inc., 2003), p. 876.

28. Roy F. Baumeister, and David A. Butz, "Roots of Hate, Violence, and Evil," in *The Psychology of Hate*, ed., Robert Sternberg (Washington, DC: American Psychological Association, 2005), p. 87.

29. Edward B. Royzman, Clark McCauley, and Rozin, Paul, "From Plato to Putnam: Four Ways to Think About Hate" in *The Psychology of Hate*, ed., Robert Sternberg (Washington, DC: American Psychological Association, 2005), pp. 3-35.

30. *The Psychology of Hate*, p. 7.

31. Robert Sternberg, "A duplex theory of hate and its development and its application to terrorism massacres, and genocides," *Review of General Psychology*, 7, (2003), pp. 299-328.

32. Sternberg, "Understanding and Combating Hate."

33. "Understanding and Combating Hate."

34. Merton, *"Honorable Reader,"* p. 123.

35. Alford, "Hate Imitation of Love," p. 237.

36. Staub, "Origins and Evolution of Hate," p. 53.

37. Susan Opotow, "Hate, Conflict, and Moral Exclusion," in *The Psychology of Hate*, ed. Robert Sternberg (Washington, DC: American Psychological Association, 2005), p. 127.

38. Harry Stack Sullivan, *Conceptions of Modern Psychiatry* (New York: W.W. Norton & Co., 1953), p. 15.

39. Merton, *New Seeds*, p. 72.

40. *New Seeds*, p. 74.

41. Thomas Merton, *No Man is an Island* (New York: Harcourt, Brace & Company, 1979), p. 35.

42. Merton, *New Seeds*, p. 75.

43. Merton, *"Honorable Reader,"* p. 123.

44. Thomas Merton, *Thomas Merton in Alaska: The Alaskan conferences, journals, and letters* (New York: New Directions, 1989), pp. 153-154.

45. *Thomas Merton in Alaska*, p. 154.

46. Merton, *New Seeds*, p. 112.

47. Allan N. Schore, *Affect Dysregulation and Disorders of the Self* (New York: W.W. Norton & Company, Inc., 2003), p. 31.

48. *Affect Dysregulation and Disorders of the Self*, p. 273.

49. Merton, *Disputed Questions*, p. 207.

50. Daniel N. Stern, *The Interpersonal World of the Infant: A View From Psychoanalysis and Developmental Psychology* (New York: Basic Books, 1985), p. 270.

51. John Bowlby, *Attachment and Loss. Vol. I: Attachment* (New York: Basic Books, 1969), p. 346.

52. Allan N. Schore, *Affect Regulation and the Repair of the Self* (New York: W.W. Norton & Company, Inc., 2003), p. 39.

53. *Affect Regulation and the Repair of the Self*, p. 39.

54. Merton, *New Seeds*, p. 67.

55. *New Seeds*, p. 74.

56. Merton, *"Honorable Reader,"* p. 126.

57. Robert Kegan, *The Evolving Self: Problem and Process in Human Development* (Cambridge, MA: Harvard University Press, 1983), pp. 19-20.

58. Merton, *No Man is an Island*, p. xx.

59. *No Man is an* Island, p. xxi.

60. Thomas Merton, *The Inner Experience: Notes on Contemplation* (San Francisco: HarperCollins, 2003), p. 22.

61. Merton, *No Man is an Island*, p. xxiii.

A Bricoleur in the Monastery: Merton's Tactics in a Nothing Place

Fred W. Herron

The ability of Thomas Merton to unsettle us and re-organize our sense of "spiritual spaces" accounts in no small part for his continued appeal more than thirty-five years after his death.[1] The last several years have sparked questions about his suitability as a role model for young people in the light of some ill-considered reflections on his trip to Asia and his relationship with "M," the student nurse with whom he fell in love in the spring of 1966.[2] His positions on war and peace, racial justice, and monastic living were guaranteed to tweak the noses and the assumptions of many along the way. Two examples, set fifty years apart, may serve to make the point. English Benedictine Aelred Graham criticized Merton in 1953 for his "mysticism for the masses" and for his projection of his personal experience into his writing.[3] Fifty years later Mary Jo Weaver argued that "it seems fair to want a deeper acknowledgement of his experience with 'M'" than Merton allows and suggested that he seemed at times to Weaver, "neurotic, over-published, and extraordinarily self-centered."[4]

Merton himself was aware of the discomfort he caused many and commented on it in a variety of ways. After a somewhat disappointing physical exam he was to remark that "[a]s an ikon, I am not doing too well."[5] He was careful to discourage people from turning him into a plaster-cast model of piety for the edification of young people. His continual ability to prompt, chide and even infuriate people who approach his work from a variety of perspectives is not much more surprising than this ability to confirm the preconceived notions of so many of those who approach his works from such widely disparate and sometimes contradictory points of view as well.

How are we to account for the comments of one self-proclaimed "conservative" Catholic bookseller who remarked to me that Merton is consistently among her store's bestsellers and the remarks of a number of veterans of the 1960s (if you can remember them, you weren't there) who comment that they are still "turned on" by how far ahead of his time Merton was? The writings of French Jesuit historian, theologian and ethnologist Michel DeCerteau, along with others who share his perspective regarding the nature of everyday life and "the politics of the quotidian" offer some insights into these seemingly disparate responses.[6] The object of this discussion is to highlight several key insights which DeCerteau and others who follow his line of thought have to offer, especially regarding the notion of *bricolage,* and then to consider two points of intersection between the visions of DeCerteau and Merton.

The Bricoleur

Claude Levi-Strauss brought the term "bricolage" into academic discourse when he used it to describe the scientific workings of mythic reflection.[7] The French term refers to something made or put together using whatever materials happen to be available. A *bricoleur* is a handyman or jack-of-all-trades in contrast to a tradesman. The term describes a person adept at odd jobs and repairs who does not begin work with a planned-out project, dedicated materials, and accepted procedures but must make do with whatever is at hand. Levi-Strauss argues that like "bricolage" on the technical plane, mythical reflection can reach brilliant unforeseen results on the intellectual plane.

DeCerteau took up this term and placed it within the context of his study of the everyday throughout history. He was concerned with how ordinary men and women, whose voices are heard only as the background murmur of official history, live their lives each day. He was especially interested in the activities of groups of people who lacked power. He wondered how the powerless made creative use of the culture imposed upon them.

DeCerteau, for example, points to the imposition of European culture and Christianity upon indigenous Americans. He notes that, "Submissive, and even consenting to their subjection, the Indians nevertheless often *made of* the rituals, representations and laws imposed on them something quite different from what their conquerors had in mind; they subverted them not by rejecting or altering them, but by using them with respect to ends and references foreign to the system they had no choice but to accept."[8] He argues that they did this through the various religions which they fashioned and which preserved the content of their beliefs and practices in the form of a European Catholicism. Slaves in the New

World decided what they would do with the Christian religion imposed upon them. They used it as a means of preserving their Yoruba religious traditions. So both slave owners and priests were happy to see them revering the Catholic saints. What they did not realize, however, was that they were revering the saints as representations of their traditional deities. So Mary, St. Barbara and Lazarus were used to translate and preserve slave devotion to the great Yoruba Orisishas: Oshun, Shango, and Babaluaiye.[9]

After citing a host of other similar examples, DeCerteau argued that all of these variations on bricolage are examples of *tactical practices*. He draws a distinction between these and others that he calls *strategies*. He argues that *strategies* are exercised by subjects, in established places and situations, who are in control of their lives and destinies. These include social or institutional domains such as governments, churches and academic institutions. *Tactics*, on the other hand, are the "art of the weak" living in foreign territory. In these cases people make do and get by in lands and cultures that are beyond their control and not of their making. Tactics are "ruses" or "surprises." They are "clever tricks" that allow and enable the weak to work within "the order established by the strong" by taking advantage of "cross cuts, cracks, and lucky hits."[10] DeCerteau pointed to the ruses of the weak as primordial realities that were present in ancient Greek, Islamic, and Chinese cultures. He went so far as to argue that there appeared to be a link between them and the deceptions of plant and animal camouflage. He spoke of the "permanence of a memory without language, from the depths of the oceans to the streets of our great cities."[11] Those without power, he argued, use subversive tactics in a space which is not their own. This kind of subversion is viable for even the most disadvantaged and victimized groups.[12]

The space of the disadvantaged is always the space of the Other. They must use alternative tactics within a terrain imposed and organized by laws they did not create. DeCerteau argues that "it operates in isolated actions, blow by blow, takes advantage of 'opportunities' and depends on them, being without any base where it could stockpile its winnings, build up its position, and plan raids. What it wins it cannot keep." These "nowhere" places or "nonplaces," as he described them, are of tremendous strategic value. A non-place is the necessary precondition for those without power to create their own community. On the other hand, such a non-place suggests the only possible place from which to critique and undermine normative culture, language, and the meaning we take for granted when embedded in a particular place.[13]

Ada Maria Isasi-Diaz echoes this approach in discussing the stance of Hispanas/Latinas and Mujerista theology. She notes that, "often I know that we, Hispanas/Latinas, let [those with power and privilege] think they are dominating us while we in the interstices create a meaningful *cotidiano* that makes our lives worth living …. In other words, *nos burlanos del opresor* for though they exploit us, we in turn not only survive despite them, but also change their material world and are learning to influence their discourse about the world at large and even about themselves." That is, "we mock the oppressor by tricking/evading the oppressor." This happens by "turning the confinement/spaces to which we are assigned into creative/liberating spaces." To put it another way, she argues, "we are trying not to let the will of the masters (and mistresses) define the tiniest space which initially was not ours but which little by little we turn into our own, partially because masters and mistresses are scared to come into them once we inhabit them."[14] Isasi-Diaz is careful to note that "the mischieviousness of mockery is a most healthy antidote for any sense of 'victimhood' that we might be tempted to embrace."[15]

Merton as Bricoleur

It seems clear that there are points of intersection between this vision of the *bricoleur* and a balanced view of Thomas Merton. While there was never anything artless about Merton's writing, there was a studied and dedicated openness to going to the places where his prayer, his reading, his correspondence, or the challenges of the day took him. One would be hard pressed to imagine him as the author of a systematic theology. The "voice of the present moment" was too compelling for that.[16] Merton's procedures were his own; his tools were those that were the ones at hand.

At the same time he was comfortable making use of the materials at hand. Those materials ranged from the literature of the world to the writings of the Fathers of the Church. Nothing human was alien to his vision and nothing was beyond the ability to be used to make the point that all creation reflected the presence of the Creator. Merton found in the cultural movements and aspirations of the day, as well as in the rich Catholic imaginative and spiritual tradition, what Marie-Dominique Chenu called *pierre d'attente*, toothing stones that jut out from a wall in order to mesh with an eventual addition.[17] True *bricoleur* that he was, Merton was able to see the points of intersection between those various cultural and religious traditions and the next steps in the construction of the Christian community. He saw links to other religious traditions at a time when elements of the Catholic community were only beginning to emerge from the great citadel of faith and embrace the "wide country" of "the holy commonwealth of contemplation."[18] Looking at the world from the wide country of the monastery, he could reflect that Gethsemani "taught me how to live. And now I owe everyone else in the world a share in that life. My first duty is to start, for the first time, to live as a member of a human race which is no more (and no less) ridiculous than I am myself."[19]

The "no place" of the monastery is "the burning promised land," "the place of silence," and "the place of wrestling with an angel." It is the place where God has given him "roots in eternity."[20] But Merton was never to find one true "abiding place."[21] A little more than decade after describing Gethsemani as "the four walls of my new freedom" he was to say: "My monastery is not a home. It is not a place where I am rooted and established in the earth."[22] William Shannon wisely remarks that "Gethsemani roots him, not where Gethsemani is, namely in this earth, but elsewhere, that is to say, in eternity. Gethsemani points to home, but is not itself 'Home.'"[23]

The unforeseen quality of his searching and Merton's particular kind of *bricolage* can be attested to by the dramatic change and growth which he experienced throughout all his spiritual seeking. This was never clearer than in the arc of his life in Gethsemani. Much that happened in his monastic life from 1941 to 1958 was chronicled and the source of profound edification for a generation of his readers. A lesser literary artist, a different kind of spiritual person, would have been content to rest in the citadel that was, for a time, his spiritual home. His experience at "Fourth and Walnut" led him through the looking glass and challenged him to articulate an astonishing awareness of his solidarity with all the rest of humanity. It was, he said, "like waking from a dream of separateness."[24] Claude Levi-Straus argued that *bricolage* can achieve brilliant unforeseen results. Merton seems bowled over, thunderstruck, by the unsought and unforeseen "liberation," "relief," and "joy" in his realization that "I *am* like other men," a part of the human race "in which God Himself became incarnate." He is overwhelmed by the startling awareness that "[t]here is no way of telling people that they are all walking around shining like the sun."[25]

The reflections of Michel DeCerteau serve to cast much of Merton's writings in a particularly pointed slant of light. DeCerteau was interested in the activities of the powerless. He focused on the ways that the powerless made creative use of the surrounding culture. Drawing on his research he marked a distinction between *strategies*, the works of social or institutional domains in which their operations were carried out, and *tactics*, the "art of the weak" who live in foreign territory.[26] Tactics are employed by those without power in a space not really their own. They inhabit "nowhere" places or non-places which take on tremendous strategic value.

Compare this vision with Merton's description of life as a monk. The life of a monk, he says, "appears to be completely useless."[27] But he reminds us that the contemporary world calls us to and rewards the useful, but that this is largely "the usefulness of suckers."[28] Merton defies the conventional wisdom and refuses to define people by their functions. For the monk, "'Being' always takes precedence over 'doing' and 'having.'"[29] He notes the unique palace of nowhere which the monk inhabits, arguing that the monk is one "who at once loves the world yet stands apart from it with a critical objectivity which refuses to become involved in its transient fashions and its more manifest absurdities."[30]

The monk's "nowhere place" makes him "a marginal person … essentially outside of all establishments."[31] This position, outside of contemporary technological society and its tendencies to dehumanize, places him in a unique spot to take advantage of the "cross cuts, cracks, and lucky hits" which emerge and to offer them as a vision of authentic humanity rooted in the image of God. This is the point he makes in his final talk in Bangkok when he defines a monk as "essentially someone who takes up a critical attitude toward the world and its structures… somebody who says, in one way or another, that the claims of the world are fraudulent."[32] His reaction to the challenges of technological society was not to adopt a piecemeal approach. Rather it was to argue for *metanoia*, a total personal transformation. This vision was possible for Merton precisely because he adopted a stance in this "no place." He hints at radical nature of this vantage point in a letter written to Daniel Berrigan dated October 10, 1967:

In my opinion the job of the Christian is to try to give an example of sanity, independence, human integrity, good sense,

as well as Christian love and wisdom, against all establishments and all mass movements and all current fashions which
are merely mindless and hysterical …. The most popular and
exciting thing at the moment is not necessarily the best
choice."[33]

Gethsemani was such a "nowhere place" for Merton. He described
it in a talk to the novices at Gethsemani as a "total non-entity," "a
null and void nothing place."[34] While he jokingly agreed with one
novice who referred to the monastery's main building as looking
"like a barrel factory," he quickly qualified that remark by noting
that "God knows how or why, but prayer here has been valid."[35]
It became clear that this "nothing place," when seen through the
eyes of a contemplative poet open to the grace of God, was indeed
consequential and spoke of things beyond itself where time and
timelessness intersect.[36]

In the preface to the Japanese edition of *The Seven Storey Mountain* Merton concludes that it is his task to "take my true part in all
the struggles and sufferings of the world… to make my entire life
a rejection of, a protest against the crimes and injustices of war
and political tyranny which threaten to destroy the whole race of
man and the world with him."[37]

The paradox for the *bricoleur*, as it was for Merton as well, is
that this "no place" becomes the very place from which he or she
can critique and undermine the normative culture, language, and
meaning that is taken for granted when embedded in a particular
cultural space.[38] This happens by affirming solidarity and communion with others through a compassionate identification with
their brokenness. Merton maintains that "[t]he monastic life today stands over against the world with a mission to affirm not
only the message of salvation but also those most basic human
values which the world needs most desperately to regain: personal
integrity, inner peace, authenticity, identity, inner depth, spiritual
joy, the capacity to love, the capacity to enjoy God's creation and
give thanks."[39]

Merton makes this point more explicitly in his discussions of
non-violence. The roots of all violence, he argues, are to be found
in the denial of our common human condition. The distorted vision of humanity which results leads us to project our own
unadmitted evil onto the other.[40] Peacemakers, observing the world
from their "no place," are able to see the common humanity which

transcends these divisions: "Christian non-violence is not built on a presupposed division, but on the basic unity of man." Ultimately, Merton argues, Christian nonviolence is rooted in his firm belief in "the total solidarity of all."[41]

Merton frequently associates himself with the *bricoleur* who acts as a "sign of contradiction" to a society that calculates human worth in terms of achievement and accomplishment. The hermit, he argues, exists, "outside all our projects, plans, assemblies, movements."[42] He is a reminder that God's ways and the world's ways are not the same or even compatible, reminding the followers of Christ that they are pilgrims with "no abiding place" on this earth.[43]

Ada Maria Isasi-Diaz approaches the role of the *bricoleur* in a slightly different way. She notes the benefits brought by the "mischievous use of mockery" in helping the bricoleur to avoid any sense of victimhood.[44] The most notable and charming example of this appears in Merton's poetry dealing with the mechanization of Gethsemani life. In his poem "CHEE$E" he remarks, "Poems are nought but warmed-up breeze, / *Dollars* are made by Trappist Cheese."[45] His anti-poem to his friend Robert Lax called "A Practical Program for Monks" provides an example that is a little less comic and substantially more satiric: "Each one's own business shall be his most important affair, and provide his own remedies" and "The monastery, being owner of a communal rowboat, is the antechamber of heaven. / Surely that ought to be enough."[46] Even here in the monastery Merton projects a stance of "no place" to look critically at the life of the Gethsemani community.

Merton moves beyond humor and satire and makes use of irony to accomplish the ends to which Isasi-Diaz points. His prose poem on the dropping of the first atomic bomb on Hiroshima, *Original Child Bomb*, appears to be, in large part, a detailed factual description of the events culminating in the use of the bomb. At many turns, however, Merton provides ironic commentary on the events he describes. For example, he notes that Harry Truman "knew a lot less about the war than many people did."[47] The decision to drop the bomb as "a demonstration of the bomb on a civil and military target"[48] suggests that this "demonstration is a sanitized, bureaucratic description of the enormous destructive capabilities of the bomb."[49] "America's friendly ally," the Soviet Union, would not be told about the creation of the bomb because they are "now friendly enough."[50] Hiroshima is "Lucky" because it had escaped bombing up until this time.[51] The list goes on and on, and the focus of the irony gathers steam and centers around two key sets of images. The first cluster of images identify the bomb with a child: "'Little Boy' was . . . tucked away" and "the Original Child that was now born," for example. The second focuses on images that have religious associations such as "Trinity," "an atmosphere of devotion" surrounding the event and the "act of faith" of the observers.[52] The topic lends itself to a stance that is critical and that encourages a different interpretation when looking at humanity from the standpoint of the image of God.

Robert Nugent has highlighted Thomas Merton's difficulty with the Trappist censors concerning his writings on war and peace and the challenge this offered to obedience.[53] Writing to W.H. Ferry in December, 1961 he acknowledged that he was having "a bit of censor trouble" which he hoped to avoid by having his materials circulated along with Ferry's writings. This he did not believe was a violation of censorship rules.[54] Writing to James Laughlin, Merton denied that he was engaging in some "wild subversive activity," arguing that circulating his writings in this way would not be wrong unless it had been expressly forbidden.[55] In response to Dom Gabriel Sortais's letter of May 26, 1962 ordering him "to abstain from writing in any way whatsoever about the subject of nuclear war," Merton missed no opportunity to forward copies of the Cold War Letters to Jim Forest, Daniel Berrigan, Dorothy Day and others.[56] At about the same time Merton remarked in his journal that "If I am to write an article asked for by the *Nation* it must be super-cagey, censored by the Cardinal in N.Y (or some other ordinary acceptable to the Canons)."[57] Such caginess is the hallmark of the practiced and intentional *bricoleur*. He carefully and relatively skillfully operated from this "nowhere place" and continued to distribute his writings in a way which appears to be almost classic *bricolage*.

Articulation from No Place

Thomas Merton took up the challenge of *bricolage*, implicit in the gospel, through his willingness to enter into a searing search for the real in his writings and his life. That search reflects a deep sense of faith in the image of God central to humanity and in Christ the great physician who came to heal all who are wounded. It leads to a kind of personal humility that causes him to resist turning himself into any sort of icon and that is quick to notice any kind of institutional idolatry. It is precisely the golden calf that is the prime and easy target for the *bricoleur*.

It is this approach which DeCerteau recommends as the logical response of the Christian community to the challenges of *bricolage*. Rather than resist the challenges of tactical *bricolage*, he argues that our religious tradition is called to mediate these "other desires." He uses the term "articulation" to describe this sort of Christian engagement with culture. Here he does not mean "articulation" as either translation or re-expression. Instead he uses it to mean, "to join flexibly" as in "articulated" buses or sculptures. The articulation or "writing" of and within the tradition involves "insinuating" the desires and operations of Christianity into our contemporary institutions, practices, and systems of knowledge.[58]

It is precisely this critical stance that leads Merton, as *bricoleur*, to advocate for a truly "transcultural awareness." He is quick to say that a self-critical attitude toward one's own culture, one of the true strengths of Western culture, is an essential stance to take.[59]

This provides the opening, similar to the one DeCerteau describes, to the divine truly present in the other. This is what Merton means when he says that "We must, then, see the truth in the stranger, and the truth we see must be a newly living truth, not just a projection of a dead conventional idea of our own—a projection of our own self upon the stranger."[60] When this begins to happen, we can start to become aware of a relationship like that which he experienced at Fourth and Walnut that exists between ourselves and every other human being. It is then that we are "fully 'Catholic' in the best sense of the word," he remarks, possessing a vision and an experience "of the one truth shining out in all its various manifestations, some clearer than others, some more definite and more certain than others."[61]

Ultimately, Merton argues, "the path to final integration ... lies ... beyond the dictates and programs of any culture."[62] The Christian is called to live in a "no place" in which "a transcultural integration is eschatological." This will require, in the final analysis, "a disintegration of the social and cultural self, the product of merely human history, and the reintegration of that self in Christ, in salvation history, in the mystery of redemption, in the Pentecostal 'new creation.'"[63] This, too, is the ultimate end of all *bricolage*.

Notes

1. I am indebted for this understanding of "spiritual spaces" to Graham Ward, "Michel DeCerteau's 'Spiritual Spaces,'" *The South Atlantic Quarterly* 100:2 (Spring, 2001), pp. 501-517.

2. "Letter to Bishop Donald Wuerl," www. Merton.org/Letter/index.asp (accessed 6/23/05) and Deborah Halter, "Whose Orthodoxy is it?" *National Catholic Reporter* (March 11, 2005). For a useful evaluation by a younger Catholic see Michael Herron, "'No Offense, but ...' Thomas Merton and the New Catechism," *National Catholic Reporter* (October 28, 2005), pp. 21a-22a.

3. Aelred Graham, "Thomas Merton: A Modern Man in Reverse," *Atlantic* 191 (January, 1953), pp. 70-74.

4. Mary Jo Weaver, "Conjectures of a Disenchanted Bystander," *Horizons* 30/2 (2003), pp. 291, 285.

5. Thomas Merton, *Conjectures of a Guilty Bystander* (Garden City, NY: Doubleday, 1968), p. 330.

6. Michel DeCerteau, *The Practice of Everyday Life*, vol. 1 (Berkeley: University of California Press, 1984); Graham Ward, (ed.), *The Certeau Reader* (Oxford: Blackwell, 1999); and Vincent Miller, *Consuming Religion: Christian Faith and Practice in a Consumer Culture* (New York: Continuum, 2005), p. 155.

7. Claude Levi-Strauss, *The Savage Mind* (Chicago: University of Chicago Press, 1966), p. 17.

8. *The Practice of Everyday Life*, p. xiii.

9. Joseph Murphy, *Santeria: An African Religion in America* (Boston: Beacon Press, 1988). For a similar perspective see Thomas Merton's reflections on cargo cults in *The Geography of Lograire* (New York: New Directions, 1969). Kenelm Burridge raises some interesting questions in this regard in his "Merton, Cargo Cults and *The Geography of Lograire*," in Victor A. Kramer, (ed.), *The Merton Annual*, vol. 17 (Louisville, KY: Fons Vitae, 2004), pp. 206-215.

10. *The Practice of Everyday Life*, pp. 37-38. Leonard Cohen makes a similar comment in his song "Anthem," "There is a crack, a crack in everything/ That's how the light gets in." I am grateful to Dr. Paul Pearson for reminding me of this verse.

11. *The Practice of Everyday Life*, pp. 38, 40.

12. For one example, see the application of this theory to people with autism and other related disorders in Ine Gevers, "Subversive Tactics of Neurologically Diverse Cultures," *Journal of Cognitive Liberties* 2 (Spring/Summer 2000), pp. 43-60.

13. Michel DeCerteau, *The Mystic Fable*, vol. 1 (Chicago: University of Chicago Press: 1992).

14. Ada Maria Isasi-Diaz, "Burlanda al Opresor: Mocking/Tricking the Oppressor: Dreams and Hopes of Hispanas/Latinas and Mujeristas," *Theological Studies* 65 (June, 2004), p. 346.

15. "Burlanda al Opresor," p. 346.

16. Thomas Merton, "Rain and the Rhinoceros," in *Raids on the Unspeakable* (New York: New Directions, 1964), p. 23.

17. Joseph A. Komonchak, "The Church in Crisis: Pope Benedict's Theological Vision," *Commonweal* 132 (June 3, 2005).

18. Donald Grayston, *Thomas Merton: The Development of a Spiritual Theologian* (New York: Edwin Mellen, 1985), p. 177.

19. Thomas Merton, *The Sign of Jonas* (New York: Harcourt, Brace, Jovanovich, 1953), pp. 322-23. I am grateful to Michael Herron for pointing me to this remark.

20. *The Sign of Jonas*, p. 345.

21. See Fred Herron, *No Abiding Place: Thomas Merton and the Search for God* (Lanham, MD: University Press of America, 2005).

22. Thomas Merton, *The Seven Storey Mountain*, (New York: Harcourt, Brace, 1948), p. 772 and Robert E. Daggy, (ed.), *"Honorable Reader": Reflections on My Work* (New York: Crossroad, 1989), p. 65.

23. William H. Shannon, *Silent Lamp: The Thomas Merton Story* (New York: Crossroad, 1992), p. 9.

24. *Conjectures of a Guilty Bystander*, p. 140.

25. *Conjectures of a Guilty Bystander*, p. 158.

26. *Practice of Everyday Life*, pp. 37-38.

27. Thomas Merton, *The Silent Life* (New York: Farrar, Straus and Cudahy, 1957), p. viii.

28. "Rain and the Rhinoceros," p. 22.

29. Thomas Merton, *The Monastic Journey* (Kansas City, MO: Sheed, Andrews and McMeel, 1977), p. 44.

30. Thomas Merton, *Contemplation in a World of Action* (Garden City, NY: Doubleday, 1971), p. 227.

31. Thomas Merton, *The Asian Journal of Thomas Merton* (New York: New Directions, 1973), p. 305.

32. *Asian Journal*, p. 329. See Paul R. Dekar, "What the Machine Produces and What the Machine Destroys: Thomas Merton on Technology," *The Merton Annual*, vol. 17, pp. 216-34.

33. Thomas Merton, *The Hidden Ground of Love: The Letters of Thomas Merton on Religious Experience and Social* Concerns, ed., William H. Shannon (New York: Farrar, Straus and Giroux, 1985), p. 98. For a discussion

of Merton and technology see Paul R. Dekar, "What the Machine Produces and What the Machine Destroys."
34. Thomas Merton, *T.S. Eliot and Prayer* (Creedence Cassette).
35. *T.S. Eliot and Prayer.*
36. Mark Van Doren, "Introduction," in *Selected Poems of Thomas Merton* (New York: New Directions, 1967), p. xiii. See also Deborak P. Kehoe, "Early Reflections in a 'Nothing Place': Three Gethsemani Poems," in Victor A. Kramer, (ed.), *The Merton Annual*, vol. 17 (Louisville: Fons Vitae, 2004), pp. 61-75.
37. *"Honorable Reader,"* p. 65.
38. *The Mystic Fable.*
39. *Contemplation in a World of Action*, p. 81.
40. See Thomas Merton, *Ishi Means Man: Essays on Native Americans* (Greensboro, NC: Unicorn Press, 1976), pp. 26-27.
41. Thomas Merton, *The Nonviolent Alternative* (New York: Farrar, Straus and Giroux, 1980), pp. 209, 257.
42. Thomas Merton, *Disputed Questions* (New York: Farrar, Straus and Cudahy, 1960), p. 199.
43. See *No Abiding Place: Thomas Merton's Search for God.*
44. "Burlanda al Opresor," p. 346.
45. Thomas Merton, *The Collected Poems of Thomas Merton* (New York: New Directions, 1977), p. 800.
46. *Collected Poems*, pp. 797-98.
47. Thomas Merton, *Original Child Bomb*, (New York: New Directions, 1962), p. 2.
48. *Original Child Bomb*, p. 5.
49. *Original Child Bomb*, p. 5.
50. *Original Child Bomb*, p. 6.
51. *Original Child Bomb*, p. 7.
52. *Original Child Bomb*, pp. 26, 40, 13, 15.
53. Robert Nugent, S.D.S., "The Silent Monk," *America*, 194 (May 15, 2006), pp. 8-12.
54. *The Hidden Ground of Love*, p. 203.
55. *The Hidden Ground of Love*, p. 204.
56. "The Silent Monk."
57. Victor A. Kramer, (ed.), *Turning Toward the World: The Journals of Thomas Merton*, vol. 4, 1960-1963 (New York: Farrar, Straus and Giroux, 1996), p. 187.
58. Michel DeCerteau, "The Weakness of Believing: From the Body to Writing, a Christian Transit," in *The Certeau Reader*, pp. 215-243 and "How Is Christianity Thinkable Today?" *Theology Digest*, 17 (Winter, 1971), p. 344. For a reflection on the implications of DeCerteau's vision

see Frederick Bauerschmidt, "The Abrahamic Voyage: Michel deCerteau and Theology," *Modern Theology* 12 (January, 1996), pp. 1-26 and Jeremy Aherne, "The Shattering of Christianity and the Articulation of Belief," *New Blackfriars* 77 (November, 1996), p. 501.

59. *Conjectures of a Guilty Bystander*, p. 62.

60. *Collected Poems*, p. 385.

61. *Contemplation in a World of Action*, p. 212.

62. *Contemplation in a World of Action*, p. 217.

63. *Contemplation in a World of Action*, p. 216.

Kindred Spirits in Revelation and Revolution: Rachel Carson and Thomas Merton

Monica Weis

In considering the theme of Revelation and Revolution, one could focus on many different incidents in Thomas Merton's life when a significant spiritual insight effected a dramatic change in attitude or behavior. One thinks of his epiphanic experience at Fourth and Walnut when Merton realized how intimately he was linked with every other human being; or those years in the late 1950s and early '60s, termed by some scholars his "turning toward the world," when, as the fruit of long periods of contemplative prayer, Merton became increasingly aware of how closely issues of social justice were tied to his monastic vocation of silence and solitude. It is to these early years of the 1960s I want to turn, to look at a little-discussed moment of revelation and revolution in Merton's life—specifically to January 1963 when Merton felt compelled to write a letter to Rachel Carson.

Let me set the scene. Since 1939 DDT had been used success-fully to eradicate mosquito larvae; during World War II, our mili-tary regularly sprayed the Pacific islands with this chemical be-fore an invasion. When malaria was significantly reduced in de-veloped countries, DDT's inventor, Paul Müller, was awarded a Nobel prize. By the mid-1950s most U.S. municipalities were spray-ing DDT in neighborhoods to eradicate tent caterpillars, gypsy moths and the beetles responsible for Dutch elm disease.[1] Yet all was not well.

Rachel Carson in 1945 had submitted an article to *Reader's Digest* detailing the disruptive influence of DDT on the delicate balance of nature. Despite the fact that she had been an occasional con-tributor to the magazine for almost ten years and had once sought a position as its science editor, her article was not accepted. As Carson's biographer Linda Lear comments, "The *Digest*...found pesticides an unpalatable subject, and Rachel turned her attention to other research subjects."[2]

Now, in the early 1960s when a friend in Massachusetts asked her to investigate why all the song birds in her yard had died along with the mosquitoes, Carson was persuaded to tackle this question. *Silent Spring*, published in three installments in *The New Yorker* beginning June 1962, and in a single volume by Houghton Mifflin that September, called for a major paradigm shift in our thinking. Considerable hell broke loose. Negative comments from scientists, politicians, and chemical company executives—a veritable international controversy—threatened to destroy her. Carson's writing and scientific career seemed to be at an end. Targeted in a vicious campaign to discredit her scientific integrity, Carson was vilified as a "hysterical female," a "pseudo-scientist," "probably a communist," a "bird and bunny lover" and a charlatan researcher.[3]

The controversy over *Silent Spring*—what Vice President Al Gore has termed the "power of the writer against the power of politicians"[4]—fueled public debate and "people began to think about the chemicals they were handling, what they were doing to the environment, and what scientists weren't telling them....they began to question the very direction of technology."[5] Rachel Carson—the mouse that roared—was heard.

Forty-plus years later, we can verify that *Silent Spring* became a catalyst for our current environmental movement. Carson's "third eye" allowed her to see beneath the surface to a new truth about nature, namely, the interdependence of all creation: soil, air, water, animals, and human beings. Prior to 1962, the word "environment" was not a public policy term; two years earlier, conservation matters had been only peripherally mentioned at both the Democratic and Republican conventions.[6] But concern over nuclear fallout, the pesticide-contaminated cranberry scandal of 1959, and widespread infant deformities in Europe due to the drug, thalidomide, had created public readiness for a new message.[7] Carson's meticulous research, combined with her lyrical explanation of the dangers of pesticides, not only put the issue of pesticides into the public debate, but directly led to the establishment of the Environmental Protection Agency in 1970, and a ban on the production of DDT in 1972. Widely regarded as the most influential book in the last fifty years, *Silent Spring* is credited by Thomas J. Lyons and former Vice-President Al Gore, among others, with inaugurating a new era of environmental concern, a watershed moment of new vision and activism. In presenting Rachel Carson posthumously with the Presidential Medal of Freedom in 1980, President Jimmy Carter said: "she created a tide of environmental consciousness that has not ebbed."[8]   More recently, Gary Kroll has claimed that *Silent Spring* was "so much more than an anti-pesticide tract. It was an essay of ecological radicalism that attempted to wake up a populace quiescent to the techno-scientific control of the world."[9]

Thomas Merton became aware of Carson's book and, through the efforts of Ann Ford, secured a copy soon after it hit the bookstores. On January 12, 1963, before television interviews with Rachel Carson had persuaded the American public to support her position, Merton wrote to Carson, congratulating her on her "fine, exact, and persuasive book."[10]   Merton had for some time been concerned about racism, war, nuclear weapons, and the dangers of technology.[11] He had been in contact with James Forest of *The Catholic Worker*, peace activist Daniel Berrigan, and non-violence advocates Jean and Hildegard Goss-Mayr. Peace and the moral bankruptcy of the Vietnam War were uppermost in his mind. And yet, Merton paused to initiate a connection with Rachel Carson. Why might this be? What revelation of justice was tugging at Merton's heart?

A careful reading of Merton's letter to Carson reveals several points of resonance with Rachel Carson, namely, her prophetic stance; her ability to view the significance of research on the macro scale of human decision-making; and her belief in the interdependence of all creation. When Merton writes that *Silent Spring* is "perhaps much more timely even than you or I realize," he is sensing in Carson a kindred spirit who is offering both information and insight at the cutting edge of an issue—information with far-reaching consequences, and profound insight into our responsibility for the earth. "Though you are treating of just one aspect, and a rather detailed aspect, of our technological civilization," writes Merton, "you are, perhaps without altogether realizing, contributing a most valuable and essential piece of evidence for the diagnosis of the ills of our civilization."

Merton also realized that Carson's research was a quite good illustration of how we not only disregard the value of small things such as garden pests, but also exhibit "portentous irresponsibility" on the grand scale, namely in world politics and war. He comments:

[W]e dare to use our titanic power in a way that threatens not only civilization but life itself. The same mental processing…seems to be at work in both cases, and your book makes it clear to me that there is a *consistent pattern* running through everything that we do, through every aspect of our culture, our thought, our economy, our whole way of life. What this pattern is I cannot say clearly, but I believe it is now the most vitally important thing for all of us…to arrive at a clear, cogent statement of our ills, so that we may begin to correct them…. [I]t seems that our remedies are instinctively those which aggravate the sickness: *the remedies are expressions of the sickness itself.* I would almost dare to say that the sickness is perhaps a very real and very dreadful hatred of life ….

Merton, himself, was astute at reading the signs of the times and delineating the long-range implications of human activity. In the later part of the 1950s and into the '60s, he had been reflecting and writing on the rights of indigenous people, the dangers of atomic energy and nuclear war, the Christian responsibility for peacemaking, and the urgency of non-violence as a means toward peace.[12] Indeed, fifteen months earlier, Merton had made a definitive entry into the struggle against war with an essay on the madness of war published in *The Catholic Worker*—"The Root of War is Fear."[13] Most of this essay appears as a chapter in the theologically updated and expanded *New Seeds of Contemplation*.[14] With rhetorical conviction, Merton castigated us for our "fictional thinking" bent on creating "a scapegoat in whom we have invested all the evil in the world" and challenged Western civilization to relinquish its false notion of superiority and accompanying hatred of the "Other."[15]

In Merton's mind, our propensity for nuclear war and our desire to eradicate garden pests spring from the same hubris. To make his point to Carson that we have relinquished wisdom in favor of technology, Merton creates an analogy between our radical actions to exterminate the Japanese beetle, that "dire threat," and our ability to exterminate the enemy through nuclear war. Both, insists Merton, rely on the same logic. Once we have labeled a non-human species or human being as "Other," we arrogantly believe in our right to eradicate the undesirable. "In order to 'survive' we instinctively destroy that on which our survival depends."[16] Despite the danger to nature, to ourselves and to our children, government leaders and politicians are bent on convincing us that our actions are "harmless."

While Merton traces our "awful irresponsibility" and instinctive propensity for destructiveness to "the doctrine of the 'fall' of man and original sin"—a blindness that contemporary nature writer Barbara Kingsolver has recently dubbed our "crisis of perception"[17]—Merton also acknowledges our incarnational status. "The whole world itself, to religious thinkers, has always appeared as a transparent manifestation of the love of God, as a 'paradise' of His wisdom, manifested in all His creatures, down to the tiniest, and in the most wonderful interrelationship between them....That is, to say, man is at once a part of nature and he transcends it. In maintaining this delicate balance, he must make use of nature wisely." Our vocation, writes Merton, is "to be in this cosmic creation, so to speak, as the eye in the body," a vocation to defend and preserve the "delicate balance" in nature. Unfortunately, laments Merton, "man has lost his 'sight' and is blundering around aimlessly in the midst of the wonderful works of God."

Such a statement in the 1960s emphasizes Merton's own prophetic awareness of our unique human dignity and interdependence with all creatures on this planet. Grounding his thinking, as he admits to Carson, in the writing of psychologist Erich Fromm and Zen scholar D.T. Suzuki, Merton distances himself from a Cartesian mechanistic and compartmentalized view of the world. He reiterates the importance of maintaining a "cosmic perspective"[18]—a broad vision that sees all creation as relationship, and human dignity springing from a true sense of our shared creaturehood. Merton would have us reject hubris in favor of humility, a word whose root is *humus*, earthiness—a recognition of the clay and stardust that we are. This paradox of plainness and an exalted dignity often appears in Merton's poetry, for example "O Sweet Irrational Worship," in which he proclaims: "I have become light, /Bird and wind, My leaves sing, I am earth, earth ..."[19]

Merton's letter to Rachel Carson is more than a congratulatory message to a well-known writer; it is a revelation of his long-held incarnational yet ever-expanding vision. Such expansion is critical to deep spiritual growth. If one pitches a tent in the wilderness, for example, one gains a certain perspective on the world through the tent flaps; if one shifts those tent pegs, the vision can be enlarged. Merton's letter to Carson marks such a significant enlargement of vision. Having focused his social justice writing on right relationships among people—topics of racism, rights of indigenous people, the dangers of atomic energy and technology, as well as the moral imperative for making peace through non-violent means—Merton is now articulating a new insight: responsibility for the earth. Indeed, I want to emphasize that reading *Silent Spring* is a graced moment in Merton's life—a moment of both revelation and revolution—because it appears to have allowed him to see how human justice is related to eco-justice.

I use the word "appears" deliberately because this letter to Carson is Merton's first "public" utterance—as much as a personal letter is "public"—about non-violence to the environment. It might seem that Carson is solely responsible for shocking or widening Merton's vision of social justice to include all species of creation, non-human as well as human. However, I would argue that Merton's life experiences—his early childhood in France, the events recorded in *The Seven Storey Mountain*, his long-time fascination with Gandhi, many poems, and his *Journals*, as well as his own commitment to contemplation—predisposed him to this particular moment of increased awareness, what Thich Nhat Hanh calls "engaged spirituality."[20]   Nevertheless, I would also insist that Merton's letter to Carson represents a defining moment that sets the stage for a revolution in his thinking, namely, a deepening sense of environmental justice.

In 1963 when he wrote to Rachel Carson, Merton had been a Trappist monk for more than twenty years. His academic training in literature, his natural gift for writing, and his extended experience in theology and contemplation made him a responsive reader of *Silent Spring*. Although from different backgrounds and fields, Carson and Merton had discovered important characteristics of life on this planet. Carson's professional life, which involved intense training in observation, led to her vision of the interdependence of all creation and the human challenge of acting for wholeness; Merton's monastic life, which also involved intense training in awareness, led to a vision of our complete dependence on God, our interdependence with each other, and the challenge of acting in non-violent ways toward all creation. Carson's discipline was marine biology; Merton's, silence and solitude. Carson's practice of the scientific method prepared her to confront the problem of dying song birds; Merton's practice of regular communal prayer and extended periods of contemplation prepared him to embrace the world and its problems with compassion and justice. Carson's love for the world, coupled with a love of words, enabled her to write graceful, persuasive, astute books that contributed to the field of nature writing and, in the case of *Silent Spring,* triggered modern environmental thinking;[21] Merton's love for the world, coupled with a fascination for words and commitment to the Word, enabled him to inform thousands with his writing on spirituality, prayer, East-West dialogue, and stretched him in his later years to see how justice for human beings must of necessity involve justice for the planet.

In both writers, there is a sense of responsibility for environmental health that comes from attentiveness to their surroundings and commitment to a coherent vision of the cosmos. In both writers, there is what eco-critic Jonathan Bate has called *ecopoesis*—a deep longing for belonging.[22] In such sensitive writers, argues Bates, the rhythm of words—their syntactic connections and linguistic overtones—are intimately related to the "song of the earth itself."[23] Both Carson and Merton are pondering the essential question: "How shall we live? How shall we/can we belong?" In the light of new scientific data, both writers see the urgency of attempting an answer to that question. For Carson, the answer can be found in human action: diminishing the use of chemical pesticides, in favor of biological controls; for Merton, the answer is beginning to dawn that non-violence toward the earth means we must develop an ecological conscience.

And where does that answer take him? Prior to 1963, Merton's journals, letters, and notebooks are filled with notations about spirituality and the delights of the natural world; in the late 1950s there are increasing references to civil rights, non-violence, the dangers of technology, war and nuclear proliferation. After January 1963, a new topic joins this catalogue of concerns: our responsibility for the health of the planet. It appears in reading notebooks, in journal entries, in letters, and in book reviews. Let me be more specific by offering examples.

In the mid-1960s, Merton spent time reading Kenneth Jackson's books on early Celtic nature poetry. [24] He was captivated by Jackson's research into the influence of the rustic, simple life of the solitary in the woods on Irish poetry. It is clear from multiple and extensive entries in his notebooks that Merton felt affirmed in his own desire to live as a hermit by discovering he shared some insights about nature and contemplation with the early Irish monks. In one his of working [reading] Notebooks, he comments:

"The ultimate significance of the hermit's relationship with Nature is something that transcends both nature and hermit....Bird and hermit are joining together in an act of worship; the very existence of nature was a song of praise in which he himself took part by entering into harmony with nature."[25]   In another notebook dedicated to ideas for poems and notes for *Cables to the Ace*, Merton waxes lyrically about creation and includes himself as integral to its continuous unfolding:

> My worship is a blue sky and ten thousand
> crickets in the deep wet grass of the field.
> My vow is the silence under their
> Sound. I support the woodpecker & the dove.
> Together we learn the norms. The plowed & planted field
> says: it is my turn. And several of us
> begin to sing. [26]

Here Merton not only celebrates the splendor of nature and his intent to interact responsibly with it—symbolized by his commitment to the woodpecker and the dove—but he also admits how his worship and nature's praise of God are intertwined. The field initiates a moment of celebration, yet the word "my" is unclear: does it indicate the field's turn or Merton's turn? It matters not; "several of us begin to sing." Surely, the Celtic harmony with nature, which Merton so valued, is evident in this jotting.

Not long after, Merton confides in his journal how glad he is that "on Rum (Hebrides) now they allow no one to live except those protecting the wildlife and trying to restore the original ecology. This is wonderful!"[27]   Equally important, as Merton comments in another working notebook, is our obligation to heed the call of wilderness prophets like John Muir who could write with lyrical rhapsody about the trees of the North American forests and decry the white man's axe that sealed their doom. [28]

And, of course, mention can be made of Merton's elegant description of his life at the hermitage published posthumously as *Day of a Stranger*.[29]   In these journal pages, which offer a salute to the wilderness, Merton celebrates the "ecological balance" of his hermitage with its "precise pairs of birds."[30] There he could savor the "mental ecology, too, a living balance of spirits in this corner of the woods"[31]—writers from East/West, North/South. With the woods as his home, he could live fully the Benedictine ideal of an integrated life, captured so profoundly in this famous catch-phrase: "What I wear is pants. What I do is live. How I pray is breathe."[32]

However, one paragraph of Merton's journal description that does not appear in *Day of a Stranger* is especially worth noting. In this section, he deplores

> non-ecology, the destructive unbalance of nature, poisoned and unsettled by bombs, by fallout, by exploitation: the land ruined, the waters contaminated, the soil charged with chemicals, ravaged with machinery, the houses of farmers falling apart because everybody goes to the city and stays there.... There is no misery to compare with that which exists where technology has been a total success.[33]

This statement echoes an earlier journal entry in which Merton laments how he personally used calcium chloride to kill some troublesome ants. Unfortunately his actions also killed the "beautiful whistling ... titmice.... What a miserable bundle of foolish idiots we are! We kill everything around us even when we think we love and respect nature and life. This sudden power to deal death all around us *simply by the way we live,* and in total 'innocence' and ignorance, is by far the most disturbing symptom of our time."[34] Merton would agree with Thoreau that we need the tonic of wildness.

Merton also began counseling his correspondents about our responsibility for environmental justice. In a January 1964 letter to Jim Frost, a high-school sophomore, Merton was prompted to write: "[W]e Americans ought to love our land, our forests, our plains, and we ought to do everything we can to preserve it in its richness and beauty, by respect for our natural resources, for water, for land, for wild life. We need men and women of the rising generation to dedicate themselves to this.[35] To an Italian graduate student inquiring about his values, Merton shared his belief in the sacramentality of nature: "God manifests himself in his creation, and everything that he has made speaks of him. . . .The world in itself can never be evil." [36]

In the last year of his life in a still more extensive letter to Barbara Hubbard, Director of the Center for Living in New York City, Merton distinguished between what he termed a millennial consciousness and an ecological consciousness.[37] A millennial consciousness invests all our hope in technology and commercial progress—and is doomed to intensify the world's problems. On the other hand, there is hope for our planet if we develop an ecological consciousness, that is, an attitude built on authentic awareness of our interconnectedness with all creation and our Christian responsibility of stewardship.

Merton enlarges on this theme in two book reviews published just months before his accidental death in Thailand. In a critique of two scholarly books on scripture and desert spirituality, Merton adds his advocacy for compassion toward all our brothers and sisters in the planetary community.[38] He writes:

> If the monk is a man whose whole life is built around a deeply religious appreciation of his call to wilderness and paradise, and thereby to a special kind of kinship with God's creatures. .., and if technological society is constantly encroaching upon and destroying the remaining 'wildernesses'. . . .[T]he monk should be anxious to preserve the wilderness in order to share it…. [Monks] would seem to be destined by God, in our time, to be not only dwellers in the wilderness but also its protectors.[39]

In a footnote to this paragraph Merton further muses that it "would be interesting to develop this idea" because hermits have a "natural opportunity" to act as forest rangers or fire guards in "the vast forests of North America."[40] It might be noted that at some monasteries, monks have literally placed some of their properties and land in public trust. Redwoods Monastery in California, for example, is part of a collaborative effort to manage the headwaters of the Mattole River and preserve the old growth forest and nearby salmon runs; Holy Trinity Monastery in Arizona invites birders to enjoy its 1.3 mile trail around its pond.[41]

A subsequent 1968 book review, devoted to a critique of Roderick Nash's *Wilderness and the American Mind*, reveals Merton's at his ecological best.[42] After skillfully summarizing the Puritans' negative attitude toward nature, the Transcendentalists' view of its healing power, John Muir's commitment to preserve wilderness for its own sake, Theodore Roosevelt's impulse to preserve hunting opportunities to support the cult of virility, and Aldo Leopold's principles for ethical land use, Merton astutely comments that the savagery which the Puritans had projected "out there" onto the wilderness has turned out to be savagery within the human heart. Our challenge, he writes, is to adopt Aldo Leopold's notion of an ecological consciousness: "A thing is right when it tends to preserve the integrity, stability, and beauty of the biotic community. It is wrong when it tends otherwise." For Merton, this is the essential challenge of contemporary living and he concludes his review with a piercing question:

> Can Aldo Leopold's ecological conscience become effective in America today? The ecological conscience is also essentially a peace-making conscience. A country that seems to be more and more oriented to permanent hot or cold war making does not give much promise of developing either one. But perhaps the very character of the war in Vietnam—with crop poisoning, the defoliation of forest trees, the incineration of villages and their inhabitants with napalm— presents a stark enough example to remind us of this most urgent moral need.

One might be prompted to comment: how curious this flurry of activity and ecological commitment after January 1963. And yet, not so curious. Rachel Carson had written a landmark book that influenced millions. Her revelation began a revolution in American thinking that birthed our current notions of eco-justice. Along the way she touched the consciousness and heart of Thomas Merton, writer and monk, with a revelation of justice for the planet that engendered its own ongoing revolution of love in thinking and writing—a revolution of love that expanded to include not just human beings but the entire planetary community.

Notes

1. Bruce Watson, "Sounding the Alarm," *Smithsonian* (September 2002), pp. 115-177. See also Linda J. Lear, "Rachel Carson's *Silent Spring*," *Reflections*, Oregon State University, 9:2 (May 2002), pp. 3-7.

2. Linda J. Lear, *Rachel Carson: Witness for Nature* (New York: Henry Holt and Co., 1997), pp. 118-119. Lear makes the point that this rejection by *Reader's Digest* was fortunate because when Carson returned to the subject of pesticides in the 1960s, she did so not as a federal employee but as a private citizen.

3. Watson, p. 116 and Lear, p. 5.

4. Al Gore, Introduction to *Silent Spring* (Boston: Houghton-Mifflin, 1994), p. xv.

5. Lear, *Rachel Carson*, quoted by Watson, p. 115.

6. Gore, p. xv.

7. Lear, *Reflections*, p. 4.

8. J. North Conway, *American Literacy: Fifty Books that Define our Culture and Ourselves* (New York: William Morrow & Company, 1993), p. 243, and Thomas J. Lyons, *The Incomparable Land: A Guide to American Nature Writing* (Minneapolis: Milkweed Editions, 2001), p. 13. See also Al Gore's Introduction to *Silent Spring*.

9. Gary Kroll, "Ecology as a Subversive Subject," *Reflections*, Oregon State University, 9:2 (May 2002), pp. 10-12.

10. Thomas Merton, Letter to Rachel Carson, 12 January 1963 in *Witness to Freedom: Letters in Times of Crisis*, ed. William H. Shannon, (New York: Farrar, Straus & Giroux, 1994), pp. 70-71. All subsequent unidentified quotations are from this letter.

11. Merton had already published "Nuclear War and Christian Responsibility" in *Commonweal* (February 9, 1962), "We Have to Make Ourselves Heard" in *The Catholic Worker* (May/June 1962), "Peace: A Religious Responsibility" in *Breakthrough to Peace*, edited by Merton and published by New Directions, September 1962, and "Original Child Bomb" (New Directions, 1962). He was also periodically disseminating his "Cold War Letters" from October 1961-62. See Patricia Burton's *Merton Vade Mecum* (The Thomas Merton Foundation, 1999) for a complete listing of letters, poetry, and publications.

12. See *Merton Vade Mecum* for a complete listing of letters, articles and books on these topics.

13. Thomas Merton, *Passion for Peace: The Social Essays*, ed., William H. Shannon (New York: Crossroad Publishing Co., 1995), pp. 11-19.

14. Thomas Merton, *New Seeds of Contemplation* (New York: New Directions, 1961), pp. 112-122.

15. Merton, *Passion for Peace*, p. 14; *New Seeds*, p. 114.

16. Merton, *Witness to Freedom*, p. 71.

17. Barbara Kingsolver, *Small Wonder* (New York: HarperCollins, 2002).

18. Merton, *Witness to Freedom*, p. 71.

19. Thomas Merton, "O Sweet Irrational Worship" In *The Dark Before Dawn: New Selected Poems of Thomas Merton*, ed., Lynn R. Szabo (New Directions, 2005), p. 96.

20. Thich Nhat Hanh, *Peace is Every Step: The Path of Mindfulness in Everyday Life* (New York: Bantam, 1991). Merton's belief in non-violence can be traced to his early awareness of Gandhi when Merton was a student at Oakham and reaches new fulfillment with the publication of *Gandhi on Non-violence* (New York: New Directions, 1965).

21. Carson's earlier full-length publications, *Under the Sea-Wind* (1941) and *The Sea Around Us* (1951) not only made her famous but enabled her to retire from government service in order to write full-time.

22. Jonathan Bate, *The Song of the Earth* (Cambridge MA: Harvard University Press, 2001), p. 212.

23. Bate. *The Song of the Earth*, p. 76.

24. Kenneth Jackson, *Early Celtic Nature Poetry* (Cambridge, 1935) and K.H. Jackson, *A Celtic Miscellany*, (London 1951).

25. Thomas Merton, *Working Notebook #14* (June 1964), Thomas Merton Center, Bellarmine University, Louisville, KY, p. 5.

26. Thomas Merton, *Working Notebook #15* (1965-August 1966), Thomas Merton Center.

27. Thomas Merton, *Dancing in the Water of Life* (Journals 5 1963-65); ed., Robert E. Daggy; San Francisco: HarperSanFrancisco, 1997), p. 165.

28. Thomas Merton, *Working Notebook #19* (July 1966-68), Thomas Merton Center.

29. Thomas Merton, *Day of a Stranger*, ed., Robert E. Daggy, (Salt Lake City: Gibbs. M. Smith, 1981).

30. Merton, *Day of a Stranger*, p. 33.

31. Merton, *Day of a Stranger*, p. 35.

32. Merton, *Day of a Stranger*, p. 41.

33. Merton, *Dancing in the Water of* Life, pp. 239-40.

34. Thomas Merton, *Turning Toward the World* (Journals 4; 1960-63); ed., Victor A. Kramer; San Francisco: HarperSanFrancisco, 1996), p. 312.

35. Thomas Merton, *The Road to Joy: Letters to New and Old* Friends, ed., Robert E. Daggy (New York: Farrar Straus & Giroux, 1989), p. 330.

36. Merton, *The Road to Joy*, p. 347-348.

37. Merton, Letter to Barbara Hubbard, 16 February 1968 in *Witness to Freedom*, pp. 73-75.

38. Louis Merton, 'Wilderness and Paradise: Two Recent Books', *Cistercian Studies* 2:1 (1967), pp. 83-89; reprinted in Thomas Merton, *The Monastic Journey: Thomas* Merton, ed., Patrick Hart; (Kansas City, MO: Sheed, Andrews, and McMeel, 1977), pp. 144-150.

39. Merton, 'Wilderness and Paradise', p. 89.

40. Merton, 'Wilderness and Paradise', p. 89, n.

41. Redwoods Monastery is part of the Upper Mattole River Cooperative, an entity of public, private, federal, state and non-profit organizations working together to manage over 4,000 acres of the Mattole headwaters and its corresponding old growth forest and endangered salmon refuge. Holy Trinity Monastery in the San Pedro River Valley, Arizona invites birders to enjoy its 1.3 mile trail around their ponds. The Carmelite Monastery in Wyoming is part of the greater Yellowstone Coalition to

preserve the regional ecosystems. The Chicago Little League plays on five acres originally owned and operated since the 1960s by the Marian Fathers of the Immaculate Conception Abbey. In 2005 the National Council of Churches as part of its Eco-Justice Program, committed itself to managing its public lands in a way that will "sustain our cultures and economies and God's glorious web of life." Recently, Holy Spirit Monastery near Atlanta joined city, church, and environmental organizations to fund wetlands adjacent to the monastery dubbed the Greenway Acquisition to preserve this wilderness area in perpetuity.

42. Roderick Nash, *Wilderness and the American Mind,* (New Haven: Yale UP, 1967). "The Wild Places," *Catholic Worker,* (June 1968) and *The Center Magazine* (July 1968) 40 – 44; reprinted in *Preview of the Asian* Journey, ed., Walter Capps (New York: Crossroad Publishing Co., 1989), pp. 95-107. All subsequent unidentified quotations are from this review.

The Thomas Merton—John C.H. Wu Letters: The Lord as Postman

Lucien Miller

Introduction

The hitherto unpublished manuscript of these letters between Thomas Merton and John C.H. Wu (Ching-hsiung Wu, 1899-1986) marks a hidden yet seminal movement among the religious encounters between East and West in the twentieth century. Writing to Thomas Merton at the midway point of their correspondence (March 14, 1961—August 18, 1968), John C.H. Wu observes: "Between true friends the Lord Himself serves as the postman."[1] Wu's comment epitomizes the consciousness that he and Merton come to share regarding the true nature of the ninety letters they exchange:[2] theirs is a threefold encounter between self and other, Christianity and Asia, the human and the divine.

Working together on *The Way of Chuang Tzu*, Thomas Merton and John C.H. Wu discovered a project and a friendship willed by God. Both published prior to their relationship—autobiographies that were simultaneously on the Catholic best-sellers book list,[3] and both were simultaneously presently writing works on Asian philosophies and religions.[4] Opposites in politics, brothers in the spirit of hermit and extrovert, and mourners over the loss of a woman, they inspire, teach and console each other through a correspondence of six and one-half years.

Part I: Relationships

As we begin to read the letters, it is interesting to observe that it is Thomas Merton who initiates a correspondence for which John Wu has been silently waiting. Writing to Wu to request his help with a translation of the Chinese philosopher, Chuang Tzu [Zhuangzi].[5] Merton asks for Wu's guidance in the study of the Chinese Confucian Classics and Taoist mysticism. Merton is familiar with Wu's books and feels Wu is "exactly the kind of person who would be of immense help."[6] John Wu is ecstatic. He receives Merton's letter on the feast of St. Joseph, opening it after Mass while still on his knees before the Blessed Sacrament. He tells Merton that he has been waiting for Merton to take the initiative, believing their friendship is fated, and he is quite happy to serve Merton as his "altar boy."[7]

As their correspondence unfolds, direct address and signatures indicate the two men are soon on familiar terms, with Merton signing off as "Tom"[8] and Wu jokingly calling himself "your old good-for-nothing in Christ."[9] Before long Merton and Wu are fast friends, locked in their mutual translation enterprise and sharing the revelations of the Asian Holy Spirit.

Merton's initial need for Wu is professional—he seeks a specialist in ancient Chinese literature and culture.[10] Wu solicits a preface by Merton for a book Wu is doing on St. Térèse of Lisieux and Lao Tzu.[11] Soon, the two men discover through their mutual professional interests an admiration and need for one another. There are minor differences, quirks in personality and contrasting passions that appear along the way. Wu meets Merton's Abbot, James Fox, and writes Merton: "Ever since I came to know him, I have been in love with him. (He is your Joseph, Father.)"[12]—a comment which may have galled Merton, who struggled mightily with his Abbot. Merton informs Wu about issues of peace and war he writes about in *The Catholic Worker* which cry out for attention,[13] but Wu reads them not as personal calls to action for peace and justice, but as the reflections of a true mystic. Merton tries to draw out Wu on the Vietnam War, but Wu does not respond.[14]

From the start, Wu is candid and open regarding himself. Merton may admire his writing on St. Thérèse and Lao Tzu, but Wu laments "the yawning gulf" between his writing and his sinful self.[15] Wu agrees when Merton discerns that Wu's spirit is akin to the "playful samadhi" of the Chinese Zen (Chan) Master, Hui-Neng, combining light-heartedness and deep seriousness.[16] But in fact, as Wu tells Merton,[17] for several years he has been depressed over the death of his wife, Teresa Teh-lan Li (1899-1959), and feels he has been "nailed to the Cross with Christ."[18] He is deeply consoled by Merton, who is "indescribably moved" upon reading Wu's later published description of Teresa's "death in Christ,"[19] and calls it an Asian epiphany of Christ the Savior.[20] From time to time Wu deals with another mysterious depression that seems unrelated to the loss of his wife. There are moments of calm and peace writing calligraphy[21] followed by days of ashes,[22] and "the darkest tunnel so far" when he discovers compassion for those who are suicidal.[23] In Wu's Preface to his *The Golden Age of Zen* he writes: "There is no telling how much the friendship of this *true man* [Merton] has meant to me during all these lonely years of my life."[24]

For his part, Merton empathizes with Wu's suffering, deeply admires him, and comes to need his support when faced with a personal crisis of his own. In the first year of their correspondence, Merton remembers Wu in his Easter Masses, asking the Lord "to give you every blessing and joy and keep ever fresh and young your 'child's mind' which is the only one worth having. May He grant us as you so well say to be both inebriated and sober in Christ, Confucians and Taoists."[25] A year later, Merton offers Mass for Wu's intentions, for China and all Wu loves.[26] Wu's visit to Gethsemani the same year is a grace for Merton and the monastic community.[27] In Wu, Merton encounters the spirit of Chuang Tzu, and it is to Wu that Merton insists on dedicating *The Way of Chuang Tzu*.[28] Merton misses Wu deeply when the latter moves to Taiwan and writes that he keeps trying to get over his consternation that Wu is gone.[29] When Wu returns to New Jersey, Merton rejoices, eagerly looking forward to having Wu revisit Gethsemani.[30]

A poignant moment of personal want surfaces when Merton writes Wu, "As to me, I need your prayers, life is not always easy!!! I am in trouble, so please pray and get the saints at it too."[31] Although we cannot be certain, in all probability in this letter Merton is hinting about his relationship with "M," the student-nurse with whom he fell in love in March 1966, when he was hospitalized while recovering from back surgery. The relationship unfolds over the spring and summer of 1966, and Merton last sees "M" October 27 of that year.[32] In Wu's September 6, 1966 to Merton, he mentions receiving Merton's August 27, 1966 letter, but the latter is missing from the Merton-Wu manuscript. In his footnotes to the Merton-Wu letters, John Wu Jr. suggests his father may have destroyed Merton's August 27 letter to forestall a scandal.[33] There is no extant correspondence between Wu and Merton after Wu's September 6, 1966 letter until Wu writes again, January 2, 1967.

Merton's appeal for Wu's support and Wu's September 6, 1966 letter reflect the deep trust and intimacy Merton and Wu share. In his letter, Wu comforts and encourages Merton, echoing the role Merton often plays as Wu's friend. If we read Wu's letter as referring to "M," its meaning is clear.

Quoting Merton's missing August 27, 1966 letter (which I assume refers to "M"), Wu assuages Merton's agony by assuring Merton he is experiencing the way of the Cross and following the way of Tao: "It is so characteristic of you to write: 'It is a little hard to laugh off the heartbreak of another person.' Indeed, Father *Misericordieux* (I mean Compassionate), this is the worst cross to a man of boundless generosity like yourself. The simplest way out would be to turn the heart into steel. But this is the coward's or the cynic's way. Your way, I am sure, is [to] let the Lord beat your heart into pulp, so that it is no longer your heart but the Heart of God with its all-embracing Compassion. This is the Way of Tao in which you are so steeped, the Way of knowing the masculine but sticking to the Feminine."[34]

In a posthumously published private journal entry which Wu would not have seen, Merton reviews his affair with "M" and says most of the pain of loneliness he felt for "M" on Holy Thursday and Good Friday of 1966 came out, "but very obliquely," in the poem he wrote describing his hospital stay, "With the World in My Bloodstream."[35] Merton's reference to his suffering over "M" in the poem may have been oblique to Merton, but it seems that it was transparent to Wu. When Wu reads a copy of the poem sent by his son, Francis, he writes Merton that the poem is "a poetic version of 'beating the heart into pulp.'" "Even your hospitalization is fruitful," Wu assures Merton, citing the prophet, Isaiah (*Isaiah* 32:15): "Together with oxygen *the Spirit is poured upon you from on high, and the wilderness becomes a fruitful field.*" Quoting the closing lines of "With the World in My Bloodstream":

> While the frail body of Christ
> Sweats in a technical bed
> I am Christ's lost cell
> His childhood and desert age
> His descent into hell.[36]

Wu marvels "at the God who is working in you" and concludes that in becoming a fruitful field and descending into hell, "The poet has become a Divine Poem."[37]

We are left wondering what Merton may have said about "M" and her anguish in his missing letter. It is hard to imagine that she found her heartache redemptive, as Wu found Merton's. Wu's attention however, is on his friend, Merton, not on the woman he leaves behind. What is significant is the way he responds to Merton's plea with a firm but timely sense of Asian grace. Here Wu reveals his instinctive awareness of the mutual flowering of Eastern and Judeao-Christian spiritualities when planted in a shared garden of Gethsemani. Compassion is self-bruising, Wu affirms. Merton's descent into hell and beaten heart are intimations of the Heart of God and the Way of Tao. Such inter-religious insights move Merton throughout the course of his correspondence.

Reviewing his first year of contact with Thomas Merton, Wu is deeply grateful for a divine gift of friendship.[38] Gradually, he comes to view Merton as his spiritual father, and himself as Merton's son.[39] For his part, Merton finds it is Wu who, like a spiritual father, spurs him forward with "my own vocation to see things Asian in their simplicity and truth." When Wu honors Merton's move to the hermitage with the Chinese pseudonym "Mei Teng" or "Silent Lamp,"[40] Merton feels he has been "'baptized' Chinese" by Wu with a Chinese name he must live up to, for "a name indicates a divine demand."[41] In the very last letter Wu wrote to Merton the year Merton died, Wu asks: "But need I tell you that your friendship has sunk so deep into my psyche that it has become a part of me?"[42]

Merton and Wu share an affinity for one another and similar personality characteristics. In many respects they are soul mates. In reading the letters, we find Wu often identifies with Merton. He tells Merton that the whole time he was reading an article Merton sent him on Mystics and Zen[43] he felt "as though every word came from my real self."[44] Sometimes Merton triggers in Wu an awareness of something latent within himself. Merton's comment in an introduction to Christian mysticism linking the spiritualities of St. Thérèse of Lisieux and the German Rhineland mystics such as Meister Eckhart, John Tauler, and Henry Suso strikes Wu with a sudden illumination. The Rhineland mystics "are really Chinese," says Wu, in that their spirituality is Chinese. And now that Merton has likened their spirituality to St. Thérèse's "little way" Wu understands "the secret of the magical power the divine witch of Lisieux has exercised on me."[45] "Every word of yours finds an echo in me," he tells Merton, who he says is "in a conspiracy with the Holy Spirit to enlighten me."[46] Reading Merton makes him realize that, like Merton, he has been haunted all his life by the desert within, and that it is the Lord who had led them both into this desert where they "meet and take delight in each other." "The Lord has whispered to me," adds Wu, "'Seek first the desert, and everything else, including the friendship of my modern Prophet Thomas Merton will be added unto you.'"[47] When Merton moves into his hermitage, Wu writes that he himself is by nature a hermit and that in solitude they are now closer than ever and "[y]ou are more mine."[48]

At the close of their second year of correspondence, December 1962, Merton and Wu exchange two letters on the paradox of sanity and madness. Both are attracted, on the one hand, to the "madness" of the poet and the recluse. Merton especially is drawn to persons who are marginal or social misfits or radical critics. They rejoice together in the "insanity" of the Gospels and Chuang Tzu which is really the deepest sanity. In his Christmas letter, Merton tells Wu that the world cannot silence the Christ-child nor Chuang Tzu for "[t]hey will be heard in the middle of the night saying nothing and everybody will come to their senses." As for himself, Merton claims that "the very name of Chuang Tzu restores me to sanity." "Anything but his quiet debunking view is plain insanity." Merton delights in his discovery of the "mad" Nicaraguan poet, Alfonso Cortes, who writes "the most amazingly sane poetry" and who reminds Merton of Chuang Tzu, for "in his madness he accuses all the right things for the right reasons." Allying himself with both Chuang Tzu and Cortes, Merton encloses in his Christmas letter to Wu "another poem of a madman you know well [Merton]: he beats out his poems on the back of a saucepan, on top of a little hill, while the snakes dance in the woodshed."[49]

Merton's "Chineseness" in his Christmas letter amazes Wu. He muses that he will not know why Merton is so Chinese in the way he thinks until they both get to Heaven. Even Merton's use of "madman" is typically Chinese, reminding Wu of the Tang poets. He simultaneously views Merton's "madness" in both Asian and Christian terms. Wu claims St. Paul was also very Oriental, like Merton, when St. Paul affirmed the sanity-madness paradox, saying "If we were out of our mind, it was for God; if we are sane, it is for you . . . ." He links Paul's "madness" with a traditional Chinese notion of intoxication, translating St. Paul's phrase as, "if we are *drunk* . . . if we are sober." Expanding on his drinking metaphor, Wu tells Merton that no one can be a saint who has not been filled "by the intoxicating Spirit of Love. And, Father, you have drunk like a whale." With his "overwhelming hospitality," "our

Divine Host" and "mad Lord" has urged Merton to "bottoms up"[50] over and over again, and Merton's resistance, even worse than Wu's, has been "almost nil." Only a "dead-drunk man" like Merton can understand Wu's own "timeless moment of void."[51] Three years later, Wu wraps up the theme of madness, concluding that: "Only a contemplative like you can burn with such Christ-Love as you have radiated in all your letters. You are mad with the very madness of Christ; yet this madness is a mysterious blend of the Fire of Love and the Water of Wisdom."[52]

There is one feature of the relationship that we find peculiar to Wu, and that is an admiration for Merton that sometimes borders on adoration. That extreme degree of respect partly stems from the intensity and flamboyance of Wu's personality, but mainly results from Wu's appreciation for Merton's understanding of Asian thought and culture.

There are many examples of Wu's awe for Merton the person coupled with Wu's esteem for Merton the student of the East. At one point in his collaborative project with Wu translating the Chuang Tzu text, Merton tries to learn a little Chinese. Knowing Merton's intellectual prowess, Wu imagines Merton making great strides studying Chinese and comments: "the fire of your spiritual wisdom turns every bit [every Chinese written character] into *light*, informing all information."[53]   The truth is Merton had no time to study Chinese and got practically nowhere learning Chinese characters. What is noteworthy is Wu's utter confidence in Merton's light-transforming wisdom. For Wu, meeting Merton face to face the first time at Gethsemani, and walking and talking with him and sharing silence are blissful experiences.[54] He wants Merton's "holy hands" to touch up his translations of Chinese Buddhist texts.[55] Praising what he calls Merton's "Integral Humanism," Wu remarks that since the apex of Merton's pyramid is in heaven, "you [Merton] could not be otherwise than universal".[56] Indeed, Merton is a masterpiece, created by the Divine Artist using nature and grace, a "sublime" landscape of "towering peaks hidden in clouds and mists," of flowing streams merging "with the infinite Void," and an "ineffable" blend of Confucianism and Taoism.[57] "All things you do and write, Father, are poetry; and you are His great Haiku," writes Wu.[58] "Every time I receive a letter from you, I feel as though I had a new satori!" he exclaims. "A subtle and indefinable peace begins to seep into my soul and fills it with a deep and inexplicable satisfaction."[59] "If this is attachment, let there be more attachment!" Wu chortles.[60] Reading Merton's *New Seeds of Contemplation*, Wu feels like he is "strolling on a mountain, breathing the pine-scented air."[61] Sending Merton a newspaper clipping where a photograph of Merton and another of Pope Paul VI appear side by side, Wu tells Merton he likes to see the two famous figures together, as they represent "the two aspects of Christ—the inner and the outer. You are supporting his diplomatic efforts ontologically."[62]

Part II: Christianity and the East

Poor Merton! How his ears must have burned! And how he must have loved it! How did Wu get this way, an altar boy idolizing his priest? We might also ask, what is it that Merton discovers in Wu? While never effusive, Merton clearly needs and respects Wu, loves him and learns from him.

As noted previously, Wu, like so many readers, identifies with Merton spiritually and emotionally. Prior to letter writing, Wu is deeply touched by Merton as monk and spiritual writer. But why does Wu say that he has been waiting for Merton to write? There is in Wu an intuitive sense that their encounter is providentially ordained. Before their correspondence begins, Wu has made a significant discovery: Merton understands the East. Through subsequent letters, while at the same time reading unpublished or recently published Merton writing on Asia, Wu awakens more and more profoundly to the awareness that Merton grasps the spirituality of Chinese Taoism, Confucianism, Buddhism and Chinese poetry in a contemplative Christian sense that is uniquely his own. Equally momentous for Merton is the fact that Wu approaches the Gospel through Asian spirituality. Wu's findings, and his revealing and teaching his own understanding, must have thrilled Merton, as Wu brings out a latent awareness in Merton. Equally momentous for Wu is that his waiting has come to an end.

Let us turn to the practical evidence of Wu's and Merton's grasp of things Chinese, and then move to Wu's theory of the mind of Thomas Merton through which he makes sense of Merton's and his vision of the Christian need for the East.

At one point barely two months after they have initiated correspondence, Merton comments to Wu: "Now I enjoy the quiet of the woods and the song of the birds and the presence of the Lord in silence. Here is Nameless Tao, revealed as Jesus, the brightness of the hidden Father, our joy and our life. All blessing to you, joy and grace in Him."[63] We do not know Wu's reaction, but we can surmise that he is deeply moved with the awareness that Merton has penetrated the mystery of Tao through the visible Christ who reveals the invisible Source. "To have seen me is to have seen the Father," as Christ says to Philip in the Gospel of John.[64] Wu is ardent about the *Logos*, the Word-Event that is Christ in the Judeo-Christian scriptures and which he sees in classical Chinese texts.[65] Both Merton and Wu respond to this Word-Event, Christ, with the whole of their beings. In his very first letter to Merton, Wu speaks of Lao Tzu and Chuang Tzu, the forefathers of Taoism, and tells Merton that "the Logos of God who enlightens everyone coming into this world illuminated their minds." Through Lao Tzu and Chuang Tzu, God prepared both the Chinese mind and the modern "post-Christian" mind to recognize the True Light. Conversely, says Wu, we cannot fully understand the Taoists nor the Confucianists unless we are one with the Word incarnate."[66] In his second letter to Merton, dated Good Friday, 1961, Wu reiterates his conviction about the Logos and Tao. While reading Merton's *The Wisdom of the Desert*, Wu is constantly reminded of the moral intuitions and spiritual insights found in sayings and anecdotes by Chinese Sages such as Lao Tzu, Chuang Tzu, Confucius, Mencius and Buddha. This experience reveals to Wu a thrilling truth: "*The Tao Incarnate* is absolutely the *Same Tao* who was from the beginning with God and is God. Before Lao Tzu was, He *is*" (Wu italics).

Assuming this close identification between Logos and Tao, Wu readily points out to Merton his awareness that the post-Christian West needs the spirituality of the East to re-discover Christ and to be re-Christianized. The natural wisdoms of the East are meant by God to remind Christians of a richer heritage that either they are unaware of or have forgotten.[67] Indeed, Wu surmises, the ancient would be better Christians than many today, because had they heard Christ's teachings they would have understood them, while Christians have lost their ear for the words of the Gospel and the "'impractical' living counsels of the Living LOGOS" [Wu capitals]. Were Christ's sermons or Paul's letters to be submitted to chancery offices today, says Wu, many passages would be considered heretical.[68] Merton concurs with Wu in his belief that Christians need the East and that a whole new orientation is required. An erroneous sort of "supernaturalism" and blind adherence to legalistic formulas, gestures and rites have impaired living and understanding the Gospels. Allowing that many of his fellow priests would not understand his perspective, Merton speaks of a need at present for the "wonderful natural wisdoms that came before Christ" and that are fulfilled in Christ and the Gospel, so that Christians may themselves achieve the fulfillment Christ requires of them.[69]

One concrete example of Merton's East-West integrative approach that impresses Wu is Merton's teaching on self-nature or the person as void. According to Merton, in the West the person is commonly viewed as a divided self—an individual empirical ego and an inner real self. The truth, says Merton, is:

What is most ourselves is what is least ourself [*sic*], or better the other way round. It is the void [emptiness] that is our personality, and not our individuality that seems to be concrete and defined and present, etc. It is what is seemingly not present, the void, that is really I. And the "I" that seems to be I is really a void ... It is the No-I [not I] that is most of all I in each one of us. But we are completely enslaved by the illusory I that is not I and never can be I except in a purely fictional and social sense.

And of course there is yet one more convolution in this strange dialectic: there remains to suppress the apparent division between empirical self and real or inner self. There is no such division. There is only the Void which is I, covered over by an apparent I. And when the apparent I is seen to be void it no longer needs to be rejected, *for it is I.* How wonderful it is to be alive in such a world of craziness and simplicity."

Merton adds, poking fun at his analysis: "I get this way from sleeping nights in the hermitage and watching the stars."[70]

Wu, in contrast, terms Merton's analysis a "transparent perception" penned by the "Not I." Merton is "Father Void," a wizard, pointing to the moon. "With this fundamental insight" about the nature of self as void, says Wu, "we can spin the Buddhist scriptures" like boys playing tops. As he signs off, Wu extends Merton's East-West insight as to human self-nature to the divine nature of Ultimate Self: "With filial love in the Word Who is the Void."[71] Here Wu links Christ the Word with Buddhist emptiness (Void), intimating but not explaining this mysterious and provocative analogy.[72]

Wu's study of Tang Chinese Buddhism, *The Golden Age of Zen*, and Merton's role in its formation reflect the shared vision of East-West encounter we find throughout the Merton-Wu correspondence. In terms of their production, *The Golden Age of Zen* and Merton's *The Way of Chuang Tzu* mirror one another, as Wu longs for Merton's assistance with his work, while Merton absolutely requires Wu's for his.[73] Wu very much wants Merton's input and criticism as he writes,[74] and he sends manuscripts of chapters, asking for "a sound beating" from Merton the Master.[75] Merton begs off the editing job, claiming incompetence as well as being too busy.[76] He gently finds fault, saying Wu's statements sometimes miss his target, his choice of words may be inappropriate, or more explanations are needed for the general reader. Later he compliments Wu on the readability of his revisions, especially in one section where he is charmingly informal and spontaneous.[77] Wu feels Christ himself has praised him.[78] Merton believes in the worthiness of Wu's book project, and he revels in reading material he considers magnificent. "It is a wonderful book," Merton concludes, "and certainly one of the best things on Zen that has come out. It provides a very welcome change of pace and perspective from Suzuki, and throws such abundant light on Chinese Zen, it is going to be invaluable."[79] In a subsequent letter to Wu, Merton says students of Zen will find the book indispensable.[80]

What Wu really wants from Merton is an Introduction to his book that is similar to the one Merton writes for *The Way of Chuang Tzu*.[81] "Am I asking too much?" he asks, pleadingly, adding with emphasis, "*O Father, hermit or no hermit, I need your help.*"[82] Again and again he begs and cajoles Merton for the Introduction. When at last Merton sends the Introduction to Wu in Taiwan, and its arrival is delayed in the mail, Wu comments: "Our friend the Devil is trying to hinder the publication of this book, whose aim is to open the door of Our Church."[83] Upon reading the Introduction when it does arrive, Wu is elated. He finds Merton's comparative study of Christianity and Zen "a living bridge between East and West," and "a masterful summing up of the spirit of Zen."[84] In his own Preface to the book, Wu generously suggests *The Golden Age of Zen* may be regarded as a long footnote to "the profound insights embodied in his [Merton's] introduction."[85] We have here an indication of Wu's high hopes and expectations. *The Golden Age of Zen*, like *The Way of Chuang Tzu*, may unbolt closed doors and provide access to Asian spiritualities helpful for the reawakening of Christian contemplation.

Part III: Wu's Theory of Merton's Mind

We glean from various remarks Wu makes during the first two years of their correspondence the emergence of a general theory of Merton's intellect. As he dialogues with Merton or reads his letters and writing, Wu observes Merton's mind in action and comments on its qualities and the way it works. Perusing Merton's *Disputed Questions* as well as *The Thomas Merton Reader*, Wu remarks:

> Your mind is like a crystal not only in its transparent clarity, but in the wonderful fact that every unit of it possesses the characteristic features of the whole. And is this not how the Creator Himself works? There is no atom which does not reproduce more or less faithfully the structure of the solar system!"[86]

Because of this transparent clarity, Merton's vision is genuine. He exemplifies Goethe's ideal thinker: "one who can divide so deeply that he can unite, and [who is] united so deeply that he can divide."[87] There is a mystical quality about Merton's mental processing, which Wu terms "catholicity." He likens Merton's intelligence to a dancer who somehow dances while suspended over a cliff and dances on flat ground at one and the same moment. Like St. Thomas Aquinas, Merton in his writing stretches the Mystical Body of Christ to the ultimate limit, yet does no more "than register the necessary growth toward the full stature of Christ." Merton's mind and writing have "the beauty of the Golden Mean," and "the spontaneity of the inevitable."[88]

Wu's general theory reflects and illuminates his specific perceptions of Merton as a perfect blend of East and West, and his concrete encounters with a mind that is simultaneously Asian yet centrally Christian in spirituality. In his first letter to Merton,[89] Wu immediately cites particular examples which reveal that Merton is "Asian" in disposition or background, or that he is a gifted interpreter of Asian matter, particularly Chinese. The monk-writer has a natural gift for "seeing the essential in everything," a capacity which is complemented by the gifts of the Holy Spirit. Studying Chinese material, Merton's mind becomes transparent "like a fire burning white-hot," and he grasps Chinese ways of thinking with penetrating insight. In certain ways Merton is both Confucian and Taoist. The practice of monastic obedience enables Merton, says Wu, to recognize that Confucian rites are an external expression of what is internal. Faithfully carrying out daily tasks in the monastery means that Merton has "*lived* Confucianism" [Wu emphasis], and knows rites not as something imposed externally, but rising from within.[90] Certain works by Merton on Western subjects sound Asian to Wu. A book like *Seeds of Contemplation* reveals a similarity between Merton's mode of thinking and the Taoist patriarchs, Lao Tzu and Chuang Tzu. When Merton writes in *Seeds*, "The Holy Spirit is sent from moment to moment into my soul," Wu proclaims the sentiment is exactly what Chuang Tzu would have written were he a Christian. Merton's phrase, "selflessness is my true self," declares Wu, "sums up Lao Tzu and Buddha and the best of Hinduism." *Seeds of Contemplation* is a remarkable book from an Asian perspective, and "may be called a bridge between East and West."[91]

In yet higher praise, Wu terms Merton's *The New Man* a "perfect synthesis of East and West," which echoes the non-dualistic thinking of the Chinese sages. He believes this parallel is due to Merton's habit of reading contemplatively, absorbing whatever he reads in terms of personal experience and understanding. Reading *The New Man* Wu finds echoes of the "Oriental Sages" and gains a new understanding of their insights. "You are so deeply Christian that you can't help touching the vital springs of the other religions—Hinduism or Buddhism." Calling Merton a major prophet of the age, he tells him, "You need not bother about improving your knowledge of Chinese. You *are* Chinese, because you are universal."[92] When Merton remarks in his "Mystics and Zen Masters" article that for Hui Neng (638-713), the Sixth Patriarch of the Chinese Zen sect of Buddhism, "*all life was Zen*,"[93] Wu writes, "It couldn't be better put. Did I not say that my Father Louis was a Chinese?"[94] Merton's remarks in that article so move Wu that he experiences non-duality in a union of minds. He ticks off Merton's achievement as follows: Merton's "explanation of 'Mind' as 'Spirit' and of Prajna as *Light*, the Light that illumines all," his "discernment of the empirical self from the *Real Man* in the Chuangtzean sense," his concept of "pure affirmation," his differentiation "between *is* and *has*," his "awareness of full spiritual reality," his "speaking of the 'true face' as 'a discovery of *genuine identity* in and with the One,' his "repeated insistence on all-embracing catholicity as the earmark of a true Catholic," and his reservations on a Buddhist metaphor for enlightenment, "The mirror has no stand." The cumulative effect of encountering Merton's acuity of vision, says Wu, is it "wrought in me the transcending of the subject-object relationship. There is no longer Father Louis or John Wu, but the Vagabond Spirit, the Divine Rascal Who comes and goes like the Wind."[95]

Merton's "Buddhism," or rather, his understanding of Buddhism, is something which particularly strikes Wu, sometimes leaving him "speechless," as when he re-reads *Mystics and Zen Masters* years after he read it the first time, and finds Merton's interpretation of "Zen enlightenment" as "an insight into pure being in all its actual presence and immediacy." Wu exclaims that Merton's perception is the very point of his own work on Buddhism he is currently writing and now he no longer cares if it gets published.[96] Wu's discovery of what might be termed "Merton's Buddhism" is important, because what is striking is not Merton's contribution to knowledge of Buddhism *per se*, nor the question of his being a Buddhist scholar or Buddhologist—which he most decidedly is not. What is significant is Merton's existential grasp of Buddhism as a Christian contemplative. In effect, Wu, the Buddhist scholar, is saying that Merton, monk and poet, understands Buddhism better than he does. Equally important today is the fact that Buddhologists and Asian specialists who are not steeped in the Gospels of Jesus and the Christian contemplative traditions like Merton, miss Merton's contribution entirely.

Wu's reasoning is partly playful. Early in their correspondence, while commenting on Merton's *Seeds of Contemplation* as a text Buddhists of the Rinzai school would prefer, Wu jokes that he suspects Merton must have been a Zen Master in a previous life, and that in the present one he will attain Buddhahood.[97] Merton knocks the Buddhahood ball back to Wu's court, saying: "If I once reached Buddhahood and redescended to my present state, all I can say is that I made a really heroic sacrifice." Continuing the joke and admitting his attraction to the hermit life and things Chinese, Merton adds: "Whatever I may have been in previous lives, I think more than half of them were Chinese and eremitical."[98] Furthering the banter about identity in later letters, Wu refers to some sketch Merton makes of himself and declares: "The 'Old Rice Bag' [Merton's nickname for himself] looks very much like Hui Neng."[99]

While Wu loves to tease Merton, there is no doubt he profoundly esteems Merton's Buddhism. Merton's "fundamental insights" are likened to rivulets forming a sea of understanding.[100] Indeed, notes Wu, as other Asian specialists such as Father William Johnston S. J. have observed, many of Merton's works are "full of Zen," even those not dealing directly with Zen,[101] including ones such as *Seeds of Contemplation* written when Merton was young and may not have heard of Zen.[102]

Speaking only partly in jest, Wu says whether Merton is among his Gethsemani monks or goes one day to visit Zen monks in Japan, he might "serve as the occasion for their awakening to the Logos." Merton is the answer to the famous Zen *koan*, "What is your Original Face before you were born." "For you, Father, you are already *yourself*, the 'Original Face;' who is everywhere, including Japan, and nowhere, not even in Gethsemani."[103] Sometimes Merton's observations serve to confirm Wu's views—e.g. the Zen masters are the heirs of Lao Tzu and Chuang Tzu,[104] or clarify passages that were formerly obscure,[105] or make connections between Buddha's teachings and Zen that Chinese masters overlook.[106] While collaborating with Merton on his project translating Chuang Tzu, Wu is also writing chapters on various Zen masters for his *The Golden Age of Zen*. Merton's *The Way of Chuang Tzu* "opened my eyes to many things," says Wu, and "helped me to understand these monks of towering stature."[107] He believes *The Way of Chuang Tzu* reveals "the original affinities between Zen and Chuang Tzu."[108] After reading Merton's "The Zen Koan" in *Mystics and Zen Masters*, Wu concludes: "it can no longer be doubted that you have a clearer understanding of the whole damned thing than any of the modern Zennists, so far as I know."[109]

Conclusion

After exploring the unpublished letters between Thomas Merton and John C.H. Wu, we can readily agree with Wu's statement with which we began this essay: "Between true friends the Lord Himself serves as the postman." The encounter is providential for both. They need one another professionally for writing *The Way of Chuang Tzu* and *The Golden Age of Zen*, and each relies on the friendship, trust and encouragement of the other. They share a spiritual affinity for solitude and an attraction to that which is offbeat or original in poetic temperaments and spiritual masters East-West. Merton understands Asian spiritualities as contemplative monk and poet. Wu finds Christ in ancient Chinese Taoism and Buddhism. Both agree that Western Christianity needs the East, and that a reawakening to the Gospel can occur through an encounter with Asian traditions. In Merton, Wu discovers a mind of transparent clarity, a mystical intelligence able to hold both ends of a paradox in one hand. The monk is a synthesis of East and West, who like Wu sees the West in the East and the East in the West. Wu discovers Merton's Buddhism, his "Asian" or "Chinese" self, and helps him to see Asia more clearly. Merton names Wu's playfully profound *samadhi* and conspires with the Holy Spirit to bring Wu to enlightenment. In the last analysis, the encounter and interaction between Thomas Merton and John C.H. Wu uncovers what is latent in each. Merton becomes Father Void and Wu discovers the Logos in the East.

Notes

1. Letter dated 11/16/65.Thomas Merton, John C.H. Wu, "The Thomas Merton—John C.H. Wu Correspondence," unpublished manuscript. I wish to thank John Wu, Jr. and Jonathan Montaldo for generously providing access to this manuscript and for encouraging research and writing on this project.

2. Merton wrote thirty-seven letters, Wu fifty-three. Thirty-one of Merton's letters to Wu are published in whole or in part in Thomas Merton, *The Hidden Ground of Love: Letters on Religious Experience and Social Concerns*, ed. William H. Shannon (New York: Farrar, Straus and Giroux, 1985), pp. 611-35.

3. Thomas Merton, *The Seven Storey Mountain* (New York: Harcourt, Brace, 1948). John C.H. Wu, *Beyond East and West* (Sheed and Ward, 1951).

4. Thomas Merton, *Mystics and Zen Masters* (New York: Farrar, Straus and Giroux, 1967). *Zen and the Birds of Appetite* (New York: New Directions, 1968). John C.H. Wu, *The Golden Age of Zen* (New York: Image Books Doubleday, 1996, (Orig. 1967).

5. Zhuangzi. 莊 子. Merton and Wu's collaborative translation project culminated in Merton's *The Way of Chuang Tzu* (New York: New Directions, 1965). For a study of the project and Merton's book, see Lucien Miller, "Merton's *Chuang Tzu*," available through the Thomas Merton Center, Bellarmine University, Louisville, Kentucky.

6. 3/14/61.

7. 3/20/61.

8. 3/14/61; 12/12/61.

9. 12/27/62.

10. 3/14/61.

11. 4/15/61. Wu's study was published as an essay, "St. Thérèse and Lao Tzu: a Study in Comparative Mysticism," in *Chinese Humanism and Christian Spirituality: Essays of John C.H. Wu*, ed. Paul K. T. Sih (Jamaica, NY: St. John's University Press, 1965).

12. 12/7/65.

13. 12/12/61.

14. 6/9/65.

15. 8/4/61.

16. 1/31/65; 2/5/65.

17. 5/25/61; 3/9/62.

18. 12/27/62.

19. See *The Golden Age of Zen*, pp. 214-15.

20. 12/28/65.

21. 1/1/66.

22. 1/10/66.

23. 3/26/66.

24. John C.H. Wu, Preface, *The Golden Age of* Zen.

25. 4/1/61.

26. 6/7/62.

27. 7/10/62.

28. 6/9/65.

29. 7/11/66.

30. 9/12/67.

31. 8/5/66.

32. See *Learning to Love: Exploring Solitude and Freedom*, ed. Christine M. Bochen, *The Journals of Thomas Merton*, Vol. 6, 1966-1967; (San Francisco: HarperCollins, 1997). pp. 150-51.

33. John Wu, Jr., "Footnotes to Merton-Wu Letters," unpublished manuscript. Footnote dated 9/6/66.

34. 9/6/66.

35. *Learning to Love*, p. 122.

36. Thomas Merton, "With the World in my Bloodstream," in Thomas Merton, *Collected Poems* (NY: New Directions, 1977), pp. 617.

37. 9/6/66.

38. 12/19/61

39. Undated card, December 1964.

40. Mei Teng 昧 燈. 12/17/65.

41. 12/28/65. Later on, Merton mocks himself with the epithet "Old cracked Mei-Teng" (2/7/66).

42. 1/26/68.

43. Published as "Mystics and Zen Masters" in Merton's *Mystics and Zen Masters* (New York: Farrar, Straus and Giroux, 1967), pp. 3-44.

44. 3/31/63.

45. 3/9/62. [**Unidentified Merton work**: Wu's reference to Merton's *Introduction to Christian Mysticism*.] For Wu's writing on St. Thérèse of Lisieux see "St. Therese & Lao Tzu," in Wu's *Chinese Humanism and Christian Spirituality*. St. John's U Press, 1965, and his book, *The Interior Carmel*. New York: Sheed & Ward, 1952.

46. 12/26/62.

47. 12/27/62.

48. 11/16/65.

49. 12/20/62.

50. "Bottoms up." *gan bei* 乾杯.

51. 12/27/62.

52. 2/5/65.

53. 3/9/62.

54. 6/30/62.

55. 7/17/62.

56. 12/26/62.

57. 11/16/65.

58. 11/16/65.

59. 12/7/65

60. 1/1/66.

61. 1/21/66.

62. 1/24/66.

63. 5/19/61.

64. John 14:9.

65. "Word-Event" is a term coined by the late Japanese Dominican and master of Christian-Buddhist encounter, Shigeto Oshida, O.P., of the Takamori Community, Japan, for an experiential reading of Sciptures. See "The Mystery of the Word and Reality" (1981: Unpublished essay).

66. 3/21/61.

67. Dated "First Friday," 4/61.

68. 12/17/64.

69. 4/1/61.

70. 1/31/65.

71. 2/5/65.

72. A further East-West insight Merton and Wu share is an understanding of Zen and Tao. Both detest Western popular Buddhism's tendency to reduce Zen to *zazen* or sitting meditation and the solving of *koan*. Merton terms such simplifications a "stinking skeleton" (6/23/63). Wu and Merton find a fundamental likeness between Tao and Zen

and a oneness in modality that, says Wu, traditional devout Buddhists do not acknowledge (12/2/65).

73. See my "Merton's *Chuang Tzu*" for Wu's role in the creation of *The Way of Chuang Tzu*. Merton's *The Way of Chuang Tzu* is published in 1965. Wu's *The Golden Age of Zen* is published in 1967.

74. 6/13/65; 8/6/65.

75. 8/14/65.

76. 7/11/65.

77. 12/28/65.

78. 12/31/65.

79. A review of the 1996 reissue of *The Golden Age of Zen* (originally published in 1967) praises Wu's book for its detailed characterizations of Tang dynasty era Zen, wealth of background information, and contextualizations of famous sayings of ancestral teachers. See Frank J. Hoffman, "*Zen Keys; The Golden Age of Zen,*" *Philosophy East and West.* Vol. 48, No. 1 (Jan., 1998), pp. 165-67. Another finds it prophetic. See John A. Lindblom, "John C.H. Wu and the Evangelization of China," in *Logos*, Vol. 8, Number 2 (Spring 2005), pp. 130-64. Wu's decidedly Christian perspective links Buddhism, Taoism and Christian contemplative or mystical traditions. Wu and Merton, both pioneers in Christian-Asian religious encounter, offer alternative visions largely ignored in scholarly secular studies. For Buddhist scholarship illuminating the field Wu introduces, see Stanley Weinstein, *Buddhism Under the T'ang* (Cambridge: Cambridge University Press, 1987); Steven Heine, *The Koan: Text and Contexts in Zen Buddhism* (Oxford: Oxford University Press, 2000); Heinrich Dumoulin, *Zen Buddhism: A History* (New York: Macmillan, 1988).

80. 9/12/65. The book was rejected several times by various publishers before eventually being published by the College of Chinese Culture Press and the National War College in Taiwan, in co-operation with the Committee on the Compilation of the Chinese Library, Yang Ming Shan, 1967.

81. 8/12/65; 12/2/65.

82. 11/19/65.

83. 9/6/66.

84. 9/19/67. Merton's Introduction in *The Golden Age of Zen* is republished as "A Christian Looks at Zen" in Merton's *Zen and the Birds of Appetite*, pp. 33-58.

85. John C.H. Wu, Preface, *The Golden Age of Zen*.

86. 12/16/62.

87. 3/31/63.

88. 8/14/65.

89. 3/20/61.
90. 3/20/61.
91. "First Friday," April 1961.
92. 11/28/61.
93. See "Mystics and Zen Masters" in *Mystics and Zen* Masters, p. 21, [Merton emphasis].
94. 3/31/63.
95. 3/31/63.
96. 3/26/66.
97. 5/25/61.
98. 5/29/61.
99. 12/27/64.
100. 8/14/65.
101. 8/3/65.
102. 12/7/65.
103. 12/27/64.
104. 2/5/65.
105. 5/11/65.
106. 8/14/65.
107. 2/2/65.
108. 11/16/65.
109. 1/19/66.

From the "Political Dance of Death" to the "General Dance": The Cold War Letters of Thomas Merton

John P. Collins

Introduction

In *The Sign of Jonas*, Thomas Merton has an entry dated February 10, 1950 in which he describes a beautiful day, "Today it was wonderful. Clouds, sky overcast, but tall streamers of sunlight coming down in a fan over the bare hills." Then Merton describes a pasture full of starlings that have been become frightened along with the crows by a descending eagle. Not far away were buzzards circling awaiting the final outcome. The eagle is unsuccessful in its attempt to strike the starlings as they flew away to safer ground. Merton writes, "[The starlings] were there moving about and singing for about five minutes. Then, like lightening, it happened . . . . [A] hawk came down like a bullet, and shot straight into the middle of the starlings just as they were getting off the ground. They rose into the air and there was a slight scuffle on the ground as the hawk got his talons into the one bird he had nailed." Merton laments, "It was a terrible and yet beautiful thing, that lightening flight, straight as an arrow, that killed the slowest starling." In the passage, Merton describes the "guttural cursing" of the crows and the circling of the vultures, "lovers of dead things." The hawk remained in the field devouring its lone prey and "nothing else came near him. He took his time." As Merton meditated on the hawking practices of the lords of the Middle Ages he mused, "and I also understood the terrible fact that some men love war."[1]

And so it was that a decade later, Thomas Merton gave full flight to a series of 111 letters designated as the "Cold War Letters." These letters began in October, 1961 and extended to October, 1962. The term "Cold War," of course, refers to the power struggle between the United States and Russia following the Second World War.

It is the purpose of this article to give the reader a flavor and a sampling of Merton's thoughts about the threat of nuclear war and related problems because the same issues resonate with us today albeit in a different context. Many people would agree that our chances of being devastated by a dirty bomb, a nuclear bomb or through chemical/biological warfare are greater today than in the 1960s. Merton is quite candid about various war issues with his correspondents and the writer frankly at times finds the letters more instructive than his essays on war.[2] Having combed through the 111 letters, the writer has identified for purposes of this essay three themes: The Threat of Nuclear War; The Silence of American Catholics Including the Church Hierarchy and the Moral Theologians; Thomas Merton's Views about Peace Movements and Pacifism. The themes are representative of the disunity and strife that Merton so clearly articulated both in the Cold War Letters and his numerous essays. Although the paper will focus on the "Cold War Letters," linkages will be made to his essays for contextual purposes when necessary. Reference to the Merton essays on war can be found in the fine bibliography prepared by Patricia A. Burton.[3]

During 1961-1962, Merton had a problem with the censors and he was informed by his abbot, Dom James Fox, on April 26, 1962 "that he was no longer to publish books or articles on the issues of war and peace." Although Merton followed the dictates of the Order by not publishing articles on war, he privately circulated unpublished letters in mimeographed form to his friends.[4]

William Shannon observes:

> "The Year of the Cold War Letters" needs to be singled out as a unique year in the life of Thomas Merton. Articles on war and peace are interwoven with Cold War Letters to form a literary fabric out of which emerges a fairly clear image of Thomas Merton the peacemaker.[5]

Before beginning with the letters it is instructive to summarize "The Cold War Letters: Preface" in which Merton states his purpose as well as some disclaimers. Merton asserts that the letters intended for his friends are in raw form without any careful corrections. He goes on to say that the letters "form part of no plot" or "incite to no riot" and "they suggest no disloyalty to government." Further the letters were written in haste and sometimes "often distorted by indignation" because he has a "frank hatred of power politics" and a "contempt for those who use power to distort the truth or to silence it altogether." In a compelling statement Merton also declares:

> . . . . [D]uring the Cold War, if not during World War II, this country has become frankly a warfare state built on affluence, a power structure in which the interests of big business, the obsessions of the military, and the phobias of political extremists both dominate and dictate our national policy. [6]

Merton further states that the people of this country have been lulled into passivity and ignorance and "blindly follow any line that is unraveled for them by the mass media." He refers to a possible lost civilization through nuclear war but, moreover, he rails against the "suicidal moral evil and a total lack of ethics and rationality with which international policies tend to be conducted."[7] He mentions the so-called "well-adjusted" men who promote the insanity and one could conjecture that this is a reference to Adolph Eichmann who also was well-adjusted and "well-balanced."[8] There is no lack of moralists, Merton claims, and by taking his stand against theologians and even bishops, he is not turning against the Church or Christ. Rather, he is in line with the popes, "particularly Pius XII and John XXIII, who have repeatedly pleaded for rational and peaceful ways of settling disputes." Merton concludes his Preface proclaiming that "[t]he burden of protest in these letters is simply that such a state of affairs is pure madness" and "that to accept it without question as right and reasonable is criminally insane."[9]

William Shannon reminds us that Catholic clergy speaking out against war in the 1960's was a rare phenomenon. Shannon goes on to say that, indeed, Merton felt that he was "called to be a prophet" but he had no illusions about how "poorly equipped" he was for the role.[10] Abraham J. Heschel has this to say about the role of a prophet:

> The prophet was an individual who said No to his society, condemning its habits and assumptions, its complacency, waywardness, and syncretism. He was often compelled to proclaim the very opposite of what his heart expected. His fundamental objective was to reconcile man and God.[11]

Prophet or not, Thomas Merton certainly was a lone voice for his generation regarding the ominous threat of nuclear war. Through the themes presented in this article it will be evident that man not only has a propensity for self-destruction, the political dance of death, but indulges himself in an embarrassed silence about the possibilities of this self-destruction. The silence is occasionally broken by feeble attempts of protest led by people without clear mission and without spiritual direction. The only hope for mankind is a "flight from disunity and separation, to unity and peace in the love of other men." [12] The promise of unity and harmony is the focus of the concluding section of this article— "The General Dance"—Merton's attempt in Abraham Heschel's words "to reconcile man with God."

The Political Dancd of Death: The Threat of Nuclear War

The title of this article refers to the "Political Dance of Death" and the writer will attempt to take the reader from the stains and disunity of this war dance to the joys of the "General Dance" which may be interpreted as harmony and unity guided by the Holy Spirit. More about this "General Dance" later but for now let us examine Merton's reference to "The Political Dance of Death" in his essay entitled, "Peace: A Religious Responsibility" which is found in the book, *Breakthrough to Peace.*This book is a compilation of essays from contemporary writers about the threat of nuclear war. Merton states:

No one seriously doubts that it is now possible for man and his society to be completely destroyed in a nuclear war. . . . Indeed, this awful threat is the chief psychological weapon of the cold war. America and Russia are playing the paranoid game of nuclear deterrence, each one desperately hoping to preserve peace by threatening the other with bigger bombs and total annihilation. Every step in this political dance of death brings us inexorably closer to hot war. [13]

Merton's examination provides an apt context for the series of Cold War Letters that have been selected to demonstrate Merton's abhorrence of war, primarily nuclear war, as well as his occasional references to chemical-biological war. To one of his many correspondents, Elsa Englander from Austria, Merton writes:

There is no question that we live in an age of revolutionary change, perhaps even of cataclysm. . . . If by miscalculation or accident, or even by the pride and fury of men, war breaks out again, then there is every danger that nothing at all will be left of what was valuable and great in Europe. And all the wonderful possibilities of North America will be destroyed. It is a shame that we have such great capabilities and so little wisdom. [14]

Merton reflects on the more cosmic aspects of war in a letter to John Whitman Sears thanking him for his recent paper titled, "The Arms Race as a Chain Reaction." He remarks, "I think you have hit the nail on the head, as also Fromm and others have. It is a question of insanity." He goes on to say:

Yet looking at it [the arms race] on another level as a spiritual problem, it really becomes apocalyptic. I know men are seriously asking themselves now whether this sort of thing has happened somewhere before, and whether on other planets somewhere there have been races which have reached a point of development where they ended by destroying themselves.[15]

Man's separation from God through the hatred and violence of war is graphically explained to Rabbi Steven Schwarzchild in a sad commentary by Merton in which he cites God's loneliness, not his wrath:

[I]t is not [God's] wrath, exactly, it is His loneliness. His lostness among us. That He waits among us unknown and silent, patiently, for the moment when we will finally destroy Him utterly in His image . . . And leave Him alone again in the empty cosmos.[16]

In a gentler note stressing the possibility of moving along the continuum from insanity to sanity, Merton pens a letter to the Mayor of Hiroshima on or about the anniversary date of the dropping of the bomb:

In a solemn and grave hour for humanity I address this letter to you and to your people. I thank you for the sincerity and courage with which you are, at this time, giving witness for peace and sanity . . . . Man should use political instruments in behalf of truth, sanity, and international Order. Unfortunately the blindness and madness of a society that is shaken to its very roots by the storms of passion and greed for power make the fully effective use of political negotiation impossible.[17]

Merton demonstrates his concerns about the tremendous financial burden caused by military buildups in a letter to George Dunne: "I am . . . much concerned about the economy of our own country: not that I know much about it. But one doesn't have to know the first thing about economics to know that this present war economy spells ruin . . . . I am speaking primarily of the economic collapse of a totally wasteful and destructive system."[18]

An Embarrassed Silence

An "[e]mbarrassed silence, despondent passivity, or crusading belligerence seem to be the most widespread 'Christian' response to the H-bomb," according to Thomas Merton.[19] The next series of letters will focus primarily on the silence of American Catholics including the Church hierarchy and the moral theologians. To highlight the plight of the Church, and its silence the following letter to Erich Fromm is illustrative:

All these questions [of evil] float about in my mind, but my personal conviction is that when everyone else in my Church (except the Popes who have after all spoken quite clearly condemning nuclear annihilation bombing) seems to want to stay silent and perplexed, or worse still encourages nuclear war as the "lesser evil," it has become my clear duty to speak out against this crime and to denounce the steps taken to perpetuate it, while refusing all cooperation and trying to get others to do the same. [20]

Merton continues his criticism of the silence of Catholics and the Church hierarchy in a letter to Monsignor John Tracy Ellis denouncing the passive attitude of so many American Catholics concerning nuclear war. He states: "They make no distinction between out-and-out pacifism which refuses to serve even in a 'just war' and the Christian obligation, pointed out by the recent Popes, to avoid the criminal tragedy of nuclear annihilation of civilian centers, even for the best of causes." Merton makes the point that there has been the usual we are good and they are evil paradigm by stating "much popular thought in this country simply goes along with the immoral and secularist attitude that since communism is evil, we can do anything we like to wipe it out and thus prevent it from gaining ground and overwhelming us."[21]

The misperception of American Catholics as the good people fighting the forces of evil in the world was an interesting note in Merton's letters. In writing to Ethel Kennedy, he declares: "The great illusion is to assume that we are perfectly innocent, peace-loving and right while the communists are devils incarnate. I admit they are no angels and they have been guilty of some frightful crimes against humanity." He criticizes "the 'good' people, the right-thinking people, who stick to principle all right except where it conflicts with the chance to make a fast buck." [22] In the same letter, Merton voices his concern about the Church not being articulate in its position relative to nuclear war even though Pius XII issued clear principles about it. Merton states, "If as Christians we were more certain of our duty, it might put us in a very tight spot politically but it would also merit for us special graces from God, and these we need badly."[23]

In a letter to Jesuit theologian John Ford, Merton speaks of the division of the theologians and the silence of the bishops:

> Sure, the theologians are divided, and the bishops rely on the theologians. But can't the theologians and the bishops say something? . . . Father, my heart is very sick with the feeling that we don't give the impression of caring at all what happens to man, the image of God . . . . But of one thing I am convinced: the vital importance of a forceful and articulate Catholic position, in this country, in favor of peace, rather than the permissive and silent attitude that seems to prevail at the moment.[24]

At this point in my analysis, perhaps, it would be instructive to note commentaries about John Ford, S. J. from John T. McGreevy, eminent Catholic historian, in his book, *Catholicism and American Freedom*. He cites Ford's condemnation of Hiroshima and Nagasaki bombings as "the greatest and most extensive single atrocity of all this period .... Twenty years later Ford would regret wartime Catholic 'complacency and conformity' in the face of a 'moral issue that was staring us in the face.'" It is interesting to note that John Courtney Murray, according to McGreevy, congratulated Ford on his position and another priest. Father Francis Connell, agreed with Ford, stating, "there is apt to be too much rationalizing even among priests in defense of governmental activities, and theologians should make a stand on principles without respect of persons."[25]

According to McGreevy, Father John Ford applied his natural law arguments regarding the defense of human life to military tactics. McGreevy writes:

In 1944, at the height of the war, Ford published a powerfully reasoned forty-nine page attack on the American and British practice of bombing civilian targets, an essay that became a landmark in the literature of military ethics. So-called 'obliteration bombing,' . . . violated the 'Catholic view that to take the life of an innocent person is always intrinsically wrong, that is, forbidden absolutely by natural law.'[26]

Regarding a preemptive nuclear attack, Merton notes in another letter to Monsignor Ellis that in the journal, *Theological Studies*, American theologians have been trying "to squeeze around the traditional limitations of the 'just' war, in order to show that by Catholic standards a preemptive nuclear attack is really only defense." Merton cites the immorality of the nuclear bomb dropped on Hiroshima even though it was considered morally acceptable by many. He goes on to say that our political leaders and some theologians argue that a limited war is legitimate and if it leads to an all out war then that too can be justified because of the circumstances.[27] In further correspondence with Ellis, Merton affirms that the moral theologians should be advising President Kennedy against a preemptive first strike against Russia and its "frightful consequences" and its immorality.[28]

The moral theologian, John Courtney Murray, is described by Merton in a letter to W. H. Ferry as a learned theologian who can make very fine distinctions in his arguments about the plausibility of a limited war which is "a reasonable war, a nice kind of war, in which the limits set down by Catholic moral theology and Pius XII are respected by the Pentagon."[29]

Merton underscores the moral passivity and silence of American Catholics and especially the clergy in his essay "Theologians and Defense," asserting that there is an "all too general . . . apathy and passivity among the clergy and the faithful. Perhaps it is exact to say that they are afflicted with a kind of moral paralysis."[30]

Peace Movements and Pacificism

Thomas Merton abhorred war, spoke against it, and reproached the church hierarchy about their "moral paralysis."[31] Excerpts from the following letters focus on Merton's views and reservations about the peace movements and their inherent weaknesses. Also this group of letters has been selected to reveal Merton's views of pacifism and where he stood with the issue.

Merton was generally supportive of the Quakers and Mennonites in regards to their peace efforts. In a correspondence to Allan Forbes, Jr., Merton praises Quaker and Mennonite peace activity. He states, "It seems to me that the long-standing Quaker position on peace is one of the most reliable and stabilizing forces we have at the moment."[32] He goes on to say that the peace positions have spiritual as well as political importance. He adds that the "unilateral disarmament" position of the peace movements is unrealistic but serious negotiations should begin by the United States and the Soviet Union in regard to disarmament and both parties should cast away the propaganda machines in regards to the issue. In Merton's view the importance of this political process may prevent a future nuclear holocaust. However, he declares that the spiritual dimension articulated by the Quakers as a matter of conscience about the evils of war may "start a chain reaction in the moral order." [33]

Merton regarded the Mennonite tradition with the same enthusiasm as he had for the Quakers. In a letter to Maynard Shelly, editor of *The Mennonite*, Merton expresses his respect for "Mennonite tradition of peaceful action and non-violence." He further states, "Though not a total pacifist in theory myself, I certainly believe that every Christian should try to practice non-violence rather than violence and that some should bind themselves to follow only the way of peace as an example to the others."[34]

In regards to the question of pacifism, Merton made a distinction between absolute pacifism and nuclear pacifism in an essay titled "Religion and the Bomb" originally published in *Jubilee* in May, 1962. While not subscribing to the notion of absolute pacifism, which is an unqualified objection to war for any reason including a defensive war, as exemplified by the United States declaration of war following the Pearl Harbor attack by the Japanese, Merton encouraged his correspondents and friends to be nuclear pacifists, that is, opposed to the first-strike mentality prevalent at the time. In the same essay, he makes the point that pacifist movements "tend to attract a certain number of professional oddballs." Also there is the chance of exploitation by the communists but that should not deter one from favoring a policy of nuclear disarmament "without being a Red, a beatnik or a 'pacifist.'"[35]

Further testimony of Merton's position on pacifism can be examined in a letter to Dorothy Day: "It is true that I am not theoretically a pacifist. That only means that I do not hold that a Christian *may not* fight, and that a war *cannot* be just." However, Merton is quick to explain to Day that his statements are more in the realm of theory and "that in practice all the wars that are going around...are shot through and through with evil."[36]

In a series of cold war letters to James Forest, Merton is clear about peace movements. Forest was very active in various peace movements, and was one of the founders of the Catholic Peace Fellowship, an affiliate of the Fellowship of Reconciliation.[37] In his criticism of peace movements, Merton mentions to Forest that "hidden aggressions and provocations" are prevalent in the movements caused by elements of non-religious people or persons who are not developed spiritually. The danger, of course, is that the opposition may harden their views when confronted with people tainted with these hidden aggressions who themselves are supposedly opposing aggression.[38] In another letter to Forest, Merton speaks of the superficiality of peace movements although they have potential. He is quick to say, however, that he may lack perspective and that "everything is superficial now."[39] In further correspondence with Forest, Merton states that:

> [t]he "peace movement needs more than zeal. It certainly needs to be organized on a very clear basis . . . . It is not going to do any good for a lot of excited people to mill around without purpose and without definite means of making their protest clear and intelligible. Especially if a lot of them are not too clear themselves what they are protesting about.[40]

Further criticism of peace movements by Merton to Forest underscores activism: "The trouble with movements is that they sweep you off your feet and carry you away with the tide of activism and then you become another kind of mass man."[41]

However, Thomas Merton held out hope for the viability of peace movements. In his essay, "Preamble: Peace—A Religious

Responsibility," Merton emphasizes that opposition to war is imperative and religious protest is "badly needed."[42] In another essay, "Moral Passivity and Demonic Activism," Merton clearly states the "need for strong peace movements, both as a protest and a 'brake' to slow down the accelerated rush toward war."[43]

One can conclude, therefore, that Merton had little regard for peace movements as they were rendered impotent through the lack of spiritual direction and purpose. However, he articulated the potential of peace movements and protests if they had clarity of purpose led by people who were developed spiritually.

Conclusion: The General Dance

Thomas Merton's "prophetic" voice articulated through the Cold War Letters signaled man's alienation, division, and disunity. According to Merton it was original sin "which alienated each man from God, from other men and from himself."[44] Further, Merton contends that the "moral evil in the world is due to man's alienation from the deepest truth, from the springs of spiritual life within himself, to his alienation from God."[45] "[M]an was created as a contemplative" and the fall from Paradise was a fall from the unity of his contemplative vision to alienation, division, and disunity.[46]

William Shannon conjectures that it was Merton's "deep contemplative vision" that led him to write about social issues. This contemplative vision empowered Merton to call for unity and "to see the oneness we share with all God's people—indeed with the whole of God's creation."[47] Merton calls upon us to see the Holy Spirit in our enemy and stranger. "We must find [the Holy Spirit] in our enemy, or we may lose him even in our friend. We must find him in the pagan or we will lose him in our own selves."[48] The Holy Spirit as a pathfinder to unity is exemplified in his letter to Maynard Shelly, when Merton states:

> There must be a total love of all, even of the most distant, even of the most hostile. Without the gift of the Holy Spirit this is mere idealism, mere dreaming. But the Spirit who knows all things and can do all things, He can be in us the power of love that heals, unites, and redeems, for thus the Blood of Jesus Christ reaches all men through us. [49]

In a prophetic call to unity, Thomas Merton warns that "time is rapidly running out" and that "every possible effort must be made for the abolition of war." [50] Further, he asserts that Christians are obliged to seek information, sacrifice, work, and cooperate to bring about a peaceful world because "[w]e cannot expect a peaceful world society to emerge all by itself."[51] Throughout Merton's Cold War Letters and his essays there is a sense of urgency to persist with the negotiation process through "intelligent political action"[52] as the rising tide of military power will certainly, in the end, leave God "alone again in the empty cosmos."[53]

The spirit of negotiation can only take place by recognizing that fear is the root of war. In the essay, "The Root of War is Fear," Merton asserts, "For only love—which means humility—can exorcise the fear which is at the root of all war."[54] Later in this essay he states:

So instead of loving what you think is peace, love other men and love God above all. And instead of hating the people you think are warmakers, hate the appetites and the disorder in your own soul, which are the causes of war. If you love peace, then hate injustice, hate tyranny, hate greed—but hate these things *in yourself*, not in another.[55]

Merton's call for unity through the intercession of the Holy Spirit is to enter in harmony with the cosmos. Victor A. Kramer interpreting Merton's last chapter titled, "The General Dance," in *New Seeds of Contemplation* states that harmony is a way for all of us to get closer to God and "if we truly believe in the Incarnation, we must be prepared to see the mystery and presence of Christ in *all* persons."[56] Lawrence Cunningham comments that in this chapter, one senses "the goodness of creation, the gift of Christ's incarnation, and a general sense of the human person as part of the great gift of God which is creation and re-creation." [57]

Merton urges, "if we could let go of our own obsession with what we think is the meaning of it all, we might be able to hear His call and follow Him in His mysterious, cosmic dance."[58] Further, Merton wants us to understand the "phenomena of life" and states that "no despair of ours can alter the reality of things, or stain the joy of the cosmic dance which is always there." Hopefully, there is still time for mankind to turn from the war hawks and their Political Dance of Death to Merton's plea for unity and harmony through the General Dance. He concludes in *New Seeds of Contemplation*: "Yet the fact remains that we are invited to forget ourselves on purpose, cast our awful solemnity to the winds and join in the general dance."[59]

Notes

1. Thomas Merton, *The Sign of Jonas* (New York: Harcourt, Brace, 1953), pp. 274-75.

2. In his book, *Silent Lamp* (New York: Crossroad, 1992), William H. Shannon speculates about the possible impact of the *Cold War Letters*. He states: "Quite a number of copies of *The Cold War Letters* circulated in the famous yellow cover. Several copies were put into the hands of various bishops at the Second Vatican Council in Rome. It is tempting to think that this work, as well as Merton's other writings on war and peace, exerted a positive influence on the council fathers when they came to write the section (arts. 77-82) on war and peace in *Gaudium et Spes* (The Pastoral Constitution on the Church in the Modern World)." Shannon mentions the bishops' stance on nonviolence, condemnation of total war etc—"all these stances resonate with positions on these issues that Merton had taken in his articles and letters during what we might call his 'year of the Cold War letters.'" (p.215). A few pages later Shannon remarks, "Just a year after Merton's war-writing 'industry' was shut down, Pope John XXIII published his encyclical *Pacem in Terris*, which contained a number of things Merton had been saying. Merton promptly wrote to the abbot general, Dom Gabriel Sortais, expressing mock relief that Pope John had not been an American Cistercian. For the American censors would never have approved the Pope's peace encyclical" (p.223).

3. Patricia A. Burton, *Merton Vade Mecum*, 2nd ed. (Louisville, KY: The Thomas Merton Foundation, 2001), pp. 161-164.

4. *Witness to Freedom, Letters of Thomas Merton in Times of Crisis*, ed. William H. Shannon (New York: Farrar, Straus & Giroux, 1994), p. 17.

5. *Witness to Freedom*, p. 18.

6. *Witness to Freedom*, pp. 19-20.

7. *Witness to Freedom*, pp. 20-21.

8. Thomas Merton, *Raids on the Unspeakable* (New York: New Directions, 1964), pp. 45-49.

9. *Witness to Freedom*, pp. 21-22.

10. Thomas Merton, *Passion for Peace, The Social Essays*, ed. William H. Shannon (New York: Crossroad, 1995), p. 3.

11. Abraham J. Heschel, *The Prophets* (New York: Harper & Row, 1962), p. xv.

12. Thomas Merton, *New Seeds of Contemplation* (New York: New Directions, 1961), p. 78.

13. *Breakthrough to Peace,* Introduction by Thomas Merton (New York: New Directions, 1962), p. 91. It was the intention of Thomas Merton and publisher, James Laughlin to publish the works of well-known authors on the dangers of nuclear war. Merton was originally to be the editor of the book but "he changed his mind" about being named editor after he had been given his orders to no longer publish writings about "war and peace." Therefore the book has no official editor but Merton still carried out the responsibilities. He also wrote the introduction and contributed a rewrite of one of his earlier essays which is quoted in the text. This essay is "perhaps the clearest statement of his position on nuclear war." *The Thomas Merton Encyclopedia,* eds. William H. Shannon, Christine M. Bochen and Patrick F. O'Connell (Maryknoll; New York: Orbis Books, 2002), p. 32.

14. *Witness to Freedom,* p. 32. Cold War Letter 28, February 4, 1962.

15. *Witness to Freedom,* pp. 303-304.Cold War Letter 89, June 23, 1962.

16. *Witness to Freedom,* pp. 35-36. Cold War Letter 41, February 24, 1962.

17. *The Hidden Ground of Love, The Letters of Thomas Merton on Religious Experience and Social Concerns,* ed. William H. Shannon (New York: Farrar, Straus & Giroux, 1985), p. 380. Cold War Letter 98, 1962.

18. *Witness to Freedom,* p. 69. Cold War Letter 110, October 30, 1962.

19. Thomas Merton, *Peace in the Post-Christian Era,* ed. Patricia A. Burton (Maryknoll, New York: Orbis Books, 2004), p. 3.

20. *The Hidden Ground of Love,* p. 319. Cold War Letter 5, December, 1961.

21. *The Hidden Ground of Love,* p. 175. Cold War Letter 6, December 7, 1961.

22. *The Hidden Ground of Love,* p. 445. Cold War Letter 10, December, 1961.

23. *The Hidden Ground of Love,* p. 446. Cold War Letter 10, December, 1961.

24. *Witness to Freedom,* p.30.Cold War Letter 23, January, 1962.

25. As quoted in John T. McGreevey, *Catholicism and American Freedom* (New York: W.W. Norton and Company, 2003), p. 228.

26. As quoted in *Catholicism and American Freedom,* p.227.

27. *The Hidden Ground of Love,* p.176. Cold War Letter 29, February 4, 1962.

28. *The Hidden Ground of Love,* pp. 177-178.Cold War Letter 53, March 10, 1962.

29. *The Hidden Ground of Love,* pp. 205-206.Cold War Letter 26, January 30, 1962.

30. *Peace in the Post-Christian Era,* p. 88.

31. Thomas Merton, *Passion for Peace*, p. 73.

32. *Witness to Freedom*, p.61. Cold War Letter, 97, August, 1962.

33. *Witness to Freedom*, pp 61-62. Cold War Letter, 97, August, 1962.

34. *Witness to Freedom*, p.23. Cold War Letter 4, December, 1961.

35. *Passion for Peace*, p. 74.

36. *Hidden Ground of Love*, p. 145. Cold War Letter 86, June 16, 1962.

37. *The Hidden Ground of Love*, p. 254.

38. *The Hidden Ground of Love*, pp. 263-264. Cold War Letter 31, February 6, 1962.

39. *The Hidden Ground of Love*, p. 270. Cold War Letter 101, August 27, 1962.

40. *The Hidden Ground of Love*, p. 265. Cold War Letter 61, March 28, 1962.

41. *The Hidden Ground of Love*, p. 266. Cold War Letter 69, April 29, 1962.

42. *Peace in the Post-Christian Era*, p.3.

43. *Peace in the Post-Christian Era*, p. 108.

44. Thomas Merton, *The New Man* (New York: Farrar, Straus and Giroux, 1961), p. 149.

45. *Peace in the Post-Christian Era*, p. 127.

46. Thomas Merton, *The Inner Experience: Notes on Contemplation*, ed.William H. Shannon (San Francisco: HarperSanFrancisco, 2003), p. 35.

47. *Passion for Peace*, p. 4.

48. Thomas Merton, *The Collected Poems of Thomas Merton* (New York: New Directions, 1977), p. 384. This passage is taken from the essay, "A Letter to Pablo Antonio Cuadra Concerning Giants," which "likens the two world powers of the Soviet Union and the United States to the figures of Gog and Magog in Ezekiel, and looks to the 'Third World,' particularly to Latin America, as providing hope for renewal should the two giants destroy each other . . . . Despite its use of symbolism, it clearly is an essay rather than a poem; it remains from an earlier conception of *Emblems of a Season of Fury* as a combination of verse and prose, perhaps because it serves as a kind of transition to the group of translations, the first of which are of poems by Cuadra." *The Thomas Merton Encyclopedia*, p.133.

49. *Witness to Freedom*, p. 23

50. *Peace in the Post-Christian World*, p. 162.

51. *Peace in the Post-Christian World*, p. 93.

52. *Peace in the Post-Christian World*, p. 93.

53. *Witness to Freedom*, p. 36. Cold War Letter 41, February 24, 1962.

54. *New Seeds of Contemplation*, p. 119.

55. *New Seeds of Contemplation*, p. 122. Also Pax Christi, a United States peace group, states that Americans must overcome its stereotype of Iran in order to assess better President Bush's claims that the Muslim nation is building nuclear weapons. Dave Robinson, Executive Director of U.S. Pax Christi, has just completed a 12-day visit to Iran and commented, "Enemy imaging dominates the U.S media. This makes Americans 'easy targets' for accepting a U.S. 'preventive war' against Iran rather than a negotiated solution." Mr. Robinson was part of a delegation of mostly U.S. peace activists organized by the Fellowship of Reconciliation, an international interfaith peace movement (Catholic News Service, May 6, 2006).

56. Victor A. Kramer, *Thomas Merton, Monk and Artist* (Kalamazoo, MI: Cistercian Publications, 1984), p. 63.

57. *Thomas Merton: Spiritual Master*, ed. Lawrence S. Cunningham (New York: Paulist Press, 1992), p. 251.

58. *New Seeds of Contemplation*, p. 296.

59. *New Seeds of Contemplation*, p. 297.

Landscapes of Disaster:
The War Poems of Thomas Merton

Patrick F. O'Connell

Although Thomas Merton's best known poem, and certainly one of his best, is his elegy to his brother, John Paul, killed in action in 1943,[1] and although Merton's writings on war and peace, in both prose and verse, during the last ten years of his life are among the most influential of his works,[2] relatively little attention has been paid to the fact that during the period preceding his entrance into the Abbey of Gethsemani in December 1941, the very week America entered World War II, Merton wrote a substantial number of poems concerned with this war. The fact that these poems have not been considered as a group is not surprising, since they are scattered through three different volumes of verse, *Thirty Poems* (1944), *A Man in the Divided Sea* (1946),[3] and the posthumously published *Early Poems: 1940-1942* (1971),[4] and they are concerned with a period before the direct involvement of the United States in the hostilities, although for Merton, born in France and educated largely in England, this initial phase of the war had a greater immediacy and urgency than it would have for most native-born Americans. Though not all of these war poems are fully realized, they display a remarkable variety of frames of reference and strategies of analysis, so that considering them as a group provides an opportunity both to observe Merton's struggles with the moral, political and spiritual issues of war at this critical point in his own life, and to see him trying to articulate these struggles in poems that are aesthetically coherent and intellectually and emotionally effective. What follows is an analysis, in roughly chronological order, of Thomas Merton's premonastic war poems,[5] highlighting the particular approach to the war taken in each poem.

* * * * * * *

Probably the earliest of the war poems, simply entitled "Poem 1939" (*MDS* #2),[6] takes what might be described as a cosmic perspective on the conflict that began with the German invasion of

Poland on September 1 of that year. Written in three fairly regular trimeter quatrains,[7] it opens with an image of universal order symbolized by the constellations:

> The white, the silent stars
> Drive their wheeling ring,
> Crane down out of the tall black air
> To hear the swanworld sing. (ll. 1-4)

In the first two lines, the stars are depicted as having their own perfect, self-contained pattern, perhaps a reminiscence of Henry Vaughan's celebrated image of eternity as "a great ring of endless light" in his poem "The World."[8] Even the assonance of "white," "silent" and "Drive" and the echoing effect of "wheeling ring" reinforce this impression of celestial accord. Yet the parallel verb phrase in the two following lines reveals that the heavens are not detached from or indifferent to what is taking place on earth; the "silent stars" are depicted as listening "to hear the swanworld sing," a striking image of the beauty of the earth recalling the kennings of early English verse;[9] the metaphorical implications of the verb "Crane" suggest both a kinship and a contrast between stars and earth, perhaps to the advantage of the earth, as swans are generally considered more beautiful than cranes. The impression is that the celestial world, while perfect in its own way, is nevertheless drawn to the earth because of a melody, a harmony, available only there, in the "swanworld" which is also, more pertinently, the world of human beings.

But as the rest of the poem reveals, the stars listen in vain, for earthly order, unlike that of the heavens, is contingent on human decisions and actions, and is at best precarious in what has become a fallen world. In fact the image of the "swanworld sing[ing]" itself carries an element of foreboding, because in the classical tradition the swan is said to sing only when it is dying.[10] The middle stanza reflects the world situation in 1939, during the opening phase of the war in Europe:

> But the long, deep knife is in,
> (O bitter, speechless earth)
> Throat grows tight, voice thin,
> Blood gets no regrowth, . . . (ll. 5-8)

The swan has been stabbed, its throat constricts so that its "thin" voice is difficult if not impossible to hear, and it is in any case "speechless" with bitterness at its betrayal and perhaps with surprise as well. Its blood pours forth profusely and cannot be replaced, "no regrowth" providing an ironic verbal echo to "Throat grows tight" in the previous line. The staccato effect of the stanza's two final lines, with articles omitted, presents an almost clinical description of the dying process. The appealing picture of cosmic order complemented by earthly harmony in the opening stanza has been shattered by human discord and violence.

The final stanza personalizes the situation: "As night devours our days, / Death puts out our eyes" (ll. 9-10). Surrounded by so much destruction, it becomes impossible to see the light, to perceive the truth. For eyes blinded by death, night is regarded simply as a monstrous power of darkness that "devours" the daylight. As the stars hear no music from the earth, so in turn the earth has become unable to perceive the pattern of the stars. The poem concludes in a sort of anti-Pentecost in which "Towns dry up and flare like tongues / But no voice prophesies" (ll. 11-12). The towns which have caught fire, presumably from aerial bombing, recall the tongues of flame that descended on the apostles, but now there is no prophecy, no proclamation of the Word of God. The forces of destruction have apparently usurped and reversed the creative action of the Holy Spirit. The final silence is the opposite of the contemplative silence of the stars; the earth ravaged by war, blinded, speechless and apparently bereft of any source of insight into its tragic condition, fails to reflect and participate in the cosmic order of the "wheeling ring" of the heavens; darkness, for the time being at least, has overcome light.

* * * * * * *

"The Dark Morning" (*TP* #4),[11] a second poem from 1939,[12] also consisting of three stanzas written in the rhymed quatrains that Merton would soon leave behind, takes a very different approach that might be labeled "psychospiritual," though it too begins with natural description:

> This is the black day when
> Fog rides the ugly air:
> Water wades among the buildings
> To the prisoner's curled ear. (ll. 1-4)

The opening "weather report," presented in very simple words (only "ugly" has more than one syllable), is less simple in meaning that may initially be apparent. The use of the definite article in the first line (not "*a* black day" but "*the* black day"[13]) implies that it is a day that has been anticipated, and the personification of the fog, which "rides" on the air, suggests that the forces of darkness are abroad and that the blackness of the day is of more than meteorological significance, an impression reinforced by the cacophony of the harsh plosives in "black," "Fog" and "ugly." The parallel personification in the two final lines of the stanza (reinforced by their identical placement in two successive lines and by the slant rhyme of "rides" and "wades") suggests that here water is not to be taken as a sign of life or renewal but as another agent of darkness, finding its way through flooded passageways until it reaches its apparent its goal, "the prisoner's curled ear." Presumably the meaning is that the noise of the storm and its rushing water fills his ear so as to drown out all other sounds. The status and situation of "the prisoner" are not as yet further identified, but it is at least clear that he is unable to escape or evade the water's invasive presence. As vision is obscured by the darkness, so hearing is immersed in the sounds of the storm.

Yet the second stanza reveals that the prisoner is in fact quite receptive to the message of the storm:

> Then rain, in thin sentences,
> Slakes him like danger,
> Whose heart is his Germany
> Fevered with anger. (ll. 5-8)

The rhythm here switches to anapestic, a quickness that perhaps reflects the sound of the falling rain striking the already flooded streets (an aural and even visual impression of raindrops that would also explain how water could be said to "wade" in the previous stanza). In any case the rain's message, its "thin sentences" (a description that may refer to both the sight and the sound of the falling rain, but also to the lack of substance in its "words"), are said to satisfy the prisoner's thirst, but to do so "like danger." That is, the prisoner has a thirst, an attraction, for danger, which the storm "slakes": the power of darkness represented by the water is welcome to the prisoner, whose heart is "Fevered with anger." The rain provides a kind of counter-revelation, the opposite of sun, light, illumination, words of darkness and disillusion, perhaps emotionally satisfying lies that allay, or justify, or rationalize, or excuse his anger, or do all at once. They claim that the storm, the blackness, is the most authentic reality, so that his own inner turmoil corresponds to the upheavals of the outer world. For the prisoner's "heart is his Germany": his enemy, his attacker and betrayer, is not external to himself but is identified with his own interior passions. Like the Merton of the opening page of *The Seven Storey Mountain*,[14] he is a prisoner of his own disordered desires, and his feverish inner conflict leaves him open to the seductions of the dark rain that pours in from the day deprived of all light.

The final stanza recapitulates the first two, reemphasizing the sense of imprisonment, with one significant difference:

> This is the dark day when
> Locks let the enemy in
> Through all the coiling passages of
> (Curled ear) my prison! (ll. 9-12)

The "dark day" (altered from "black day" of the otherwise identical first line of the poem) symbolizes the despair of the prisoner's state, held captive by his own "Germany" which he had evidently struggled against to no avail, unable to free himself from what Merton will later describe as the false self of egotistical desires,[15] and powerless to keep out the tempter's voice that confirms his own hopelessness by claiming it is the true condition of the world. It is the voice of the serpent that whispers in Eve's ear in *Paradise Lost*, the insinuating voice that traces the labyrinthine pathways to the prisoner's cell which are also the "curled" channels of his ear, an appropriately twisted path for a twisted message. But in the final words of the poem the speaker no longer refers to "his" but to "my prison." He has recognized that the condition he had analyzed in the first two stanzas also applies to himself – he too is imprisoned by his anger, longing for the dark rain's "thin sentences" to penetrate the "coiling passages" of his own ears. He has realized, as Merton repeatedly emphasizes in his prose works from this same period,[16] that as a sinner he shares in the culpability for the conditions that have made the war possible. This evidence of self-knowledge is then, paradoxically, a slight but genuine countersign to the hopelessness that has dominated the poem up to this final confession.

* * * * * * *

"The Philosophers" (*EP* #1)[17] uses literary parody to make its point about the worldviews that have led to the current conflict. The speaker is evidently a plant:

> As I lay sleeping in the park,
> Buried in the earth,
> Waiting for the Easter rains
> To drench me in their mirth
> And crown my seedtime with some sap and growth,...(ll. 1-5)

This opening section, a long subordinate clause clearly organized into parallel verbal phrases, is marked by the contrast between the participles modifying "I," which are passive and receptive ("sleeping," "Buried," "Waiting"), and the dynamic, active infinitives associated with the rain ("To drench . . . / And crown"), which is thus to bring potency into act, as the outer flow of the water evokes a responsive flow of the sap within. The specification of "Easter rains"[18] suggests that the vitality of rebirth in spring is analogous to and a sign of the spiritual renewal found in the resurrection of Christ. The speaker waits to be inundated not just by water but by the joy associated with this celebration.

The section that follows opens with the main clause of this first sentence, which contains a radical shift in focus and tone that will continue through most of the remainder of the poem:

> Into the tunnels of my ears
> Two anaesthetic voices came.
> Two mandrakes were discussing life
> And Truth and Beauty in the other room. (ll. 6-9)

These "anaesthetic voices" represent a counterforce to the power of the rains, conveying not vitality but its opposite, not only without feeling but inducing a lack of feeling, serving as instruments of anaesthesia. There may also be a pun in which "anaesthetic" refers to an atrophy of the aesthetic sense, an insensitivity to or denial of the reality and meaningfulness of beauty – despite the fact that this is the subject of the voices' discussion.[19] The mandrake roots, considered to have a human shape,[20] are appropriately personified as speakers here, but as the mandrake, or mandragora, is used both as a narcotic and as a poison, their words are hardly to be taken at face value. The reference to "the other room" is rather odd for an underground locale, but it is apparently an allusion to Emily Dickinson's poem #449, "I died for Beauty,"[21] in which the speaker is "In an adjoining Room" (l. 4) to one who died for Truth, and says "We talked between the Rooms" (l. 10). The mandrakes' conversation, of course, covers these very topics, though their words reflect Dickinson less directly than a source that she herself probably was alluding to, "Beauty is truth, truth beauty, – that is all, / Ye know on earth, and all ye need to know" – the famous final lines of John Keats' "Ode on a Grecian Urn,"[22] which each of the two mandrakes reworks to articulate its own twisted "philosophy":

> "Body is truth, truth body. Fat is all
> We grow on earth, or all we breed to grow."
> Said one mandrake to the other.
> Then I heard his brother:
> "Beauty is troops, troops beauty. Dead is all
> We grow on earth, or all we bleed to grow."[23] (ll. 10-15)

The first statement reduces all to matter – if body is truth and truth body then the spiritual dimension is denied and the only growth is in quantity, in marked contrast to the holistic sense of "growth" in the first section of the poem, which suggests an analogy be-tween material and spiritual development. Here greed and glut-tony reign; successive generations are no more than a succession of bodies. The second mandrake's version is not just materialistic but militaristic and even nihilistic: power and violence are the only beauty recognized and death is ultimately triumphant.

This poem might seem to be only tenuously related to the war being waged at the time of its composition, except that the final lines, in which the speaker once again voices its own perspective of organic development counter to the reductive proclamations of the previous lines, conclude with a reference to conflict between the mandrakes:

> As I lay dreaming in the earth,
> Enfolded in my future leaves,
> My rest was broken by these mandrakes
> Bitterly arguing in their frozen graves. (ll. 16-19)

These lines recapitulate the movement of the entire poem, with the first line a compressed version of the two opening lines and the second emphasizing once again a sense of organic development. The lyric tetrameters of these two lines give way to the unmetrical rhythms of the two final lines which summarize the central sections of the poem, with one crucial piece of additional information. Even though there might seem to be little real difference between them, the mandrakes are described as engaging in a bitter disagreement, which suggests that their views may be reflective of the military conflict currently in progress, in which case the materialistic philosophy of the first brother could be taken to represent the hedonistic worldview of the Western democracies, and the militarism of the second brother the totalitarianism of the Fascist powers. The distinct yet similar variations on Keats' lines suggests that the two are thus more closely linked than they are willing to admit, though the second does appear much more aggressive and frightening than the first. As the slant rhyme of "future leaves" and "frozen graves" indicates, the real contrast is between the pessimistic materialism the two brothers have in common and the expectation voiced by the speaker of a renewal that is both natural and supernatural.[24]

* * * * * * *

The poem entitled "Two British Airmen" (*EP* #3),[25] and subtitled: "(Buried with ceremony in the Teutoburg Forest)," written in rhyming couplets and probably dating from October 1939,[26] takes a historical approach to the war, setting it in the context of patterns of conflict dating back to classical times. The fliers of the title have apparently been shot down or crashed in the Teutoburg Forest in northern Germany, the site of a catastrophic defeat of three Roman legions by Germans in the first decade of the common era.[27] The poem opens with a focus on the warriors whose rest has been left undisturbed for 1900 years, a situation about to be changed:

> Long buried, ancient men-at-arms
> Beneath the beechtrees and the farms
> Sleep, and syntax locks their glory
> In the old pages of a story. (ll. 1-4)

The cumulative effect of "Long," "ancient" and "old" is to emphasize the gap, psychological as well as chronological, separating the as yet vaguely described past events from contemporary consciousness, a remoteness increased by the "dead" language in which the story is preserved.

In the second section of the poem, this distance is suddenly bridged by the experience of the two airmen of the title, described in their own words:[28]

> "We knew that battle when it was
> A curious clause in Tacitus,
> But were not able to construe
> Our graves were in this forest too;
> And buried, never thought to have found
> Such strange companions, underground." (ll. 5-10)

They begin by looking back to their schooldays, when the story of the Roman defeat as told by the Roman historian Tacitus[29] was of at most mild interest because of its grammatical structure; the event itself was too far removed from their own experience to generate much in the way of empathy or vicarious identification with the human drama of the battle. They had no premonition at the time that their own destiny would be to be buried in the same location. The use of "construe," which carries both the specific connotation of grasping the meaning of the Latin and the more general sense of "understand" or "interpret," marks the point of transition from schoolboy indifference to military engagement: war, and death in war, is no longer a historical curiosity of merely academic interest. Suddenly what was distant in time and space has become intensely relevant as the Roman soldiers are recognized as "strange companions" whose fate and burial site they now share. While the transition from "ancient men-at-arms" to contemporary "airmen" provides evidence of "progress" in the technology of violence, death remains death and war is still war – there is a sense of kinship in the sudden awareness of how little has changed over the centuries.

The poem then switches from the words of the dead airmen to those of the people burying them, who would of course be Germans living in the area:

> "– Bring his flag, and wrap, and lay him
> Under a cross that shows no name,
> And, in the same ground make his grave
> As those long-lost Romans have.
> Let him a speechless exile be
> From England and his century,
> Nor question these old strangers, here,
> Inquisitive, around his bier." (ll. 11-18)

Attention remains focused on the affinity of the dead airmen with the dead Romans, specifically identified for the first time in the poem, who are apparently the "inquisitive" "old strangers" (echoing the airmen's reference to "strange companions" above) seen gathered around the gravesite, disturbed by the reopening of the earth in which they have lain; they are neither to be questioned (about their own experiences), nor, evidently, to be answered (satisfying their curiosity about what is happening). The airmen are to be consigned to the same oblivion in which their buried predecessors have been left for all these centuries, at least as far as the speaker of this section is concerned. They too are to be "speechless exile[s]," not only cut off from their homeland but removed from time, from history, made contemporaries in death, as it were, with the "long-lost Romans," slain by the ancestors of the Germans now at war with Britain. Their very identities have been obliterated, as their nameless crosses attest. But the reference to the cross has another dimension, noteworthy even while remaining unexpressed. The opening couplet briefly notes that each flier is wrapped for burial in a British flag, and interred beneath a cross: national and religious symbols are juxtaposed here with no sense of tension between them, even though the buried and the buriers presumably have the religious symbol in common. The cross is reduced to its conventional function as a gravemarker, with no notice taken of the fact that the cross does in fact distinguish the gravesites of the airmen from those of the Romans, one difference amongst all the similarities.

The significance of this omission becomes evident in the final section of the poem, in which the speaker returns to his own voice:

> Lower, and let the bugle's noise
> Supersede the Parson's voice
> Who values at too cheap a rate
> These men as "servants of their state."
> Lower, and let the bombers' noise
> Supersede the deacon's voice:
> None but perfunctory prayers were said
> For the unquiet spirits of these dead. (ll. 19-26)

These final lines may initially seem to have wandered away from the main theme, as the comparison with the Romans is not mentioned at all. The speaker instead criticizes the parson officiating at the gravesite for identifying the dead airmen simply as "servants of their state," and ironically calls for the sound of the bugle, associated both with military funerals and with military engagements, to drown out the parson's banal superficialities; the speaker's comment that this appraisal values the men "at too cheap a rate" suggests that he at least recognizes that they have a more significant identity – that they are not simply functionaries of a political entity. Likewise he calls for the sounds of war and destruction to "Supersede" the graveside prayers of the deacon, "perfunctory" platitudes which fail to mediate any genuine encounter with God. In fact it is here that the true significance of the poem is revealed. The poem is not just about how things haven't changed over the course of two millennia, but also about how they should have changed. It is about the incongruity, indeed the scandal, of German Christians officiating at the gravesite of British Christians and not noticing any contradiction in the fact that they are fighting a war against one another. The evident irrelevance of religious affiliation on both sides makes them more like the Romans and Germans of the first century than the accident of a shared burial site. The dead airmen are finally described as "unquiet spirits," not truly laid to rest, because the deeper issues of their loyalties and identities have been left unresolved. The poem is ultimately about the failure of a conventional Christianity that has become an adjunct to national identity to advance contemporary civilization beyond the point where pagans had left it almost 2000 years earlier.[30]

* * * * * * *

"Iphigenia: Politics" (*TP* #13)[31] uses classic myth rather than ancient history to illuminate the current international situation. Iphigenia was the daughter of Agamemnon, leader of the Greek forces during the Trojan War, who was sacrificed for political expediency, to obtain favorable winds in order to sail to Troy. This destruction of innocent life becomes the paradigm for the destruction of innocence in all wars and in this war in particular. The scene of political betrayal is set in the opening section not on a beach but in a meeting room:

> The stairs lead to the room as bleak as glass
> Where fancy turns the statues.
> The empty chairs are dreaming of a protocol,
> The tables, of a treaty;
> And the world has become a museum. (ll. 1-5)

The room was apparently the scene of some past diplomatic activity, and has been preserved as it was arranged for that event. The comparison "as bleak as glass" is enigmatic at this point, but will be clarified later in the poem where the glass will be identified as mirrors and the bleakness seen as a reflection of the events that have taken place there. The main impression is one of emptiness and lifelessness: the statues may appear to be alive, but it is a mere fancy;[32] the furniture is described as "dreaming" of some political agreement, but this is just as surely a product of fancy as the turning of the statues. The reference to a museum in the final line here would seem to pertain quite aptly to the room itself, but is expanded to encompass "the world" – as though this room somehow represents the world in microcosm, its bleakness a reflection of a similar static lifelessness beyond its walls.

The three parenthetical lines that follow seem to have no connection to what has preceded. (The link will come only in lines 14 ff.) They are a précis of Euripides' drama *Iphigeneia at Aulis*,[33] in which the girl to be sacrificed to win the favor of the gods is rescued by the goddess Artemis:

(The girl is gone,
Fled from the broken altar by the beach,
From the unholy sacrifice when calms became a trade-wind.) (ll. 6-8)

The Iphigenia story is an archetypal image of war's duplicity and brutality, its willingness to destroy even one's own children for political and even economic (cf. "trade-wind") ends, in which even religion may be implicated, as the "broken altar" suggests. But in Euripides' version it is also a counter-image of hope, a claim that the girl is not dead, that the powerful fail to execute their design, that the apparent success of *realpolitik* is actually itself illusory.

But for the time being this sentence is simply a parenthetical aside. The focus returns to the "empty upper rooms" in the following verse paragraph:

The palaces stare out from their uncurtained trouble,
And windows weep in the weak sun.
The women fear the empty upper rooms
More than the streets as grey as guns
Or the swordlight of the wide unfriendly esplanade. (ll. 9-13)

The identification of the buildings as "palaces," in the plural, is suggestive: it hints at a link between past and present, between the palace of the ancient myth, the house of Agamemnon at Argos, and the building that houses the room of the opening lines, which would then also be a palace. Even though they are uninhabited, the buildings are ironically personified here as embodying the despair they project. The windows are eyes which stare and even weep, but which also reveal the "trouble" behind them, a variation on the "bleak as glass" image earlier in the poem. Amidst this emptiness it is somewhat of a surprise to encounter "the women" in line 11, the first human figures in the poem – other than the vanished girl in the previous section. Their fear of the "empty upper rooms" is not yet explained, but it outweighs the threat of the streets, described in a carefully balanced pairing of simile and metaphor, drawn from modern and ancient weaponry – the dull grimness of "streets grey as guns" and the glitter of "swordlight," both instruments of death but still considered less dangerous than the palace rooms.

The explanation that follows serves as well to link the contemporary situation to the classical myth:

> Thoughts turn to salt among those shrouded chairs
> Where, with knives no crueler than pens, or promises,
> Took place the painless slaying of the leader's daughter. (ll. 14-16)[34]

The ancient pattern is replayed in contemporary Europe, but nowadays the "unholy sacrifice," the violation of innocence for the sake of power, is likely to take place not on the beach but in an office or meeting hall, in the "empty upper rooms" that the women find so fearful. Yet the description here is filled with problematical elements. "Thoughts turn to salt" may simply indicate that sad recollections lead to tears, but with its echo of the earlier line "fancy turns the statues," it also recalls the story of Lot's wife fleeing Sodom and being turned into a statue, a pillar of salt, for looking back at the destruction: here it seems to suggest that an attempt to see clearly what has happened paralyzes thought and so should be avoided. The chairs are described as "shrouded" because they are covered with dust cloths, but the word of course also recalls the shroud covering a dead body, as well as the idea of concealing a deed, "shrouding" it in secrecy. The equation of knives with "pens, or promises" is likewise ambiguous: it can be read to say that the spoken and written word can be just as cruel, just as deadly, as actual weapons, but the phrasing ("no crueler") also lends itself to a kind of palliation or mitigation of the knife as no worse than the pen. This would correspond with the reference to the "painless slaying" of the girl in the next line, an apparent effort to make the killing sound less offensive. It becomes apparent at this point in the poem that the perspective is not consistent throughout – there is no indication here that the girl has escaped, no revulsion at an "unholy sacrifice." The effect is that of a Greek tragic chorus, perhaps composed of the women mentioned in the previous section, oscillating from one point of view to another, with one chorus member or another contributing to a "mosaic" with an associative rather than logical progression, encompassing a range of responses from horror to acquiescence, from propaganda to prophecy.

This choric effect becomes more evident in the following section, which adopts a first-person-plural voice:

> O, humbler than the truth she bowed her head,
> And scarcely seemed, to us, to die.
> But after she was killed she fled, alive, like a surprise,
> Out of the glass world, to Diana's Tauris. (ll. 17-20)

Here the girl is said to be "humbler," lowlier, less powerful, than the truth – implying that the truth is likewise lowly and powerless. The peacefulness of her death, without struggle or resistance, is emphasized, but the claim is unconvincing,[35] a state of denial, an effort to minimize the outrage (in both an objective and subjective sense). Likewise the claim that after dying "she fled, alive" is compromised by the speakers' own passive acceptance of the injustice, their acquiescence in the crime. The weak comparison "like a surprise" suggests that this is just rhetoric, and unconvincing rhetoric at that, a facile parroting of official propaganda, a refusal to think lest one be turned into salt.

This effort to mouth the "party line" cannot be sustained indefinitely however. In the following section a progressive disillusion sets in:

> Then wind cheered like a hero in the tackle of the standing
>   ships
> And hurled them bravely on the swords and lances of the
>   wintry sea –
> While wisdom turned to salt upon the broken piers. (ll. 21-23)

The first line maintains a positive, enthusiastic perspective, as the sound of the wind in the rigging suggests the warrior's shout of enthusiasm going into battle. The cheer is a response neither to the girl's death or to her putative restoration to life but to the opportunity to head into war, made possible by her sacrifice which brought favorable winds. But the following line is more ambiguous: the wind has in fact hurled them into the hostile environment of the "wintry sea," imaged as an army with weapons at the ready. Nature is depicted as hostile after the unnatural act of sacrifice. Finally the interpretation turns completely negative in the third line, which recalls both line 14 ("Thoughts turn to salt . . .") and line 7 ("broken altar"): the salt suggests the sea spray thrown against the piers by the wind, as well as salt tears and the pillar of salt – but in any case it is clear that wisdom has not accompanied the ships on their expedition. When thought turns to salt, propaganda takes its place and truth is denied; when wisdom has turned to salt, actions take place that are shortsighted and unsound. But the departure of the ships has apparently freed the chorus from the influence of the callous arbiters of political power, though not from their fear of "the empty upper rooms" first expressed back in line 11. They now chant:

> This is the way the ministers have killed the truth,
>   our daughter,
> Steps lead back into the rooms we fear to enter;
> Our minds are bleaker than the hall of mirrors:…(ll. 24-26)

The first line here seems finally to come to terms with what has happened, to recognize the fact that in war, truth is always the first casualty, truth that is not merely the "leader's daughter" but "our daughter"; the chorus seems to be acknowledging their own personal loss, their own stake in the disaster. However, it is still not clear if truth is dead, in which case they are unable to see and speak the truth, or if truth has indeed come back to life as Euripides' version of the Iphigenia myth would have it. Are they speaking the whole truth when they place the blame solely on "the ministers," or are they trying to absolve themselves of any complicity in the crime? To discover the truth, they must return to "the rooms we fear to enter," to look in the mirrors and see themselves as they actually are, to acknowledge that they too reflected to some degree the political opportunism they now distance themselves from.

The poem as a whole is not only about the way "Politics" sacrifices truth to apparent (but ultimately illusory) political advantage, but the way in which ordinary people – the "chorus" – consent to such policies when they seem advantageous, and try to dissociate themselves from those same policies when their true consequences become evident.

The reference to "the hall of mirrors" – the famous room in the Palace of Versailles where the treaty bringing World War I to an end was signed – suggests a specific (though not exclusive) application in the context of the new conflict: the French population approved the settlement of 1919, but now blame the politicians after the Fall of France, without acknowledging the elements of injustice in the original treaty that eventually contributed to Germany's declaration of war and subsequent invasion. The chorus must confront their own past by facing themselves in these mirrors and so acknowledging their own complicity; they must enter the scene of former triumph that has now become a sterile, lifeless museum. Their only path to salvation is up the stairs to confront the past and come to terms with it, to restore truth not "Out of the glass world" but within it. Any effort at avoidance is futile, since they carry around the bleakness, the emptiness and despair associated with the room, within themselves.

But the poem ends without a resolution, with a repetition of line 5: "And the world has become a museum" (l. 27). The atmosphere of the room has pervaded the entire world because it has taken over the inner world, "Our minds." The poem develops a triadic relationship between three spaces: room and world are identified in lines 1-5; lines 6-26 seek to break this relationship by interposing the mind, but the attempt fails: only by returning to the room can the room's hold on the world and on the mind be broken, but this does not happen because it requires the moral courage of an honest self-examination that is not undertaken. The poem concludes with an identification of room, mind and world: all are in the grip of bleak despair. The repeated declaration of the final line takes on apocalyptic overtones as it proleptically anticipates that the lifelessness of the Hall of Mirrors, the sterility and callous inhumanity it represents, will spread throughout the entire world as the war extends its power over physical and moral life.[36]

* * * * * * *

"The Night Train" (*TP* #6)[37] describes an imagined journey through wartime France that transposes the actual world situation into the quasi-surreal landscape of a dream. It opens with a rapid passage through what are eventually revealed to be successive phases of the war:

> In the unreason of a rainy midnight
> France blooms along the windows
> Of my sleepy bathysphere,
> And runs to seed in a luxuriance of curious lights. (ll. 1-4)

The "unreason" of the opening line seems to signal the bizarre logic of a dream, but may also suggest the fact that the actual situation of the war is irrational, representing the triumph of the Nazis' rejection of rational principles, so that the nightmarish quality of the ensuing description is only too appropriate. The train is described as "my sleepy bathysphere,"[38] a submarine craft that may initially seem to be referring simply to the rainy weather outside the train's windows, but also suggests that this journey is a descent beneath the surface of waking observation to confront a deeper level of awareness revealed through his dreaming. The immediate scene observed from the train window seems to reveal the vividness and vitality of the French spring, but within two lines the period of blooming is over and has been succeeded by the ambiguous period of "run[ning] to seed" – which could suggest seeds of future growth but commonly carries connotations of degeneration and decline. The laconic reference to "a luxuriance of curious lights" adds to the ambiguity – luxuriance suggests abundance, but also excess, and the "curious" nature of the lights implies they are somehow odd, abnormal, not simply the usual lights of cities and towns that "bloom" as the train passes through them, but unexpected, as yet unexplained illumination that at this point is only curious but that will take on an ominous meaning as the poem develops.

These opening lines make no overt reference to the current political situation, nor does the second section of the poem, though the sense of menace becomes somewhat more apparent here:

> Escape is drawn straight through my dream
> And shines to Paris, clean as a violin string,
> While spring tides of commotion,
> (The third-class pianos of the Orient Express)
> Fill up the hollow barrels of my ears. (ll. 5-9)

The journey is now discovered to be one of escape, though from whom or what remains as yet unspecified. The goal is to reach Paris, envisioned as a safe haven; the route of escape is described as "straight," "shin[ing]," and "clean as a violin string," all suggestive of the rails reflecting the light of the train's headlight as they stretch out toward the goal. Yet the possibility of escape seems compromised by the fact that forces of disorder are present on the train itself, now identified as the "Orient Express," the setting of any number of fictional intrigues: the "bathysphere" is being flooded by the rising tide of disruptive noises from the "third-class pianos" (both coming from a third-class carriage of the train and of less than superior quality), which threaten to overwhelm the calm resolve symbolized by the purity of the violin string mentioned earlier. The speaker's own inability to resist this disorder is evident from his description of his ears as "hollow barrels," empty of anything more substantial and so susceptible to being controlled by the hectic, disruptive sounds. Escape seems much more problematic at the end of this section that at its beginning, and the illusory quality of the speaker's initial hope would be particularly evident to any reader in 1941, when the poem was written, since Paris had in fact been occupied by the army of the Third Reich since June of 1940,[39] a fact of which the dreamer is apparently ignorant at this stage of his journey.

But full awareness of the war and its consequences emerges in the long central section of the poem that now follows:

> Cities that stood, by day, as gay as lancers
> Are lost, in the night, like old men dying.
> At a point where polished rails branch off forever
> The steels lament, like crazy ladies.
> We wake, and weep the deaths of the cathedrals
> That we have never seen,
> Because we hear the jugulars of the country
> Fly in the wind, and vanish with a cry.[40]   (ll. 10-17).

The true state of affairs has now become evident. The stance of courage and devil-may-care insouciance of the cities in daylight evokes a bygone era, a chivalric pose that cannot be sustained, and certainly is not sustaining. In the face of the darkness of war and of enemy ideology the cities which had appeared to be powerful defenders prove to be moribund. They shrivel up like old

men and are lost – lost to the invading enemy but also representing lost hopes, lost convictions, a loss of direction that encompasses
the speaker as well. The single straight path to Paris of the previous section proves to have been an optical illusion, for now the
tracks split, and which if any direction leads to safety has become
unclear, and as they are said to "branch off forever" the choice of
direction is definitive, irrevocable. The clean clear sound of the
violin string is replaced by the screeching of wheels against rails
like the keening of "crazy ladies," counterparts to the dying old
men which the cities have become, perhaps a reminder of women
who have lost lover or spouse or child to the horrors of war. The
harsh sound is said to "wake" the speaker, though whether from
or within the dream is unclear and perhaps immaterial. Certainly
the nightmarish succession of violent images continues and in-
creases in intensity. The deaths of the unseen cathedrals (because
passed in the darkness?) suggests the destruction of faith, or at
least of the signs of faith, a persecution in which a religious and
even cultural legacy is desecrated by a new barbarism. This causal
connection between main and subordinate clause here suggests
that destroying the cathedrals is equivalent to ripping out "the
jugulars of the country," the very lifeblood of the nation which is
carried away by the wind with a cry of anguish that echoes the
lament of the rails themselves. This grotesque image suggests that
the attack is that of a savage beast, going for the jugular, rather
than of human beings.

The remainder of the poem then turns its attention to other
passengers on the train, who are also awakened by the wild sounds:

> At once the diplomats start up, as white as bread,
> Buckle the careless cases of their minds
> That just fell open in the sleeper:…(ll. 18-20)[41]

The implication is that the diplomats have slept through their ap-
pointed time, have lost their opportunities to avert war. They too
are on the train, not in control of its movements but carried along
like everyone else, drawn inevitably to whatever destruction awaits
at the end of the journey. They are said to be "white as bread,"
pale with fear, but perhaps also, in a kind of counter-eucharistic
image, able to provide no real sustenance. Their very minds are
described as being like unsecured briefcases that have "fallen open"
in the sleeping cars (have they been talking in their sleep?) and are

now "Buckle[d]" too late, after their secrets have been exposed. They are depicted as reading the truth of their mutual fates in one another's expressions:

> For, by the rockets of imaginary sieges
> They see to read big, terrible print,
> Each in the other's face,…(ll. 21-23)

That the light by which they perceive the facts of the situation is said to be cast by "the rockets of imaginary sieges" is a puzzling declaration: why would the sieges be described as "imaginary"? The answer would seem to lie in the diplomats' complete misperception of the nature of the current war. Expecting that it would be conducted through interminable trench warfare like the 1914-1918 war, which would give them ample time to engage in various diplomatic maneuvers, they were totally unprepared for the actual blitzkrieg which bypassed the "impregnable" Maginot Line and captured Paris in a matter of weeks. The jugulars of the country have been ripped out yet they are still thinking in terms of long sieges. But if the sieges are imaginary, so must the rockets be (unlike the "curious lights" mentioned earlier which must refer to burning cities), so in fact the message they read on one another's faces must also be in their imaginations, a projection of their own fears. They have resigned themselves to their supposedly inevitable fate and play out their predetermined roles like characters in a B-movie melodrama (appropriately taking place on the Orient Express).

The tragedy of the first part of the poem has modulated into a kind of almost buffoonish cloak-and-dagger parody, as the final lines suggest. They are reading the "big, terrible print"

> That spells the undecoded names
> Of the assassins they will recognise too late:
> The ones that seem to be secret police,
> Now all in place, all armed, in the obvious ambush. (ll. 24-27)

The whole final section of the poem is a satiric depiction of the inadequacies of politicians, who project themselves as victims of inevitable forces, powerless to prevent their own doom when in fact the scenario is a product of their own imaginations – though no less true for all that, as it becomes a kind of self-fulfilling prophecy. Their passivity and inadequacy will lead to their own destruction, but what they think they see in one another's faces is really within themselves. They are responsible for their own failure to work to prevent war. They have slept when they should have been awake, and now the consequences are suffered not merely by themselves but by the entire country. They come across as totally self-absorbed and oblivious to the larger ramifications of their actions, or their failure to act. Whereas "we" wake to mourn the deaths of the cathedrals, they are totally fixated on what is to happen to themselves. This lack of a broader vision and sense of responsibility serves as evidence of why diplomatic efforts to avert war were unsuccessful. Because of their failure of vision and failure of imagination, they have doomed not merely themselves but the country. Whether they will actually be assassinated by the secret police or whether this is simply a figment of their overheated imaginations, they have failed to prevent a catastrophe that extends far beyond the outcome of their own individual dramas.

* * * * * * *

The French setting of the previous two poems continues in "Dirge for a Town in France" (*MDS* #25),[42] which takes an elegiac approach to the war, and probably incorporates reminiscences from Merton's own memories of his early years in southern France. It might initially seem that this poem has no connection with the war, which is never explicitly mentioned, but to write a poem with this title in 1941 unrelated to the crisis France was enduring would be as unlikely as writing a poem entitled "Dirge for a Town in Iraq" in 2006 that is not concerned with the current situation there.

The opening section of the poem presents an interesting pattern:

> Up among the stucco pears, the iron vines,
> Mute as their watered roses, their mimosas,
> The wives gaze down among the traceries
> Of balconies: the one-time finery
> Of iron, suburban balconies. (ll. 1-5)

The human figures of the wives in the central line are surrounded on both sides by two lines of description: they are embedded in their environment, removed from contact with the street below. The opening pair of lines contrast the elaborate artificiality of the house décor, the "stucco pears" and "iron vines" of line 1, which have the appearance of organic growth and vitality, but only the appearance, with the actual living, cared-for ("watered") flowers of line 2. Yet the point of contact between plants and people is their shared muteness: the "wives" are also alive, vital amid the faux vegetation that surrounds them, but they are unable to communicate that vitality – domesticated, like their flowers, kept isolated and apart on their once elegant but now increasingly shabby balconies. The scene has a static quality as the women "gaze" with a fixed stare at some unspecified object, "down" at the street from which they are removed. No overt destruction is depicted, but rather a certain impression of sterility is conveyed that suggests limited resources to resist forces of disorder. Even the repeated references to "iron," usually connoting firmness and strength, here seem more constricting then protective.

The following section, likewise five lines, provides a contrasting description:

> Down in the shadowy doors,
> Men fold their arms,
> And hearken after the departing day
> That somewhere sings more softly
> Than merry-go-rounds in distant fairs. (ll. 6-10)

The scene shifts to the street below and the focus from "the wives" to "Men" (not defined by their domestic relationships), who are less enclosed by their surroundings, but also stand in isolation, half-hidden in the doorways, in neither domestic nor public space, with folded arms that suggest inactivity, perhaps even a sense of withdrawal from action and a resignation to the present situation. But whereas no indication of the women's inner lives was provided (as yet), the men "hearken after the departing day" as though hoping for some message, some revelatory insight. There is a tension between "hearken," which is usually associated with a newly present source of information, and "departing," which suggests the information is soon to be no longer available, a sense reinforced by the phrasing "hearken after" rather than the more usual "hearken to." What is departing is both the light of day, source of illumination, and the faint sounds of music with which it is identified, barely perceptible music that emphasizes the difference between here and "somewhere" else, with no indication of where that "somewhere" might be. The sound is compared to that of "merry-go-rounds in distant fairs": the initial basis for the comparison is quantitative, the degree of sound volume, but the focus will shift to the vehicle of the comparison itself, the carousel which is the image of childish innocence and joy, and the fair that is the occasion of celebration, of community festivity. The analogy is an attractive one, implicitly contrasted to the evident grimness of the present, but it is more equivocal than it initially appears: certainly "softly" is not a descriptor that would be appropriate to carousel music up close, where it would sound loud and rather garish. This incongruity raises the question whether the distance, in time as well as space, has the effect of romanticizing the music, whether the longing for a bygone era, nostalgia for childhood innocence, leads to a distorted perception.

This question hovers unarticulated in the background of the brief section that follows, two pairs of parallel lines that focus on natural phenomena that do not prompt the music, or the recollection:

> O, it is not those first, faint stars
> Whose fair light, falling, whispers in the river;
> And it is not the dusty wind,
> Waving the waterskirts of the shy-talking fountain, …(ll. 11-14)

These are the most lyric, "musical" lines of the poem, with the alliteration of "first," "faint," "fair," "falling," "fountain" and of "whispers," "wind," "Waving" and "waterskirts," as well as the assonance of "whispers" and "river" and the movement from monosyllables to trochaic disyllables (associated with the "falling" light) to trisyllabic dactyls (associated with the movement of the water in the fountain). But this music is explicitly distinguished from the sounds of the carousel: the "*fair* light" of the stars recalls, yet is specifically dissociated from, the "distant *fairs*" that the men "hearken after." The earlier synaesthesia of light and sound is gently reprised here in the "whispers" of starlight in the river, the reflection of celestial light, with its own quiet message, that goes unnoticed in the men's concentration on discerning some revelation from what is distant and disappearing. Likewise when the "dusty wind" causes the spray of the fountain, in a particularly effective image, to undulate like skirts, and is itself presumably purified by its contact with the water, the fountain is described as "shy-talking," also communicating a disregarded message in the quiet sound of the water falling back into its basin.

The first line of the following verse paragraph completes the meaning of lines 11-14, and if joined with them would preserve the five-line stanzaic structure, but its removal to the following section reflects the separation of the starlight and fountain and their "music" from that of the carousel:

That wakes the wooden horses' orchestra,
The fifing goldfinch, and the phony flute,
And the steam robins and electric nightingales
That blurred the ding of cymbals,
That other time, when childhood turned and turned
As grave as sculpture in a zodiac. (ll. 15-20)

The main emphasis here is on the "unnatural" elements of the music of the carousel: the "phony flute" is the most obvious "false note" here, but all the birds are artificial and the songs are mechanical. Like the "stucco pears" and "iron vines" of the opening line, they are simulacra, imitations of genuine life, as are the "wooden horses."[43] The music is not truly revelatory, not to be depended on; consequently the "hearkening" of the men is misdirected, no solution to their present situation. Previously, the sound of the merry-go-round had "blurred the ding of cymbals," perhaps coming from a nearby band shell, but associated with military music, so that obscuring the sounds of clashing cymbals could be taken to represent a failure to attend to a more aggressive music with its suggestions of approaching conflict, a failure of perception being "echoed" by a preoccupation with the same source of sound now, a culpable failure in the name of an ersatz innocence to recognize artifice and to become aware of more ominous background sounds which its music "blurred."

The specification of "That other time" sounds vague and prosaic, but actually does refer to a different, contrasting period, a time before the present death-in-life has become apparent, a time of (illusory) carefree existence. Yet even then the children on the merry-go-round appear anything but merry themselves. The individual children are assimilated into the personified abstraction of "childhood" and are described as "grave" – not only serious, but suggesting the demeanor of the tomb. The revolving of the carousel is compared to the revolution of the constellations, the cyclic pattern which elsewhere in Merton's verse serves as an image of order and cosmic harmony, but here the "zodiac" suggests a kind of futility, a return to the starting point, a fatalistic, determinist attitude very different from the impression made by the stars reflected in the river in the previous section. The sculpture, images from pagan mythology that remain static and lifeless even while moving, convey an impression of ominousness rather than of innocent joy, wonder and vitality: the façade of celebration, of festivity masks a kind of hopelessness.

The artificiality characteristic of the remembered fair of the past is even more evident in the town of the present, to which the speaker now returns:

> And yet the mystery comes on
> Spontaneous as the street-lights, in the plane trees:
> The trees, whose paint falls off in flakes,
> Elaborate as the arches
> Of a deserted opera! (ll. 21-25)

The "mystery" of these recollections that arrive at dusk is compared to the street-lights which seem to come on automatically, with no human intervention, but this is of course an illusion – they are pre-set, far from "Spontaneous." In fact, as the last three lines of this segment graphically indicate, the whole scene is comparable to an elaborate stage set in which the trees are reduced to props, and dilapidated ones at that, forming a canopy or archway over a stage. The nostalgic "song" of the departing day is ultimately as empty of reality as the faded grandiosity of a deserted opera house, once filled with theatrical, hyper-emotional music. The implication is that the whole recollection of the fair and its carousel is a self-indulgent, self-deceptive construct, a hearkening back to a supposed time of innocence that never really existed, at least in the form given it by these memories. It is a comforting evasion of present responsibility by indulgence in cheap nostalgia for an imaginary idyllic paradise, a retreat into "tradition" that does not empower or inspire responsible action now. It is of a piece with the gesture of the folded arms and the loitering in the shadowy doorways.

As the poem begins to draw to its conclusion, the figures and images of the opening lines recur, in the same order, responding to the arrival of the night:

> The roses and mimosas in the windows
> Adore the night they breathe, not understanding;
> The women dream of bread and chocolate

In their aquariums
Of traceries, and lace, and cherubim; . . . (ll. 26-30)

Whereas the wives and the flowers were initially aligned with one another, here their responses diverge. The flowers show a genuine spontaneity (unlike the street-lamps) and acceptance, a natural alternative, with supernatural overtones, to the inadequate human attitudes. The darkness is not feared or shunned but accepted and worshipped. The flowers and the night air form an interconnected whole. Initially the connotations of "not understanding" might seem to be negative, a failure to recognize that the present situation is not "adorable"; but the workings of a discriminating mind, an analytic approach to reality, are not necessarily a plus. There is no need on the part of flowers to "understand" – they act appropriately without having to think. Their intuitive, holistic, synthetic approach, an apophatic inspiration – in-breathing – of the night, is more authentic and more life-giving than a reductive rationalism could ever be. The women, on the other hand, "dream" of a return to normalcy, to everyday, ordinary life as it used to be, symbolized by food: bread and chocolate, necessity and modest luxury. The evident lack of these items is the first indication, still oblique but clear enough, that a wartime situation is being described. They are described as being in "aquariums," an image of enclosure and containment, which makes it impossible for them to "breathe" the night as the flowers do. The framework of the aquariums is made of traceries (repeated from line 3), lace (evidently the intricacy of the ironwork on the balconies) and cherubim – apparently further decorative adornment on the houses, plasterwork putti, artificial angels to go with the artificial fruit mentioned earlier. But cherubim are the angelic order associated most specifically with the adoration of God, so that the genuine adoration of the flowers is juxtaposed with artificial images of adoration. Thus the women are isolated from authentic, life-giving interchange with their world, able neither to breathe nor to adore.

The third and final response to the night's arrival is described in the final verse paragraph:

But the men die, down in the shadowy doors,
The way their thoughts die in their eyes,
To see those sad and funny children
Run down the colonnade of trees

Where the carnival doesn't exist:
Those children, who are lost too soon,
With fading laughter, on the road along the river:
Gone, like the slowing cavalcade, the homeward horses. (ll. 31-38)

It is unclear whether the reference to the men's deaths is intended to be taken literally – there is no indication of fighting, and they are still located in the same doorways, so they may have simply given up, surrendered to despair and resigned themselves to death. This reading is supported by the link with "The way their thoughts die" – the light in their eyes is extinguished not by sudden violence but by the loss of something to live for. This "death" is said to be caused by a vision of the children looking for the phantom carnival, presumably not actual children in the present but their own younger selves, their memories of themselves. They are letting go of the comforting fantasies of their own past embodied in the fair and the carousel – the effort to grasp at a sustaining vision is finally seen to be futile, and they have nothing it put in its place. The children are perceived as sad because they are pursuing an illusion, and funny because they are not yet aware of the gap between anticipation and result; they will discover nothing at the end of the colonnade of trees, already described as a stage set with flaking paint. They are "lost too soon" because their innocence, the capacity of children to experience communion with creation, to develop a revelatory awareness, is frustrated by the adult world. Their laughter is "fading" into the distance, but also fading away to be replaced by the attitude "grave as sculpture" described earlier. Ironically they are running "along the river," where the first stars whisper, an alternative source of meaning, but one they are apparently oblivious to in their preoccupation with reaching the carnival, an inadequate "liturgy" that cannot meet their deepest yearnings. In the final line, the "slowing cavalcade" suggests that the merry-go-round is coming to a stop and the horses are heading "home," not into the town but away from it, receding into the distance with the entire ephemeral vision they represented.

The question remains: what does all this have to do with World War II? What is obliquely suggested is that the foundations on which the town and its inhabitants built their identity, symbolized by the fair and its carousel, were inadequate to sustain them when the time of crisis arrived: the women dream of normalcy while the men despair at the loss of the vision that proved to be no more than a fantasy. The apparently joyful and carefree music of the past is replaced by, or transformed into, a dirge, a funeral song. Since there is no mention in the poem of occupying troops, the town in question is probably in Vichy France, the puppet regime established by the Germans in the south, where Merton himself had lived. Thus the focus on the town's memories may be intended more specifically to parallel Vichy's appeal to past tradition as its sustaining force, a nostalgia for past glories as inadequate as the yearning for "distant fairs," which likewise have disappeared and were insubstantial to begin with.[44] The poem critiques a false appeal to past innocence that is no substitute for a mature willingness to endure the testing of the present situation. It is finally a portrait of the superficiality of the town's moral and spiritual resources as revealed by the crisis of war and military defeat.

* * * * * * *

In the piece simply entitled "Poem"[45] and beginning "Light plays like a radio . . ." (*EP* #5),[46] perhaps Merton's most bleak and apparently hopeless war poem, natural images usually symbolic of a sacramental vision are co-opted by and identified with forces of disintegration and destruction, with no countermovement, no promise of eventual reversal and restoration. Except for a single parenthetical line, the poem could be read simply as a description of a particularly violent storm, but it is actually a grim fantasia on the etymology of *blitzkrieg*, in which invasion of the German army is imaged as a seemingly irresistible force of nature, obliterating all before it. But a careful reading of the poem makes clear that the despairing perspective of the poem is not to be identified as Merton's own but as that of the poem's morally compromised speaker.

The opening lines provide an ominous prelude to the storm's arrival:

> Light plays like a radio in the iron tree;
> Green farms fear the night behind me
> Where lightnings race across the western world. (ll. 1-3)[47]

The enigmatic simile of the first line is perhaps best interpreted as a variation of the synaesthetic linking of light and sound in "Dirge for a Town in France." Here light, which in a religious context is traditionally identified with spiritual illumination, even with the divine Logos (see John 1:1-9), is likened to a mechanical instrument for providing information, but not revelation.[48]   Likewise the "iron tree" in which the light plays is a profoundly ambiguous image: it is unclear if "tree" is to be taken literally and "iron" figuratively, or whether it refers to an iron structure (a radio tower, perhaps?) that resembles a tree. Iron is a symbol of strength, but as with the "iron vines" in "Dirge" it seems to exclude actual life and the capacity for growth. It may be a deceptive image of power and security, particularly when it is recalled that lightning is attracted to iron. It seems to contrast with the "Green farms" of the following line, representing fertility and vitality, but personified as threatened by the approach of night with its lightning storms. While there is nothing in these lines that definitely indicates the storm is to be interpreted allegorically, the description of the "lightnings rac[ing] across the western world" carries at least a suggestion of something more portentous than a simple, even if severe, meteorological event. We also note that the speaker is positioned in the midst of the landscape, between the green farms and the approaching darkness. He is not a detached, omniscient observer but a participant in the unfolding drama, a fact that will increase in significance as the poem develops.

The non-realistic dimension of the description becomes more apparent in the second verse paragraph:

> Life, like a woman in the moving wheat,
> Runs from the staring sky
> That bends upon the earth like a reflector. (ll. 4-6)

The allegorical figure of Life[49] is depicted as trying to evade detection by "the staring sky," a hostile, threatening image. Wheat frequently carries sacramental, eucharistic connotations in Merton's poetry, but here seems to offer no shelter or protection. The image of the sky "That bends upon the earth like a reflector" suggests low-hanging storm clouds completely enclosing the earth, a claustrophobic image of an impenetrable barrier blocking access to the heavens beyond it. On a more symbolic level it hints that the sky and its attendant phenomena are a reflection of what is happening on the earth itself, that the weather is a symbolic representation of earthly events – which proves to be precisely the meaning assigned to the storm in the next section of the poem:

The last column of sun
Is enfiladed in the battle-colored woods.
Rain fills the valley with a noise of tractors,
(For the tanks are come), ... (ll. 7-10)

In the first three lines here the weather is being described in terms of war, but in the fourth, the only "literal" statement in the entire poem, it is evident that in fact the reverse is the case. The setting sun is envisioned as in full retreat like a thin column of troops spread out across the entire horizon of woods, "battle-colored" either from the gunsmoke gray of the twilight or the bloody red of the sunset, or both. The imagery then shifts incongruously from military to agricultural as the sound of the rain is likened to that of tractors, suggesting that the heavy downfall is leveling the wheat stalks. But it is at this point that the veil of natural imagery is momentarily pulled aside and the actual situation is briefly indicated: the sound is not in fact that of heavy rain nor of tractors but of tanks. What is being described is not simply the arrival of a thunderstorm, a natural event, but of an army of "storm troopers," of "lightning war," a most unnatural event. This sudden, startling shift of perspective comes as a shock to the reader who had up to this point assumed that an actual storm was being described. The effect of using this figurative language to describe a military invasion is deeply problematic: is it meant to imply that the war is just as inevitable, just as much a force of nature as a storm itself, that it can no more be evaded or resisted than severe weather? What implications does this analogy carry, and what does its use reveal about the speaker and his own attitude toward what is taking place? These are issues that will become more urgent as the poem continues.

The consequences of the "storm" are evident in the next verse paragraph:

Until the land lies murdered in my naked windows
And the whole horizon's compass
Thrashes with the winds, like harvesters
Pulling down my million acre prairie. (ll. 11-14)

Here what would be metaphorical in the figurative frame, the "murder" of the land by the storm, is a factual description in the literal frame, the invasion of tanks and troops. Wherever one looks, in any direction, there is total devastation; not a single field but the entire land has undergone this bitter, destructive harvest. The speaker here emerges as a kind of collective personality, not a particular individual but the embodiment of the entire populace to whom the "million acre prairie" belongs. His "naked windows," on the figurative plane perhaps referring to shutters being ripped away by the force of the storm, suggests on the literal level that he is forced to confront the full dimensions of the catastrophe.

In the following section, he emerges from shelter to view the effects of the storm:

> At last, when restless doors fall still,
> And let me out to trample the wet light,
> I breathe in anguish
> Cold and hunger on the watersmelling sky. (ll. 15-18)

Light has returned, but it is now "wet light," prostrate, vanquished, trodden underfoot even by the speaker. The aftereffects of the storm are described both as interior anguish – mental and spiritual destitution – and exterior deprivation: cold and hunger. But all are "breathe[d] in": the very air itself has been affected, and the "watersmelling sky" still perceives the consequences of the storm and senses that the severe weather could reactivate itself on short notice should the occasion arise. Here is the natural analogy to military occupation: the storm has completed its work but ongoing oppressive conditions now dominate the land. The speaker's response is to dig in the earth – not for planting and sowing of seeds but for burial:

> Earth turns up with a dark flash, where my spade
> Digs the lovely stranger's grave;
> And poppies show like blood.
> The woman I saw fleeing through the bended wheat:
> I know I'll find her dead. (ll. 19-23)[50]

The "dark flash" from the ground, the glint of light reflected from the spade, or a spark where it strikes rock, is an echo of the lightning in the darkness of the night before – not evidence of vitality, not genuine light. The flowers, which should be signs of life, are imaged as the blood the earth itself has shed. This is the context for the speaker's act of digging the grave for the "lovely stranger," the personification of Life seen running through the wheat earlier in the poem. But the speaker's behavior here is in fact quite strange.

He digs the grave first, then goes to look for the woman. This is not the normal sequence of activity. The speaker had remained a passive observer up until this point, had made no effort to shelter the "stranger" at the time of crisis, and now digs the grave before finding a body. Does this say something about the speaker's attitude and character? Is there a kind of acquiescence in what has happened, a presumption of irreversible defeat? Is the fact that "Life" was a stranger to him part of the problem here? The very awkwardness of the syntax in the final two lines seems to reflect an uneasy attempt to justify his action (and lack of action) – first the identification, grammatically suspended, then the complete sentence, which is not simply a factual statement but a claim based on no concrete evidence. It is as though he is being questioned about his premature action of grave-digging, and responds by defending himself with an unsubstantiated assurance. He finally appears as spokesman for a kind of defeatist mentality that presumes the worst and acts on this presumption.

The conclusion of the poem casts doubt on the reliability of the description that preceded it – the presentation of the invasion as storm makes it appear to be an inevitable and irresistible force of nature, but it is the outcome that makes it advantageous and self-justifying to regard it as such, since there is no way to deal with a storm but to let it happen. The poem is finally less about the enemy than about the speaker and his perceptions, his justification for his own impotence and ineffectiveness. The storm imagery is evidence of a failure of imagination, an acquiescence to the rhetorical framework of the enemy. The poem is deeply disturbing not just because of the invasion but because of the response to and interpretation of the invasion. It can be considered as Merton's reflection on the predominant French reaction to the Fall of France: we "know" that Life itself has died, and all that's left for us to do is to dig the grave and bury her. All vestiges of hope have been abandoned. It is a victory not just of German arms but more profoundly of the German "vision," the force of blitzkrieg "rac[ing] across the western world."

* * * * * * *

"The Pride of the Dead" (*MDS* #17)[51] begins with a kind of oblique presentation of the *"sic transit gloria mundi"* topos: powerful leaders and warriors of the past now appear as pathetic, insubstantial shadows of their former selves:

> The doors are down before the ancient tombs
> And wind dies in the empty gate.
> The paper souls of famous generals
> Complain, as dry as leaves, among the stones of Thebes. (ll. 1-4)

The setting is identified as the famously fought-over seven-gated city of Oedipus,[52] contested by his sons Eteocles and Polyneices, as related in Sophocles' *Antigone* and elsewhere. The greatest heroes of the generation preceding the Trojan War, the "Seven against Thebes," fought there, but the specifics are not emphasized in this poem: the city is presented more as a representative of antique fame, now gone. The celebrated gateways that in their day would have been closely guarded to protect the city's wealth are now "empty" – with no glory and wealth to protect. Likewise the doors of the tombs have fallen open and allow the wraiths of the ancient heroes to emerge in the hushed stillness of the windless day. Theirs are "paper souls," two-dimensional, insubstantial shadows of their former selves: worldly power and reputation were not equivalent to spiritual maturation, and even their complaints are now as nearly imperceptible as the rustling of dry leaves.

The open doors of the tombs permit a glance at the gravesites within:

> The jars of gravel that was one time corn,
> The wineskins that the mourners left them,
> They know will all be dry forever,
> These tired emperors, stitched up for good,
> As black as leather. (ll. 5-9)

The provisions left in the tombs have long since disappeared, and the bodies have likewise dried up and turned "black as leather." The dead are here described not just as "generals" but as "emperors," presumably having become rulers through successful military conquest, but they are "tired" emperors, worn out by their labors but unlikely to be refreshed by this sleep. Up to this point in the poem, then, the focus is on the ultimate emptiness and insignificance of past military and imperial glory, which cannot be sustained by grain or wine or any other material substance.

The thematic switch in the longer central section of the poem comes as a surprise, then. Their obsolescence has suggested no relevance or relatedness between these dead figures and contemporary people or situations, but now a representative "emperor" figure, no longer just complaining but commanding, orders that they be recalled by the playing of a dirge:

> So we are startled by the leaf-speech of some skinny Alexander:
> "Strike from the harpstrings of the rain
> Bars of a dirge.
> Pacify the ancient dead
> For fear they be allowed to love the thin, salt smell of life,
> And drift across the rims of graves
> Like smoke across a crater,
> And loiter in your windless squares,
> And scare the living, hiding in the rubble of the ruined
>   treasuries." (ll. 10-18)

The demand is not for a literal musical performance, since it is to be played on "the harpstrings of the rain," but rather to be remembered and honored, not dismissed as of no present significance. The Alexander figure calls not for a paean or an ode, a commemoration of their mighty deeds, but for a dirge, a song of mourning that could "Pacify the ancient dead," allow them to find rest and peace. The alternative is that they will be drawn to "the thin, salt smell of life," perhaps a metonymy for sweat, or blood, trying to find sustenance from what is still alive. They would emerge from their graves like smoke from a volcano, perhaps a harbinger of more violent eruptions still to come, to "loiter in your windless squares," a description recalling the dying wind in the gates of Thebes. Suddenly there is a point of similarity, rather than of contrast, that is confirmed by the description of the people in the following line, "hiding in the rubble of the ruined treasuries." The present is now revealed as a time of war, of destruction; the phrase "ruined treasuries" perhaps recalls the so-called Mycenaean treasury discovered by Schliemann, one of the great archeological finds of the ancient Greek world, but here refers to its contemporary equivalent, modern bank buildings[53] now reduced to rubble comparable to the stones of ruined Thebes. Thus the singing of a dirge for the conquerors of the past becomes a way of reminding oneself that the current conflict is part of a long pattern of violence and inhumanity; it becomes a mourning song not only for the past but for the present, a warning, an object lesson of the insubstantiality of human ambition.

In the final section of the poem, the single voice swells into a chorus:

> The paper souls of emperors,
> Frisk on the stones as sharp as leaves, and sing:
> "Draw back upon our night some windless morning,
> And hang it like a shroud upon your burning country,
> And strike us, from the tinny harpstrings of the rain
> Bars of a dirge." (ll. 19-24)

The first two lines here are a restatement of lines 3-4, but now the paper souls sing rather than complain: a kind of jauntiness, a grotesque playfulness has emerged. They call upon their modern listeners to pull back the morning like a curtain to reveal the night behind it, to face the darkness that is the true state of affairs that must be recognized and accepted. The windless morning can then be transformed from a curtain into a shroud, its white light no longer a sign of life and hope but useful only as a symbol of death, now the death of "your burning country," sharing the fate of Troy and other sacked cities. The recurrence of the command for a dirge to conclude the poem now becomes a call for a mourning song for the destroyed country of the present rather than the dead of the past – or rather the two are united. The dirge is no longer a way to keep the dead pacified but to recognize the triumph of the dead, of death itself. The dead return to walk the earth because their "way," the way of power through destruction, has returned to the earth. They are familiar with what is happening, so they belong on the scene. The "pride" of the dead at first seems to refer to their demand for attention, a desire to be commemorated, not left in oblivion, but by the end of the poem it seems to suggest that they take satisfaction in having no illusions: they see the actual state of affairs, the darkness that is true reality. Yet as "paper souls" their viewpoint is necessarily two-dimensional, lacking any depth; their claim that the "windless morning" is only a façade, surface drapery to be pulled away, is in fact a temptation to despair, to accept as normative the world of "our night," a world of destruction and war in which only the dead could take pride.

* * * * * * *

At 79 lines more than double the length of any of the other war poems, "The Bombarded City" (*MDS* #18)[54] is also the only poem of this group that explicitly mentions the effects of war in its title.[55]

But the content of the poem itself is far from the realistic description that the reader might be led to expect. It is rather a quasi-surreal phantasmagoria of shifting images in which the obliterated city is imagined as a kind of ghost town, a place of taboo which is to be left uninhabited. The voice of the poem is monitory, issuing repeated warnings to avoid the site, though the reason behind the warning only becomes evident in the later sections of the poem.

The opening verse paragraph makes immediately clear that what is being depicted is not a realistic cityscape but a symbolic transmutation of the scene into a psychic terrain:

> Now let no man abide
> In the lunar wood
> The place of blood.
> Let no man abide here,
> Not even in a dream,
> Not in the lunar forest of this undersea. (ll. 1-6)

The rhythms of the warning have a kind of hypnotic power, with their slant rhymes concluding the first three lines, the variant of the first line in the fourth (with only the reference to space at the end of the line 4 replacing the reference to time at the beginning of line 1), and the repetition of "Not" to open the last two lines. Obviously the same site cannot simultaneously be "lunar," "wood" and "undersea" – especially when it is a city that is ostensibly being described. The "logic" of the poem, as with others in the group, is that of a nightmare. Yet each of the terms has its own appropriateness: the craters of the bombed city might well recall the pocked surface of the moon, and the devastation suggests the acts of a madman, in the grip of lunacy. The forest represents a pre-civilized, even pre-human world from which cities emerged over the course of history, and back toward which the world at war seems to be tending; as "the place of blood" the wood is associated with elemental savagery, of beasts or of pagan rites like those of the druids. Finally it has been, as it were, submerged totally in violence, inundated by death, a shipwreck which has apparently left no survivors.[56]

The speaker expresses a kind of primal terror, a sense of the uncanny, from which no one is exempt:

> Oh you who can a living shadow show
> Grieving in the broken street,
> Fear, fear the drowners,
> Fear the dead!
> But if you swagger like the warring Leader
> Fear far more
> What curse rides down the starlit air,
> Curse of the little children killed!
> Curse of the little children killed! (ll. 7-15)[57]

There seems to be a kind of atavistic "survivor's guilt" at work here, in which the very fact of being alive in a place that death pervades makes one an intruder, a profaner trespassing on sacred, forbidden ground. Even to walk the streets grieving does not exempt one from the fear, not of death, but of the dead – the guilt of being alive when others no less deserving of life have been deprived of theirs. The experience is one of being haunted by the dead, by the memory of the dead. But what the consequences of this haunting actually are, and how this relates to the speaker's urgent command to leave the place, is as yet unclear. Of course those who were actually responsible for these deaths, for the killing even of innocent children, should be more fearful in proportion as their guilt is greater, but the working out of the "curse" remains mysterious. The speaker then repeats lines slightly revised from the opening section as a kind of refrain: "Then let no living man, or dead, abide / In this lunar wood, / No, not even in a dream" (ll. 16-18). The added specification of "no living man, or dead" is odd here, unless the two categories correspond to the two groups addressed in the previous section, and "dead" refers not to physical death but to the kind of moral deadness that characterizes the swaggering followers of the "warring Leader" who call down upon themselves the curses of the dead children.

The physical description of the ruined houses maintains the surreal tone of the previous lines:

> For when the houses lean along the night
> Like broken tombs,
> And shout, with silent windows,
> Naked and windy as the mouths of masks,
> They still pour down
> (As conch-shells, from their curling sleep, the sea)
> The air raid's perished roar. (ll. 19-25)

The parenthetical comparison here bears a complex relationship to the rest of the verse paragraph: it makes clear the basic point, that the "perished roar" of the air raid can be "heard" echoing from the houses in the same way that the sea can be "heard" in a shell; but there is a delicate beauty in the interposed line, in which the double alliteration of "conch-shells" and "curling sleep" and the final assonance of "sleep" and "sea" is the antithesis of the alliteration and rhyme of "pour" with "perished roar"; and yet the juxtaposition of the sound of the bombardment and the sound of the sea reinforces the earlier references to "this undersea" and its "drowners."

The passerby is warned once again not to linger, in fact not to pay attention to this impression:

> But do not look aside at what you hear.
> Fear where you tread,
> And be aware of danger growing like a nightshade
> Through the openings of the stone.
> But mostly fear the forum,
> Where, in the midst, an arch and pediment,
> Space out, in honor of the guilty Warlord,
> A starlit area
> Much like the white geometry of peace: … (ll. 26-34)

Again the effect is carried largely by the repetition of sound, the repetition in successive lines of "hear," "Fear," "where," "aware"; of "growing," "openings," "stone"; the consonance of "fear" and "forum"; the seductive but specious attraction of the regular iambic pentameter line that closes the section. Here there is a glimmering of what is to be feared in the ruins of the destroyed city. The journey to the center of the city, to the forum, is a journey to a monument, which cannot be that of the Leader who has attacked this place, but must be of some previous ruler of the city itself, who had made some conquest of his own commemorated on this triumphal arch.[58]   There is thus a suggestion of a cycle of violence, of a perpetuating of the killing in which each generation finds its justification in the atrocities of the enemies of a previous generation. What is to be feared from the dead, then, is the summons to avenge their deaths, to do to others what they have done to you. This space around the monument resembles "the white geometry of peace," but it is a peace of the victor, a peace of conquest and capitulation, a peace that lasts only until the subjugated have re-gathered their strength enough to renew the conflict. This is the danger growing through the stones like the poisonous nightshade; it is the appeal of the forum, the recollection of past glory confronted with present devastation, that is most to be feared, the seductive appeal of a "peace" whose terms are dictated by one's own side.

The long section that follows declares that even after the enemy leader is dead the "claims" of the dead will still not be satisfied:

> O dread that silent place!
> For even when field flowers shall spring
> Out of the Leader's lips, and open eyes,
> And even while the quiet root
> Shall ravel his murdering brain,
> Let no one, even on that holiday,
> Forget the never-sleeping curse.
> And even when the grass grows in his groin,
> And golden-rod works in his rib,
> And in his teeth the ragweed grins,
> As furious as ambition's diligence:
> And when, in wind,
> His greedy belly waves, kneedeep in weeds,
> O dread the childish voices even then,
> Still scratching near him like a leaf,
> And fear the following feet
> That are laid down like little blades,
> Nor face the curses of the innocent
> That mew behind you like a silver hinge. (ll. 35-53)

This description of the Leader's ultimate capitulation to nature[59] is filled with verbal music, such as the alliteration of "grass grows . . . groin," or the combined alliteration and assonance of "when, in wind, / His greedy belly waves, kneedeep in weeds." It is reassurance that a conqueror's triumph is never permanent, that "all flesh is grass" (Is. 40:6), that "all is vanity" (Eccl. 1:2). But even this is not enough to satisfy the "curses of the innocent," the obsessive call to avenge the death of innocents by the death of other innocents.

As the following section suggests, such an attitude cannot bring genuine peace but only a dream of peace, the illusion of peace:

> For even in the dream of peace
> All men will flee the weedy street,
> The forum fallen down,
> The cursed arenas full of blood,
> Hearing the wind creep in the crannied stone:
> Oh, no man can remain,
> Hearing those souls weep in the hollow ruin. (ll. 54-60)

This section seems to look into the future, after another round of violence has destroyed the forum and filled the arenas with blood and yet not brought peace and rest to the dead. The bombarded city has become a necropolis, a city of the dead, a city haunted by death, controlled by death, demanding a death for a death:

> For there no life is possible,
> Because the eyes of soldiers, blind, destroyed,
> Lurk like Medusas of despair,
> Lay for the living in the lunar door,
> Ready to stare outside
> And freeze the little leaping nerves
> Behind the emperor's sight. (ll. 61-67)

The blind stares of the soldiers paralyze the emperor's[60] ability to see clearly, to base policy on something other than the vindicating the honor of his own troops. Likewise the voices of the dead children have a similar effect:

> And there no life is possible
> Because a weeping childvoice, thin
> Unbodied as the sky,
> Rings like an echo in the empty window:
> And thence its sound
> Flies out to feel, with fingers sharp as scalpels,
> The little bones inside the politician's ear. (ll. 68-74)

The parallelism between these two culminating verse paragraphs makes the theme of the poem clear. Whether it be an emperor's obligation to his maimed troops or a politician's[61] responsibility to his country's dead children, the rationalization is the same: a justification, when justification is required or desired, for taking vengeance in the name of justice. The poem ends where it began, with the same warning, but now the reasons for that originally enigmatic warning have become evident. Even in the early days of the war, Merton, much like Simone Weil in her essay on the *Iliad* that he would read many years later,[62] had the wisdom to challenge the prevailing notion that suffering death can serve as a justification for inflicting death.

> Oh let no man abide
> In the lunar wood,
> The place of blood.
> Let no man abide there, no,
> Not even in a dream. (ll. 75-79)

* * * * * * *

"Lent in a Year of War," the opening poem of *Thirty Poems*,[63] puts war in an eschatological context. It begins with brief character sketches of its two contrasted but ultimately allied figures. The first is the authority figure, whose identity consists of empty external show:

> One of you is a major, made of cord and catskin,
> But never dreams his eyes may come to life and thread
> The needle light of famine in a waterglass. (ll. 1-3)[64]

The major is a figure of blustering self-importance without substance, Merton's version of the "hollow man" of T.S. Eliot's poem.[65] He is not merely clothed in but "made of" cord and catskin – the cord presumably suggestive of military braid but also used to tie together a stuffed figure like the Guy Fawkes effigy in "The Hollow Men," while "catskin," derived in one of its meanings from the "quatreskin," four rows of ermine used to trim the finery of British aristocrats, might also bring to mind a cat whose nine lives are all spent, so that only the skin remains, an outward façade bereft of inner vitality. He is utterly oblivious to the possibility of moving beyond the death-in-life of his present state, in particular the possibility of regaining the capacity to perceive reality. Merton's evocative and extraordinarily compact image of the "needle-light" can be understood in two complementary ways: the light seems to be identified both with the thread which passes through the needle's eye and with the needle itself. Thus to "thread the needle-light of famine" would be to see clearly enough to allow light to be passed through a needle's eye, a reminder of the verse in the Gospel associating the passage of the camel through a needle's eye with a rich man's salvation (Mk. 10:25),[66] the light in this case being the light "of famine," a recognition of the suffering of innocent victims of war, an awareness that is a necessary preliminary to passing through the needle's eye himself, renouncing his privileged status and identifying with the starvation endured by those displaced by the war. But this same light would then penetrate his own eye as well, enlightening him to the truth of others' pain, and so function as a "needle-light," a sharp, piercing, painful wounding that would also heal. Such a transformation is made available "in a water-glass," an image of the Lenten fast, which has the power to renew life and vision through a vicarious participation in the physical and spiritual hungers of others. But of course this is presented as what could happen, not what does happen: the possibility of such a conversion doesn't even occur to the major, whose eyes remain blind and lifeless, oblivious to the suffering inflicted by the war as he is oblivious to Lenten asceticism and its potential consequences.

The second figure is less pretentious, a representative of the common man:

> One of you is the paper Jack of Sprites
> And will not cast his sentinel voice
> Spiraling up the dark ears of the wind
> Where the prisoner's yell is lost. (ll. 4-7)

Flimsy, two-dimensional, perhaps to be associated with the Jack in a deck of cards[67] as well as with mythical spirits that have little physical substantiality, he is a less imposing figure than the major; while on one level they may represent different levels of the military hierarchy, the identification of the second figure as a "Jack of sprites" suggests that the pair may also be intended to represent different dimensions of the human person – the major the physical, reduced and distorted to the biblical *sarx*, "the flesh," and Jack the spiritual, the soul shrunk from spirit to sprite. What they share is an abdication of responsibility. While the major won't see, Jack won't speak; he rejects the role of "sentinel" who could speak out on behalf of the prisoner whose own voice is lost "in the dark ears of the wind." Neither the pompous officer nor the ordinary sentry is willing to recognize the needs of or assume personal responsibility for victims of the war.

The pair is given the opportunity to defend their inactivity, and in the process reveal, in an ironic inversion of Matthew 25, that the hungry and the imprisoned that they ignored is none other than Christ himself:

> "What if it was our thumbs put out the sun
> When the Lance and Cross made their mistake?
> You'll never rob us our Eden of drumskin shelters,
> You, with the bite of John the Baptist's halter,
> Getting away in the basket of Paul,
> Loving the answer of death, the mother of Lent!" (ll. 8-13)

Their self-justification begins with a willingness to admit the result of their activity but a refusal to grant it any significance, an aggressive stance that continues throughout their speech. Even granted that it was they who brought about the eclipse of the sun at the time of the crucifixion (like fingers extinguishing a candle), their response is, "So what . . .?" They separate this plunge into darkness from the "mistake" of the crucifixion itself – an error attributed not to human agents but to the inanimate instruments of Christ's death, thereby excluding any culpability for themselves or anyone else. They cling to a myth of innocence, a presumptuous claim to remain in an unfallen world that is theirs by right, so that they rebuff as robbery any attempt to deprive them of it; but tellingly it is "our Eden of drumskin shelters," paradise as a military camp in which they describe themselves as living inside of drums, unable to see or to hear anything other than the rhythms of battle. They liken their critic successively to John the Baptist and to Paul, ominous, even threatening comparisons given that the first lost his head for speaking truth to power (see Mk. 6:14-29) and the second had to flee for his life from political authorities in Damascus (see Acts 9:23-25, 2 Cor. 11:32-33), and of course was eventually martyred himself. It is particularly noteworthy that they speak of the Baptist's "halter," though in the gospel it is not John but Judas with whom the hangman's noose is associated[68] – they project onto John the identity of betrayer which properly belongs to themselves. Alternatively, the halter could be identified with reins used to restrain and control wild behavior (such as Herod's in taking his brother's wife), its "bite" the prick of the harness bit. In any case, John's bold speech contrasts with Jack's refusal to raise his "sentinel voice," while Paul's blindness and recovery of vision is the antithesis of the major's lifeless eyes. But according to them, it is really their accuser who is "Loving the answer of death, the mother of Lent." It is true that the death of Christ gives birth to Lent, to the period of fasting and mortification, a death to self that is a sharing in the paschal mystery as Paul tells the Galatians: "I have been crucified with Christ. It is no longer I who live but Christ lives in me" (Gal. 2:19-20). Death is indeed "the answer" in that Christ's death is the source of redemption. But the speakers' meaning is rather that to observe Lent, to acknowledge the need for repentance and a change of heart, is to wallow in a cult of death, an obsession with death, with perhaps even the threatening implication that in acting like the Baptist and Paul the speaker is courting death, so that to kill him would simply be to give him what he is asking for. In fact this attempt to deflect criticism of their own action, or inaction, is a desperate effort to deny their own guilt, to conceal that it is actually they who are in love with death, in league with death. Their argument is a tissue of accusations and self-justifications that inadvertently reveals a desperate effort to lay claim to a specious innocence, an evasion of responsibility for the suffering of others that extends from Calvary to the latest atrocity of total war.

The final lines of the poem suggest the ultimate futility of such a strategy:

> Thus, in the evening of their sinless murders,
> Jack and the Major, sifting the stars for a sign
> See the north-south horizon parting like a string! (ll. 14-16)

The oxymoronic "sinless murders" is of course not an expression of objective fact but of subjective rationalization, a refusal to acknowledge the evil of the killing they have participated in. In looking for a sign in the stars they seem to accept the determinism of astrology that relieves them of the burden of personal freedom, a preference for fate rather than faith. But the sign they do see as they face (presumably) toward the east, is the unraveling of the horizon, the separation of the sky and the earth, the apocalyptic moment of judgement when all their evasions will be definitively revealed. Their worldview itself is about to unravel, and their closed system of unconvincing rationalizations about to be exposed.

Thus this poem undermines the kind of blasé attitude that is always ready to shift the blame to someone else. Lent, especially Lent in a year of war, is a time to prepare to meet the Lord who identifies with "the least of these," victims of violence and oppression throughout history. It is an opportunity, missed by Jack and the Major, for profound repentance, for recognizing and confessing that I am responsible for Christ's death, that I am responsible for war, that by my own sinfulness I have contributed to an environment where others suffer. I can ignore the needs of others or take responsibility for them and act on their behalf; I can speak out like the Baptist and Paul or defend my own callous disregard like Jack and the Major. "Wars and rumors of war" are the sign that they overlooked, a recapitulation of Christ's sufferings that can and should function as a call to conversion and compassion.

* * * * * * *

Along with comments in his journals and his autobiography, and his posthumous novel *My Argument with the Gestapo*, which they resemble in many respects, this group of premonastic poems on the early stages of World War II furnishes significant insights into Merton's political and spiritual attitudes in the years between his baptism and his entrance into monastic life. They are not of course "typical" war poetry such as came out of the previous world war, written by, or as if by, participants, whether in a patriotic mode associated with Rupert Brooke or John McCrae's "In Flanders Fields" or from the grittier, more disillusioned perspective of Wilfred Owen, Siegfried Sassoon and other combatants.[69] The only military voices heard in Merton's poems are the dead airmen alluding to Tacitus and the semi-allegorical figures of Jack and the Major, discoursing of Biblical events; the only descriptions of battle are couched in the metaphorical terms of "Light plays like a radio . . ." or the surreal phantasmagoria of "The Bombarded City." The various non-realistic frames Merton uses – dream, myth, parody, ghost story, archetypal symbols and the rest[70] – are not only appropriate for someone viewing the war from thousands of miles away,[71] but they provide effective vehicles for probing the psychological, moral and spiritual dimensions of the war, which were Merton's principal concerns. As his prose writings of the period also make clear, Merton viewed the war not simply as a struggle between the forces of light and the forces of darkness, but as a sign of the loss of moral and religious clarity and conviction in Western

"Christian" society as a whole.[72] These poems, then, are not descriptions of actual warfare, of which Merton had no first-hand knowledge, but of the ways that this war, and all wars, are both revelation and consequence of ethical and spiritual failure: a recognition of personal moral responsibility for social disintegration ("The Dark Morning"); an awareness of the absence of adequate communal values ("Dirge for a Town in France"); a critique of political policies devoid of ethical concern ("Iphigenia: Politics," "The Night Train," "The Bombarded City"); above all an indictment of the hollowness of a conventional Christian rhetoric not incarnated in Christian action ("Poem 1939," "The Philosophers," "Two British Airmen," "Lent in a Year of War").

An attentive reading of these poems as a group makes evident both their consistency of perspective and the considerable variety of ways Merton takes to articulate that perspective in effective, coherent, aesthetically satisfying literary forms. Considering these poems together also provides a context for reading the most powerful and most personal of the war poems, "For My Brother, Reported Missing in Action," with its plangent question, "And in what landscape of disaster / Has your unhappy spirit lost its road?" (ll. 9-10), and shows that this was not the first time that the poet had visited and surveyed such landscapes—nor would it be the last.

Notes

1. "For My Brother, Reported Missing in Action, 1943," in Thomas Merton, *Thirty Poems* (Norfolk, CT: New Directions, 1944), [pp. 7-8], and Thomas Merton, *Collected Poems* (New York: New Directions, 1977), pp. 35-36; for a discussion, see Patrick F. O'Connell, "Grief Transfigured: Merton's Elegy on His Brother," *The Merton Seasonal*, 18:1 (Winter, 1993), pp. 10-15.

2. For Merton's writings on war and peace see Thomas Merton, *Passion for Peace: The Social Essays*, ed. William H. Shannon (New York: Crossroad, 1995); for an overview of the material see the articles "Hiroshima"; "Holocaust"; "Just War, Theory of"; "Nonviolence"; "Peace"; "Vietnam"; "War" in William H. Shannon, Christine M. Bochen and Patrick F. O'Connell, *The Thomas Merton Encyclopedia* (Maryknoll, NY: Orbis, 2002), pp. 205-206, 206-207, 235-37, 330-33, 354-55, 508-10, 516-19.

3. Thomas Merton, *A Man in the Divided Sea* (New York: New Directions, 1946).

4. Thomas Merton, *Early Poems: 1940-1942* (Lexington, KY: Anvil Press, 1971).

5. "Fable for a War" (*Collected Poems*, pp. 712-713), which despite its title is in fact a pre-war poem, and one that Merton did not see fit to include in any of his published volumes, will not be discussed. In his autobiography, Merton comments, "In November 1938, I acquired a sudden facility for rough, raw Skeltonic verses—and that lasted about a month, and died. They were not much, but one of them took a prize which it did not deserve" (Thomas Merton, *The Seven Storey Mountain* [New York: Harcourt, Brace, 1948], p. 235). The poem, which won Columbia's Mariana Griswold Van Rensselaer Award, was "Fable for a War," which according to this chronology would therefore have been written before the end of 1938, in the aftermath of the Munich Pact (signed September 29), and in any case was published in June, 1939, more than two months before the outbreak of hostilities, both in *Columbia Poetry* (New York: Columbia University Press, 1939), pp. 60-61, and in *The New York Times*, on Sunday, June 18, 1939, in an article entitled "2 Columbia Poets Named for Awards" (36). "Fable" consists of five six-line stanzas that are indeed "rough" and "raw" if not exactly "Skeltonic"; in *The Seven Mountains of Thomas Merton* (Boston: Houghton Mifflin, 1984), Michael Mott describes it as "a propaganda poem" and adds, "It is hard to say what kind of promise this shows" (pp. 128-129).

6. *Man in the Divided Sea*, 16; *Collected Poems*, pp. 61-62.

7. The third line in the first stanza is a tetrameter.

8. Henry Vaughan, *Complete Poetry*, ed. French Fogle (Garden City, NY: Doubleday Anchor, 1964), p. 231.

9. See J. A. Cuddon, *A Dictionary of Literary Terms* (Garden City, NY: Doubleday, 1977), pp. 344-345 (which includes mention of the term "swan road" for "sea").

10. This notion, from which the expression "swan song" arises, was known at least as far back as the time of Pliny the Elder, who refutes it in the tenth book of his *Historia Naturalis*, c. 32; see Pliny, *Natural History*, 10 vols., trans, H. A. Rackham, Loeb Classical Library (Cambridge, MA: Harvard University Press, 1938-44), 3.333.

11. *Thirty Poems*, p. [2]; *Man in the Divided Sea*, p. 116; *Collected Poems*, p. 29.

12. In Merton's own copy of *A Man in the Divided Sea*, which also includes a slightly revised and reordered text of *Thirty Poems* as an appendix, now at the Thomas Merton Center, Bellarmine University, Louisville, KY, beneath each poem its date is written. See also Ross Labrie, "The Ordering of Thomas Merton's Early Poems," *Resources for American Literary Study* 8 (1979), 115-17, which draws on a 1951 letter, written

by Merton's secretary, providing the year of composition for almost all the poems in Merton's first three collections (presumably based on this copy of *A Man in the Divided Sea* for the first two).

13. An earlier version of the poem, found in the Van Doren File at Columbia University, reads "dark" for "black" in line 1.

14. *Seven Storey Mountain*, p. 3.

15. See Thomas Merton, *New Seeds of Contemplation* (New York: New Directions, 1961), pp. 34-35.

16. The idea that moral responsibility for the war is shared by all sinners is found in Merton's journal as early as September 30, 1939: "The whole world is filled with the blood and anger and violence and lust our sins and self-will have brought upon us, my own sins as much as anybody else's: Hitler, Stalin are not alone responsible. I am too, and everybody is, insofar as he has been violent and lustful and proud and greedy and ambitious" (Thomas Merton, *Run to the Mountain: The Story of a Vocation. Journals, vol. 1: 1939-1941*, ed. Patrick Hart [San Francisco: HarperCollins, 1995], p. 31; see also p. 186 [April 1940]; Thomas Merton, *My Argument with the Gestapo* [Garden City, NY: Doubleday, 1969], pp. 76-77, p. 119; *Seven Storey Mountain*, p. 248, p. 250).

17. *Early Poems*, p. 1; *Collected Poems*, p. 3.

18. An earlier version of the poem reads "spring rains."

19. The poem was originally entitled "The Aestheticians."

20. See Genesis 30:14-16, and John Donne's poem, "Go and catch a falling star, / Get with child a mandrake root,..." (John Donne, *Complete Poetry*, ed. John T. Shawcross [Garden City, NY: Doubleday Anchor, 1967], p. 90).

21. Emily Dickinson, *Complete Poems*, ed. Thomas H. Johnson (Boston: Little, Brown, 1960), p. 216; in his journal entry for March 18, 1941, Merton writes, "The first insult of the day...was when I found the letter from *New Yorker* saying a poem containing a parody on 'Beauty is truth etc....' was a parody of Emily Dickinson and their readers would mostly be unfamiliar with that poem 'of hers' so they couldn't use it. I never read a line of Emily Dickinson" (*Run to the Mountain*, p. 322). If this last statement is literally true then there is a remarkable coincidence of phrasing; it may rather be an overstatement in reaction to the failure to recognize the more central parody of Keats. An earlier version of the poem, found both in the Fitzgerald File at St. Bonaventure University and in the Van Doren File at Columbia University, reads "in the neighbor room," even closer to Dickinson's "adjoining room."

22. John Keats, *Poetical Works*, ed. H. W. Garrod (New York: Oxford University Press, 1956), p. 210.

23. The published text reads "breed" here, as in line 11, but an earlier version of the poem, found both in the Fitzgerald File at St. Bonaventure University and in the Van Doren File at Columbia, reads "bleed", a superior reading in the context; the repetition of "breed" is evidently a mistranscription, though it is also found in a March, 1941 letter to Robert Lax (*When Prophecy Still Had a Voice: The Letters of Thomas Merton & Robert Lax*, ed. Arthur W. Biddle [Lexington: University Press of Kentucky, 2001], p. 72).

24. In *Thomas Merton: Monk and Artist* (Kalamazoo, MI: Cistercian Publications, 1987), Victor A. Kramer suggests that Merton's decision to open the volume of *Early Poems* with this piece "indicates his fondness for it" (p. 39); in George Kilcourse's opinion, "Such parody is difficult to suppose as the work of a promising poet" (George Kilcourse, *Ace of Freedoms: Thomas Merton's Christ* [Notre Dame: University of Notre Dame Press, 1993], p. 58); Mott concurs that it "is not a strong poem, whatever it is" (*Seven Mountains*, p. 170). No previous commentator has considered how the parody relates to the thematic point of the poem.

25. *Early Poems*, pp. 2-3; *Collected Poems*, pp. 4-5.

26. The germ of the poem is found in a journal entry for October 6, 1939, at the conclusion of a discussion of empty gestures that substitute for genuine charity: "In the war—yesterday the Germans buried, with military honors, three unknown English airmen brought down in a fight over the Teuterborg Forest. A substitute for charity: it got some outlet in the pomp and bugles and speeches of a stupid military funeral. And by the way—Bill Hemmings who sat in the back row at Oakham, next to me, when we read Tacitus, and who was my studymate one term—we read of the battles in the Teuterborg Forest: he wrote two years ago he was in the R.A.F. Was he one of these men?" (*Run to the Mountain*, p. 44). Merton apparently read of the men in an article from *The New York Times* of October 6, 1939, dated the previous day from Osnabrueck, with the headline "Nazis Honor 3 Britons / Killed in Air Battle" and subtitled "Eulogy is Delivered and Full / Military Rites Observed" (p. 10). The article notes that the airmen's plane had been shot down the previous week over "Teutoburg forest" and that the bodies were burned beyond recognition; they were buried in the Cloister Cemetery in coffins covered with the Union Jack, and eulogized both by a German officer and by a military chaplain wearing decorations from the last war. Excerpts from both addresses are given; the chaplain is quoted as saying, "In the flower of their life these three airmen passed away obedient to their military duty. For us it will be a duty and an honor to care for their graves in this cemetery. May they rest here in peace in God's holy earth!" Merton's spelling "Teuterborg" is also found in the subtitle of a draft

version of the poem at Columbia University, which reads "(Buried in the Teuterborg Forest, 1939)," as well as in the subtitle in a draft typescript otherwise identical to the printed version in the New Directions Files at Harvard University, and in the typescript of *Early Poems* made by Sr. Thérèse Lentfoehr in the summer of 1968, which suggests that the spelling was altered late in the process of preparing the edition of *Early Poems*.

27. In the battle, which took place in September, 9 A.D., three Roman legions, upwards of 18,000 men, under the command of Publius Quinctilius Varus, were ambushed by Germanic forces led by Arminius, a former Roman ally, and almost completely wiped out. For an imaginative reconstruction of the battle, along with a thorough discussion of its social and political context and consequences and a summary of recent archeological discoveries at the battle site, see Peter S. Wells, *The Battle That Stopped Rome: Emperor Augustus, Arminius, and the Slaughter of the Legions in the Teutoburg Forest* (New York: Norton, 2003). Kalkriese, the actual battle site, discovered in 1987, is located between the Ems and Weser Rivers near Osnabrück in northwest Germany; it is in fact some twenty miles north of the area near Detmold that was given the name Teutoberger Wald in the seventeenth century (after the rediscovery of the *Annals* of Tacitus, source of the name) and that features an outsized statue of Arminius which is a major tourist attraction (see Wells, p. 35). A more technical discussion of the archeological evidence for the battle site is found in Wolfgang Schlüter, "The Battle of the Teutoburg Forest: Archeological Research at Kalkriese near Osnabrück," in J.D. Creighton and R.J.A. Wilson, eds., *Roman Germany: Studies in Cultural Interaction, Journal of Roman Archaeology*, Supplementary Series 32 (1999), pp. 125-159.

28. In the draft version of this poem at Columbia, first-person plural forms have been altered to third-person plural: the typewritten "We knew the battle" in l. 5 has been altered in pencil to "They knew this forest" and "Our grave was in this forest" in l. 8 is likewise altered in pencil to "Their grave was in this dark earth". In the Harvard draft, which appears to be later than the Columbia draft because it incorporates some of the latter's penciled revisions in its typed text, the first-person plural forms have been restored.

29. Tacitus, writing almost a century after the event, does not describe the battle itself but the visit in 15 A.D. of the Roman commander Germanicus to the battlefield, where he buried the remains of the slain legionaries (see Wells, pp. 42-43, and Tacitus, *Annals*, 1:60-62, in Tacitus, *The Histories and The Annals*, 3 vols., trans. Clifford H. Moore and John Jackson, Loeb Classical Library [Cambridge, MA: Harvard University

Press, 1931], 2:347, 349). The catastrophe is also discussed by the historians Velleius Paterculus (a contemporary who may have known both Varus and Arminius), Dio Cassius (early second century) and Lucius Annaeus Florus (mid-second century) (see Wells, pp. 38-42).

30. In *Thomas Merton, Monk and Poet: A Critical Study* (New York: Farrar, Straus, Giroux, 1978), George Woodcock calls this poem "an oddly Housmanesque little elegy" (p. 35), perhaps thinking of the conversation between the dead farmer and his living friend in "Is my team plowing," or the shades gathered around the newly dead young man at the conclusion of "To an Athlete Dying Young" (see A. E. Housman, *Collected Poems* [New York: Holt, Rinehart and Winston, 1965], pp. 42-43, 32-33); given Merton's disparaging comments about Housman during this period (see *Run to the Mountain*, p. 437 [October 11, 1941]), any echoes are probably not deliberate. Mott call it "a fine poem despite all the echoes of other poems by other poets" and considers it "the first poem that would continue to mean something to" Merton (*Seven Mountains*, p. 146).

31. *Thirty Poems*, pp. [8-9]; *Man in the Divided Sea*, pp. 128-129; *Collected Poems*, pp. 36-37.

32. A working draft of this poem at Columbia University that is clearly a source for the final version reads "turns to statues" in line 2, which may possibly be the correct reading – i.e. fancy turns its attention to statues in the room.

33. See Euripides, *Iphigeneia at Aulis*, trans. W. S. Merwin and George E. Dimock, Jr. (New York: Oxford University Press, 1978).

34. In the draft version "chairs" in l. 14 is preceded by x'd out "statues" and the final version of l. 16 is added in pencil above cancelled "Or smiles, Agamemnon slew his charming daughter". The draft version also interlines "swords" in pencil above cancelled "knives" in l. 15, an alteration that was not used in the final version, perhaps because of the more metaphorical "swordlight" two lines earlier.

35. In the original reading of the draft version, this claim is made by Agamemnon himself; the first-person plural forms and the consequent choric effect are part of a penciled rewriting of the final eleven lines of the poem.

36. George Woodcock considers this poem, along with Merton's elegy on Lorca, as the "best of the poems…from the pre-monastic days," and identifies Iphigenia as "the truth which politicians kill, in this way creating a future holding terrors as fearful as the vengeance that finally awaited Agamemnon" (*Thomas Merton, Monk and Poet*, p. 37).

37. *Thirty Poems*, pp. [3-4]; *Man in the Divided Sea*, pp. 118-119; *Collected Poems*, pp. 30-31.

38. In a journal entry for October 30, 1939, Merton includes "bathysphere" among the words "of out of the way and uninteresting things, expressing our interesting civilization" (*Run to the Mountain* pp. 74, 75).

39. For initial comments on the fall of France from July 1940, which begin, "I wish I had something I could write down about the war, and make sense. I wish I knew something I could say about France," see *Run to the Mountain*, pp. 235-236.

40. Both *Thirty Poems* and *A Man in the Divided Sea* read "head" in l. 16; Merton's copy of *A Man in the Divided Sea* emends to "hear"; the correct reading is found in *Collected Poems*.

41. An earlier version of the poem, found in the Van Doren File at Columbia University, includes an extra line following line 20: "And lock them under pillows:".

42. *Man in the Divided Sea*, pp. 46-47; *Collected Poems*, pp. 84-85.

43. George Kilcourse considers the carousel to be a wholly positive image, "a strong metaphor of childhood," an "archetype of fantasy and imagination," and suggests that the poet identifies "the child's imaginative life with the true or inner self"; though he quotes lines 11-20, he does not comment on the contrast between the natural sounds of the stars and fountain and the artificial noise—the "phony flute" etc.—of the carousel, nor does he consider that the children are part of the memory of the adult men standing "in the shadowy doors," so that the "stark contrast" between the "paradise consciousness" of the children and "the adult despair, or capitulation" is actually quite problematic (*Ace of Freedoms*, pp. 70-72).

44. See Merton's comments in his journal for October 26, 1940: "There is a fear, not that the war will end civilization, but that the reaction after the war will. Now everyone is keyed up to a great effort: but the fear is that, after all is over, everybody will fall down and die of a mortal lassitude and the sickness of disgust. Maybe everyone will just die of weariness and shame and hopelessness. That was what was frightening about France. As if they just gave up in disgust, willing to do nothing but die of *accidie*" (*Run to the Mountain*, p. 243).

45. In a draft version of this poem at Columbia University, the title "The Storm in the Afternoon" is written in pencil above cancelled "Poem"; in a second draft, the original typescript of which is in the New Directions Files at Harvard University and the carbon at Columbia, this new title is part of the typed text. It is unclear whether it was deliberately or inadvertently omitted in the published version.

46. *Early Poems*, pp. 4-5; *Collected Poems*, pp. 6-7.

47. Kilcourse sees the opening lines of this poem as an example of "writing [which] often labors as self-consciously poetic, even imitative,

or worse derivative of Donne, Hopkins, Eliot, and others whose metaphysical conceits Merton envied," though he does not specify how these lines bear out his critique (*Ace of Freedoms*, p. 56); Woodcock, in contrast, considers this "[o]ne of the best war pieces," and cites the opening lines as marked by "the kind of arresting cluster of sharp visual images that will later characterize Merton's poetry at its best" (*Thomas Merton, Monk and Poet*, p. 35).

48. In the Harvard draft the opening line reads "Light is more artificial than a radio, in the iron tree"—a clear indication that the comparison is intended to be a negative one.

49. The Harvard draft reads "like a lady" in line 4, with "lady" subsequently canceled and "population" interlined above in pencil.

50. In both drafts, line 21 (beginning "The poppies" rather than "And poppies") precedes line 19, which reads "And earth ... my shovel". In line 20 of the Harvard draft "stranger's" is cancelled and replaced in pencil by "summer's". A text of the two final lines identical to the printed version is cancelled in the Columbia draft and replaced in pencil by "The Summer I saw running through the bended and embattled corn: / I know I'll find her dead." The typed version of the Harvard draft is substantially identical with the revision of the first draft, but "summer I saw flying" is cancelled and replaced in pencil by "nations I saw flying" and in the following line "them" is written in pencil below cancelled "her". It is clear that the revisions of the Harvard draft tend toward a more overtly "political" reading than that found in the text printed in *Early Poems*. Whether the apparently earlier version of the poem was selected purposely or inadvertently as copy text for the published volume cannot be ascertained, but the alterations found in lines 1, 4 and 22 of the drafts have a certain literalistic stiffness that may make the poem's meaning clearer but do so at the expense of the quality of the verse.

51. *Man in the Divided Sea*, p. 33; *Collected Poems*, p. 75.

52. Two earlier versions of the poem are found in the Van Doren File at Columbia University, the first with authorial corrections in both pen and pencil, the second substantially a clean copy of the first with its ink corrections; in line 4 the first version initially read "stones."—"of Asia" is added in pen, then "Asia" cancelled and "Caucasus" added in ink, then cancelled in pencil and "Thebes:" written above; the second version reads "of Caucasus."

53. Line 18 of the first Columbia draft originally read "banks!" cancelled in pen and replaced by "factories!" interlined below, subsequently cancelled in pencil and "treasuries" added in pencil above; this is the one penciled alteration that is also found in the text of the second draft.

54. *Man in the Divided Sea*, pp. 34-36; *Collected Poems*, pp. 75-78.

55. See the descriptions of the bombing of England in the journal entries for October 27, 1940 and November 28, 1940 (*Run to the Mountain*, pp. 244-46, 264-65).

56. Ross Labrie comments on this stanza, "While lunar imagery is sometimes presented positively in Merton's poetry, here in this surrealistic setting it is sinister and frightening, particularly the 'lunar forest of the undersea,' an image that recalls Poe. Instead of illuminating the subconscious, however, as Poe would have done, Merton here uses the nightmarish scene to show the actual terror of war as greater by far than that of horrible fantasies about it that could grip the mind. Moreover, the imaginative image of the bony lunar light piercing the dark subconscious conveys an impression of death far more powerfully than would have been the case with an explanatory statement" (Ross Labrie, *Thomas Merton and the Inclusive Imagination* [Columbia: University of Missouri Press, 2001], p. 157); see also the brief comments on the "syntactical experimentation" in the poem in Labrie's earlier book, *The Art of Thomas Merton* (Fort Worth: Texas Christian University Press, 1979), p. 116.

57. In a typescript of the poem at Columbia University, line 11 reads "swagger / like the warring flier" with "/" added to make two lines and "warring" added in pencil after multiple cancellations including "warring leader" written in pen and cancelled in pencil. A second typescript, in the Van Doren File at Columbia, reads "But if you swagger / Like the warring flier or his leader" (two typed lines) for line 11 in the published version.

58. In the first Columbia typescript, lines 32-34 originally read: "Space out a starlit area / To imitate the white geometry of peace: / For the stone and fallen conqueror / The guilty statue overturned." The two final lines were then cancelled in pen and replaced by "In honor of the guilty winner"; then the three remaining lines were cancelled in pencil and replaced by the published lines 32-34, with the exception of "winner" rather than "Warlord" in line 32 and "To institute" rather than "Much like" in line 34. The second Columbia typescript likewise reads "winner" rather than "Warlord" in line 32.

59. Note the similar imagery in "Dirge for the Proud World," ll. 4-6, 13-14 (*Thirty Poems*, p.[18]; *Collected Poems*, pp. 49-50).

60. The second Columbia typescript reads "flier's" for "emperor's" in line 67.

61. The second Columbia typescript reads "airman's" rather than "politician's" in line 74. It is evident that in the earlier drafts there is more explicit attention to the role of the actual bomber; it appears that

Merton eventually decided to move away from a realistic to a more mythic set of images.

62. See "Pacifism and Resistance in Simone Weil," in Thomas Merton, *Faith and Violence* (Notre Dame, IN: University of Notre Dame Press, 1968), pp. 76-84.

63. *Thirty Poems*, p. [1]; *Man in the Divided Sea*, p. 113; *Collected Poems*, p. 27.

64. Labrie comments in *The Art of Thomas Merton* that "The army major in 'Lent in a Time of War' is largely a creation of sound.... The high-pitched 'i' and 'e' sounds intensify the feeling of acuteness appropriate to the crises of war and famine, while the image of the 'needle-light' works at the same effect visually" (p. 113); Labrie considers this "compact and tense" poem among the best in Merton's first volume (p. 112).

65. T. S. Eliot, *The Complete Poems and Plays, 1909-1950* (New York: Harcourt, Brace & World, 1962), p. 56; the figure may also show the influence of Dylan Thomas: in his journal entry for February 9, 1941, Merton mentions that Thomas "gets some shattering effects by speaking of fleshly organisms being put together like things being carefully made of wood and string and sacking and so on" (*Run to the Mountain*, p. 306); see for example lines 10-12 of "When once the twilight locks no longer": "That globe itself of hair and bone / That, sewn to me by nerve and brain, / Had stringed my flask of matter to his rib"; and line 6 of "My hero bares his nerves": "And these poor nerves so wired to the skull" (Dylan Thomas, *Collected Poems* [New York: New Directions, 1953], pp. 4, 11).

66. See also the tenth line of the fourth part of Dylan Thomas' "Altarwise by Owl-Light": "My camel's eyes will needle through the shroud." (*Collected Poems*, p. 82).

67. Merton may also be recalling Hopkins' reference to "This Jack, joke, poor potsherd, patch, matchwood, immortal diamond" in the penultimate line of "That Nature Is a Heraclitean Fire and of the Comfort of the Resurrection" (Gerard Manley Hopkins, *Poems and Prose*, ed. W. H. Gardner [Baltimore: Penguin, 1953], p. 66). Dylan Thomas also uses the term in a number of poems: see *Collected Poems*, pp. 15, 76, 84.

68. Merton makes the connection in a journal entry from Gethsemani on Good Friday, 1941: "The world is hanging itself like Judas, with a halter" (*Run to the Mountain*, p. 348).

69. See Paul Fussell's classic discussion of the literature of World War I in *The Great War and Modern Memory* (New York: Oxford University Press, 1975).

70. These poems are thus sharply differentiated from the documentary style of the poetry on the Second World War Merton wrote in the 1960s, *Original Child Bomb* (*Collected Poems*, pp. 291-302), "Chant to Be Used in Processions around a Site with Furnaces" (*Collected Poems*, pp. 345-49) and, to a somewhat lesser extent, "Epitaph for a Public Servant" (*Collected Poems*, pp. 703-11), though they show a remarkable affinity with such Vietnam-era poems as "The Great Men of Former Times" (*Collected Poems*, pp. 623-624) and "Fall '66" (*Collected Poems*, pp. 644-645).

71. It should be noted that these elements could be and were frequently incorporated into the predominantly realistic verse of the World War I poets, as Fussell points out and as Merton himself was no doubt aware.

72. See the article on *My Argument with the Gestapo* in *The Thomas Merton Encyclopedia*, pp. 311-314.

Lax, Merton and Rice on War and Peace

James Harford

Thomas Merton and his two long-time friends, Robert Lax and Edward Rice—as far back as their undergraduate days, and then throughout their lives—wrote voluminously about the absurdity and cruelty of war, and of the importance of peace activism.[1] Much of the writing was in biting, satirical letters to each other, or in articles for *Jubilee*, the magazine that all three worked on for fifteen years, while they often published elsewhere on the subject as well.

The 30s and 40s

An early example of Merton's satire is his prize-winning poem on fascism, "Fable for a War," from Columbia's 1939 annual poetry volume. An excerpt:

> The old Roman sow
> Bears a new litter now
> To fatten for a while
> On the same imperial swill.
> The cannibal will dig
> And root out Spanish bones beside the pig.
>
> Germany has reared
> A rare ugly bird
> To screech a sour song
> In the German tongue:
> Tell me if there be
> A sparrowhawk for such birds as he?
>
> ...Europe is a feast
> For every bloody beast:
> Jackals will grow fat
> On the bones after that.
> But in the end of all
> None but the crows can sing the funeral.[2]

Lax, Merton and Rice were each editors-in-chief of the Columbia humor magazine *Jester* at one time or another in the 1938-40 period. Their levity, however, was mixed with savage sarcasm about the stirrings of war. One Christmas issue had a "Peace on Earth" cover that showed Mussolini, Hitler and Franco riding camels and gazing at the Star of Bethlehem while cradling bombs.[3] Inside was an 8-page folio of the Goya sketches of wartime horror in Spain. They even ran a "Stop the War" ad as WWII was looming.

Lax, always the gentlest of the three, wrote this poem in longhand, circa 1941:

> I believe that all the people should stop their fight
> I believe that one should blow
> A whistle or sing
> Or play on the lute
> Or say very quietly into a microphone
> That whatever they think they are doing it is wrong[4]

As World War II approached, most men who were eligible marched lock-step into the military, and their patriotism soared as they enlisted. Rice was one of those, and was ready to join. He expected to be drafted and was planning to join the Marines, but he had bad eyes that would plague him all his life, and he was declared 4-F. Not willing to serve as a combatant were Lax and Merton, whose detestation of war was palpable. Neither had disqualifying physical ailments—although both were borderline hypochondriacs—but it was their pacifist convictions that held sway.

Lax eventually got conscientious objector status,[5] but first had to undergo the same humbling experience that befell many another young American in those months, and he wrote Merton about it, using a racial epithet that was, unfortunately, common for the times:

> Oh, Myrtle....Among the draft they did force me naked in a room with a thousand jigs in a similar condition and direct me harshly to piss in a Dixie cup which I could not. They did fumst me and pummel me and direct me to an impractical truck. They did transfix me with needles, startle me with bright lights, pound my kneecaps, and sound with unsharpened pencils my ears.[6]

On one of my visits to him on Patmos, in 1997, Lax gave me a paper he had kept since writing it out in 1941, 36 years earlier:

> My objection is to taking human life. My desire is to help preserve lives that are endangered...My belief is that a single God, good and loving, rules the universe. I believe that His authority extends to every event, large and small. I believe that in this scheme man is particularly blessed with a conscience to advise and a will to choose between good and evil action. The religious writings in harmony with this belief and which seem to me of great importance are The Ten Commandments, the 23rd Psalm and the Lord's Prayer. These express for me the goodness of the Lord and the proper faith and right behavior of man."[7]

Merton's despair over world militarism was voiced not only towards his country, but to the whole of mankind, in "An Argument: Of the Passion of Christ," which was published in *Thirty Poems*, the first volume of Merton poetry published by *New Directions*, in 1944. This is the fourth and last stanza of the poem.

> The cry that rent the temple veil
> And split the earth as deep as hell
> And echoed through the universe,
> Sounds, in bombardments, down to us.
> There is no ear that has not heard
> The deathless cry of murdered God:
> No eye that has not looked upon
> The lance of the crucifixion:
> And yet that cry beats at the ears
> Of old, deaf-mute interpreters,
> Whose querulous and feeble cries
> Drown stronger voices, and whose eyes
> Will let no light of lances in:
> They still will clamor for a sign![8]

Disillusioned by the bellicosity of his adopted country, Merton inserted a scathing passage in his 1947 poem, "Figures For An Apocalypse III," addressed to his friends back in New York with this sub-title: "Advice to my Friends Robert Lax and Edward Rice, to get away while they still can." This is the fourth stanza:

Time, time to go to the terminal
And make the escaping train
With eyes as bright as palaces
And thoughts like nightingales.
It is the hour to fly without passports
From Juda to the mountains,
And hide while cities turn to butter
For fear of the secret bomb.
We'll arm for our own invisible battle
In the wells of the pathless wood
Wounding our limbs with prayers and Lent,
Shooting the traitor memory
And throwing away our guns—
And learning to fight like Gedeon's men,
Hiding our lights in jugs.[9]

In "A Letter to America" he expressed deep disappointment with what he considered the excessive militarism of his adopted land. This poem started out on a high note:

America, when you were born, and when the plains
Spelled out their miles of praises in the sun
What glory and what history
The rivers seemed to prepare.

And then turned ominous:

How long are we to wake
With eyes that turn to wells of blood
Seeing the hell that gets you from us
With his treacherous embrace![10]

Merton looked back on that period in *The Seven Storey Mountain*, writing that, "If I had objected to war before, it was more on the basis of emotion than anything else," but now "God was asking me, by the light and grace He had given me, to signify where I stood in relation to the actions of governments and armies and states in this world overcome with the throes of its own blind wickedness." He would be willing, he said, to serve as a stretcher-bearer, "so long as I did not have to drop bombs on open cities, or shoot at other men."[11] His entry into the Trappists made this moot.

In 1951 Merton offered, in the prologue to *The Ascent to Truth,* an apocalyptic view of the world that might well have been written today:

The human race is facing the greatest crisis in its history, because religion itself is being weighed in the balance. The present unrest in five continents, with everyone fearful of being destroyed, has brought many men to their knees.[12]

The Jubilee Years

Throughout its fifteen year lifetime, the magazine *Jubilee*, started and edited by Ed Rice, with strong contributions from both Lax and Merton, relentlessly carried anti-war messages to its readers. Typical was the April, 1957, issue which led off with a Rice quote of St. Augustine: "And if anyone either endures or thinks of war without mental pain, his is a more miserable plight still, for he thinks himself happy because he has lost all human feeling."[13] Rice, himself, edited a seven page article titled "War & Peace" illustrated by a stark Georges Rouault lithograph from his *Miserere* series. The piece offered a somber summary of the expected terrifying consequences of nuclear warfare. Nobelist Harold Urey wrote: "Scientists have repeatedly stated that no adequate defense against the atomic bomb is to be expected in the future." In a Bikini test report was found: "...the radiological effects have no parallel in conventional weapons...contaminated ships became radio-active stoves and would have burned all living things aboard them." A quote from Lt. Gen. James M. Gavin said that, "Current planning estimates run on the order of several hundred million deaths...depending on which way the wind blew."[14] Catholic comment was from Jules-Gerard Cardinal Saliège: "Are we drunk or are we insane? Ten million men were killed in the first world war, forty million in the second; if a third world war comes there is every indication that far more than a hundred million will die. You can truthfully say that the devil is calling the tune...." The oft-stated argument for or against "just war," which dates back to St. Augustine, was given an airing for *Jubilee* readers. "It is possible for a nation to engage in a just war...." stated Reverend Francis Connell of Catholic University. Absolutely not, said Alfred Cardinal Ottaviani, who wrote "...the conditions which theoretically make it justified and permissible are never present...."[15]

Merton himself rejected the label "pacifist," believing that a just war was, at least theoretically, sometimes the only alternative. In practice, however, he said, the just war concept was irrelevant in an age when nuclear destruction was possible. He wrote Rice on February 28, 1959, that he would review a book on the dropping of the bomb on Japan under a pen name.

What then have I done? This. I have set down in a swirl and written a short address of the book with my own hand...but this has not been done without subterfuge and an assumed name. Which assumed name is not making I think its last appearance because under it also I can publish like articles...outside my official ken.[16]

He used his own name later that year for a book that included the powerful "Chant To Be Used In Processions Around A Site With Furnaces." The whole poem is one long flow ending with this:

Do not think yourself better because you burn up friends and enemies with long-range missiles without ever seeing what you have done.[17]

Towards the end of 1961 Merton wrote Lax, in their special jargon, about plans for publishing new material on peace, and added jabs at the belligerency of Catholics:

From all parts I make together paperbacks of peace for New Directions.... It is articles of peace by Erich Fromms and Lewis Mumfords...and finally sly jibes about peace from English Cathlick intellectuals very witty and sly indeed, saying war is much sin, and it is, baby, it sure is. This the popes have all said...also Cardinal Ottaviani.... But not so our yonder folk catholic and suburban fathers who all cry out dead rather than red it is physical evil to smash reds with bombs and is moral evil, like sin, to be beat by reds and have to suffer prison. How new the gospel has become in these our purlieus. Choice of evils, choose the one which makes most sore the enemy and violate every type of human decency.[18]

His cynicism about America's war stance is reflected in this excerpt from another letter to Lax at Christmas time:

Here with the ship of state already half submerged and with
waters up to our beard standing nobly on the tottering
captain's bridge, We Santa Claus salute you.[19]

The Sixties

It was in 1962, that Merton—with the collaboration of both Lax
and Rice—went all out in his attack on the international war psy-
chosis. It started with an apocalyptic note to Lax on New Year's
day:

> We are in an awfully serious hour for Christianity, for
> our own souls. We are faced with the necessity to be
> very faithful to the Law of Christ, and His truth. This
> means that we must do everything that we reasonably can
> to find our way peacefully through the mess we are in.
> ....We have to try to some extent to preserve the sanity
> of this nation, and keep it from going berserk which will
> be its destruction, and ours, and perhaps also the destruc-
> tion of Christendom.
>   I wanted to say these few things, as we enter the
> New Year, for it is going to be a crucial year....

Unfortunately, Merton was often obliged to maintain anonymity
when writing about war, as for his *Jubilee* article in March of that
year titled "Testament to Peace, Father Metzger's thoughts about
the duty of the Christian."[20] Father Max Josef Metzger had been
executed in 1944 by Hitler's Gestapo for trying to get letters out of
Germany to bishops in various countries through a Swedish lady,
who turned out to be a Gestapo agent. He "died for Germany just
as heroically and just as wholeheartedly as any soldier who fell on
the battlefield. And he died for peace," wrote Merton, without
author credit.

In spite of his efforts at remaining anonymous, Merton was beginning to get national attention. On April 12, 1962 a Merton prayer
was read to the Congress by Frank Kowalski, Democrat from Con-
necticut, who addressed "this Congress, our President, our military forces, and our adversaries." It concludes using this sentence:

> Grant us prudence in proportion to our power,
> Wisdom in proportion to our science,
> Humaneness in proportion to our wealth and might.

Ironically, it was in the same month, April, 1962, that Merton wrote Jim Forest about the latest, and firmest, clampdown on his peace writings: "Now here is the ax. For a long time I have been anticipating trouble with the higher Superiors and now I have it. The orders are, no more writing about peace...I am hoping to get the book [*Peace in the Post-Christian Era*] through on the ground that it is already written."[21]   In fact, it took forty-two additional years, until 2004, before the book finally came out.

It was not possible to halt some of Merton's peace works that were on the way to press. And so *Jubilee*, in May, 1962, carried a striking seven pager by the monk, leading off with a pitch-black first page set off by **Thomas Merton** in bold white type and the title, **RELIGION AND THE BOMB** in even larger white type.[22] The article is vintage Merton, the polemicist, so impassioned that he wrote his friend, Ping Ferry, that

> I do not realize how strident I have been until I get into print. The one in this month's *Jubilee* will set a whole lot of people on their ear, and I guess it is my fault...[T]here are smoother ways of saying the same thing. I lash out with a baseball bat. Some professor of non-violence I am. Oh well....[23]

The article is not only strident but—it must be said—exaggerative, making it seem that a U. S. nuclear first strike may have actually been a possibility. "The interests of the West, the NATO, and the Church are all confused with one another," he wrote, "and the possibility of defending the West with a nuclear first strike on Russia is sometimes accepted without too much hesitation as 'necessary' and a 'lesser evil.'

Merton's peace-writing momentum kept building and in October, 1962, he co-opted Bob Lax's occasional broadside publication, PAX, with "Original Child Bomb." As much a political tract as poetry, it was written in numbered journalistic-style paragraphs. Some readers evidently did not get the satire, which included four citations of Admiral Leahy's prediction that the bomb would never explode. The reporting is a bit sloppy. Alamogordo, site of the first nuclear bomb test, is misspelled twice. An excerpt:

> ....So it was decided Hiroshima was the most opportune target, as it had not yet been bombed at all. Lucky Hiroshima! What others had experienced over a period of four years would happen to Hiroshima in a single day![24]

A translation of that poem into French had already been set in type when the Abbot General of the Trappists, Dom Gabriel Sortais, vetoed its publication. "I suppose he is one of those people who is convinced that France has to have the bomb and maintain her honor with the *force de frappe*...." Merton wrote acidly to the nun who would have done the translation into Portuguese.[25]

The official Trappist wraps were reapplied in 1964, when Merton was told by the secretary of Dom Gabriel's successor, Dom Ignace, that he was forbidden to republish some of his articles on nuclear war, including some that had been permitted. In his journal he lumped in other grievances:

> Thus, I am still not permitted to say what Pope John said in *Pacem in Terris*. Reason: "That is not the job of a monk, it is for the Bishops.".... A grim insight into the stupor of the Church in spite of all that has been attempted, all efforts to wake her up. It all falls into place. Pius XII and the Jews, the Church in South America, the treatment of the Negroes in the U.S., the Catholics on the French right in the Algerian affair, German Catholics under Hitler.... The whole thing is too sad and too serious for bitterness.... [S]ilent complicity is presented as a greater good than honest, conscientious protest.... I refuse complicity.... In any case, I have been definitely silenced on the subject of nuclear war.[26]

James Finley, who was a novice under Merton at Gethsemani, remembers going to see him once when he was in the midst of writing *Seeds of Destruction*. "They told me," he said, "to take out the part about nuclear warfare. How can I call it *Seeds of Destruction* if I have to take out the destruction?"[27]

Ed Rice continued to be an ally in publishing Merton's writings on peace in *Jubilee*. In 1965, for example, he printed "Gandhi And The One-Eyed Giant"—an allusion to the likening of the white man's callous entry into Africa in virtual blindness. Merton had admired Gandhi as far back as his school days at Oakham and here he related the sainted Indian's principles to those of another much-revered man, John XXIII:

> They are pertinent for everybody, but especially for those who are interested in implementing the principles expressed by another great religious mind, Pope John XXIII, in *Pacem in Terris*. Indeed this encyclical has the breadth and depth, the univer-

sality and tolerance, of Gandhi's own peace-minded outlook. Peace cannot be built on exclusivism, absolutism and intolerance. But neither can it be built on vague liberal slogans and pious programs gestated in the smoke of confabulation. There can be no peace on earth without the kind of inner change that brings man back to his "right mind." Gandhi's observations on the prerequisites and the disciplines involved by *satyagraha*, the vow of truth, are required reading for anyone who is seriously interested in man's fate in the nuclear age.[28]

In 1965, he called out Gandhi's legacy to the world, quoting his very words:

The evils we suffer cannot be eliminated by a violent attack in which one sector of humanity flies at another in destructive fury. Our evils are common and the solution of them can only be common. We are not ready to undertake this common task because we are not ourselves. Consequently, the first duty of every man is to return to his own right mind in order that society itself may be sane.[29]

Bob Lax, too, was much influenced by Gandhi and was, himself, on a perpetual mission to preach the gospel of peace in his poetry. He once told his friend Anthony Bannon that, "The whole idea of non-violence, what Gandhi called *ahimsa*, is of prime importance to me. I try in my poetry to make it a kind of a song that evokes a picture of this peaceable kingdom." In another talk with Bannon he said that:

Art is a way of profoundly reflecting and communicating the concept and reality of peace…. Peace is the work of the artist as well as the statesman, and any work of art at best—poem, picture or concerto—provides a pattern for, and is an instrument of peace. The artist is above all a peacemaker and prophet of peace. It is with this understanding and by his authority that he functions in the world.[30]

Lax got a passionate message from Merton in late 1965 after the monk had received a letter from some women who had been fasting to influence the Vatican Council on peace initiatives:

…I am fallen on the floor with sighs and transports because I have receive from the women who fasted in Rome for peace a paper they all writ, while fasting, they signed it all with fasting fingers saying be our friend. How should I not be friend of these fasting ladies who have moved the whole Council up ten notches closer to God and make them speak of peace and kept silence the American Bishops from jumping up and yelling about bombs and war. They have shut up that fool Bishop Hannon with their fasting and they deserve praise, let them think of me any time they want I am ready to be thought of kindly by such ladies. Tomorrow Mass for the peace, but the mists of bad feeling are all over this country let me tell you it smell bad here in Denmark.[31]

A few weeks later, his exasperation with the U. S. government was beyond toleration; he wrote again to Lax: "We American citizens have had enough of President Johnson and of Secretary McNamara as hoped also of J. Edgar Hoover. That for the govt."[32] He had hoped that Vatican II, spurred by John XXIII's strong message, would move peaceful actions by national governments, including his own. He wrote Sister Thérèse Lentfoehr, in the last days of 1965, that, "The big thing now is to get people to understand the real importance of the Council teaching on war and peace—and the Pope's insistence on the same ideas."[33]

In August, 1966, the Vietnam War peaking, Merton wrote an article for *Jubilee* about the Buddhist monk, Thich Nhat Hanh, preceded by Hanh's own essay which was illustrated by a grisly photo showing the self-immolation of a Buddhist monk that had occurred in 1963. "In the Buddhist belief," wrote Nhat Hanh, "life is not confined to 60 or 80 or 100 years; life is eternal...To express will by burning oneself, therefore, is not to commit an act of destruction but to perform an act of construction, i.e., to suffer and to die for the sake of one's people."[34] Merton wrote on the following page that,

This is not a political statement. It has no ulterior motive, it seeks to provoke no immediate reaction "for" or "against" this or that side in the Vietnam war. It is on the contrary a human and personal statement and an anguished plea for Thich Nhat Hanh who is my brother. He is more my brother than many who are nearer to me by race and nationality, because he and I see things exactly the same way. He and I deplore the war that is ravaging his country. We deplore it for exactly the same reasons: human reasons, reasons of sanity, justice and love. We deplore the needless destruction, the fantastic and callous ravaging of human life, the rape of the culture and spirit of an exhausted people. It is surely evident that this carnage serves no purpose that can be discerned and indeed contradicts the very purpose of the mightly nation that has constituted itself the "defender" of the people it is destroying.[35]

Merton could not resist quoting some fellow Americans at the peak of U. S. involvement in the Vietnam war—a General who said the way to peace was to "bomb North Vietnam back into the Stone Age," and Cardinal Spellman, who had addressed the troops in Vietnam, deploring the home protesters, with the statement, "My country right or wrong." In the same article he cited the Vatican Council's proclamation that even without nuclear, chemical and bacteriological weapons modern war can be "savagery far surpassing that of the past" involving entire populations. He likened the human race to "an alcoholic who knows that drink will destroy him and yet always he has 'good reasons' why he must continue drinking." Written thirty four years before another U. S. President afflicted with that same addiction led the country into war in Iraq, the Merton words cut hard in the re-reading. He was not, however, in favor of burning draft cards ("I just do not know if their position is comprehensible to a lot of frightened and confused people") although he backed "responsible" dissent. He also praised the Pope Paul's "clear and firm protest against war and injustice" at the UN, calling it a "most serious and highly credible reminder that instruments for peaceful conflict solution are at hand."[36]

Lax showed what was for him a rare cynicism in a 1967 poem about international peace negotiations that was handwritten to his South Dakota friend Gerry Lange, on stationery that carried PAX in big letters at top and bottom:

> We say:
>
> They don't trust
> us
>
> I say:
>
> Can you blame
> them?

They say:

They don't trust
us

I say:
Can you blame
us?

We talk
& they talk
about

"confidence-
building
measures"

I say:

name one

(silence)

I say:

Change the
tone
in the way
we talk
of
them
&
to
them

You say:

is that
all?

I say:

Try that
& I'll give
you another
one
tomorrow[37]

Merton's journal entries sometimes became as angry as his letters to his friends in 1967, as in this entry:

> "...I think the world of the U.S.A. in 1967 is a world of crass, blind, overstimulated, phony, lying stupidity. The war in Asia gets slowly worse—and always more inane. The temper of the country is one of blindness, fat, self-satisfied, ruthless, mindless corruption....[38]

Vietnam was not the only theater of war that concerned Merton. He wrote his lawyer-friend John Slate, who had been a Columbia classmate, in 1967 that

> This Israel-Arab war sounds very nasty indeed. Things feel like 1939. Hope I am wrong. Lax is in Patmos. Should he get out of there? Patmos, Greece, will reach him. Let me know if something specially dramatic happens—I may or may not hear things here. Maybe first thing I will know—I will be going up in a radioactive cloud all mixed up with the Gold of Fort Knox and the fissionable materials treasured there.[39]

He did not absolve his fellow American Catholics from their culpability by any means, delivering this blast in a letter to Lax as the Vietnam war was still being waged in 1968:

> When you come to ol'Kaintuck don't let on you are coming to see me. Frantics are burning my books in L'ville (honest, have writ to papers, "will burn *Seven Storey Mountain*: Merton is commie red atheist contra Vietnam war pitznik)...Catlick papers all full of turmoil over your friend...
>
> [signed] Beppo Zampiglione[40]

Rice, after *Jubilee* folded in 1967, began traveling, and went to see Merton in 1968, some time after returning from Asia. He wrote in his Merton biography, *The Man In The Sycamore Tree*, about how deeply affected his friend was by the pictures he brought back of Vietnam scenes, including one picture of a mother and baby horribly scarred by napalm burns. Merton, wrote Rice, "looked at it a long time, wondering not only about the tragic burns on the two victims, but what had happened to the interior sensibilities of the young American men who could drop such a weapon without an apparent thought of the consequences."[41]

Throughout the year 1968, the last one of his life, Merton fulminated in his journal over the Vietnam War. He kept up on national affairs with the help of people who sent him news clips—Dan Berrigan, Ping Ferry, Jay Laughlin, John Howard Griffin, Victor Hammer, Carolyn Hammer [librarian at University of Kentucky] probably Ed Rice and Jim Forest. He talked also to Dan Walsh who, he says, "has a lot of inside knowledge of the Democratic Party." That Walsh's knowledge was sometimes irresponsible gossip is indicated by his comment to Merton that LBJ's resignation "was all a ruse, that he would be drafted at the convention and thereby circumvent Bobby Kennedy."[42] It is doubtful that anyone with Merton's spiritual credentials went on record with more severity about his country than the monk. He used phrases in his journal like "incredible barbarity" "killing utterly defenseless people" "the moral sense of this country is eroded" "the country is under judgment...."[43] Few editorialists used harsher words than Merton did in accusing President Johnson of "unconvincing fraud" over his action at the time of the Pueblo incident.[44] It must have hurt him deeply to receive the criticism he got from some Catholics. "A devout Catholic is burning my books," he wrote, "I must be godless, as I wish to save lives rather than kill Commies for Christ."[45]

He still harbored hope that his fellow citizens would come to their senses, but worried that they might not:

> I have never had such a feeling of the strange madness that possesses the country. And yet there is still some hope—based not on reason but on a basic good will and a luck that might still hold. Or is there a basic good will? Has it all been mortgaged to a police state? Are we already *there*? We may be![46]

Legacy

Merton's views on peace and war have had profound effect on tens of thousands, maybe millions, of people worldwide in the decades since his death. Some of the monk's wisdom gets new attention as fresh statements are published. This was quoted by Merton's old friend, Jim Forest, himself a man who has devoted his life to international peace, in 1996—probably 30 years after it was written—in the introduction to to the Japanese printing of *The Seven Storey Mountain*:

I reject this ["their ideology of matter, power, quantity, movement, activism and force"] because I see it to be the source and expression of the spiritual hell which man has made of his world: the hell which has burst into flame in two total wars of incredible horror, the hell of spiritual emptiness and sub-human fury which has resulted in crimes like Auschwitz and Hiroshima....

...by being in the monastery I take my true part in all the struggles and sufferings of the world....

...It is my intention to make my entire life a rejection of, a protest against the crimes and injustices of war and political tyranny which threaten to destroy the whole race of man and the world with him. By my monastic life and vows I am saying *no* to all the concentration camps, the aerial bombardments, the staged political trials, the judicial murders, the racial injustices, the economic tyrannies, and the whole socio-economic apparatus which seems geared for nothing but global destruction in spite of all its fair words in favor of peace.[47]

In a lighter vein, but no less profound, is this poem by Bob Lax, which I re-discovered in a pile of his letters sent to me from Greece. With Lax's characteristic simplicity, it was written longhand to his publisher, Emil Antonucci, on a piece of 3 by 8 cardboard. An audience at the Princeton Public Library reacted with audible amusement when I read it recently:

war/
peace

mmmmm

rrrrr

mmmmm

rrrrr

rrrrr

mmmmm

rrrrr

mmmmm

mmmmm

rrrrr

mmmmm

rrrrr[48]

Lax's horror of war and killing was certainly equal to Merton's. In fact, he had a respect for life that included all beings—even insects. My daughter Jennifer recalls that, when she visited him on Patmos in 1994, he would not let her dispose of a spider on the window sill. He had her put a glass jar over it, slip a card underneath, and release it outside.

In 1999, the year before Lax died, his *peacemaker's handbook* came out—just three poems, single words strung down 104 pages in both English and German. Here's a portion of the first one, which went 16 pages, untitled:

how
to
start
the
day
right

tips
from
the
mas
ters:

1: lie
in
bed
for
a
while

&
look
at
the
ceil
ing

2.

3.

4.

5.

be
present
to
the
mo
ments
as
they
pre
sent
them
selves
to
you

-

bring
peace
to
the
mo
ment

let
the
mo
ment
bring
peace
to
you

-

When I finished reading this poem, I realized that I was, indeed, at peace. I derived peace, as well, and considerable satisfaction when, in 2004, Merton's *Peace in the Post-Christian Era* was published with a stirring, memory-jogging introduction by Forest: "While Thomas Merton would be pleased that forty-two years later this labor of love is at last in bookshops and libraries, it would distress him that, far from being a poignant memento of a bygone era, it remains both timely and relevant."[49]

Recollections of George W. Bush's actions in Iraq come all too vividly to mind when reading, for example, this Merton remark quoted by Forest: "Indeed the big powers have been content to use the UN as a forum for political and propagandist wrestling matches and have not hesitated to take independent action that led to the discrediting of the UN whenever this has been profitable to them."[50]

Notes

1. From a paper presented at the 9th General Meeting, *International Thomas Merton Society*, San Diego, June 9-12, 2005, and from James Harford's book, *Merton & Friends A Joint Biography of Thomas Merton, Robert Lax and Edward Rice* published by Continuum International, 2006.

2. *Columbia Poetry 1939*, Columbia University Press, pp. 60-61; reprinted in *The Collected Poems of Thomas Merton* (New Directions, 1977), pp. 712-713.

3. *Jester*, December, 1938, front cover.

4. Found by the author in a pile of Lax writings, now in the Lax archive, Friedsam Library, St. Bonventure University, Olean, NY.

5. In a *Catholic Worker* remembrance of Lax in Jan., 2001, p. 7, Tom Cornell wrote that he had been trying, in the 1950s, to get the Selective Service System to make him a CO by reason of his Catholic convictions. He didn't want to go to jail, and he wanted to fill out the application well so other Catholics would find it easier to be CO's. He asked Lax for counsel. "He [Lax] had sought conscientious objector status as a Jew, arguing his claim from the Torah rule that fruit trees must be spared." and, says Cornell, "He had no heart for battle...He sat there, and all he could say was he didn't know if he would do the same all over again, but again....He wasn't going to make my mind up for me, and he wasn't going to make believe the question was any less difficult than it is."

6. Lax to Merton, Apr. 2, 1941, Lax Columbia Archive.

7. Interview with Lax, Patmos, May, 1997

8. Merton, "An Argument Of the Passion of Christ," Stanza iv, 1944, taken from *30 Poems* (New Directions) in *Collected Poems*, pp. 53-54.

9. Merton, "Figures For An Apocalypse III 1947," fourth stanza, in *Collected* Poems, pp. 139-140.

10. Merton, *30 Poems*, in *Collected Poems*, pp. 151-152.

11. Thomas Merton, *The Seven Storey Mountain* (New York: Harcourt & Brace, 1948), pp. 311-312.

12. Thomas Merton, *The Ascent for Truth* (New York: Harcourt & Brace, 1951), p. 3.

13. *Jubilee*, April, 1957, p. 1.

14. p. 15.

15. p. 19.

16. Merton letter to Rice, February 28, 1959, Rice Georgetown Archive.

17. Merton, *Collected Poems*, p. 349.

18. Merton to Lax, November 27, 1961, *When Prophecy Still Had a Voice: The Letters of Thomas Merton & Robert Lax*, ed., Arthur W. Biddle (Lexington: The University Press of Kentucky, 2001), pp. 232-233.

19. Merton to Lax, Christmas, 1961, Biddle, p. 234.

20. *Jubilee*, March, 1962, pp. 22-25

21. Merton letter to Forest, *The Hidden Ground of Love* (New York: Farrar Straus & Giroux, 1985), p. 266.

22. *Jubilee*, May, 1962, pp. 7-13: *Passion for Prayer*, pp. 65-79.

23. Merton to Ferry, May 8, 1962, *The Hidden Ground of Love*, p. 211

24. Merton, *Collected Poems*, p. 295.

25. Merton to Sister M. Emmanuel de Souza e Silva, November 2, 1962, *Hidden Ground of Love*, p.189.

26. Merton, *A Vow of Conversation, Journals, 1964-1965*, ed., Naomi Burton Stone (New York: Farrar, Straus & Giroux), p. 28, March 3, 1964.

27. Talk by James Finley to *8th International Thomas Merton Society Conference*, Vancouver, June 7, 2003. *Seeds of Destruction*, MacMillan, 1967

28. Merton, "Gandhi and the One-Eyed Giant" in *Gandhi on Non-Violence* (New York: New Directions, 1965), p. 20; *Jubilee*, January, 1965, pp. 12-17.

29. Merton, *Gandhi on Non-Violence*, p. 72.

30. Interview with Bannon, Rochester, November 18, 1999.

31. Merton to Lax, November 10, 1965, Biddle, p. 315.

32. Merton to Lax, December 28, 1965, p. 316.

33. Merton to Lentfoehr, December 30, 1965, MCA.

34. Thich Nat Nhat Nanh, *The Buddhists, Jubilee*, August, 1966, pp. 7-13

35. Merton, "Nhat Hanh is My Brother", *Jubilee*, August, 1966, p 11; *Faith and Nonviolence* (Notre Dame, IN: UND Press, 1968), p. 106.

36. Merton, *Peace and Protest, Continuum*, Vol. 3, No. 4, Winter, 1966, pp. 509-512.

37. Lax to Lange, 1967, Harford personal file.

38. Merton, *Learning to Love* (San Francisco: HarperSanFrancisco, 1997), p. 239.

39. Lax to John Slate, June 6, 1967, Merton Columbia Archive—*Road to Joy*, p. 303.

40. Merton to Lax, March 15, 1968, Merton Columbia Archive—*When Prophecy Still Had a Voice*, pp. 387-388.

41. Rice, *The Man in the Sycamore Tree* (New York: Doubleday, 1970), p. 89.

42. Merton, *The Other Side of the Mountain*, April 6, 1968 (San Francisco: Harper Collins, 1998), p. 76.

43. Merton, *The Other Side of the Mountain*, p. 33.

44. Merton, *The Other Side of the Mountain*, p. 47.

45. Merton, *The Other Side of the Mountain*, p. 67.

46. Merton, *The Other Side of the Mountain*, pp. 69-70.

47. Forest, in *Catholic Peacemakers*, Vol. II, Roland G. Musto, Garland Publishing, 1996, p.753.

48. Lax to Antonucci, August 31, 1969, Harford personal file.

49. Thomas Merton, *Peace in the Post-Christian Era* (Mary Knoll: Orbis, 2004), p.vii.

50. Merton, *Peace in the Post-Christian Era*, p. 21.

Comrades for Peace:
Thomas Merton, The Dalai Lama and
the Preferential Option for Nonviolence

Joseph Quinn Raab

1. Introduction:

The United States Conference of Catholic Bishops, in its 1993 document *The Harvest of Justice is Sown in Peace*, asserted that the Christian tradition "possesses two ways to address conflict: nonviolence and just war. Both share [a presumption against the use of force and] the common goal to diminish violence in this world."[1] The defense of peace, it said, is a moral obligation, but the how of defending peace offers moral options. One finds these two ways affirmed as well in Buddhist traditions. A recent essay by Tessa Bartholomeusz convincingly demonstrates that even Buddhism, widely regarded as a pacifistic tradition, does not *de facto* reject the use of violent force and possesses a more muted but active just-war tradition.[2] Both Thomas Merton and the Dalai Lama advocate strongly for the nonviolent option, even with deference to the possibility of justifying the use of violent force from an orthodox Christian or Buddhist perspective. The powerful polemical writings of Merton on peace are complemented by the practical proposals of His Holiness the Dalai Lama[3] and together they strengthen the tendency in Catholic social teaching to make normative the preference for the nonviolent option over the use of armed force to achieve conflict resolution in our atomic age.

In this article I recall the encounters between the two most famous monks of the twentieth century and then seek to explicate succinctly the religious sources of their common commitment to nonviolence, with a special emphasis on its monastic character. Finally, I will offer some reflections on the contribution of their legacy to the growing momentum of the nonviolent option in Christian theology and practice. I am especially indebted here to Scott Appleby who convincingly demonstrates this growing momentum,[4] even while a popular image of the "Christian right" suggests a more jingoistic trend in mainstream Christian thought and practice.[5]

2. The Encounter:

It was only weeks before his death that Thomas Merton met the Dalai Lama in Dharamsala, India on November 4, 1968. Initially Merton was surprised by the impressive physical stature of the Dalai Lama, apparently expecting to meet someone more like the diminutive Tibetan rimpoches that dotted the Himalayan landscape.[6] The Dalai Lama was struck by Merton's spiritual depth and humility but more directly by the bulk and width and practicality of Merton's fat leather belt. They immediately enjoyed each other and laughter and levity permeated their weighty religious discourse.[7] They met twice again over the next four days and in this brief time they forged a genuine friendship by discovering a profound spiritual bond. The Dalai Lama would later recall: "although we did not know each other very long, in his large hearted faith and burning desire to know, I felt the inspiration of a kindred spirit."[8]

Throughout their dialogues Merton sought clarification from His Holiness Tenzin Gyatso on the doctrines of *dzogchen, samadhi,* and *boddhicitta* and the practical methods of meditation cultivated in the Vajrayana tradition. In turn, the Dalai Lama probed Merton with questions concerning the details of Cistercian monastic life, initiation practices and vows, the Christian conception of the spiritual journey and its stages of illumination. Only at their third and final meeting did Merton breach a more political topic with the question of correlations between Marxism and Monasticism. To one looking back on Merton's account of their dialogue from a twenty-first century perspective, perhaps the most fascinating element is the conspicuous absence of any mention of the issue of nonviolence, an issue that has now come to represent a central component of their legacy. The Dalai Lama, however, did recall that they spoke about spiritual beliefs as important factors in the pursuit of world peace.[9] But their mutual attraction and connection was only derivatively based on a shared ethic concerning conflict resolution; it was based primarily on the similar structure and aims of their monastic lives of prayer and contemplation and on what the Dalai Lama characterized as their quest for "mental peace." The contemplative ground of their dialogue nourished their common purpose, as the Dalai Lama later identified it, as "comrades" in that struggle for peace and social transformation.[10]

3. The Source of an Ethic:
Merton's Apocalyptic Christianity

For as much as Merton readers like to celebrate his 'embrace of the world' and his being "at home in the world" after his Louisville experience, we must recognize that Thomas Merton remained at his core a radically eschatological Christian. John Dominic Crossan, in describing the eschatological nature of *Q* and of the early Jesus movement, defines eschatology as "one of the great and fundamental options of the human spirit. It is a profoundly explicit 'no' to the profoundly implicit 'yes' by which we usually accept life's norms, culture's presuppositions, and civilization's discontents."[11]   Likewise, John Kloppenborg describes the eschatological form of early Christian discipleship as marked by one's "separation from family and rejection of the norms of macrosociety, [by one's embrace of] poverty, homelessness, and even martyrdom. More positively, it is understood as imitation of the merciful and generous God."[12] It is in this apocalyptic Christian tradition that dates from the earliest Jesus movement that Merton stands and within which his attitude toward the world must be understood.

Less than five years before his death Merton wrote:

It is my intention to make my entire life a rejection of, a protest against the crimes and injustices of war and political tyranny …. By my monastic life and vows I am saying *NO* to all the concentration camps, the aerial bombardments, the staged political trials, the judicial murders, the racial injustices, the economic tyrannies, and the whole socio-economic apparatus which seems geared for nothing but global destruction in spite of all its fair words in favor of peace.[13]

Merton's eschatological voice did not project the apocalypse into the indeterminate future, but proclaimed the kingdom already present as a transforming leaven in the post-lapsarian human world. This realized eschatology would inform the way Merton looked at everything, from monasticism and mysticism to modernity, from the patristic period to the peace movement of the 1960s. Thus he could write in *Peace in the Post-Christian Era*:

[T]he Christian attitude to war and peace is fundamentally eschatological. The Christian does not need to fight and indeed it is better that he should not fight, for insofar as he imitates his Lord and master, he proclaims that the messianic kingdom has come and bears witness to the presence of the *Kyrios Pantocrator* in mystery even in the midst of the conflicts and turmoil of the world.[14]

The imitation of Christ, for Thomas Merton, should include not only his monastic vows but, if necessary, imitating the way Christ responded to the violence committed against him. The Christian, he writes, "is bound to imitate the Savior who, instead of defending himself with twelve legions of angels (Matt. 26:25), allowed himself to be nailed to the Cross and died praying for his executioners."[15]

Merton supports his view that not only Christ but Christ's disciples should respond to violence with patient endurance and forgiveness by making a point that scandalizes many literal-minded Christians who read the Apocalypse (Revelation) as justifying the use of force on behalf of so-called Christian nations for the defense or advancement of national interests: He writes: "The book of the New Testament that definitely canonizes this eschatological view of peace in the midst of spiritual combat is the Apocalypse, which sets forth in mysterious and symbolic language the critical struggle of the nascent Church with the powers of the world, as typified by the Roman Empire."[16]

Christianity, however, has a dual tradition of both a realized and a futurist eschatology. The Kingdom is both already and not yet fully present in this world. As much as we are redeemed and living in the Spirit we are also pilgrims preparing for death, in need of fuller conversion and greater transformation. The nonviolent option in the face of conflict and the willing embrace of martyrdom, as Merton presents it, belongs to the tradition of realized eschatology, while the just war option, I would suggest, belongs more appropriately to the futurist tradition that permits lesser evils for the avoidance or elimination of greater ones and for the perceived promotion of the common good. This dual eschatological tradition runs through monasticism as well, and through every believer, including Thomas Merton.

Merton takes care in his writings to explicitly affirm Catholic just war tradition by recognizing its rational merits. But he tries to show how modern warfare and what we now call "weapons of mass destruction" make the practical application of this logically viable theory virtually impossible.[17] This alerts him to the need to argue against modern warfare akin to the way the Magisterium has consistently argued its case against abortion; namely that affirming a moral prohibition against it need not rest on faith alone or strictly religious principles, but can be supported by logical argument in the dialectical fashion accessible to reasonable people, religious and non-religious alike. To show this Merton adeptly addresses the perennial problem of conflating the ten just war principles to the single one of just cause (only one of seven criteria that need to be met in order to justify entering a war; there are three more for carrying out military campaigns justly). Once a nation has justified its causes for war, he argues, the means employed in the service of victory, regardless of their moral merit, are all too easily justified as necessary for obtaining the desired result.[18] The consistent violation of just war principles during war-time, such as prisoner abuses, countless civilian casualties, disproportionate measures of retaliation employed in the service of victory and disproportionate damage, confront us with the realization that while just causes for entering a war can be logically supported, we may never have seen a just war carried through to term. In short, Merton's position is largely apocalyptic, but it is also a critically sound engagement of just war thinking and explicates a persuasive and overwhelming preference for the nonviolent option, while refraining from an unconditional pacifism or condemnation of the just war principles.

4. The Source of an Ethic:
The Dalai Lama's Universal Compassion:

Tenzin Gyatso, the current Dalai Lama, tells us in his autobiography that his predecessor, Thupten Gyatso the 13th Dalai Lama, forcibly expelled an invading Manchu army in 1911-1912 and later undertook an ambitious campaign to modernize Tibet, one that included strengthening its military defenses.[19] The 13th Dalai Lama, in his last written testament, had also warned of the future destruction of Tibet and the repression of Vajrayana Buddhism. By the time Tenzin Gyatso came of age the Tibetan world had changed dramatically and the prophecy of his predecessor had come to fruition. On November 17, 1950, at the age of fifteen, the current Dalai Lama assumed temporal leadership of a nation of six million people on the brink of war with China.

Nonviolent resistance was not the Dalai Lama's initial plan. He knew the Tibetan army numbering 8,500 was no match for the 80,000 soldiers of the Chinese People's Liberation Army that had invaded the Chamdo district of Tibet a month earlier, and at this early stage of occupation he had taken no official position and armed resistance had not been entirely ruled out. Some of his closest advisers, including his elder brother Taktser Rinpoche, abbot of Kumbum Monastery, advised him to enlist the military support of Britain and the United States. His Holiness was aware that "although the Buddha forbade killing, he had indicated that under certain circumstances it could be justified"[20] and this may have assuaged his conscience as he began to look outside Tibet for support against the Chinese. He sent delegations to Nepal, India, Britain and the United States appealing for assistance, only to receive none. But his brother's talks with the U.S. consulate in India continued and seemed to keep the possibility of U.S. military support alive. His Holiness then began to weigh the ethics, practicality and possible results of such a U.S.-Tibet alliance in war against the Chinese, and he backed away from what seemed to him to be an ill-fated and bloody course of action.

The Dalai Lama's own account of these events suggests that his embrace of the nonviolent response to Chinese occupation was arrived at by a careful consideration of traditional just war principles. That is to say, the Dalai Lama's initial option for nonviolent resistance was based on his belief that the necessary conditions for overriding the strong Buddhist presumption against the use of violent force could not be met in this situation. He had just cause and legitimate authority to invoke war, but he was not convinced of the probability of success, or that the destruction caused by the war would be outweighed by the good it could achieve (proportionality), or that he had exhausted all peaceful alternatives (last resort).[21] Given these serious doubts he opted for continued negotiation and nonviolent resistance. However, since he made that initial choice his preference for a more universal nonviolent ethic has been strengthened over the past several decades, largely by his further appropriation of his monastic aim of realizing in himself the *mahakaruna* (the great or universal compassion).

The Buddhist monastic aim of realizing the great compassion of the Buddha is in many respects correlative with the Christian monastic aim of a realized eschatology. In his interview with Paul Wilkes, the Dalai Lama speaks of Buddhism in terms reminiscent of Merton's apocalyptic voice when he says "true religion must be a sort of destroyer. Compassion and tolerance, these we can call destroyers of anger. Destroyers of hatred."[22]   The cultivation of the virtue of humility or patience (what the Buddhist calls *ksanti*) is essential to the realization of the eschatological fullness of wisdom and compassion (*prajna* and *karuna*). *Prajna* is born of the recognition that everything that exists is radically interdependent and each person who exists shares responsibility both for what is and for what ought to be. This radical interdependence of identity makes impossible the purging of evil through a sacrificial scapegoat or the objectifying of an enemy as purely evil while we perceive ourselves as good. Hence the major religious justifications for violence dissolve.[23]   The recognition of the complex multiple causality of self-constitution leads to compassion for the enemy out of a shared guilt and shared responsibility for the evil of unnecessary violence in the world. Illustrating this point, the Catholic philosopher Charles Taylor suggests that while there is no simple remedy for the cycle of violence:

> There can be moves, always within a context, whereby someone renounces the right conferred by suffering, the right of the innocent to punish the guilty, of the victim to purge the victimizer. The move is the very opposite of the instinctive defense of our righteousness. It is a move that can be called forgiveness, but at a deeper level, it is based on a recognition of common, flawed humanity.... It opens a new footing of co-responsibility to the erstwhile enemy.[24]

The Dalai Lama speaks of this same renunciation in terms of detachment. After recalling the story of a Tibetan nun who in 2002 reported her experience of brutal torture under the Chinese, and after goading the Dalai Lama with a pessimistic account of the progress he had made with China since 1951, Evan Solomon in a recent CBC interview asks His Holiness, isn't it time for a different way: "Is this not a perfect case for a just war?"[25]   But the Dalai Lama did not waver from his nonviolent ethic in his response, urging continued dialogue and putting a more hopeful spin on recent events concerning the question of Tibet. Evan Solomon then personalized the question and asked whether if Mr. Solomon's

daughter were attacked, he would not be justified in a violent response against that attacker: after thoughtful consideration the
Dalai Lama answered that with the motivation of protecting one's
child one may intervene "with a stick or even gun. But, not kill
that person, preferably...not shoot the person in the head, but
something like in the leg. That, I think, is the proper way." Then
the Dalai Lama took the opportunity to speak about detachment
and universal compassion.

> Attachments based on biological impulse or the attachment to
> country, or the attachment to matters, or possessions, or the
> attachment to one's name—these are narrow minded—focused
> on one particular sort of object.... Now, the other kind of feel-
> ing of intimacy or closeness, that we call compassion, it's not
> biased, even towards your own enemy or neutral people, see
> even towards your enemy, through discipline and reasoning,
> you can develop...that compassion. So, the practitioner tries
> to increase...to widen that understanding of compassion and
> love, and that automatically reduces that narrow, single-
> pointed, biased sort of love or compassion. So, that's the way.
> Of course, it's not easy.[26]

5. Reflections on the Legacy of Friendship:

In a recent essay Scott Appleby argues that momentum has been
developing within both Christian theology and praxis toward a
normative nonviolent ethic of peace-building. He states, "today
nonviolence is seen by significant numbers of Christians not merely
as an option, but as a non-negotiable dimension of Christian discipleship."[27] The legacy of Thomas Merton and the Dalai Lama
contributes significantly to this growing trajectory.

In 1974 the Benedictine Confederation founded the organization called Monastic Interreligious Dialogue (MID) as a response
to a request from the Vatican to pursue mutual understanding
among spiritual traditions. Following the MID's conference at the
Parliament of World Religions in Chicago in 1993, the Dalai Lama
suggested that a more extensive and in-depth encounter between
Buddhist and Christian monks ought to take place and he proposed the Abbey of Gethsemani as the location for this meeting, in
honor of his friend the late Thomas Merton. Since the historic
meeting in 1996 at Gethsemani, the work of the MID has been

largely a continuation of the friendship between Thomas Merton and the Dalai Lama, and peacebuilding, both personally and socially, is integral to the work of the MID. [28] The fruits of these labors are collected in the published talks from these gatherings in *The Gethsemani Encounter: A Dialogue on the Spiritual Life by Buddhist and Christian Monastics* and in *Transforming Suffering: Reflections on Finding Peace in Troubled Times*, and in an audio compact disc entitled "Compassion." The immediate aim of the MID is to foster understanding between Buddhist and Christian monks and nuns but a residual effect of this enterprise has been a broader consciousness—raising concerning the importance of the traditional spiritual resources, Buddhist and Christian, for cultivating both personal and social peace and transformation. Indeed, Donald Mitchell reminds us that *The Gethsemani Encounter* was "chosen as a selection for the Book of the Month Club, received the 2002 Frederick J. Streng Book Award, and was even touted on *Sports Center* by Phil Jackson."[29] Obviously, the work of the MID is reaching the wider public and contributing to a broader consideration of the potential of these wisdom traditions for offering guidance for social change in troubled times.

But the question remains, if nonviolence is increasingly understood as a non-negotiable dimension of discipleship (whether Buddhist or Christian) does this mean that the just war principles are obsolete for seriously devoted practitioners? Both Thomas Merton and the Dalai Lama, largely because of the degree to which each has realized in himself the aims of his monastic practice, find that fewer and fewer conditions or exceptions could apply to the normative ethic of nonviolence. This is not to say, however, that they deny absolutely the possibility of justifiably using violent force. Neither Thomas Merton nor The Dalai Lama go as far as their mentor Mahatma Gandhi, who hoped he would not even defend himself against the aggressive advances of a venomous snake.[30]

The American Catholic Bishops' 1983 and 1993[31] documents on war and peace reaffirmed the legitimacy of the nonviolent option, and conscientious objection, for Catholics. Furthermore, they emphasized that the strong presumption against the use of violent force is built in to the just war principles themselves, and the principles ought to be understood in this light. The teaching of the USCCB on war and peace is strictly in accord with the trajectory initiated by the Second Vatican Council, which hurled no anathemas but issued one condemnation. It condemned geno-cide, ethnic cleansing and "every act of war directed to the indis-criminate destruction of whole cities and vast areas with their in-habitants" as crimes against God and humanity (*Gaudium et spes*, pp. 79-80).

Merton would have been delighted by Pope John Paul II's con-sistent refusal to endorse war as a means to peace; though not an unqualified pacifist, he refused to deem just any military opera-tion undertaken by the U.S. government during his Papacy. The late Pope's insistence on "saying no to war" suggests that in the overwhelming majority of cases the faithful and prayerful appli-cation of just war principles ought to lead us to opt for nonvio-lence.[32]   In this way the just war principles are not at odds with but support a preference for the nonviolent option. The more ex-plicit we make this preferential option for nonviolence and the more we emphasize it, the more difficult it should be for us to justify the use of violent military force. Indeed it was the pre-sumption against war built in to the just war principles that ini-tially helped lead the Dalai Lama himself to opt for nonviolent resistance against the Chinese occupation.

As long as Christianity is both a community of pilgrims in for-mation seeking the Kingdom, and a community of the transformed who embody the message and person of Christ, as long as the Eschaton is both beyond us and realized within us, the dual tradi-tion of just war and nonviolence rightly remains. Merton's seri-ous consideration of Catholic just war tradition does not lead him to a position of unqualified pacifism. The Dalai Lama concedes that violent force may be justified in the case of defending the help-less child. They both leave room for the just war option. The just war principles, however, are meant to establish strict parameters regarding the use of force. The effectiveness of the principles, how-ever, is strictly dependent upon the personal authenticity of the one who makes the determinations as to whether their conditions have been fulfilled, and therein lies the difficulty. The problem is not with the just war principles themselves but with their vulner-ability to cooption and to ideological corruption when used by the powerful to advance interests that are dubiously equated with the common good. How many Christians saw Desert Storm and Iraqi Freedom as just and necessary wars? The Dalai Lama has not, Pope John Paul II did not, and, we can be sure, Thomas Merton would not have either.

Notes

1. National Conference of Catholic Bishops, *The Harvest of Justice is Sown in Peace* (Washington, D.C.: USCC Office for Publication and Promotion Services, 1993), p. 7.

2. Tessa Bartholomeusz, "In Defense of Dharma: Just War Ideology in Buddhist Sri Lanka," available at http://jbe.gold.ac.uk/6/bartho991.htm

3. For example, see the Dalai Lama's Five Point Plan for Tibetan-Chinese relations laid out in his Nobel Lecture from 1989.

4. R. Scott Appleby traces this growing momentum from the World Wars to the present in "Disciples of the Prince of Peace? Christian Resources for Nonviolent Peacebuilding," in *Beyond Violence: Religious Sources of Social Transformation*, edited by James L. Heft, S.M. (New York: Fordham University Press, 2003), pp. 113-145.

5. See for example, Jim Wallis, "Dangerous Religion: George W. Bush's Theology of Empire," *Sojourners* (September-October 2003), pp 21-26.

6. Thomas Merton, ed. Patrick Hart, *The Other Side of the Mountain: The Journals of Thomas Merton*, Vol. 7, 1967-1968. (San Francisco: Harper Collins, 1998), pp. 251.

7. *Merton: By Those Who Knew Him Best*, edited by Paul Wilkes (New York: Harper and Row, 1987), pp. 145, 147.

8. *The Gethsemani Encounter: A Dialogue on the Spiritual Life by Buddhist and Christian Monastics*, edited by Donald W. Mitchell and James Wiseman, O.S.B. (New York: Continuum, 1997), p. ix.

9. *Merton: By Those Who Knew Him Best*, pp. 146-147.

10. *Merton: By Those Who Knew Him Best*, p. 147.

11. John Dominic Crossan, *The Birth of Christianity: Discovering What Happened in the Years Immediately After the Execution of Jesus* (San Francisco: HarperSanFrancisco, 1998), p. 259.

12. John S. Kloppenborg, *The Formation of Q: Trajectories in Ancient Wisdom Collections. Studies in Antiquity and Christianity* (Philadelphia: Fortress Press, 1987), p.241

13. Thomas Merton, *"Honorable Reader": Reflections on My Work*, ed. Robert Daggy (New York: Crossroad, 1989), p. 65.

14. Thomas Merton, *Peace in the Post-Christian Era* (New York: Orbis Books, 2004), p. 29.

15. Merton, *Peace in the Post-Christian Era*, p. 29.

16. Merton, *Peace in the Post-Christian Era*, p. 29.

17. See *Peace in the Post Christian Era*, Chapter 7, entitled "Justice in Modern War" (pp. 58-67).

18. Merton, *Peace in the Post-Christian Era*, p. 59.

19. The Dalai Lama, *Freedom in Exile: The Autobiography of The Dalai Lama* (San Francisco: Harper Collins, 1990), pp. 31-33.

20. *Freedom in Exile, The Autobiography of The Dalai Lama*, p. 55.

21. *Freedom in Exile, The Autobiography of The Dalai Lama*, pp. 55-56.

22. *Merton: By Those Who Knew Him Best*, p. 147.

23. Charles Taylor demonstrates the correlation between physical violence and the Judeo-Christian conception of sacrificial purification or purgation in his essay, "Notes on the Sources of Violence: Perennial and Modern," *Beyond Violence: Religious Sources of Social Transformation*, ed. James L. Heft, S.M. (New York: Fordham University Press, 2003), pp. 15–42.

24. "Notes on the Sources of Violence," p. 39.

25. The CBC interview of the Dalai Lama by the journalist Evan Solomon is available at: http://www.cbc.ca/sunday/dalailama.html.

26. CBC interview.

27. "Disciples of the Prince of Peace," p. 113.

28. See *Transforming Suffering: Reflections on Finding Peace in Troubled Times*, eds. Donald W. Mitchell and James Wiseman, OSB (New York: Doubleday, 2003), pp. vii-xiii.

29. *Transforming* Suffering, p. x.

30. Mahatma Gandhi, *All Men Are Brothers: Autobiographical Reflections*, compiled and edited by Krishna Kripalani (New York: Continuum, 1999), p. 89.

31. These are The National Conference of Catholic Bishops' documents: *The Challenge of Peace* (Washington, D.C.: USCC Office for Publication and Promotion Services, 1983) and *The Harvest of Justice is Sown in Peace* (Washington, D.C.: USCC Office for Publication and Promotion Services, 1993).

32. For a sampling of John Paul II's teaching concerning the problem of war and preference for nonviolence see: http://sao.clriq.org.au/peace/jp2_peace.html#top.

The Spirit of Simplicity:
Thomas Merton on Simplification of Life[1]

Paul R. Dekar

At the time of Thomas Merton's profession at the Abbey of Gethsemani, Abbot Frederic Dunne encouraged him to continue to publish poetry and to write several works of history. In response, early during his monastic vocation, Merton published four collections of poetry, a history of the Cistercian movement; biographies of Mary Piguet, better known as Mother Berchmans, who lived from 1876-1915 and was first a nun of the Convent of the Redemption in France and then of Our Lady of the Angels in Japan and of the thirteenth-century Flemish Cistercian mystic Saint Lutgarde of Aywières; and a study of the sixteenth-century Spanish mystic John of the Cross.[2]

Merton also left us two books on the greatest of the early Cistercians, Bernard of Clairvaux: a biography to mark the eighth centenary of Bernard's death; and a collection on Bernard's spirituality.[3] This compilation included two essays that appeared first in the order's journal, *Collectanea Ordinis Cisterciensium Reformatorum*, and "St. Bernard on Spiritual Simplicity," which originally appeared as part 2 of *The Spirit of Simplicity*, published in 1948. In the "Foreword" to this early book, Merton examined the subject of this article. Merton asserted that simplicity is one of the outstanding characteristics of Cistercian spirituality and of Cistercian saintliness. Indeed, when members of the Order were seen to grow and progress in sanctity, the chief quality that they acquired was simplicity.[4]

Authorship of *The Spirit of Simplicity* is inscribed anonymously as by "A Cistercian Monk of Our Lady of Gethsemani." As a result, *The Spirit of Simplicity* is among the least-known of Merton's books. Written before Merton's meteoric rise to fame, it is nevertheless foundational not only to Merton's monastic scholarship, but also to Merton's continuing wide appeal.

A number of sources confirm Merton's authorship of *The Spirit of Simplicity*. In 1950, Merton sent a copy of *The Spirit of Simplicity* to the Benedictine scholar Jean Leclercq. While no copy exists of Merton's initial correspondence with Leclercq regarding this early research on Cistercian simplicity, Merton and Leclercq subsequently explored themes raised in the book along with Merton's ongoing search for simplification of life.[5] When in 1980 Cistercian Publications reprinted part of *The Spirit of Simplicity*, Leclercq commented on the enduring value of this area of Merton's scholarship. "This early Merton, already full of love and enthusiasm, still marked to some degree by ingenuousness, was building the solid foundation upon which would rise Merton the activist and social critic of the following decades."[6] Adding a foreword to the work's re-publication, Patrick Hart concluded,

> these studies…are as relevant today as when they were written—perhaps more so…. In fact the interest extends far beyond the monastic enclosure to the university campus, the market place and even the family household. Everywhere one hears the question: how can I lead a deeply contemplative life in the midst of my present activities? …Is union with God possible? Thomas Merton struggled with these problems in his own monastic life and finally came to the conclusion that there is a Martha, a Mary and a Lazarus in each of us, and we must learn to live together in peace, ever striving to arrive at a balanced measure in our lives…. In the final analysis, the most perfect way for each person is the total response in faith and love to one's personal call, to one's God-given vocation.[7]

In European history, the eleventh and twelfth centuries were times of renaissance and reformation. Wealthy monasteries, notably the Abbey of Cluny in Burgundy, with its church, constructed between 1088 and 1130, that was taller than the Vatican and the greatest ecclesiastical structure that had ever been built in the West, dominated the era.

The emergence of the Cistercian movement can be understood both positively, as a return to the sources of Benedictine monasticism, and negatively, as a reaction to the excessive power of Cluny. Bernard's *Apology to William of St. Thierry*, quoted several times by Merton, is the *pièce justificative* in the controversy between the Cluniac and Cistercian spirituality.[8] Of noble birth, William and his brother Simon studied at the Benedictine Monastery of Saint Nicaise at Reims. Both embraced the religious life and became abbots, Simon at St. Nicolas-aux-Bois in the diocese of Laon, and William at St-Thierry near Reims where he implemented reforms associated with Pope Gregory VII and the Cluniac movement. A long-time friendship with Bernard led William to abdicate. He became a Cistercian at Signy where he wrote on the spiritual life until his death in 1148.

The Spirit of Simplicity opens with a six-page foreword. Part One includes Merton's translation and comments on the report of the 1925 General Chapter of the Order of Cistercians of the Strict Observance. Within the text are eleven plates of twelfth-century Cistercian monasteries and the plan for typical twelfth-century Cistercian church architecture. Part Two, "St. Bernard on Interior Simplicity," has selections from Bernard, Merton's commentary and a three-page conclusion. Notable is Merton's careful reading of selections highlighting Bernard's teaching on simplicity.

Several times Merton quotes Bernard's 1127 treatise against Cluny. Bernard criticized the building of such great structures and the comfortable lifestyle of the monks. Bernard was scathing:

> Oh, vanity of vanities, whose vanity is rivaled only by its insanity! The walls of the church are aglow, but the poor of the Church go hungry. The stones of the church are covered with gold, while its children are left naked. The food of the poor is taken to feed the eyes of the rich, and amusement is provided for the curious, while the needy have not even the necessities of life.[9]

Merton did not dwell on Bernard's critique of Cluniac monasticism. He did emphasize that Bernard was *"just as strong in castigating Cistercians, who were bordering on Pharisaism in their contempt of Cluny, as the easy-going Cluniacs themselves."*[10] Believing in the need to live out of the spirit as well as the letter of Benedict's teaching on simple living, Merton commented,

> ...when Cistercians build in fake, overdecorated gothic in preference to something on simple, functional modern lines, they are unconsciously contradicting the whole Cistercian tradition and ideal in their very attempt to preserve it. On the other hand, the more functional and the less antiquarian our use of gothic styles, the more true will they be to the spirit of the purest Cistercian art.[11]

For the early Cistercians, Merton observes, simplicity consisted in *"getting rid of everything that did not help the monk to arrive at union with God by the shortest possible way.* And the shortest possible way to arrive at union with God, who is Love, is by loving Him, in Himself, and in our brethren."[12] Merton continues in order to attain charity, the love of God, the early Cistercians discarded everything, especially *"means of getting to God that were less direct."*[13]

Discerning the radical implications of the doctrine of simplicity, Merton observes how Bernard and other early Cistercians emphasized the need to simplify art, architecture and life-style. A monastic son of Bernard, Merton is seeking to recover this aspect of the *Rule of Benedict* in ways relevant to twentieth-century Christians who are often burdened with the worries of this life. "For nothing is as inconsistent with the life of *any* Christian as overindulgence. Our Lord says: Take care that your hearts are not weighed down with overindulgence. Luke 21:34."[14]

Merton defines simplicity as the perfect conversion of the will to God and a genuine humility according to which the simple person is not afraid to be thought a fool by the world, that he or she may be wise unto God. Who truly seeks God simplifies her or his life. This teaching is a re-statement of *RB* 58: 24, to which the charter documents of the Cistercian order are faithful. Monks must unencumber their lives. "If he has any possessions, he should... give them to the poor beforehand ...."

To summarize the first part of Merton's essay, simplicity is a broad theological category including qualities such as humility, obedience and charity. Merton sees the General Chapter of 1925 as a wake-up call for the spiritual children of Benedict and Bernard to ground their search for the greatest desired end, namely, the knowledge of self, uncluttered lives and ultimately union with God. By entering into the fundamental spirit of simplicity of the first Benedictines and Cistercians, and of all the saints, Merton believed that the monks of Gethsemani should give up active works and all non-essentials to concentrate on living contemplatively. By implication all Christians are to follow the path of simplicity, silence, solitude and stillness. In short, for Merton, simplicity is an essential mark of our truest humanity.

In Part Two, "St. Bernard on Interior Simplicity," Merton highlights the relationship between his call for simplicity and his understanding of anthropology: "The whole aim of the Cistercian life—and the Fathers of the Order are unanimous on this point—

is to set men apart from the world that their souls may be purified and led step by step to perfect union with God by the recovery of our lost likeness to him."[15] For Merton, practices such as simplicity, solitude and silence help monks come to perfect union of wills with God, by love. Bernard calls this union with the Holy One "Mystical Marriage." These cornerstones of Cistercian asceticism are practices by which we may all claim our full humanity as God's children in the image and likeness of God.

> ...St. Bernard has really vindicated the fundamental goodness of human nature in terms as strong as have ever been used by any philosopher or theologian. And if the first step in the Cistercian ascent to God is for the monk to *know himself* ... the whole life of such a one will consist in *being himself*, or rather trying to return to the original simplicity, immortality and freedom which constitute his real self, in the image of God.[16]

Merton is developing a key idea. Contemplation strengthens us to claim our true self and to resist cultural pressure to conform to a false self. Augustine calls the true self a divine center, Calvin a divine spark and other theologians "soul." For Merton, the "real self" or "true self" is the God-given center of our being. If we go to the heart of our lives; if we do not buy into culture's false claims, we find the risen Christ, one with us, alive in us, giving us strength to engage the powers and principalities, even death.

Merton next presents the idea of "intellectual simplicity." By this phrase he means not only eliminating all that is superfluous, unnecessary or indirect, but also concerning ourselves exclusively with *"the one thing necessary*—the knowledge and love of God, union with Him."[17] Merton acknowledges that intellectual simplicity is more than a matter of knowledge. It prepares the contemplative for the deeper and more searching simplification of life that follows, namely, obedience, purification of the will and "social simplicity."[18]

Continuing this argument in the paragraphs that follow, Merton describes the process as follows: Cistercian simplicity begins in humility and self-denial, moves through the monastic vow of obedience, is perfected by love and culminates in a spiritual unity and peace. The Holy and Undivided Trinity is reflected not only in the souls of individuals, but also in the community. God is pleased to bend down and raise up those persons who move in the direction of simplicity. By their humility they manifest unity in community. By their mystical prayer, they attain a closer and far more intimate union with God and bear such fruits of the Spirit as love.

Merton stresses returning to the sources of his life in community, the *Holy Bible,* the *Rule of Benedict* and the earliest Cistercian writings. A cornerstone of post World War II United States monastic renewal, of which Merton's books were a principal catalyst, these sources led Merton and an entire generation back to the desert saints in whom one may discern the basic realities of the interior life such as faith, humility, charity, meekness, discretion, and self-denial. To highlight this heritage, Merton wrote, in addition to *The Spirit of Simplicity,* an anthology of early monastic sayings, *The Wisdom of the Desert,* in which he declared, "What the Fathers sought most of all was their own true self, in Christ."[19]

Recovery of the earliest sources of Western monasticism led religious seekers to self-knowledge and simplicity. For Merton, recovering the purity of such practices as *lectio divina,* contemplation and simplicity would allow monks to know themselves, simplify their lives and foster love, unity, peace and "eternal union with the uncreated Simplicity that is the Triune God, that He may make perfect in us as in our Fathers the image of that Simplicity."[20]

The Spirit of Simplicity in Merton's Other Writings

Having reclaimed Merton's crucial work as translator and commentator on monastic classics, we can now briefly locate that work as part of Merton's wider literary activity. Written in the same period as *Spirit of Simplicity* and completed on July 1, 1948, *Seeds of Contemplation* reflected Merton's maturing understanding of simplicity. Less read than its revised successor, *New Seeds of Contemplation,* the original *Seeds* presents a collection of notes and personal reflections on many themes running throughout Merton's writing, including his desire for simplicity in pursuit of God and his distinction between the false self and the true self. A few brief passages suffice:

> For how can I receive the seeds of freedom if I am in love with slavery and how can I cherish the desire of God if I am filled with another and an opposite desire? God cannot plant His liberty in me because I am a prisoner and I do not even desire

to be free. I love my captivity and I lock myself in the desire for the things that I hate, and I have hardened my heart against true love.[21]

Merton stresses desiring God, "God alone" according to words on the gate that opens into the monastic quarters.[22] Simplification of life is part of the process by which we disencumber our lives of all that detracts from this one good thing. Our attachments can get the best of us and prevent us from living into our truest self. According to Merton, "For me to be a saint means to be myself. Therefore the problem of sanctity and salvation is in fact the problem of finding out who I am and of discovering my true self."[23]

Continuing his discussion of our truest selfhood in chapter 4, "We are One Man," Merton states that one goes into the desert not to escape others but to find them in God. One goes to the monastery not because it is there that one can be "holier than thou." Rather, one discovers one's true self in relation with God, nature and others.

One of the greatest paradoxes of the mystical life is this: that *a man cannot enter into the deepest center of himself and pass through that center into God, unless he is able to pass entirely out of himself and empty himself and give himself to other people in the purity of a selfless love.*[24]

Merton reiterates what he explored in *The Spirit of Simplicity*. He regards Cistercian practices such as detachment and renunciation as essential to recovery of freedom and of the true self. Reading what Merton first penned over fifty years ago, contemporaries may find chapter 18 on detachment strikingly descriptive of our lives as busy non-monastics:

...many contemplatives never become great saints, never enter into close friendship with God, never find a deep participation in His immense joys, because they cling to the miserable little consolations that are given to beginners in the contemplative way.

How many there are who are in a worse state still: they never even get as far as contemplation because they are attached to activities and enterprises that seem to them to be important. Blinded by their desire for ceaseless motion, for a constant sense of achievement, famished with a crude hunger

for results, for visible and tangible success, they work themselves into a state in which they cannot believe that they are
pleasing God unless they are busy with a dozen jobs at the
same time.[25]

In chapter 24 on renunciation, Merton writes in a way that appealed to a generation of spiritual seekers:

Life in a Trappist monastery is fundamentally peasant life. The
closer it conforms to the poverty and frugality and simplicity
of those who have to dig their living out of the land, the more
it fulfills its essential purpose, which is to dispose men for contemplation.[26]

While the time has passed during which one might characterize
Trappist monasticism as peasant life, Merton's main point remains
pertinent. Possessions, superfluous religious practices and inane
images are distractions. The contemplative must never lose sight
of her or his simple desire for union with God. Only then can one
experience ecstatic union with God and pure love.

In a later collection, *Thoughts in Solitude* (1958), Merton addresses a theme that later preoccupies him into the 1960s. He worries about technology and mass society. Machines bring new levels of noise and business to the community, thereby posing an
obstacle to communing with God and discovering one's true self.
Technology poses a wider threat:

In an age when totalitarianism has striven, in every way, to
devaluate and degrade the human person, we hope it is right
to demand a hearing for any and every sane reaction in the
favor of man's inalienable solitude and his interior freedom...
[S]ociety depends for its existence on the inviolable personal
solitude of its members. Society, to merit its name, must be
made up not of numbers, or mechanical units, but of persons.
To be a person implies responsibility and freedom, and both
these imply a certain interior solitude....

When men are merely submerged in a mass of impersonal
human beings pushed around by automatic forces, they lose
their true humanity, their integrity, their ability to love, their
capacity for self-determination.... No amount of technological progress will cure the hatred that eats away the vitals of

materialistic society like a spiritual cancer. The only cure is, and must always be, spiritual. [27]

Mass, technological society can confuse people about what is unreal and what is truly real. For Merton, society depends for its existence on the inviolability of each person, each with the capacity to find personal simplicity and solitude. One need not become a monk to go to desert places:

>...the "unreality" of material things is only relative to the *greater* reality of spiritual things....
>
> The Desert Fathers believed that the wilderness had been created as supremely valuable in the eyes of God precisely because it had no value to men....
>
> [L]ook at the deserts today. What are they? The birthplace of a new and terrible creation, the testing-ground of the power by which man seeks to un-create what God has blessed. Today, in the century of man's greatest technological achievement, the wilderness at last comes into its own. Man no longer needs God.... When man and his money and machines move out into the desert, and dwell there, not fighting the devil as Christ did, but believing in his promises of power and wealth, and adoring his angelic wisdom, then the desert itself moves everywhere. Everywhere is desert. Everywhere is solitude in which man must do penance and fight the adversary and purify his own heart in the grace of God.[28]

One figurative wilderness is the simple life. Merton writes, "The more we are content with our own poverty the closer we are to God for then we accept our poverty in peace, expecting nothing from ourselves and everything from God."[29] In this passage, poverty is less a monetary concept than a door to freedom and source of hope. When one knows that she or he has found her or his vocation, that person stops thinking about how to live and begins to live. Simplification of life allows one to hear God, find God and measure life by the embrace of God. "Solitude...has to be a communion in something greater than the world, as great as Being itself, in order that in its deep peace we may find God."[30] Merton concludes that by the gift of silence, and poverty, and solitude, where everything one touches is turned into prayer, one is enriched. The sky is our prayer, the birds are our prayer, the wind in the trees is our prayer. God is all in all and is all. So discovering God, one responds with gratitude. The natural response welling up from a life given to simplicity and solitude is gratitude.

As a point of congruence in the dual theme of self knowledge and simplicity, let me cite that well-known passage where Merton recounts his experience from 1958 at the corner of Fourth and Walnut in Louisville, Kentucky. As revised for *Conjectures of a Guilty Bystander*, Merton re-iterates his rejection of monasticism as flight:

> ... but the conception of "separation from the world" that we have in the monastery too easily presents itself as a complete illusion: the illusion that by making vows we become a different species of being, pseudoangels, "spiritual men," men of interior life, what have you.
>
> Certainly these traditional values are very real, but their reality is not of an order outside everyday existence in a contingent world, nor does it entitle one to despise the secular ... we are in the same world as everybody else, the world of the bomb, the world of race hatred, the world of technology, the world of mass media, big business, revolution, and all the rest. We take a different attitude to all these things .... But does that entitle us to consider ourselves different, or even *better*, than others?

Simplicity and other practices enable us to participate in the Divine Nature and thereby become one with the God of infinite love:

> I have the immense joy of being *man*, a member of a race in which God Himself became incarnate. As if the sorrows and stupidities of the human condition could overwhelm me, now I realize what we all are. And if only everybody could realize this! But it cannot be explained. There is no way of telling people that they are all walking around shining like the sun.[31]

So describing that particular moment of epiphany, Merton understands his vocation in an entirely new way. His calling is not to escape from the world but to engage the world at the deepest level in suffering and transformation. Whatever the circumstances that led him to Gethsemani—his wild youth, his open sexuality, his possible draft resistance, his horror at a world marked by genocide and other evils—by the time of this Louisville experience, Merton has resolved a crisis of generativity and is assuming a new calling,[32] that of nurturing a new world into being, one free of bombs, racism, the worst effects of technology, media, big business and the rest. Merton's controversial writings on social issues and inter-religious authority may be seen as the fruit of his dual affirmation of his true self and of simplicity.

Why Merton and the Twentieth-Century Monastic Revival Matter

For fifteen hundred years, the Benedictine *Rule* has offered Christians a way of living in moderation. Nowhere in the spirituality of St. Benedict is there anything that imposes a particular system of practices—prayer, psalms, praise, whatever—on believers or a particular aesthetic for the Church. Each person, each monk and each community must find his or her own way. But without simplicity one cannot fully carry out the task assigned them in the church or the world.

Merton's thinking about simplicity clearly influenced his thinking in three areas: Christian humanism; a growing protest against some forms of technology; and his emphasis on simplicity in Cistercian art. The following paragraphs briefly explore these themes.

First, Merton traced the development of Christian humanism to medieval Europe, notably the twelfth and thirteenth centuries, a period when historians have discerned the emergence of the idea of the self. Merton cited the School of Chartres for its platonizing scholars who were also deeply intrigued by the natural world; the School of St. Victor for its motto, "learn everything, you will find nothing superfluous;" and St. Thomas for his openness to Aristotle, the Arabs, and the claims of reason and nature.[33]

For Merton, monastic culture and Christian humanism emphasized love, forgiveness and the common good. By contrast, narcissism, depersonalization and totalitarian regimes such as Nazi Germany and Stalinist Russia characterized modern secular society. Merton concluded that all humanists must come together in new ways to foster a more human and desirable future. He returned occasionally to this theme, for example, in the paper he delivered at the monastic conference before he died in Thailand, where he insisted, "The whole purpose of the monastic life is to teach men to live by love."[34]

To love others, we must first know ourselves, bridling monsters deep in the depths of our being, including illusions fed by corporate advertising, greed and other forces of self-destructiveness. Merton insists that people tame their own desires, ambitions and appetites and limit themselves in appropriate ways. We may share in the limited supply of created goods without imposing a false difference between ourselves and others.[35] As we use God's given gifts mindfully, we move towards a unity, wholeness and our truest self that is at the core of our otherwise fragmented lives.

Secondly, Merton criticized a society organized around machines. Technology had come to characterize and control our lives and therefore constituted a death urge. Drawing on his reading of Lewis Mumford, Merton made plain his critique of Western civilization which had come to ignore basic human needs. This was foundational to Merton's critique of technology.[36]

Finally, Merton manifested a passionate interest in the intersection of the sacred and the aesthetic. Son of two artists, Merton lectured on sacred art in 1954. He published some of his thoughts in "Absurdity in Sacred Decoration" and in many essays such as on the Shakers and monastic traditions. His central concern was to understand various ways in which people of different religious traditions or even different vocations have conceived the meaning and method of the "way" which leads to the highest levels of religious, or metaphysical awareness.[37]

Frank Kacmarcik, arguably one of the most influential Catholic liturgical artists and design consultants in the United States during the mid-twentieth century was among those influenced by Merton on simplicity in the arts. Kacmarcik's work was marked by simplicity, meaningful proportions, timelessness, enduring quality, poetry of light and visual silence.[38] He designed two Merton books, *Monastic Peace* and *Nativity Kerygma*.[39] Without exaggerating Merton's ongoing legacy in this area, Cistercians continue to emphasize simplicity in the arts.[40]

Concluding Observations

In ancient Delphi, in Greece, carved over the portals of the temple to the sun deity Apollo, two mottos anticipate themes which later came to dominate the writings of Thomas Merton: "Moderation in all things," and "Know thyself."[41] Nearly three millennia later Thomas Merton concluded that humankind had violated both precepts. From the margins of a culture gone awry, Merton warned that enough is enough. Discover your true self. Come to your senses. You are about to plunge over a precipice. Do not imitate the small, mouse-like lemmings that, as their numbers soar, scatter in all directions and in large numbers self-destruct.[42]

In his lifetime, Merton contributed to Catholic renewal and cautioned many spiritual pilgrims against the dangers of five Ps: publicity, prestige, property, power, and perfectibility as an ideology. Since his death in 1968, Merton's writings have continued to offer sharp insights on the need for western Christians to resist cultural obsessions; simplify lifestyle; claim true selfhood through the practice of contemplation; and tame fear, the root cause of war.[43]

Notes

1. This article is a revision of a paper read at the 9th General Meeting of the International Thomas Merton Society, June 9-12, 2005.

2. In addition to Merton's poetry, other early titles by Merton included *Exile Ends in Glory: The Life of a Trappistine, Mother M. Berchmans, O.C.S.O.* (Milwaukee: Bruce, 1948); a history of the Cistercian Order, *The Waters of Siloe* (New York: Harcourt, Brace, 1949); *What Are These Wounds? The Life of a Cistercian Mystic, Saint Lutgarde of Aywières* (Milwaukee: Bruce, 1950), and *The Ascent to Truth* (New York: Harcourt, Brace, 1951).

3. *The Last of the Fathers: St. Bernard of Clairvaux and the Encyclical, Doctor Mellifluus* (New York: Harcourt, Brace, 1954); *Thomas Merton on Saint Bernard*, Cistercian Studies #9 (Kalamazoo: Cistercian Publications, 1980).

4. *The Spirit of Simplicity. Characteristic of the Cistercian Order* (Trappist: Gethsemani, 1948), p. i. I have found only two secondary sources: M. Basil Pennington, "Father Louis' First Book: *The Spirit of Simplicity*," in *Studiosorum Speculum. Studies in Honor of Louis J. Lekai, O.Cist.*, ed. Francis R. Swietek and John R. Sommerfeldt, Cistercian Studies #141 (Kalamazoo: Cistercian Publications, 1993); reprinted in Pennington's *Thomas Merton, My Brother: His Journey to Freedom, Compassion, and Final Integration* (Hyde Park, NY: New City Press, 1996), pp. 65-78; and Patrick F. O'Connell's entry on the book in *The Thomas Merton Encyclopedia* (Maryknoll, NY: Orbis, 1994), pp. 446-448. For this article, all references to "St. Bernard on Interior Simplicity" are from *The Spirit of Simplicity*.

5. Merton to Leclercq, October 9, 1950, *Survival or Prophecy? The Letters of Thomas Merton and Jean Leclercq*, ed. Patrick Hart (New York: Farrar, Straus and Giroux, 2002), p. 23. An advantage to reading the correspondence in this source is that it includes Leclercq's letters to Merton, unlike *The School of Charity. The Letters of Thomas Merton on Religious Re-*

newal and Spiritual Direction, ed. Patrick Hart (New York: Farrar, Straus, Giroux, 1990) .

6. Leclercq, "Introduction," *Thomas Merton on Saint Bernard*, p. 14.

7. Patrick Hart, "Foreword," *Thomas Merton on Saint Bernard*, pp. 8-9.

8. David Knowles, *Cistercians and Cluniacs: The Controversy between St. Bernard and Peter the Venerable* (London: Oxford University Press, 1955), p. 18. This essay also appears in *The Historian and Character and Other Essays* (Cambridge: University Press, 1963).

9. *Apologia* 28; *The Works of Bernard of Clairvaux*, ed. M. Basil Pennington, Cistercian Fathers #1 (Spencer: Cistercian Publications, 1970), pp. 65-6; for biographical details on William of St. Thierry, see http://www.catholicity.com/encyclopedia/w/william_of_st-thierry.html

10. *Spirit of Simplicity*, p. 44.

11. *Spirit of Simplicity*, p. 48.

12. *Spirit of Simplicity*, p. iii, Merton's emphasis. While I trust Merton would now encourage the practice, I have not attempted to render direct quotes inclusive in language.

13. *Spirit of Simplicity*, p. i-iv (Merton's emphasis).

14. *The Rule of St. Benedict in English*, ed. Timothy Fry (Collegeville: Liturgical Press, 1982), 39:8-9; hereafter *RB*. I *italicize* a word that emphasizes the universality of Benedict's way, as stressed by contemporary writers including Joan Chittister, *Wisdom Distilled from the Daily. Living the Rule of St. Benedict Today* (San Francisco: Harper, 1991) and Eric Dean, *St. Benedict for the Laity* (Collegeville: Liturgical Press, 1989).

15. *Spirit of Simplicity*, p. 76.

16. *Spirit of Simplicity*, pp. 89-90.

17. *Spirit of Simplicity*, p. 98.

18. *Spirit of Simplicity*, p. 125.

19. *The Wisdom of the Desert. Sayings from the Desert Fathers of the Fourth Century*, trans. Thomas Merton (New York: New Directions, 1960), p. 5.

20. *Spirit of Simplicity*, pp. 138-9.

21. *Seeds of Contemplation* (New York: New Directions, 1949), p. 17. In *Thomas Merton. The Development of a Spiritual Theologian* Toronto Studies in Theology 20 (New York: Edwin Mellen, 1985), Donald Grayston explores the amplifications, additions and key themes in the successor work, *New Seeds of Contemplation* (New York: New Directions, 1961).

22. Photo, Dianne Aprile, *The Abbey of Gethsemani. Place of Peace and Paradox* (Louisville: Trout Lily, 1998), p. 207.

23. *Seeds*, p. 26.

24. *Seeds*, p. 47.

25. *Seeds*, p. 127.

26. *Seeds*, p. 168.

27. *Thoughts in Solitude* (New York: Farrar, Straus and Giroux, 1958), pp. 12-13. Merton wrote the book in 1953 when James Fox allowed him to use for prayer, contemplation and writing an abandoned tool shed in the woods. The volume includes several prayers including perhaps Merton's most famous published prayer, one that begins, "My Lord God, I have no idea where I am going..." p. 83.

28. *Solitude*, pp. 17-20.

29. *Solitude*, p. 53.

30. *Solitude*, p. 85.

31 Thomas Merton, *Conjectures of a Guilty Bystander* (Garden City, NY: Doubleday, 1966), pp. 140-141.

32. Erik H. Erikson provided a case study of generativity, *Gandhi's Truth* (New York: Norton, 1969). See also James Fowler, *Stages of Faith* (San Francisco: Harper & Row, 1981).

33. Merton on "Christian Humanism," essays collected as part III of *Love and Learning*, ed. Naomi Burton Stone and Patrick Hart (New York: Farrar, Straus & Giroux, 1979). See also Jean Leclercq, *The Love of Learning and the Desire for God. A Study of Monastic Culture*, trans. Catharine Misrahi (New York: Fordham, 1961); M. D. Chenu, *Nature, Man and Society in the Twelfth Century* (Chicago: University of Chicago, 1968); Colin Morris, *The Discovery of the Individual: 1050-1200* (New York: Harper & Row, 1972); Matthew Fox, *Sheer Joy. Conversations with Thomas Aquinas on Creation Spirituality* (San Francisco: Harper, 1992); Patrick F. O'Connell, "Humanism," *The Thomas Merton Encyclopedia*, pp. 214-215.

34 *The Asian Journal of Thomas Merton* (New York: New Directions, 1973), p. 333.

35. *New Seeds*, p. 47.

36. Merton read books by Mumford (1895-1990), including Mumford's two-volume *Myth of the Machine* (New York: Harcourt, Brace and World, 1969-1970) about which he commented in a letter to the *New York Times* for June 11, 1967. The title of volume 1 is *Technics and Human Development*; volume 2 is *The Pentagon of Power*. For a discussion of this crucial theme in Merton's thinking, Paul R. Dekar, "What the Machine Produces and What the Machine Destroys: Thomas Merton on Technology," *Merton Annual* 17 (2004): 216-34.

37. *Mystics and Zen Masters* (New York: Dell, 1967), p. x; *Disputed Questions* (New York: Farrar, Straus and Giroux, 1976); *Seeking Paradise. The Spirit of the Shakers*, ed. with an introduction by Paul M. Pearson (Maryknoll: Orbis, 2003). In a presentation on December 11, 2004 as part of a conference on *A Hidden Wholeness: The Art of Thomas Merton*, Anthony Bannon explored simplicity as a theme in "Thomas Merton's Art of Contemplative Photography." See general articles on Merton and

"Creativity", "Shakers," and "Theory of art" in *The Thomas Merton Encyclopedia.*

38. Interview with Kacmarcik, May 12, 2003; scattered references in journals and letters. Charlotte Zalot, "The Inward, Outward and Upward Vision of Frank Kacmarcik, Obl.S.B., Liturgical Artist and Design Consultant," Ph.D. dissertation, Drew University, 2004. See also Zalot's article on Merton and Kacmarcik in *The Merton Annual,* Vol. 18.

39. Both published by Trappist: Abbey of Gethsemani, 1958.

40. Mark Irving, "Simplicity of the Cloister," *Tablet,* September 11, 2004, an account of the serenity elicited by the minimalist architect, John Pawson, who designed a new monastery in Bohemia.

41. http://www.wdbydana.com/delphi.htm.

42. In the 1967 film of Hardy's *Far from the Madding Crowd* a scene depicts a mad sheep dog leading its charge to self-destruction.

43. The Root of War Is Fear," *Seeds,* chapter 9 and *New Seeds,* chapter 16. An uncensored version appeared in *The Catholic Worker,* October 1961, reprinted in Thomas Merton, *Passion for Peace, The Social Essays,* ed. William H. Shannon (New York: Crossroad, 1997), pp. 11-19. Two pertinent analyses of contemporary culture are Ronald Wright, *A Short History of Progress* (Toronto: Anansi, 2004) and John Carroll, *Terror. A Meditation on the Meaning of September 11* (Melbourne: Scribe, 2002).

Centennial Vignettes in Homage to My Father[1]

John Wu, Jr.

Introduction

These vignettes, personal and intimate, anecdotal and idiosyncratic, and unequal in length I present in loving memory of a parent whose centennial we celebrate this year and whose presence
in my life looms larger with the years. Regretfully, because of its
already excessive length, I've not included vignettes directly related to my mother who will also be one-hundred years old in this
last year of the millennium on October 19th. For her, I've planned
something else. The stories and sketches hopefully are as enjoy-
able for you to read as they were for me to write.

In these vignettes I shall be calling my father, *dia-dia*, what we
called him in and out of the home. *Dia-dia* is the Romanized pro-
nunciation in the Shanghai-Ningpo dialect for *daddy*. In the more
common Mandarin, it would be *dieh-dieh*. The Ningpo dialect is
one we spoke at home with varying degrees of success and failure. I, being the youngest of thirteen and the most American, spoke
it totteringly, with no structural backbone at all. Whenever I
opened my mouth to attempt something intelligent in our beloved
dialect, I was often the object of derision—which continues to this
very day.

Our beloved *dia-dia* was a high-wire performer, with one foot
on earth and the other in heaven. I do not doubt for a second it
was his ambiguities and contradictions and his circus-like ability
to hold on to both and to thrive from such polarities that made
him the person he was. Scholar and man of vision, he was, in
addition, all flesh and blood and solid earth to those privileged to
have breathed the same air as he did.

In his nearly nine rich decades, he showed us the full spectrum of his humanity. Joy, enthusiasm and the simplicity of the
child filled and marked his eighty-seven years. Yet, like all great
men and women, he was also quite capable of profound sorrow
and loneliness and, on occasion, some frightful anger. Through
him, I became aware not only of the possibility but the *inner de-*

mand of fulfilling my own humanity. I came to know too the *necessity* of living in such a way that the powers within and without may be brought together to help unfold this promised fullness that comes naturally not so much in time but together with living the *life of faith.*

Our *dia-dia* left us numerous legacies, a clear indication of the depth and breadth of his existence. Yet, the one he himself might most want us to remember was perhaps his own careful attentiveness to *personal gifts* and the weighty responsibility that follows once we acknowledge their conviviality. For he believed that in our recognizing them, in living gratefully with such gifts, we come upon *meaning* and in face with divinity from whose hands such personal endowments are directly and freely granted.

These vignettes are a celebration of a man dearly loved and cherished and whose influence will gain greater strength in time. If our *dia-dia's* books and writings are not in fashion today, this fact may speak more about ourselves and the times and our rather conventional and narrow preoccupations than it does the man himself. The century we have been a part of, decades of endlessly tragic and destructive experiments with social engineering and unprecedented technological innovations that have perhaps altered our lives forever, has been an era—despite the enormous fuss made of it—arguably neither of great intellectual nor spiritual depth and ferment.

Yet, our dear *dia-dia*—remembering that his life overlapped ours too and therefore, confined by similar limitations—was able to absorb and make use of the best of what he experienced and with which he came into contact. He savored and put into practice the cream of his own traditions and those of the West as well. And if he had any personal motives, perhaps it lay in his earnest efforts to salvage and to bring light to these dark times what we have carelessly and unconscionably discarded out of hand. His uncommon foresight was that he saw angelic and godlike elements in us even while we choose to grovel as earthbound creatures unaware of the presence of wings that take us skyward and beyond ourselves. Seeing the merely earthly and to fail to see the earth in all its plenitude is a warning he might give us were he with us now.

May we not also say he remains inaccessible and an enigma because collectively we ourselves have done much to obscure in us our own innate treasures of the mind and heart? For both the disfiguring and mislaying of such treasures make it difficult to enter into the sort of intellectual and spiritual dialogue that an understanding of his life and ideas would demand. While his deep and broad scholarship will probably always remain a daunting task to anyone attempting to plumb the depths of the man and scholar, there is in addition an underlying difficult-to-get-at quality that the scholar, no matter how intellectually gifted, might still find impenetrable. That particular quality was the gift of *simplicity*, what Mencius, the immortal Confucian, called a *child-like heart* and Thérèse of Lisieux, the Carmelite saint, *the little way*. It guided his life and was reflected in nearly everything he wrote, including politics and the Law. That is the *hiddenness* without which there could be nothing but chaos and confusion. It is also something that a Harold Bloom, and many others like him for all their brilliance and quintessential knowledge, probably could never bring themselves to entertain, not to mention, fathom.

Simplicity—a virtue and state of being particularly rare among scholars and intellectuals—is that which finally defined him. My contention is that though a first-rate biographer and scholar might gain access into a good part of his life and makeup, the writer might still fail to see the *whole* person because of an inability to see the simplicity in the man. On the other hand, if you love simplicity and are childlike yet lack the wisdom of seeing the need for persistent intellectual nurturing which marked my father's life, you too might miss the man. For, being a great lover of Confucius and of Shakespeare and Dante and therefore of knowledge and learning in general, *dia-dia* was convinced it was only through the continuous flow of rich ideas that the spirit could do its best and most natural work in us. Three themes occupied his life: *nature, nurture and grace*.

To *dia-dia*'s credit, he had the intuition and deep animal sense to understand that these three basic elements had to fuse and work together in perfect balance and unity for knowledge to become whole and to complete the strict demands of rationality. In short, he believed that each component fueled and needed the others for its fulfillment. If he found the times disjointed, he saw the confusion the result of a narrowing, and even loss, of interest in our pursuing not so much the self—for which many of us have an obsession—but the *source* of the self. And this loss had deep connections with the obscuring of faith in the human person's interior self so that, in losing our way, we become strangers in our own interior castles. Hence, whatever disjointedness we may find in the world is reflected in each individual's failure, first, to *see* and then coupled with the inability to acknowledge the fundamental mystery of one's own being and that which supports our being.

These simple vignettes, I believe, reflect my *dai-dia*'s particular way of *seeing*, a way of perception that was conditioned, as I suggest above, by a natural, innate simplicity. Further, they reflect the vision of a mystic who saw, tasted and loved all the myriad diversities that make up life but who could not, at the same time, help seeing things in their *primordial undifferentiated Oneness*.

Vignette #1: Educating a Son

Funny, isn't it, how certain notions are etched into one's life. First, they vaguely stand out as indistinct relief, then become veritable litanies, possibly leading later to profound prayers surfacing from deep within the heart. They come randomly into our lives, much like seeds do, a good number dying even at the moment they fall. Yet some, without much fuss, do take root, then the few that become seedling assume some significant space without our being aware they are there, quietly taking up residence in us.

Or, we could see these notions in musical terms that appear first as simple, hardly audible notes. With time, they assume a distinct and penetrating voice singing bars of music with a resonance quite beyond what one thinks the self is capable of containing and supporting. One might even suspect that the sound originates from a geography rather unearthly, overstepping the narrow scope of the self, surely beyond an ego that craves to be merely physically and emotionally nurtured and sated. The music abides in us quietly, encouraged by other voices within vying for the right to be present and heard as any other. And their struggle for permanence makes up the dramatic nature of each individual life.

Soon enough, melodies appear, at first, simple, then more complexly melodic, and, finally, polyphonic harmonies suffuse the whole self, the result of many voices brought together by some hidden energy, an *inexplicable* Center that somehow holds. As we live with them, they take on a shape and meaning quite of its own making. In fact, if we have graciously consented for them to reside in us, willed them to take root in our inmost hearts, they change and enrich us in surprising ways. And it seems the more concealed they are and the less fuss we make of them, the more they bear the mark of *timelessness* and the deeper they penetrate us.

These are the different ways that I see *dia-dia*'s life and thought having touched our lives. In some unaccountable way, they have taken on the delicious fragrance of gardens and the recurring melodies of songs that continually remind us of some Home beyond home.

****

July, 1964. *Dia-dia* and I have just finished a simple lunch of chicken teriyaki at a tiny Japanese-Hawaiian cafeteria near the campus of the University of Hawaii in Honolulu. The unpretentious eatery is a little more than a hole-in-the-wall. Once out on the street in the stifling mid-day heat, we walk, struggling on a mild but continuous incline toward a newly built, twin-towered dormitory where many philosophers, including *dia-dia*, will consider home for the six-week summer international conference. In those weeks we would listen to and be in the privileged, no, truly still, *sacred* and enchanting, presence of such notables as D.T. Suzuki, T'ang Chun-I, Fang Thome and T.R.V. Murti from the East, and John Smith, Richard McKeon and William Ernest Hocking from the West. Being twenty-two, they were halcyon days for me, days of continuous intellectual and spiritual feasting, surely a crossroad in my young life, the closest I've ever come to being in the company of Olympian gods, of philosophers who were not yet afraid of philosophizing and who could not envision their enterprise separated from life.

My eyes are fixed in the direction we are heading. Irritated by the heat and the nondescript edifices before me, I complain on how empty-looking the whitewashed structures appear against the clear blue sky. *Dia-dia*, huffing and puffing and ordinarily not a complainer, answers with an audible sigh and a funny, favorite phrase, *"Yes, don't I know it."* At sixty-five and no longer young, he catches his breath, wipes sweat rolling down one of his cheeks onto his brightly-colored Hawaiian shirt, and says,

W*hited sepulchers*. Yes, that's what those empty-looking buildings remind me of—whited sepulchers—you know, *whitewashed tombs*. Remember what Jesus in Matthew's Gospel calls the Pharisees and the hypocrites? You know, like the tombs, the Pharisees and the hypocrites are clean and unmarked on the outside, dressed in flowing robes, but on the inside they carry nothing but decaying bones. You see, they were people wearing gorgeous garments to embellish their external selves so that they need never expose their empty selves. You see Christ could be very direct and frank in his use of language when he had a mind to be, when he wanted to make a point, to teach a lesson through a simple parable. He would have made a poor diplomat. Wouldn't have liked it at all. He said what came to his mind and didn't care what others thought of his words. He could be tactful, but he was apt to say what he had to say, often not weighing his words very carefully. But, *don't you see*, he was absolutely right about the Pharisees and people like them.

I want to say, "I see, indeed!" but being a deferent son, I hold my young, Asian-American tongue.

A spell of silence, then some small talk about how he has to get on with his paper, a formal presentation on "The status of the individual in the political and legal traditions of old and new China." We chitchat casually about matters of more immediate concern. Both of us are especially excited about our visit with Dr. Suzuki, the renowned ninety-four year-old Japanese Zen Master who had almost single-handedly brought Zen to the West. We had made arrangements to see him and his secretary, the very charming and lively Mihoko Okamura, in his hotel room off Waikiki Beach. Seemed somewhat comically incongruous to me, for nothing could be more commercial than the Waikiki section of Honolulu. Yet, on the other hand, isn't that the very charm of Zen itself to be thrown into the very heart of contradiction, in the horns of a dilemma?

Dr. Suzuki had promised to write a preface to *The Golden Age of Zen*, and *dia-dia* was now anticipating the visit with the same relish and excitement of a child dreaming of a double-dip creamy cone on a steamy summer day on Coney Island. Funny thing that neither of us ever again mentioned *whited sepulchers* or *whitewashed tombs* or Pharisees or hypocrites; yet, the seeds of what he said somehow take root in me, assuming an importance quite hidden at the time the little dialogue had occurred.

Thirty-five years later, I continue to be struck by this rather ordinary incident, a simple chitchat between father and son, on a typically hot mid-summer day in Honolulu when all one wanted to do was to laze around doing and thinking nothing special. Every so often, especially since his passing in 1986, during mostly unguarded moments, the particular ambiance and feel of that ordinary day comes back to me with particular sharpness, sometimes with a shock, being more vivid than when it first occurred— if that is indeed possible. *Dia-dia's* high-pitched voice, in clear English tinged with his quaint Ningpo accent, is, as always, strong and direct. Particularly with the words, "*whited sepulcher*," I see clearly the nearly blinding rays of the Island sun reflecting off his glasses as he turns gently to me with a broad, toothy smile. And then there is the litany I hear, not exactly in the same words always and not always in his voice but sometimes in my own, "*You're no whitewashed tomb. Be yourself—for you cannot be anyone else!*"

Was it a warning? He had often told me how he disliked, as he put it, the "goody-goodies," people who in their *external* behavior appear to be paragons of virtue and piety, yet, *interiorly*, were running on empty. He was surely not by nature judgmental nor narrowly moralistic, but he had nearly unfailing antennae in spotting affectation and detecting people with half-baked scruples and ideas. For such people, he would say, unwittingly shrink their own minds and hearts in trying to be other than their true selves. They mislay their treasures, warping their capacity for humanity and compassion. He favored such words as "mislaid" or "misplaced" probably because he had seen his own past life—particularly in his late twenties and much of his thirties before the Hound of God grabbed him—in terms of dissipation of personal gifts. An incurable optimist, walking to the drumbeat of both Christ and Mencius, he knew no divinely bestowed human treasure could ever really be lost, only *mislaid*. The source of his belief, that nature and grace worked together in us and mostly *without our knowing it*. In his case, because the world was rarely too much with him and he was almost always open to grace, the really good things nearly always took him by surprise.

Along with his ability to detect affectation was his knack in spotting genuineness. It could be of people and things, or of books and writers of which he was expert, or ancient histories and traditions, what makes and doesn't make sense in the contemporary world. Even in the Roman Catholicism he embraced wholeheartedly in his late thirties, or, perhaps, even more so *because* he felt he was a latecomer to the religion, he put his natural constitution and sharp analytical mind to good use in unfailingly understanding the difference between the baby and the dirty water. He simply had an unmistakable feel in drawing the line between the authentic and the inauthentic, of what lasts and the merely culturally ephemeral. Because he profoundly cherished his newly found religion—though he liked to say *God and it had found him*—this was all the more reason why he felt a great responsibility in keeping a keen lookout for corrosive elements that he perceived attacking it from both within and without.

Our *dia-dia* could be strongly negative with others, even with my siblings. On the other hand, being the youngest, I was surely spoiled by both of my parents and some of my siblings. Particularly after the passing of my dear mother when I was in my teens, seeing that hard discipline had little effect on me, he was forced to alter his tactics. Poor *dia-dia* tried his best to serve as our mommy, too, and in playing this impossible dual role, he nonetheless managed to soften his ways, even to tamper his natural quick temper. He mellowed considerably and, though or, perhaps, because of being a man of constant sorrows in having lost his one true love, became a sweeter and more patient and tolerant person.

In fact, to such an extent that whenever he did admonish me, particularly during the years of my rather troubled young adulthood, he handled me very gently, with great caution. He never again resorted to hell fire and damnation and he put whatever former preachiness and moralistic tendencies, which had been his wont, aside, knowing that such ways simply did not work with me. Instead, he would advise in soft, affecting *maternal* tones:

> Johnny, accentuate the positive both in yourself and in others. While it may be true that we will never be able to rid ourselves completely of our negative qualities, when we stress the positive, you naturally diminish the negative qualities in yourself and in others. By doing this, you allow natural goodness and other merits greater play for your personal growth. This is how you practice fairness. Then suddenly you will feel grace working palpably in you.

In allowing the new found gentleness to wash over him, his spirituality deepened remarkably in the last two decades of his life. He struggled always to put into practice the most profound and cherished ideas he wrote and believed in. And this struggle became most intense in the last decade of his life.

He was also, in being father and mother to me, becoming an excellent psychologist. He knew well the excessive critical bent of my character and did not want to encourage in me the argumentative nor the disagreeable, to allow such potentially pernicious influences to paralyze or infest my yet undeveloped self. He knew well also how easily I fell prey to casuistic ways. Besides, my narrow rationalistic tendencies made me ever ready to criticize others and, in so doing, hurt people irrevocably.

Once, in college, when I brought up the subject of entering the law profession as a possible future career, he somehow turned indifferent to the whole discussion. I did not know the reason for his sudden undisguised irritability towards such a conventional goal until some time later. While he did not give a definitive *no*, his lack of encouragement alone was, for me, enough to dampen treading such a path. One assumed any father would have been elated over a child following him into such a potentially lucrative trade. Not my daddy, though. Of course, he may have thought I lacked the intellectual equipment to be a success at it. On the other hand, he also understood all too well my budding, small-minded combative and manipulative spirit that he feared the practice of law might reinforce and bring to some deadly fruition and in time dominate my entire life and character.

Though this might sound ludicrous to a secular reader, yet, given the keen insight he had of me, my *dia-dia* might also have thought that my future success in the field would somehow endanger the loss of my immortal soul. For, you see, unlike other *paterfamilias*, he simply refused to place professional success very high in his scheme of values. He had himself gained such success and great fame early in life, and found it vain and sterile. He was proud of our achievements but never do I recall, except for brother Pete's call to the priesthood, his ever favoring one sibling over another because of the profession he or she was in.

Dia-dia was perhaps as fine a judge of character as a Thomas More, a lawyer himself and perhaps the one man he came close to worshipping. When I think of his lukewarm response to my study of the Law I am reminded of the story of Sir Thomas who, while Chancellor of England for Henry VIII, reproved Richard Rich for his ambitious ways. For Rich too had wanted to go into law, though likely as a steppingstone to a future political position. Instead, Sir Thomas seriously counseled Rich to remain simple, to be a teacher. Rich did not take More's warning to heart, later indeed assuming

More's old position as Chancellor of England and had a hand in More's subsequent beheading. I am of course not suggesting that I am in any way Richard Rich, but it does strike me as curious that one of the few movies *dia-dia* and I saw together was *A Man for All Seasons*, on the life of the great More. Another was "Becket."

Later, when I became a teacher, *dia-dia* was nearly beside himself with delight. He seemed to have wished all along that I take education as my calling. Frankly it is the only profession I have found genuine contentment in. As a teacher himself, he understood the limited degree to which one's cleverness could be extended before one's fraudulent ways are rudely exposed, if not by students, then surely by one's own conscience. Having been for a short time a practicing attorney himself, he did not see such safeguards in the ferocious dens that governed the practices of the legal profession. In fact, in *Beyond East and West*, we read that even before he had taken his first course at Michigan University's School of Law, he was more than aware of the overly materialistic bent of young American students of the Law. And that was 1919. He had no illusions about the actual profession as it is conventionally practiced, though he had a lifelong love of the philosophy of law; perhaps only because he knew the *source* from whence the law comes and returns and, broadly speaking, its potential as a *civilizing* tool for humankind. One of the chapters on the Law was "Law is My Idol."

Whited sepulcher. A warning? An admonishment? In reflection, I now see it as a gentle slap on a slowly-forming consciousness that he somehow knew was on the verge of awakening. How refreshing to have had a father who never spoke of the significance of being a professional success! He wanted nothing more from me than to be *myself*, to go down paths that would lead to the discovery of the true self, the self that God had mysteriously put on this earth even before the dawning of time. Perhaps his words were along the order of a Zen koan that helped place a young searching soul on some path leading to enlightenment. And the image of a whitewashed tomb, had it not in time evolved for me into a perfect metaphor, suggesting a truly important awakening: the rising from the dead from this fragile, passing earth?

And, is it not strange, my *dia-dia* himself might ask in wonderment, that even on this little planet, on this small piece of ground inhabited by countless unenlightened and laughably inept human beings such as ourselves, where we are given the chance to work out our salvation and where we seem caught in the maelstrom of time, *eternity*—if we were only free enough to let our inmost hearts play *joyously* with time—yes, even eternity, may somehow shade imperceptibly into time and give us a welcomed glimpse into *whose* image we really are and for *whom* we were made? Lucky man, my sweet *dia-dia*. He found these answers in the midstream of his journey, unwaveringly followed its Path, and never for a moment thereafter regretted what he saw and tasted with relish. With the great Spanish mystic, Teresa of Avila, surely one of his favorite saints, he could say without a trace of irony, "Solo Dios basta"— "Only God suffices."

Vignette #2: Progressive Education

My very lovable brother Stephen, our parents' tenth child and eighth boy and inimitable storyteller, tells the following anecdote which I shall do my best to reproduce, as if Steve himself were telling it. The reader must judge for itself whether it is apocryphal or not:

One day, Peter, Vincent and I (numbers 8, 9 and 10, respectively, in the family) received our monthly report cards. We were in our early teens in Rome. As usual, we went into our *dia-dia*'s study individually, one by one. Peter, being the senior of the three, felt privileged to go in first. In fact, he was beaming from ear to ear for, you see, after having struggled academically in China, he was now fast becoming the best student—at least, grade-wise—among us. He handed his report card to *dia-dia* and, when he saw all the A's, he said simply, not with much undue excitement, 'O, Peter, very good, keep it up.' Peter, as one might expect, walked away from the study a bit crestfallen, red-faced with his mouth in a pouting position.

Next, Vincent, with some justified fear, brought his grades in to show *dia-dia*. Unlike Peter, he was rarely an exceptional student not because he had less intelligence but because he could always find some daffy foolishness to occupy his broad imagination. For instance, one day with the help of a horse he was determined to trample all the flowers of Rome. He nearly succeeded and, had he not evoked diplomatic immunity—*dia-dia* at the time being Minister Plenipotentiary from the Republic of China to the Holy See—he might still be rotting in some cell today. He was not known as *buffoon* for nothing. When *dia-dia* saw his report with all the C's, he reacted in nearly similar fashion as he had toward Peter's grades: 'O, Vincent, keep it up,' even adding a cheery 'very good.' Vincent heaved a great sigh of relief, beamed from ear to ear and did a less than perfect cartwheel, knocking over a few classics as he left the study.

Finally, being my turn, I walked in, not knowing exactly what to feel or to expect. For, unlike my brothers', my grades ran the entire spectrum from A to F. My father, after careful examination and with much nodding, looked up grinning and said, 'O, Stephen, my Stephen, wonderful, wonderful, how musical you are! Yes, yes, keep it up and you may yet have a future in music!' Little did he know at the time that Francis (number 7) was the real musician in the family!

In Steve's diverse telling of the above over time, I must confess I have never, for a second, believed that such an incident took place *exactly* as he said it did, particularly when it comes to Vincent's cartwheel. On the other hand, though, the tenth child might have embellished some of the facts (as all great storytellers are wont to do). The anecdote nevertheless does represent for me our *dia-dia's* *spirit*, his true *élan*. Is it any wonder, I now ask, that one so distinguished was never seriously considered for the position of his country's Minister of Education? Obviously, he was too far ahead of his time, and likely will always be

Vignette #3: The *Tao* of Education

I remember in the mid-70s in Taipei, at a private dinner in the presence of well-known educators, the discussion turned to educational reforms. One distinguished-looking lady, a principal at a famous private senior high school, spoke glowingly of her school's newly-instituted Parent-Teacher Association, an organization that long ago had become a significant part of educational institutions in the West. The PTA however was then an innovation in Taiwan. In such polite company, the well-coifed principal obviously expected support for her words. For, after all, the Republic of China was then still under martial law, not the kind of free-for-all democracy it has since evolved into. After listening courteously, *dia-dia* cleared his throat and began to give his take on the matter. It was not something they had expected to hear.

You know, I see what you are saying very well. On the surface, the PTA looks like a wonderful idea. No one can deny it is good for parents and teachers to talk to one another, even to become friends. And, surely there's no harm in teachers finding out the family background their students come from and so on and so forth. *But...*

I think I had sensed the coming of the "*But...,*" and, with it, everyone's attention became riveted on our distinguished Chinese scholar, the Honorary President and head of the Ph.D. program in philosophy at the then College of Chinese Culture.

But, I beg to add some words on this important question. In the principle governing the Parent-Teacher Association we all think naturally how wonderful it is for parents and teachers to work together. And I agree with its importance. However, *in the spirit of justice,* there is one significant point we all seem to overlook. We fail to give enough attention to what *young students* feel about such an organization. In fact, the young don't have much of a choice in the matter, do they? *Don't you see,* at home, children already must contend with parental pressures. Then, at school, from early morning until late afternoon, they come under the strict control of teachers. Now, when two such authorities come together to set up an association with the intention of comparing notes, in fact, sometimes quite *intimate* notes, on our young people, don't you see the terrible *additional* pressure we are unconsciously inflicting on their lives?

I think the PTA, rather than being a help, just as often makes our children feel that parents and teachers are in a *conspiracy* against them, or are even being *spied against.* The better and well-behaved students may not feel the pressure too greatly. In fact, they probably welcome it. But surely it would surprise me if the great majority of the young do not have some negative feelings toward it. Frankly, it is a great wonder to me that not *more* of the young suffer psychological distress because of the kind of artificial society we have created for them. Don't you think we educators have now become too concerned with organization and control and collecting of all kinds of data on students? We have become so concerned with such things that we fail to give proper attention to the deeper needs of the young, particularly forgetting the importance of *letting them naturally grow in freedom.*

My daddy certainly had not intentionally meant to pour cold water onto an otherwise pleasant dinner party. By the time he finished, there were many red faces around him. No one present had expected an educator of his renown to make such statements on an institution that nearly everyone endorsed and thought a positive educational innovation. Though I did not feel it my place to support him, as I was his son and one of the younger people there, secretly, I felt considerable pride at his sympathetic and down-to-earth words. Without doubt, he was indeed the mystic many thought he was, but he also possessed a wonderful common sense that went so naturally with his mysticism. I thought too what unbounded faith he had in the young.

In seeing the PTA from his perspective, he was in fact suggesting that lasting educational reforms lay, first, in both parents and teachers recovering a basic understanding of their respective roles, and then having the courage to put them into practice. I believe his words merely reflected the spirit of a true and genuine *Confucian* for few ideas were more dear to him than the implementation of *cheng ming* ("the rectification of names"). On the other hand, in the way that he defended the independence and freedom of children and their innate ability to correct themselves without undue interference from either parents or teachers, he was being a true *Taoist* as well. But, like a true *Taoist*, he was no mere libertine. Rather, he disfavored extremes and excesses and regarded each person as a *sacred vessel* that, especially in the case of children with sensitive souls, ought not to be tampered nor meddled with but rather allowed to grow naturally into itself. In a sense, his attitude toward the PTA reflected in miniature the way he approached the law.

To his mind, the PTA was simply another of the countless meddlesome human institutions that, though possessed of noble principles and goals, in time, spoil and interfere with the natural processes of life. To him, such institutions excessively fussed over things and people that are often best left alone. Typically, our *dia-dia* was strongly in favor of preserving whatever was natural through moderate nurturing. He saw eye to eye with Aristotle who said, "Perfection is the enemy of the Good," and with Lao Tzu's common sense wisdom, "To be overgrown is to decay" (#55). Looking back, I believe what he said that evening simply reflected the proper proportionality of nature and nurture, of what constitutes authentic human existence. *Dia-dia* was rarely content with anything short of the perfect balancing of these two basic elements of life. Here he not only mirrored the best in his own tradition but I believe of the West as well.

Years later, I was to find in Ralph Waldo Emerson's essay, "Education," the following words that nearly perfectly reflect his thinking on the education of the young:

> I suffer whenever I see…a parent or senior imposing his opinion and way of thinking and being on a young soul to which they are totally unfit. Cannot we let people be themselves and enjoy life in their own way? You are trying to make that man another *you*. One's enough.
>
> The secret of Education lies in respecting the pupil. It is not for you to choose what he shall know, what he shall do. It is chosen and foreordained, and he only holds the key to his own secret. By your tampering and thwarting and too much governing he may be hindered from his end and kept out of his own. Respect the child. Wait and see the new product of Nature. Nature loves analogies, but not repetitions. Respect the child. Be not too much his parent. Trespass not on his solitude.

It should not come as a surprise to anyone that the great Boston Brahmin was among *dia-dia*'s favorite writers, certainly the one American writer he turned to again and again for inspiration, as bosom brother, Lin Yutang had done too. To him, there was a good deal more of Lao Tzu in Emerson than many a Chinese *Taoist*. And I do not believe we would be too far wrong to say my daddy was China's Emerson.

Vignette #4: Filial Piety, Justice and the Sacred

Besides finding perfect comfort in being both a Confucian and a Taoist, *dia-dia* was also a defender of justice. This should not surprise anyone familiar with his juristic writings and his practices as a judge in the Shanghai courts. We are told in *Beyond East and West* that what made him most happy upon completing the initial draft of the Constitution of the Republic of China in the 1940s was that, though every other part of the draft was sharply criticized, some even coming under severe attack, the section on *human rights* remained basically intact. This fact is simply a part of the public record. As a son, however much I am interested in such matters, it was his sense of fairness and equanimity as a father that strikes me at least equally as deep.

I had just turned nineteen, a typical American freshman with some fledgling interest in the intellectual life. Unlike children in other families, however, we had the benefit of our *dia-dia's* extraordinary library. At times, to whet my curiosity, I would wander into his study—with or without him present, for he did not mind this at all—to browse his collection. He never regarded my presence bothersome or intrusive and he was quite happy whenever any of us children took interest in good books. Although they were in nearly every part of the house, even cluttering the walls of the dining room, his choicest volumes were stacked high everywhere in his study in seeming disorder. Uncanny therefore that he never had much trouble locating them when they were needed.

On this particular day when he was in his study, I noticed a thin, new book with a dark-green cover, a bilingual edition of *The Hsiao Ching*, or, *Book of Filial Piety*. Looking up from his desk, *dia-dia* noticed my interest.

"Ah, yes, that's a new translation from Hsieh Papa's (Hsueh Kwang-ch'ien, whose English name was Paul K.T. Sih) St. John's University Press. You might be interested in knowing that that little book has been so important to the Chinese that some scholars believe it's the basis of Chinese culture and ethics." *Dia-dia's* sense of equanimity and breadth of learning was such that, whenever he spoke of anything Chinese, I do not ever recall his saying "*our* Chinese culture." He simply did not harbor any sense of racial or cultural superiority and was possibly the least chauvinistic person I knew. Later, while studying Chinese philosophy in Taiwan, I came under the tutelage of Professor Hsieh Yu-wei who indeed did regard *hsiao* as the basis from which all other virtues flowed. *Dia-dia* did not think so and, for that matter, neither did I, but that is altogether beside the point here.

"If you like, just take it and look through it yourself," he said. Then, coming towards me, he took the book in hand and flipped through its pages. He had already gone through it quite thoroughly, marking its pages with his characteristic red and blue underlining.

"Ah, yes, here it is." He had stopped on chapter 15. "Now, before you start in on the first chapter, I want you to spend time reading this chapter first." He handed me the book. He had stopped on the page with the chapter heading, "The Duty of Correction." I thought, well, it's about correction, something a nineteen-year-old wasn't particularly interested in. Must be on how parents ought to correct their children, I thought to myself. Nothing different from the conventional ideas I had had about filial piety up to that time. Then, the very next instant my eyes fell on words he had underlined in red. I read carefully: "Dare I ask if a son, by obeying all of his father's commands, can be called *filial*?" To which Confucius, perhaps irritated, answered, "What kind of talk is this? What kind of talk is this?" Living on the east coast and not far from New York City, I naturally imagined Confucius speaking these words with a nasal New York accent.

Again he took the book from my hands and told me to listen carefully while he read what he felt were wonderful and important words: "If a father had one son to reason with him, he would not be engulfed in moral wrong. Thus, in case of contemplated moral wrong, a son must never fail to warn his father against it; nor must a minister of state fail to perform a like service for his prince. In short, when there is question of moral wrong, there should be correction." Then, with his usual deep sigh, as if he were directing the following question to me personally, he read slowly, enunciating each syllable, *"How can you say that filiality consists in simply obeying a father?"*

As he did not particularly like the word "correction" in rendering the notion of *yu cheng*, he felt that the English word, "remonstrate" would have more fittingly conveyed the meaning.

While teaching in the Republic of China, I have brought up this incident on countless occasions to illustrate the broad, two-way dialogical ethics that I believe is inherent in classical Confucianism. I also cite it often to indicate my *dia-dia*'s eagerness in showing his son the true and broad responsibilities of children towards parents, as well as of subordinates towards their superiors, that genuine filial piety lies far deeper than mere obedience to one's superiors. Although he did not say it straightaway, I believe he pointed out that particular chapter and passage to me for he felt it illustrated a critical and central feature of Chinese ethics, that is, the dialogical intent as set forth by the ancients that, through the many centuries, has been conveniently and disingenuously forgotten by educators and others in positions of power and authority.

This particular incident captures well for me two important characteristics in my *dia-dia*'s life as man and thinker.

The first was his natural penchant for openness and objectivity, his steadfast insistence in getting to the heart of any matter, whether it be the Law or Zen or something of seeming insignificance to the untrained eye. As his child, I was often privy to seeing him reveal his thoughts and feelings to whomever he spoke and would listen to him. I cannot ever remember him compromising his position because of the person he was addressing. And the person talking seemed always *his true self.* Secondly, his maturing years—perhaps, from age thirty-five onward—found him increasingly concerned over the importance of *salvaging* basic cultural treasures of both East and West that he felt were being preempted and overtaken by the juggernaut of modernity and a too strong emphasis on technological development for its own sake.

The greatest fear he entertained was the thick encrustation he felt growing over much of ancient literatures that he always believed held irreplaceable cultural and spiritual traditions. He saw his true vocation not as a blind return to traditions but of recapturing our collective habit to see them as *living* truths needed more than ever by generations which have lost their roots. Unlike the many mystically-oriented who have little or no faith in technological progress, he typically walked the middle path and felt that technology itself could be put to good use if its progress could be directed not by blind forces but *illuminated* intelligence.

On the other hand, his wisdom informed him the only discerning guidance would come from a fully-grown humanity that knew well where our societies are heading and, most crucially, *why* they were heading that way. Being a well-known proponent of the Natural Law—to which he devoted several books—he was never able or willing to see the universe as indifferent. By the time he had passed on, it was obvious that the world, fixated on itself, was no longer asking the same basic and essential questions so dear to his own heart. He was never able to entertain the possibility of any world view that was not *eschatological* and *teleological*, that is, that did not have a beginning and a final purpose. Here, again, he was drawing inspiration from some of the richest classical traditions, East and West.

In this harshest of centuries, driven by a strikingly wanton pragmatism, ruthless social and political tyrannies of unimaginable tragic dimensions, and the ongoing absolutizing of an undirected whirlwind progress, my *dia-dia*'s life and writings can be seen as a conciliatory effort to combat such vastly impersonal and dehumanizing forces. Recovery of humanity and all that was essential to making the person truly human and noble had to begin, for him, with *metanoia*, the moral and spiritual transformation of the self, the process of recovery in which each person is regarded not as a means toward some engineered social and political end but rather as a *sacred vessel*, holy and incorruptible in itself and conceived for no other purpose than to give glory to the Creator. His underlying message for us is that we are after all no mere trash bins containing the throwaway and the ephemeral but cisterns of unimaginable delicate beauty, each uniquely fired to contain sweet nectar *from* and *for* God.

To my *dia-dia*, whatsoever heavenly, because timeless, cannot undergo permanent loss; at worst, having become strangers to the habit of living in permanency and transcendence, we allow the empirical ego with its exhausting and interminable practical concerns to steer our lives. In the meantime, our timeless treasures, temporarily mislaid, are forgotten, and we lose our way. Although a man of countless earthly enthusiasms, *dia-dia* rarely allowed himself to be made drunk for long by the transient and impermanent, which, by themselves, he saw as dead bones worth nothing *intrinsically*. With Lao Tzu, his soul brother of twenty-five hundred years ago, he understood well what truly is permanent and priceless,

> For a whirlwind does not last a whole morning,
> Nor does a sudden shower last a whole day.
> (故飄風不終朝,驟雨不終日.) (*TTC*, #23)

He was convinced the truly priceless could be found in the unbounded ranges of the universal human heart through which the Divine, *wholly free*, comes and goes according to its will. Life had taught him the difficult and cautionary lesson of not attributing excessive worth on anything other than what we each initially bring into the world. He believed in letting things simply *be*. What he did and wrote came from his heart unadorned and had the great value of being able to affect other hearts open and receptive to his own heart.

That is perhaps the reason why the specialist has never been able to understand fully either his life or writings. To the professionals—the legal experts, philosophers, educators, politicians, men and women of religion—while he certainly did not fail to address their expertise, breadth of knowledge and intellectual reason and acumen, all of which he himself certainly possessed in fair abundance but secretly regarded more as chaff than kernel, in the end he appealed to their *whole persons* and therefore to their *silence, simplicity and solitude.* He had a marvelous sense of proportion—what the Greeks called moderation and temperance, and the Chinese, *chung yung*—quietly yet unfailingly informed whatever he did. The following translation, his own, from the last part of chapter 38 of the *Tao Teh Ching* could very well summarize the man:

> Therefore, the full-grown man sets his heart upon the substance rather than the husk;
> Upon the fruit rather than the flower.
> Truly, he prefers what is within to what is without.
>
> (是以大丈夫處其厚,不居其薄;
> 處其實,不居其華.故去彼取此.)

There was such a *oneness* about him that you had to take him complete or not at all. Despite being trained in the Law, he never mastered the scourge of the twentieth-century, *compartmentalization*, of learning to live split existences, of learning to be happy in self-imposed alienation. There was something wonderfully *organic and whole* about him; hence when you dissect the man, when you analyze him and his thought in minute detail, you somehow miss the mark, ending up with the *not quite*. This, despite the fact he himself was masterly in the art of analysis, which he learned at the foot of some of the greatest legal thinkers of the twentieth-century.

Despite being trained as a legal scholar, he never allowed his profession nor academic life to dictate his path or the way he saw reality. In fact, even in his approach to the law, he appeared far less interested in furthering its positivistic and evolutionary trends than in rediscovering its *spiritual* dimensions, its very roots and substance. Without them giving it support, he was convinced the law would degenerate into mere deadweight, becoming artificial and a gross manipulation of the truth. In his writings, be it on the law or otherwise, nothing is more evident than his deeply-held conviction that all truly productive human knowledge is anchored on a *hidden source* and carries with it the hope of self-discovery which, in turn, will help us return to that source. With Lao Tzu, he would have emphatically agreed that "To go far is to return."

Ultimately, it was the universal human heart informed steadily and *inflamed ecstatically* by the unquenchable fire of love that will bring us back to our True Home. In fact, in all this, we find him solidly secure in *The Great Learning*—one of the Four Books of the Confucian canon—where we are told that, in everything, there is a *beginning and an end*. Having been imbued with a solid traditional education, he was wholly versed in the Chinese classics, his childhood bible. Even as the buds of his Christianity bloomed into gorgeous flowers, the Chinese classics remained his ever constant and faithful guide.

Vignette #5: "Ad deum qui laetificat juventutem meam" ("To God who gives joy to my youth")

My parents' coming upon their Catholic faith is well-documented in my father's *The Science of Love, Beyond East and West* and *Huai Lan Chi (In Remembrance of Lan)*, and in the writings of Dr. Paul K.T. Sih, his beloved student and godson, particularly, *From Confucius to Christ*, and in *My Twenty Years With the Chinese* by the Reverend Nicholas Maestrini. It was the latter who first gave *dia-dia* intensive formal instructions in the doctrines of his new faith. I will not say anything about it here and only refer you to their books.

To speak of my daddy and mommy without addressing the question of the *source* of their joy would be a disservice to both. Though I do not presume to know in depth the answer to this question, yet the way they lived their lives leaves us with suggestive clues as to what motivated them.

As a teenager I first began to have some inkling as to what made their individual and marital lives so very special. What I treasure dearly was their having given me, both through daily example and words, a clear glimpse of the true nature of their piety. I began to have some deeper understanding of what held my parents' lives and our large family together. Somehow, I always saw their lives in spiritual terms and, therefore, as two lives on a continuous unbroken line progressing *upward* hand-in-hand. It was primarily in seeing such paradigms in my parents that throughout my life I have never taken any other kind of progress other than moral and spiritual progress with any degree of gravity. I believe my siblings unequivocally share this feeling with me.

From my early twenties, as I became more familiar with spiritual literature, to me, the most intimate of writings, the only couple whose piety I found comparable to that of my parents was Jacques and Raissa Maritain whom my parents had befriended in Rome. The French neo-Thomist was ambassador to Italy at the time my daddy was Republic of China's Minister to the Vatican. Later, the Maritains would carefully chronicle their rich lives in separate journals describing their spiritual journey.

During their comparatively short years together in New Jersey (1951-59), my parents attended daily Mass at a cozy and unpretentious chapel—Chapel of the Immaculate Conception—with a richly-designed interior on the South Orange campus of Seton Hall University. There, *dia-dia* first taught law and then Chinese studies. Each morning they would stroll, often hand-in-hand, on a steady up-hill from our home to the little church for the 8 a.m. services. Ordinarily, the walk took no more than seven to eight minutes, but given that my mommy had feet that were bound as a child and, later, at twelve or thirteen, unbound, by that time, structural damage had become irreversible. The short walk must have seemed for her similar to a daily trekking of the Stations of the Cross. Yet, she ventured back and forth stoically, rarely complaining. A common sight upon her return home was seeing her sitting meditatively in an old armchair ritualistically rubbing her sore contorted feet. To this day, it amazes me that I personally never heard her use her feet as an excuse to miss this daily sacred ritual. In fact, it was nearly always our dear mother who, through gentle prodding, got *dia-dia* out of bed whenever he was tempted to sleep in.

On the subject of Mass and Communion and faith in general, I remember certain simple yet profound notions that became deeply fixed in my mind. If the words are not faithful to the way they were first spoken, I do think they do at least capture their tone and spirit. What follows are composite ideas gleaned over many little conversations I had with *dia-dia* over several years.

You might wonder what is the sense of going to Mass each morning. Let me tell you that I literally thrill with joy just at the thought of such an overwhelming privilege! Do you know what is the first thing your mommy and I do the moment we get to the little chapel? We kneel before the altar of God *in total emptiness and silence*. Now, what do I mean by this? Simply this. We come to God *empty-handed with loving and grateful hearts*. Since the Mass is a banquet, a joyous celebration of a meal, what better way to start the day than to *feast* with our Lord and to thank Him for this ever-healing nourishment?

We carry our worries and burdens daily to the altar and offer them to Him completely. He always knows what to do with them. And, with each new day, as we come to a deeper awareness as to what it means to be a disciple of Christ, we now see ourselves no more than instruments our loving Father has somehow chosen in his mercy, *for yet another day,* to do *his* bidding, *his* chosen work on earth. We come to him not with any great offerings of which, in and through ourselves, we have none and, if we did, they would *originally and forever* belong to him in the first place. Frankly, besides our love and sense of gratefulness he doesn't need any of the things we have or whatever else we could give him. You see, in offering our total selves to Him, we become *fully dead to the world* for the only thing we have then is an *empty self completely at his beck and call.*

As for myself, I am like a broken cistern full of cracks unable, by my own insignificant efforts, to seal the cracks nor to hold anything within me, yet in his mercy, *he pities my brokenness*, sealing those holes and making me *whole* again. Or, sometimes, I see myself as water held in a crude pot awaiting purification and, in his miraculous hands he not only purifies the water but also proceeds to change me into the finest of vintages! We are wholly grateful for the daily miracle that occurs within us. In my case, I say to myself, imagine, he can even make a decent man out of an unfit scoundrel like me!

When mommy and I approach the altar each new morning, when we offer our simple lives to him, we let *him* decide who and what will benefit from our respective work on earth. For in fact by approaching him in this simple, ingenuous way, truly like the children that we are face to face with our Father, the sometime laborious task of working for others he, without *our* knowing it, takes out of our hands. That is, it is *he who mercifully unburdens us,* and the question of what is and is not *efficacious* in what we say and do is no longer a concern at all. You cannot imagine what freedom he is capable of granting us, just for our asking. And, since God is both Father *and* Mother, how could he or she refuse any earnest requests? If

even our own mothers and fathers are touched by our plead-
ings, how could *God*—infinitely wiser than our own dear parents—not be touched by what we seek?

Don't you see, when we are still concerned about what will
and will not benefit ourselves and others, when we are forever
conscious of every little thing that occurs around us, we are
not yet living in *simplicity* and *freedom*. I did not really understand the meaning of working and living only for the glory of
Our Lord until I understood it to mean that only when we are
detached from *both* success and failure can we truly give to
others in a *selfless* way, can we truly live in joy and freedom.
The secret is to try to live our lives without motives and only
delight in the Lord. And, if we must live with some motive,
then let it be in pleasing God who has given us everything.
For when we please him, nothing else matters as he will take
care of everything else. How could your mommy and daddy
live our lives other than in inexplicable *joy*?! Even our burdens
and sufferings are all given to us as *rare gifts* with a view towards attaining the greatest of all possible good, which of
course is our *sanctification*, the only genuine goal worth pursuing.

Among all the many virtues, perhaps the one defining quality in
dia-dia's life was his commitment to his religious belief. He deci-
sively lived his newly found faith to the bone, allowing nothing
else, certainly no material concerns (of which, except for books, he
found nothing that was ultimately *not* petty and ephemeral), to
interfere with its proper work within his soul. The crowning deed
of his life, beyond all the worldly achievements including his fine
writings, lay in the inseparability of his intellectual life and his
everyday existence. I think this was made possible only because,
in the days following his religious conversion in his late thirties,
he slowly but dramatically began to discover for himself that all
words and deeds are forms of prayer, likened to sacred cables or
offerings of praise to his Redeemer. Might we not say he had once
for all embarked upon a way in which he saw his entire life as a
fragile, easily-broken string of prayers serving as steps that he ear-
nestly hoped, with the grace of God, might help him reach the
Gates of Heaven? The secret of his simplicity lay in that his *life of
reason* could not be perceived as separate from his *life of faith*, which
is far more affective than rational. Reason and faith, like the fluid,

unlabored wings of a bird in jovial flight, existed in such nearly perfect symmetry that he was able to soar effortlessly into some uncharted reaches of his soul. What bliss such joy must have been to him as well as to my mommy!

Vignette #6: "What's in a Havana, Anyway?"

Sometimes our *dia-dia* was quite capable of using earthy humor and images in driving home a philosophical point. To me it was in the classroom that he appeared most at home, where he could leave his self-consciousness behind and simply be himself. Once, teaching a class on Zen Buddhism at Seton Hall during the mid 1960s in which I was present, there occurred, at least, to my untrained mind, a rather rich and heated debate among the clever and well-informed graduate students over some delicate point. Perhaps, it was on the great historical controversy of what is of greater meaning or authenticity, *sudden or gradual enlightenment.* Or it could have been over the question of whether it was possible to "*sit oneself into a Buddha.*" It hardly matters now what had brought about the fierce and animated exchanges among the usually docile and polite classmates. It was after all a class on Zen, which was usually dominated by a good deal of meditative thought over cups of tea. Some students, in imitation of *dia-dia* and hoping to find enlightenment, had even brought along their own favorite tea.

 Dia-dia, in his fine, dark-blue Chinese silk robe and with a long Cuban cigar dangling precariously from his mouth—quite an uncommon sight, indeed, of an Asian professor at an American university—sat both beaming and with a bemused look for much of the time the intellectual skirmishes were going on. If my memory serves me right, the distinguished professor allowed it to go on for a good fifteen to twenty minutes. Finally feeling a bit antsy and exhaling a large puff of smoke that shot up to partially hide his head, he held out his left arm, a bit cocked at the elbow, and, as the class slowly came to order, he said in a clear, loud voice, "Good! Good! Very good discussion, solid exchange, excellent ideas! You really went at each other quite fiercely, quite relentlessly! Almost like lawyers!"

 You could see the students beaming, apparently flattered. A couple of moments passed as he noticed some shades of self-complacency setting in. He chuckled to himself. Seeing that the cigar was about to go out, he then poked his right hand into his robe groping for some object. And, just as quickly, there appeared his shiny Ronson lighter, a proud gift with inscription from my sister Terry. He then struck it forcibly whereby a huge flame came up perfectly—as if he had practiced it a thousand times before—to meet the foul-smelling Havana. He took a few quick strong puffs, and without skipping a beat and in implacable rhythm, continued: "I enjoyed everything you said. Everything made sense. This is a very perceptive class and every student gave reasons that, as far as I could see, were airtight, no holes."

Then, half-teasingly but carefully avoiding sarcasm, he said, "I can tell, being trained in the best schools in the West, you are Aristotelians, masters of logic and the syllogism. *But,*" and here his voice began to rise ever so slightly, "I have to confess one thing. Yes…yes. The main problem I see in the discussion is that everything really *did* make sense. You see, despite your fine arguments, heated verbal skirmishes, nothing you have said, indisputable as they stand, *has as much cosmic validity as a simple bowel movement.*" Except for a few scarcely audible and nervous snickers, near total silence greeted his words. Some embarrassing seconds followed. There was much squirming in seats, the mood quite in contrast to a few minutes earlier.

Puffing furiously now on his Havana, he first gave his characteristic slow, sweeping gaze at the entire class, chuckling impishly to himself as he did so, obviously delighted by the confusion his words had caused. Then, nodding and smiling through his scholarly spectacles from one perplexed student to another, he added, now even louder, *"Don't you see?!"* He had gently slapped the unassuming students on the face without their knowing it. And, at that second, who could have doubted that there had occurred instantaneously an imperceptible though sensational *spiritual* bowel movement rumbling through the stuffy campus?

On another occasion, this time in a class on the *Tao Teh Ching* of Lao Tzu at Columbia University, *dia-dia* asked a question to which, except for a few soft whispers, there was quite a different response—complete silence and dumbfoundness. Sipping tea from a small teapot and slowly glancing about the room from left to right, then from back to front, and seeing that there were no raised hands, my *dia-dia's* eyes finally settled near the podium on a large German shepherd which a student had brought to class. The forbidding-looking creature was dozing away contentedly and had even been heard snoring intermittently. On that day he appeared to look more like an attorney-at-law than a teacher, looking impeccable in his business suit. Pointing at the unwitting dog, he started to address the students. "Look at Lucky there, snoring away so contentedly." He called all German shepherds "Lucky" for my brother Stephen, an incurable lover of such fierce creatures, had had one in Rome that *dia-dia* did all he could to distance himself from. Like many a philosopher and poet, he did not take well to dogs because he was either fearful of them or he found them too obsequious to his liking. Naturally, he favored the independence of purring cats and would sometimes spend long intervals between studying enticing birds of all colors to break into song. He continued:

> Look at Lucky, in a world of his own, *fully* unaware of what's going on! I can guarantee, in his unconscious bliss, he is practicing perfectly what each of you highly intelligent Ivy Leaguers ought to have mastered by now—the art of *wu-wei*! *Tao* goes in, around and through him *effortlessly*. No doors or windows and none of his senses bar or interfere with the *Way* of that docile, sleeping creature. He lives the *Way* without having any consciousness of it. Most of us—even if we know something of the presence of *Tao*—only know it consciously, by our meddling minds that can't leave things alone. Don't you see Lucky is obviously no *ordinary* scholar?!

His words were greeted by loud, spontaneous hand clapping and foot stomping—more a European than American habit—which rudely jerked the dog from his sleep. "Lucky," feeling and looking slightly irritated, gave a half-sleepy, perfunctory bark, looked around and weighed in his mind for an instant if the student display was worth losing sleep over. Then, seeming to think it wouldn't be worth his while and without much fuss, the big black and gray monster returned to his blissful, delicious dreams, letting the hippie-like human creatures sitting before him go on with their silly diversion. They may have regarded it as "fun" but Lucky, obviously correctly, considered it to be much ado about nothing.

****

Dia-dia has returned to Eternity, joining his friends like the Little Flower, Dr. Suzuki and Thomas Merton and, most of all, my dear mommy, but what a lovely day of wind and moon he meant to all of us!

Fu Jen Catholic University
May 22, 1999
(revised, Summer 2006)

1. Editor's note: These remarkable remembrances about John Wu by his son are important because they provide insight both into the man with whom Merton established a paradoxical son-father / father-son relationship and also give us a portrait of a remarkable father-scholar-believer who clearly radiated insight into the knowing of the Logos, hidden yet known through words and celebration of the *Void* embraced and pondered in a simplicity of oneness.

We are indebted for John Wu Jr.'s perceptive insights and appreciative of his willingness to let us publish these vignettes here. Clearly, they reveal facets of John Wu's complex mind, wit, faith and spirit in a love which is reflected in Thomas Merton's enthusiastic friendship with this modest model of leadership.

Han Yong-Un and Thomas Merton:
Brothers in Different Guises

Daniel J. Adams

For anyone who lives in another culture over a long period of time, or is seriously engaged in cross-cultural studies, it soon becomes apparent that there are numerous similarities which can be identified among widely diverse cultures. Among these similarities are persons who seem to have the same concerns, interests, and intentions. Indeed, some of these persons even seem to have parallel careers. Two such persons are Han Yong-Un (1879-1944) and Thomas Merton (1915-1968). Although they quite literally lived on opposite sides of the earth and were totally unaware of each other's existence, the similarities between them are so striking that it seems almost natural to say that they were brothers in different guises.

At first glance, there could be no two persons whose background and life experience seem so different. Han Yong-Un was a Korean Buddhist and Thomas Merton was an American Catholic Christian. Although Han was, during much of his life, a Buddhist monk, he did marry twice. Merton never married and was a Cistercian (or Trappist) monk for all of his adult life. Han was actively involved in the politics of his time and even suffered imprisonment for his views. Merton retreated to a hermitage where he resisted active participation in the political events of the day. Although Han travelled widely for a man of his time, he preferred to be in his native land of Korea and died of natural causes in his Seoul home. Merton took a vow of monastic stability, yet he always longed to visit faraway places and he died of accidental electrocution in Bangkok, Thailand. Today it is Christians, especially minjung theologians, who look to Han for inspiration, while Buddhists, including the Dalai Lama, travel to the Abbey of Gethsemani in Kentucky to visit Merton's tomb and dialogue with the monks on the critical religious and social issues of the day.

Yet both Han and Merton were deep religious thinkers, and both championed monastic and theological reform. Both were concerned with politics and both had an uncanny ability to discern the signs of the times. Han and Merton were literary figures and they left behind a legacy of penetrating essays and deeply moving poetry. Both edited magazines which were noted for a progressive stance on cultural and religious issues. Their personal lives were similar in that Han loved three women and Merton loved two, and for each there was one woman (who remains publicly anonymous in both instances) who inspired their best poetry. Today these two men are remembered as towering figures in the cultural, political, and religious life of their respective countries. It is entirely fitting, therefore, that we see them together—a Korean Buddhist and an American Christian—as examples of the triumph of the human spirit in the service of the Ultimate who transcends all cultures, political systems, and religious traditions.

The Context of Their Lives

Han Yong-Un was born during turbulent times and his entire life and career must be understood in terms of his opposition to the Japanese occupation and colonization of Korea.[1]   He was born into poverty as the family fortunes had greatly declined due to the turmoil of the times, and he lost both parents and his older brother while still a comparatively young man. However, at an early age he showed extraordinary ability and was able to study in a private academy where he learned to read and write Chinese characters as well as study the Confucian classics.   In 1897 he became involved in the Tonghak rebellion, a popular uprising of farmers and peasants against the injustices of the upper classes. According to many accounts his father and older brother were both executed for their roles in either the Tonghak rebellion or a later popular uprising in 1906. The Tonghak rebellion was eventually put down by government forces with the help of both Chinese and Japanese troops.[2]   Han was forced to flee to the mountains where he stayed for a time at Paektam Temple before going on to Vladivostok in Russia. It was his plan to travel across Siberia and central Europe and then take a boat to America as part of a projected world tour. However, while in Vladivostok he and two other monks were suspected of being Japanese sympathizers and narrowly escaped being murdered on two occasions. Han returned to Korea and Paektam Temple and became a Buddhist monk. He also visited Japan where he came into contact with Buddhist move-

ments there and saw first-hand the results of Japan's moderniza-
tion brought about by the Meiji Restoration.

As a result of his experience and his international travels, Han
became a champion of Buddhist reform and political independence
for Korea. When Korea was formally annexed by Japan in 1910,
Han chose voluntary exile in Manchuria where he worked with
others to restore the political independence of his homeland. While
there he was shot by two Koreans who mistook him for a Japanese
agent, and as he lay bleeding from his wounds, he had a vision of
Avalokitesvara in which she urged him to return home and work
for reform. Upon his return to Korea he resumed his efforts for the
reform of Buddhism and in 1919 became one of thirty-three signers of the Declaration of Independence. Following this action he
was arrested by the Japanese authorities and served a three-year
prison sentence. Following his release he once again returned to
Paektam Temple where he wrote his famed collection of poems
entitled *Love's Silence.* For the remainder of his life he engaged in
editing several journals, writing essays for newspapers and other
periodicals, working on numerous publishing projects related to
the Buddhist reform movement, and taking part in movements
opposed to the Japanese, one of which resulted in his being imprisoned for a second time.

Han's life was characterized by considerable instability during his childhood, adolescence, and young adulthood, and it was
not until the last decade of his life that he finally settled down in a
home that he could call his own. He was an "on again, off again"
Buddhist monk who alternated between periods of quiet contemplation in remote mountain temples and frenzied political activity
in the city of Seoul. His two passions were the reform of Buddhism and opposition to the Japanese colonization of Korea, and
he expressed his view concerning both through his voluminous
writings.

Thomas Merton was born of artist parents in France, and much
of his youth was spent in Europe as his parents wandered from
place to place, finally settling in New York City.[3] His mother died
of cancer while he was still young and his father died of a brain
tumor when Merton was at a boarding school in England. From
then on he was under the care of his maternal grandparents and a
physician friend of his father's who served as his legal guardian.
Prior to beginning his university studies, Merton took the "grand
tour" which included visits to many of the religious sites of Italy.

Merton spent a disastrous year at Cambridge University and was then forced by his guardian to leave England. He returned to New York and completed his studies at Columbia University with a major in English literature. While at Columbia he became a regular on the party circuit, flirted with communism (a popular thing to do during the Spanish Civil War), had his first contact with non-Christian religions, in this case Hinduism, and underwent a dramatic conversion to the Catholic Church. He visited Cuba where he had a mystical experience in a Havana church, began writing book reviews and essays for New York newspapers, and completed his M.A. at Columbia with a thesis on nature and art in William Blake. He then began working on his doctorate at Columbia and later was teaching English literature at St. Bonaventure College in upstate New York. Following a spiritual retreat at the Cistercian Abbey of Gethsemani in Kentucky, Merton felt called to the monastic life and he entered Gethsemani on 10 December 1941, three days after the Japanese bombing of Pearl Harbor and the entry of the United States into World War II. In 1943 Merton was informed that his younger brother was killed in action when his military plane crashed into the English Channel. Merton remained a monk at Gethsemani for the remainder of his life until his untimely death in Bangkok on 10 December 1968—exactly twenty-seven years from the day he entered Gethsemani.

Merton's years as a monk were anything but calm, however, for Merton was first of all a writer and his autobiography *The Seven Storey Mountain* brought him instant fame, and brought the monastery much-needed income. The abbot recognized Merton's literary talent and allowed him the freedom to continue on with his writing. His earlier works were mostly on spiritual themes, but following a trip outside the monastery to the nearby city of Louisville, Merton underwent a kind of conversion experience, and he began to write on topics of social and political significance. These included the Cold War and the arms race, the use of nuclear weapons, the problem of racism in American society, and above all, the Vietnam War. Following Vatican Council II, Merton increasingly turned to the issue of religious and theological reform with a specific focus on the reform of the monastic life. Needless to say, he fought a running battle with his monastic superiors, the censors of the order, and others who believed that the proper task of a monk was prayer and not writing essays on social criticism. Even as his social criticism became more intense, Merton himself longed for a more contemplative life, and he began to express a desire to live as a hermit, a wish that was finally granted in 1965.

In his later years Merton became deeply involved with both the ecumenical movement and interfaith dialogue. This latter involvement culminated with his Asian journey in 1968 and his meeting with the Dalai Lama in northern India. Throughout his life he had always been searching for a true spiritual home and he even expressed a desire to live as a hermit somewhere in Asia. However, once he came to Asia he realized that his true home was the Abbey of Gethsemani, and in a postcard to a friend, he expressed his desire of returning home to his hillside hermitage.

The Desire for Religious Reform

Han Yong-Un and Thomas Merton were first of all, deeply committed to their respective religious traditions, so committed in fact, that for varying lengths of time both took monastic vows and lived in a monastery. Han spent most his monastic life at Paektam Temple located in a remote valley in the inner area of the Sorak Mountains. He also spent some time at nearby Yujom Temple. It was while meditating at Oseam Hermitage high above Paektam Temple, that Han experienced sudden enlightenment when he heard the sound of an object being blown to the ground by the wind. Han alternated between periods of meditation in Buddhist temples and the active life of politics. Merton, on the other hand, spent all twenty-seven years of his monastic life in one place—the Abbey of Gethsemani. It should be noted that this difference in monastic stability between Han and Merton is due in part to several important distinctions between Buddhist and Christian monasticism. Buddhist monks often wander from temple to temple while Christian monks tend to remain in one monastery for their entire lives. Also Buddhist monks sometimes alternate between periods of monastic life and public life in a way that, in Merton's time, was not allowed for Christian monks. What is significant about both Han and Merton is that their religious commitment and vocation lay at the very center of their lives and the way in which they lived their lives in the world.

When Han first went to Paektam Temple, Buddhism in Korea was at its lowest ebb, for it had undergone over five hundred years of suppression under the Chosun dynasty. Furthermore both domestically and internationally the political situation of Korea was precarious at best. Han believed that the salvation of the country lay in a renewed and revitalized Buddhism. At the outset there was in Han's thinking the belief that religious faith and sociopolitical action are necessarily related.[4] Religious faith forms the ground out of which sociopolitical action grows, while at the same time effective sociopolitical activity is rooted in a deep sense of religious commitment. During the experience of his vision of Avalokitesvara while in Manchuria, Han related how Avalokitesvara threw flowers at him and said, "Why don't you stir in this critical moment?"[5]

Han did stir and he began a lifelong struggle to bring about the reform and renewal of Korean Buddhism. Two works which caused an immediate sensation were an essay advocating the allowance of married monks and a collection of essays entitled "On Revitalizing Korean Buddhism." In this latter work he wrote:

> Revitalization of Buddhism must be preceded by destruction. What is revitalization? It is the child of destruction. What is destruction? It is the mother of revitalization. Everyone knows that there is no motherless child, but no one knows that revitalization cannot take place without destruction.... Destruction does not mean destroying and eliminating everything. Only those aspects of the traditional customs that do not suit contemporary times are to be amended and given a new direction.[6]

Han was convinced that true reform did not consist of cosmetic changes here and there. Rather, true reform meant sweeping away those rituals and practices that were holding Buddhism back and not allowing it to take its rightful place in contemporary society. Han wanted to see Buddhism at the center of the great sociopolitical changes that were taking place in Korean society; he was not content to see Buddhism at the margins.

Han's call for reform focused first of all upon the education of monks. He believed that they should have a general liberal arts education prior to beginning their theological studies. He also advocated educating the monks in teachers' colleges so that they could learn how to teach not only Buddhist subjects but also teach general knowledge and thus place Buddhism more in the center of current affairs. Finally, he advocated that monks spend some time studying abroad in India, China, and even in Europe and

America. He was deeply concerned that traditionalists were advocating a narrow viewpoint and that this was causing Buddhism to lose ground in the modern world. Han went so far as to say, "Those who obstruct education shall end up in hell, and those who promote education shall attain Buddhist enlightenment."[7]

Han went on to emphasize that Buddhism was the religion best suited to give humankind hope for the future, for it is a religion of wisdom and awakening. Thus it is inappropriate to simply withdraw to the temple or hermitage and forget what is happening in the world. He also believed that Buddhism was based on egalitarianism and thus in harmony with democratic liberalism. Therefore "to look at the world from the viewpoint of equality means to escape the bondage of the inequality of phenomena, and to look with the eye of truth."[8]   In addition Han espoused a view which he called "salvationism." By this he meant that salvation in Buddhism is not primarily individual, but rather, is social. Han pointed out "that the preaching of Buddha was full of mercy for the unawakened mass."[9]   It was not enough so see salvation purely in terms of the awakening of the individual, for this leads only to self-interest and individualism. Salvation is corporate in nature and cosmic in scope.

At the same time, however, Han also favored a renewal of Son (Chinese—Chan, Japanese—Zen) Buddhist meditation. He believed that meditation was important and he himself continued to practice meditation at remote mountain temples and hermitages. However, he always returned to the world of sociopolitical affairs renewed and refreshed and even more committed to the cause of religious and political reform. He was concerned that many Buddhists used Son meditation as an escape from the harsh realities of life; thus he advocated moving temples from the mountains to the cities and establishing meditation halls in urban areas.

One of the main ways in which Han encouraged reform was through the use of the Korean vernacular script, Hangul.[10]   Traditionally virtually all Buddhist literature was written in classical Chinese characters which most of the common people were unable to read. Han undertook numerous translation projects, both of Buddhist literature and general literature, and he also edited *A Dictionary of Korean Buddhism*. In preparing this latter work, Han studied over 1,511 documents and 6,802 Buddhist woodblock tablets.[11]   At the time of his death he was researching a work to be entitled *A History of the Tongdo Monastery*, the same temple where he did most of the editorial work for *A Dictionary of Korean Bud-dhism.*

Finally Han's commitment to interfaith cooperation and dia-logue should be mentioned. Unlike many Buddhists of his time, he was open to other religions and was willing to work together with them on common concerns, especially those concerns related to Korean national independence and sovereignty. He joined with Christian and Chondogyo leaders in signing the Korean Declara-tion of Independence in 1919, but his interfaith activities went be-yond political action. In 1935, for example, he helped to publish the posthumous writings of Chol Na, the chief priest of the Tangun religion, a native Korean religion which worships Tangun the mythical founder of the Korean people. In 1936 he organized a seminar for the centennial anniversary of Chong Yak-Yong, a sec-retary in the royal court who was exiled because of his conversion to Catholicism. Although deeply committed to Buddhism, Han was able to see that ultimate truth and value was not confined to any one religion but was, in fact, greater than any single expres-sion of that ultimate truth and value. At the same time, he real-ized ultimate truth and value must be lived out in a particular concrete religious tradition, and for him, that religious tradition was Buddhism.

Unlike Han Yong-Un, Thomas Merton spent his entire monas-tic career at one monastery, and with the exception of several brief trips away for medical treatment and trips to meet important reli-gious leaders such as D.T. Suzuki in New York and the Dalai Lama in India, Merton's struggle for religious and monastic reform took place in almost total physical isolation from the world around him. The order to which Merton belonged, the Order of the Cistercians of the Strict Observance, commonly called Trappists, was one of the most austere of all Catholic monastic orders. When Merton became a monk in 1941 the order observed strict silence, and most communication took place by means of sign language. Monks slept in small unheated cells on thin straw mattresses and there was a strict regimen of fasting and hard physical labor. This proved too much for Merton, however, and he suffered several psycho-logical and physical breakdowns and he was plagued throughout his life by serious gastritis. As a result he was allowed to eat meat and eggs, which were not part of the regular monastic diet, in or-der to strengthen his overall physical condition.

The succession of abbots at the Abbey of Gethsemani recognized Merton's literary gifts and he was given time for writing and study. He was also allowed a certain amount of free time for prayer and meditation. As mentioned above, in the final years of his life Merton was granted permission to make retreats at a nearby hermitage, and the frequency and duration of these increased to the point where the abbot finally recognized his vocation to live alone as a hermit.

Several turning points can be identified in Merton's struggle for religious reform. He entered the monastery, of course, to get away from the world. But in the late 1950s he made several trips to the nearby city of Louisville for medical treatment and to take care of details relating to the publication of postulant guides and other related work. He writes of one such trip in 1958:

In Louisville, at the corner of Fourth and Walnut, in the center of the shopping district, I was suddenly overwhelmed with the realization that I loved all those people, that they were mine and I theirs, that we could not be alien to one another even though we were total strangers. It was like waking from a dream of separateness, of spurious self-isolation in a special world, the world of renunciation and supposed holiness. The whole illusion of a separate holy existence is a dream. Not that I question the reality of my vocation, or of my monastic life: but the conception of 'separation from the world' that we have in the monastery too easily presents itself as a complete illusion: the illusion that by making vows we become a different species of being, pseudoangels, 'spiritual men,' men of interior life, what have you.[12]

This was the beginning of Merton's turning toward the world. He began to notice, living as he did in the American south, the problem of racism in American society. From the forests and fields of the monastery he could hear the guns from nearby Fort Knox and he became aware of the ongoing Cold War. He began to read widely and friends sent him books and magazines as gifts. His correspondence with like-minded people began to increase as did his awareness of the world and its many problems. Merton came to the realization that contemplation in the monastery and action in the outside world were inseparable.

Another turning point for Merton was the involvement of the United States in the Vietnam War. Merton was strongly opposed to U.S. involvement in the war and he began to write essays and edit books on the subject of pacifism. Forbidden to publish anything on the subject of war and peace, Merton privately circulated a collection of letters under the title *The Cold War Letters* and an increasing number of his pacifist and anti-war essays began to appear in numerous magazines and journals. A "Prayer for Peace" written by Merton was read in the U.S. House of Representatives and in 1962 Merton joined the Fellowship of Reconciliation. In the years to come his writings on the subject of war and peace would fill several volumes.[13]   More than any other event, the Vietnam War solidified Merton's commitment to a sociopolitical living out of his Christian faith.

Still another turning point was Vatican Council II (1962-1965) and its accompanying openness both to the world and to change within the Church. Life at the Abbey of Gethsemani underwent radical change. The monks were given private rooms, sign language was abolished, the daily diet improved, and there was a great deal more personal freedom allowed. The monastic orders were encouraged to undertake self-study with a view toward the reform of outdated practices. The abbey chapel was remodeled to reflect the changes in the liturgy as the use of the vernacular replaced the use of Latin. With these changes Merton began to write extensively on the need for reform in the religious life.

Merton's views on religious and monastic reform can be seen to center around several important ideas and interrelationships. First of all, Merton was thoroughly convinced of the necessity for the vocation of the monastic life with its commitment to prayer and contemplation. Second, Merton was equally convinced of the fact that the truly contemplative life by necessity bears fruit in the world of sociopolitical activity. The spiritual and social dimensions of the religious life cannot be separated or placed in opposition to each other. Both are equally necessary. Thus all true religious reform and revival bears fruit in the world, and all true social and political movements for good have their roots planted firmly in the spiritual life.

In speaking of this interrelationship Merton often uses the phrase "contemplation and action" or "contemplation in a world of action."[14]   The idea is that there is a place for what Merton refers to as "disinterested involvement."   One observer explains

Merton's views this way: "He viewed the monk as the man who takes distance from his society, who because of his commitment rejects the prevailing structures of society and can, as the result, function credibly as its critic. Therefore, he did not see how an oppressively disciplined, rigoristic system which dehumanized the monk could be much better than the oppression that characterizes the technological society that the monk rejects today."[15]   As an outspoken advocate of reform, Merton was opposed to a legalistic form of religion that was dehumanizing. Therefore, both religion and society are in need of reform.

The monk, because of his detachment from the world, is able to see things in perspective and avoid the sense of fadism that so often accompanies movements for social reform. Merton was skeptical of mass movements and asserted that "masses indeed may be called, but only individuals are chosen because only individuals can respond to a call by a free choice of their own."[16]   He saw that many persons are sucked into a movement without really knowing what they are doing. He also understood that many social activists suffer from "burnout" because they have no spiritual foundations to sustain them. Thus Merton made a careful distinction between activism (where one follows the crowd) and action (where one freely chooses a particular course of activity). Says Merton, "We must learn to distinguish between the pseudo-spirituality of activism and the true vitality and energy of Christian action guided by the Spirit."[17]

It should come as no surprise, therefore, to discover that as Merton's contemplative life deepened, his involvement in sociopolitical affairs became more intense. Indeed, following his retirement to the hermitage, Merton became even more trenchant in his social criticism and his circle of friends and correspondents around the world became ever more enlarged. Merton counted among his circle many of the leading religious figures, social critics, literary personalities, and political dissidents of his time and his published correspondence fills five hefty volumes with perhaps at least four or five more volumes of correspondence waiting to be edited and published. And yet, this man was a cloistered monk and in later life a hermit. Certainly his life was an example of contemplation in a world of action.

Merton was, unlike many of his contemporaries, deeply interested in religious and monastic renewal in non-Christian religious traditions. He was especially interested in Islam, Hinduism, Taoism, and Buddhism. He read widely in the thought and theology of these religions, corresponded with scholars and leaders of these religions, entertained many non-Christian visitors at his hermitage, and explored the various dimensions of both the divine and human personalities in an interfaith context.[18] Merton was especially drawn to Zen Buddhism and he engaged in a series of exchanges with the famed Japanese Zen scholar D.T. Suzuki.[19] On his last journey—the journey to Asia—Merton met with Hindu and Buddhist scholars in Sri Lanka, India, and Thailand. While it would seem that the culmination of this journey was a meeting with the Dalai Lama in northern India, what actually moved Merton the most was a visit to the large Buddha images at Polonnaruwa in Sri Lanka. He wrote at length concerning this experience:

> Looking at these figures I was suddenly, almost forcibly, jerked clean out of the habitual, half-tied vision of things, and an inner clearness, clarity, as if exploding from the rocks themselves, became evident and obvious.... All problems are resolved and everything is clear, simply because what matters is clear. The rock, all matter, all life, is charged with dharmakaya ...everything is emptiness and everything is compassion. I don't know when in my life I have ever had such a sense of beauty and spiritual validity running together in one aesthetic illumination. Surely, with Mahabalipuram and Polonnaruwa my Asian pilgrimage has come clear and purified itself. I mean, I know and have seen what I was obscurely looking for.[20]

Although a Christian, Merton was able to discern the presence of the Ultimate in and through these Buddhist sculptures and thus affirm the universal presence of the Divine.

The Struggle for Political Freedom

The political involvement of both Han Yong-Un and Thomas Merton can be summarized in two significant events—the March First Independence Movement of 1919 for Han, and the November 18-20, 1964 retreat at Gethsemani on the theme of "Spiritual Roots of Protest" for Merton. These two events firmly placed both Han and Merton in the political vortex of their times.

Han had, of course, been involved in anti-Japanese activities since his youth. He was firmly committed to justice for the oppressed masses of people and was especially opposed to Japanese efforts to influence Buddhism in Korea. His brief period of exile in Manchuria served to solidify his opposition to the Japanese colonization of Korea. In addition his publication of essays with an anti-Japanese theme contributed much to the independence efforts. It was, however, his involvement in the Independence Movement of 1919 that really brought him to the forefront in the political arena. It was through Han's efforts, along with those of his close friend and ally Choe In, that the thirty-three signers of the Declaration of Independence were brought together. As one observer writes of Han's efforts, "By embracing the willing, cajoling the lukewarm, and threatening the reluctant, he demonstrated his leadership."[21]

It was no easy task bringing the signers of the Declaration of Independence together, for as one writer puts it, "they were a motly lot religiously and with dispositional differences...but all were preachers of humanity, justice, and peace."[22]   Of the signers fifteen were members of Chondogyo, a religious movement which continued out of the Tonghak popular peasant movement and rebellion. Fifteen were   Christians, of which the majority were Presbyterians and Methodists. However, only three were Buddhists and one of these was Han himself. That such a small number of Buddhists were willing to affix their names to such a document serves to illustrate the need for reform and Han had considerable difficulty in persuading any Buddhists at all to join him in this important effort. Once the group was assembled there was then considerable controversy over who should sign first. The Christians favored putting the names in Korean alphabetical order while the more traditional Chondogyoists insisted on having the names in a order that reflected age and position in Korean society. Eventually a compromise was reached with each group putting forth one or two names based on traditional hierarchy and the other names being in alphabetical order. Han proposed that the abbot of Haein Temple, Paek Yong Song, sign first for the Buddhists. After considerable discussion it was finally decided to have the document signed and presented to the public on March 1, 1919.[23]

The Declaration of Independence was written by Choe Nam-Son but then Han, as a literary figure, read it through and added several finishing touches. Han also added the Three Pledges at the end of the document. These were provided so that the public, after reading the one-thousand word document, could pledge themselves to action. The Three Pledges which Han wrote and affixed to the declaration were:

One: What we undertake today is the demand of the nation for justice, humanitarianism, prosperity and existence; display, therefore, only free spirit; do not vent exclusivist ill-feelings. Two: Express willingly the rightful intention of the people until the last minute. Three: Respect the order most in all actions; make our claim and attitude fair and upright to the end.[24]

It should be noted that the Independence Movement was totally nonviolent, and that nonviolent action was a main theme of Han's Three Pledges. Indeed, the signers of the Declaration of Independence did not participate in the public demonstrations. After signing the document in a downtown Seoul restaurant, not far from the present-day Pagoda Park, they quietly awaited their arrest. The group presented a three-point resolution which said: "They shall not take legal recourse; they shall not accept private meals; and they shall not petition release."[25] In other words, Han and his fellow independence leaders knew that they would be arrested, but they asked for no special favors.

The response of the Japanese authorities to the issuing of the Declaration of Independence was both swift and brutal. All thirty-three signers of the document were immediately arrested and given prison terms. Han himself served a three-year sentence. Throughout the country 7,509 persons were killed, 15,961 were wounded, and 9,400 were given prison sentences.[26] The Independence Movement was not successful in terms of securing the political independence of Korea from Japanese rule, but it was successful in galvanizing the Korean people to political action, and from then on there was strong resistance to the Japanese

The fact that Han's prison term was so light can be explained by two factors. First, his actions were totally nonviolent and at no point did he act to incite others to violence or encourage violent actions. And second, there were a number of Koreans who were sympathetic to the independence cause but who also served under the Japanese administration. Undoubtedly some of these persons spoke out for him. Han himself, however, never accepted those who served with the Japanese, and when a group of them offered him money to buy a piece of land and build a house, he refused the offer. On another occasion when one of these persons gave his daughter a monetary gift, he walked through the rain to return it, and on still another occasion when Han met one of his former friends on the street, he refused to speak to him and said only that "you are not the same man I used to know." Han was so strongly opposed to the Japanese, that when he finally did get enough funds to buy a piece of land and build a house, he built the house facing north so that he would not have to look down the hill at the Japanese capitol building. He named his house "Ox-searching Hall" after the famed Buddhist series of paintings of the ox herder. Since Han was a well-known figure in both literary and Buddhist circles, the Japanese undoubtedly believed that he could be compromised and thus used to further their own ends. They failed, however, to correctly observe that Han was a man of absolute integrity who would not under any circumstances compromise his firmly held beliefs.

Following his release from prison, Han continued his efforts for religious reform, became involved in still other movements opposed to the Japanese, and served yet another prison sentence for leading a movement among Korean Buddhists who were opposed to an amalgamation of Korean and Japanese Buddhism. In all of these anti-Japanese activities Han remained nonviolent and never wavered in his commitment to peaceful sociopolitical change.

Following his decisive trip to the city of Louisville in 1958, Thomas Merton increasingly turned to more secular topics in his writing and the tone of his essays became more and more focused in the area of social criticism. This approach toward the world in Merton's work seemed to blossom and flourish in the 1960s, for this was a time of great intellectual and social ferment in the United States. The Catholic Church under the leadership of Pope John XXIII demonstrated a new openness toward the world and the spirit of reform was in the air. With the increasing involvement of the United States in the war in Vietnam and Indochina, the peace movement began to grow and large demonstrations took place in American cities. The civil rights movement too, was well underway, and it was obvious that there would be significant changes in race relations. Then too, a movement among youth spread throughout the nation and the "hippies" became a force to be reckoned with. Although the hippies were often associated with the use of drugs and the practice of free love, there was also an obvious searching for spiritual values and for new forms of the communal life. As all of these various movements were unfolding in the United States, Merton was quietly meditating in his hermitage and taking it all in. He read widely, corresponded with men and women throughout the world, and had a steady stream of visitors—mostly intellectuals and cultural leaders—coming to his hermitage for advice and counsel.

All of these various strands came together in a retreat held at the Abbey of Gethsemani from November 18-20, 1964. The retreat was organized by Merton around the theme "Spiritual Roots of Protest."[27] It was perhaps Merton's intention to bring together a number of leaders of what was then known as "the new left." The group was very much like the signers of the Korean Declaration of Independence—they were an extremely varied group in terms of temperament, ecclesiastical background, and political affiliation, but they were all concerned with the issues of war and peace and social justice. Included were such leaders in the peace movement as A.J. Muste of the Presbyterian-Reformed tradition, Mennonite John H. Yoder, and the Catholic brothers Daniel and Philip Berrigan. In his brief planning notes for the retreat, Merton wrote that "We are hoping to reflect together during these days on our common grounds for *religious dissent and commitment* in the face of the injustice and disorder of a world in which total war seems at time inevitable, in which few seek any but violent solutions to economic and social problems more critical and more vast than man has ever known before."[28] Merton went on to point out that the purpose of the retreat was to seek out and deepen the spiritual roots that inform peaceful protest and that these roots are "in the 'ground' of all being, in God, through His word."[29]

Moving on to the question of protest, Merton pointed out that one had to identify who or what one was protesting against, be certain for what one was protesting, and by what right one was protesting. Also considered was the how and why of protest. Involved here was the negative (protesting against...), the positive (protesting for...), and the issue of legality. Once these three issues were covered, Merton then moved on to methodology—which methods were appropriate and why. Other issues covered in the retreat included the nature of technological society, mass communications and the free flow of information, and the role of the interior spiritual life in protest. This latter point was especially important for Merton and he raised a question concerning "The meaning of *metanoia*, total personal renewal, as a prerequisite for valid nonvioient action?"[30]

The actual contents of this retreat have never been made public, in part perhaps, because of legal actions taken by the United States government against a number of the participants. It is significant that in the months following this retreat a number of the participants were arrested for nonviolent acts of protest at various government military draft boards. These included Daniel Berrigan and Philip Berrigan of the "Baltimore Four" and the "Catonsville Nine" and Robert Cunnane and James Forest of the "Milwaukee Fourteen."[31]   In each of these instances of protest, the protesters entered draft boards and scattered files and poured their own blood supplanted by animal blood to increase volume on the files. They then calmly waited for the police to arrive and arrest them. Another participant in the retreat, Thomas Cornell, publicly burned his draft card as a protest against the Vietnam War, after which he too, remained at the scene and awaited his arrest. The trials of these protesters received considerable media attention and generated controversy in the churches. Merton himself wrote on occasion that he was disturbed by "the almost total lack of protest on the part of religious people and clergy, in the face of enormous social evils" and that religious people and clergy are "no longer capable of *seeing and evaluating* certain evils as they truly are, as crimes against God and as betrayals of the Christian ethic of love."[32]

It will perhaps never be known just how much influence the November 1964 retreat had on the peace movement, but it was undoubtedly considerable and it gave Merton an opportunity to actually have a say in the formation of public policy, albeit a kind of alternative public policy of protest. It also gave Merton the occasion to stress that effective political protest must have deep spiritual roots, and where Merton thought that those roots were absent or had been betrayed, he was known to take swift and decisive action. On November 9, 1965 when a young member of the Catholic Worker movement immolated himself on the steps of the United Nations in protest of the Vietnam War, Merton was shocked and two days later requested that his name be removed as a sponsor of the Catholic Peace Fellowship.[33]   On another occasion Merton referred to an outspoken Catholic woman supporter of nuclear weapons and war as a "devout she-wolf." Merton continued to oppose racism, nuclear weapons, and the Vietnam war while at the same time waging a struggle for peace, and did so until his untimely death in Bangkok.

The Gift of Writing

Although both Han Yong-Un and Thomas Merton were religious figures and indeed, ordained monks, they were known to the public primarily through their literary efforts. It was through their books, essays, poetry, and editorial work that Han and Merton got their ideas across, for both were gifted writers and a steady literary output issued forth from their pens. Both men had amazing powers of concentration and they were able to accomplish a great deal of writing under less than ideal conditions. Han was an organizer and thus a busy man, yet he found time to write. Merton had almost every hour of the day planned out with monastic activities, yet he too found time to write. Han struggled against the Japanese censors who were always looking over his shoulder. Merton was threatened by the censors of the Cistercian Order who were concerned lest he stray too far from the traditional ideals of the monastic life. Both men were aided by sympathetic friends and colleagues in the literary world although neither was ever a member of the literary establishment. Both men also wrote under different names. Han Yong-Un was known by his pen name of Manhae meaning "Ten Thousand Seas." To his readers Merton was known by his given name of Thomas Merton, but within the monastery he went by his religious name, Fr. Louis.

Han's most common form of literary expression was the essay, and he wrote hundreds of essays on the topics of religious reform and political independence. The following sample of essay titles gives one an idea of the wide range of Han's interests: "Theism in Korean Buddhism," "Joan of Arc and Women's Hair Style" (on allowing women to wear short hair), "Korea Youth and Self-Mastery," "Free Yourself from Your Own Fetters," "A Letter on Korean Independence," "The Awakening of Women," "A History of Life after Death," "Chinese Buddhism Today," "Buddhism in Thailand," "Zen Buddhism and Life," "The Religious Movement in New Russia," "The State of Self-Detachment," "Zen Buddhism Beyond Zen," "The Anti-Religious Ideology of Communism," and "Patience." In addition Han wrote newspaper editorials on such topics as "The Resolution of Farmers under Tenancy Contracts" and other social concerns. He undertook translations such as "The History of Three Kingdoms" and "Prenatal Educa-tion." Most of Han's essays were published in vernacular news-papers and in smaller specialized magazines and journals of reli-gious and cultural interest. Some were written for intellectuals and religious specialists and others were written for the general public, but all were written from the heart tempered by a keen and critical mind.

Although not his best work, Han also wrote several novels and novellas which were serialized in the newspapers. These in-cluded *Death* which was not published until after his death. Those that were published (although not always completed) included *Black Wind, Remorse, The Iron Lady,* and *Misery.* Critics have given Han's fiction mixed reviews with the overwhelming majority agreeing that "Han the novelist does not rank high in modern Korean literature."[34] Perhaps one of the reasons for this is that Han was intentionally trying to reach a popular audience with his ideas and he believed that the serialized novel was the best way to do this. Because of this Han used his novels as vehicles for his ideas with the result that literary style was often sacrificed.

Han is best known as a poet and it is here that he has made his literary reputation, a reputation that is largely built upon on small book of only eighty-eight poems. The title is variously translated as *The Silence of My Beloved* or *Love's Silence.*[35] On the face of it, this is a book of love poems which it almost certainly is, as Han is reputed to have had a relationship with a women at the time the poems were written. However, it is much more than this for "Han's poetry operates on several levels at once.... They do indeed cut across many levels: literal, allegorical, symbolical, and mystical; they can be read as lyrical, patriotic, and religious poems...."[36] It is common in Korean poetry to use "the beloved" as a symbol for that which one longs for, be it the nation, political independence, a reformed Buddhism, or whatever. This is certainly the case with *Love's Silence* for there are numerous symbolic references through-out the poems and these become clear when the entire context of Han's life and work is taken into account.

Han was also a writer of nonfiction and compiled *A Dictionary of Korean Buddhism* and collected research for a history of Bud-dhism during the Koryo period and a history of Tongdo Temple; however, neither of these two works was ever completed.

In addition to his own writing, Han was the editor of several progressive journals of literary and social criticism and religious reform. One of these—*The Spirit*—was discontinued after only three issues, but this was a magazine founded and edited entirely by Han. Later Han was asked to take over the editorship of another magazine called *Buddhism* which ceased publication due to financial problems. Several years later he was again asked to revive *Buddhism* and once again he became the editor, a position which he held until his second period of imprisonment.

Han found it virtually impossible not to put his thoughts down in writing. Indeed, several of his most successful series of lectures were based upon ideas that were first expressed in some of his essays. Although he spent long periods in meditation at mountain hermitages and equally long periods of organizing political movements, Han always seemed to be able to find the time to write, and it is because of this that we know so much about him today.

Thomas Merton was also a compulsive writer who did much of his work early in the day between the 2:30 morning services and 7:00 breakfast. He wrote so much that it was said that "Merton literally meditated on paper." Like Han, Merton was primarily an essayist and the vast majority of his books were in fact collections of essays that had been published earlier in an odd assortment of journals and magazines both religious and secular.[37]   Most of these books were compiled by Merton himself although since his death others are now editing similar collections of his work. The subject matter of Merton's essays was also quite broad and ranged from purely religious and spiritual topics to matters of social, political, and cultural concern. He wrote extensively on literary topics and carried on a lively correspondence with such well-known writers as Boris Pasternak and Czeslaw Milosz. Although a monk, Merton also tried his hand in founding and editing an experimental journal called *Monks Pond* which ceased publication after only four issues.

One of the possible reasons that Merton wrote essays was to get around monastic censors who were acting under ecclesiastical custom to stop him from publishing on issues such as war and peace. Some essays appeared in obscure avant-garde journals which may have escaped the eyes of the censors, and still others were circulated privately and published without Merton's expressed knowledge (though almost certainly with his tacit approval). Once these essays appeared in print they eventually found their way into a collection that was published in book form.

Among the hundreds of Merton's essays the following selected titles show the wide range of his concerns: "Christian Ethics and Nuclear War," "Gandhi and the One-Eyed Giant," "Ishi: A Meditation," "Letters to a White Liberal," "Monk in the Diaspora," "Nhat Hanh is My Brother," "Poetry and Contemplation: A Reappraisal," "Religion and the Bomb," "Significance of the Bhagavad Gita," and "Vietnam: An Overwhelming Atrocity" as well as his talk "Marxism and Monastic Perspectives." One can see how he juxtaposed contemplation and action so that the two were always related. These two concerns were always expressed in Merton's work as an essayist.

Merton did, of course, write books but only one, the autobiographical *Seven Storey Mountain*, ever had immense commercial success. Some, like *New Seeds of Contemplation*, have been reprinted many times. A number of the others were written at the direction of his monastic superiors and he considered them to be vastly inferior to his later works. Merton was also a novelist but only one of his novels has ever been published, *My Argument with the Gestapo: A Macaronic Journal* and it was published posthumously. [38] Several other novels exist only in manuscript form including *The Labyrinth*, *The Man in the Sycamore Tree*, and *The Straits of Dover*. It is doubtful that these will ever be published as they were written when Merton still a student and his writing skills were unpolished.

Merton wrote several volumes of poetry which have firmly fixed his position in American letters as a minor poet. Three of his poems have become quite well-known both because of their subject matter and because of the depth of feeling that is evoked. The first, "For My Brother Missing in Action" was written shortly after Merton had been informed that his brother's air force plane was down in the English Channel. The second, "Elegy for the Monastery Barn" was written following a fire which destroyed one of the barns on the monastery farm. The third, "Chant to be Used in Processions around a Site with Furnaces" is a meditation on the death camps of the Holocaust with special reference to those who designed and built the crematoria. Merton also experimented with free verse and two of his books, *Cables to the Ace: or Familiar Liturgies of Misunderstanding* and *The Geography of Lograire*, continue to puzzle readers with multiple levels of meaning.[39]

Merton wrote at least fifty books during his lifetime and there have perhaps been as many collections of his writings edited by others to appear since his death. He wrote hundreds of essays, thousands of letters, thousands of pages of notebooks, and left behind a number of unpublished manuscripts. The Merton literary corpus is so great that a special committee—the Merton Legacy Trust—has been set up to oversee the publication of it all. Merton's former monastic secretary, Brother Patrick Hart, has made a lifetime vocation of editing and publishing Merton's work, and in a recent article has pointed out that there is still much, much more remaining to be published.[40]

What is most remarkable about the literary Merton is that he was, at the same time, a contemplative monk who made the life of prayer his primary vocation. Through the gift of writing he has shared that vocation with others, both in the past and, most significantly, in the present.

The Search for Love

Han Yong-Un and Thomas Merton shared yet another common life experience—the search for love. Both were involved in early loves that proved less than successful, and both met women in later life who satisfied their search for love and inspired them to write some of their best poetry. Yet in both cases, these women have remained anonymous and the affairs did not come to fruition in marriage.

Han was married in his teens to a young girl from a village about one-hundred kilometers from his home town. It was an arranged marriage, and from all indications the two were not at all compatible. Shortly after the marriage Han was forced into exile in the mountains due to his involvement in the Tonghak rebellion. Then he went to Paektam Temple and from there on his ill-fated journey to Vladivostok. Upon his return he went not to his home, but back to the mountains of Kangwon Province. When he finally did return home for a few months his wife gave birth to a son whom he named Po-Guk meaning "Defend the Country." After about a year he left home again to return to Paektam Temple and from then on there is no further mention of his wife and son. According to one scholar, Han remained cold toward both his first wife and his son throughout the remainder of his life.[41] Indeed, Han never returned to his hometown again, and when in later life his son sought him out, he showed him little emotion. It is obvious that the marriage was a mistake and that Han had a son simply to fulfill his filial duty to his parents by providing them with a descendant.

It was not until middle age that Han really fell in love for the first time in his life. Little is known about who this woman was except that reference is made to "the author's alleged intimacy with a certain Buddhist lady at the time."[42] At the time Han was at Paektam Temple living as a monk. Since Buddhist monks were expected to be celibate and remain unmarried, the relationship with this woman was technically forbidden. It was clear that if Han were to continue in his monastic vocation this love affair would have to end, but it did give rise to inspire Han to write his literary masterpiece, *Love's Silence*. Certainly the critics are correct to see in this work many levels of interpretation, but one cannot ignore the depth of emotion found in this collection of poems. In "Seeing Her Off" he wrote:

> She goes against her wishes
> and against mine,
> Her red lips, her white teeth and delicate eyebrows
> enchant me, but more charming
> is her cloud-like raven hair, her willow-slender waist
> and her jade-smooth ankles.
>
> She goes farther off till almost out of view.
> The farther away, the closer the heart;
> the closer the heart, the farther away she goes.
> I thought it her handkerchief waving in the distance
> but it was a cloud sailing, and smaller than a seagull.[43]

Although the relationship came to an end, it cut Han to the very heart and out of his pain he was inspired to literary greatness.

Later at age fifty-four Han married for a second time and this marriage produced a daughter whom he named Yongsuk. The family lived in Seoul in Ox-searching Hall and the marriage was a success. Han's search for love was fulfilled during the last eleven years of his life and he found the stability of a home which had been denied him in earlier years.

Thomas Merton's first experience of love was an absolute disaster. It happened while he was an undergraduate at Cambridge University. He became involved with an unmarried women, she became pregnant, and had a baby. He was then presented with paternity issues which he escaped by leaving Cambridge and the

United Kingdom for refuge in the United States. His legal guardian in London handled the legal affairs and worked out a settlement with the woman. In his will Merton stipulated that a portion of his assets be left to his guardian "to be paid by him to the person mentioned to him in my letters."[44] That person was, of course, the mother of his child. When Merton became a monk the unofficial story that was circulated by Ed Rice was that the young woman and her child were killed by a German bomb during the war; however, there is no evidence that would support such a story. Today nothing is known concerning the woman and the child and Merton made no mention of her. Once he entered the monastery and took his final vows all possibility of feminine love passed from his mind.

In 1966 at the age of fifty-one, Merton had serious back surgery at a hospital in Louisville, and several days following the surgery a young student nurse came to care for him. At first Merton resented her presence, then came to look forward to her coming, and finally fell in love with her. The feelings of love were mutual, and thus began an affair that continued over a period of a number of months.[45] Since Merton was a cloistered monk it was an affair that was carried on mainly through clandestine phone calls made at night when the other monks were asleep and letters smuggled in and out of the monastery by sympathetic friends. Perhaps friends arranged for Merton and the nurse (whom Merton identified only as M in his journals) to meet at a secluded pond deep in the woods on monastery property. In one journal entry Merton wrote, "Now I see more and more that there is only one realistic answer: Love. I have got to dare to love, and to bear the anxiety of self-questioning that love arouses in me, until 'perfect love casts out fear'."[46] It was, of course, an affair that eventually had to end, but through it Merton learned for the first time in his life what it meant to love and to be loved. His love for M also enabled him to overcome his fear of the erotic, a fear that had been with him since his youthful indiscretions at Cambridge many years earlier.[47] Throughout it all Merton was inspired to write some of his best poetry in a book entitled *Eighteen Poems* which he wrote for M but which was not published until seventeen years following his death. When it was obvious that their love would not come to full fruition he wrote:

If only you and I
Were possible.[48]

He too suffered the frustration of unfulfilled love and the wrench-ing pain of parting, but in the process he was freed to pursue his vocation as a monk and as a hermit knowing that he had learned, at long last, how to love and to be loved.

Conclusion

Han Yong-Un and Thomas Merton—brothers in different guises—continue to inspire others. Their collected writings are read, stud-ied, and debated. Seminars are held in their honor. In August of 2000 a three-day Manhae Festival was held at Paektam Temple drawing scholars and admirers from around the world. In July of 1996 an interfaith dialogue of Buddhist and Christian monastics met at the Abbey of Gethsemani to continue the work which Merton had started.[49]   Both men have made an indelible impact upon their respective religious traditions and societies through their desire for religious reform, their struggle for political free-dom, and their gift of writing. And, through their search for love, they have shown that they are normal human beings with both strengths and weaknesses.

But both men were also visionaries, who, while remaining loyal to their respective religious traditions and national identities, were able to take the cosmic viewpoint. When asked whether a Bud-dha born into modern Korea might not be a staunch nationalist, Han replied: "Buddha transcended not just life and death but also the living and the inert, time and space. His ideal being to revolu-tionize the entire cosmos, he wouldn't busy himself just with Ko-rea."[50]   Merton wrote words that were strikingly similar when he pointed out that "the saint does not represent himself, or his time, or his nation: he is a sign of God for his own generation and for all generations to come."[51]   Truly Han Yong-Un and Thomas Merton were brothers in different guises.

Notes

1. There are only brief biographical sketches of Han Yong-Un avail-able in English. Those currently in print include a "Chronology of the Life and Work of Han Yong-Un" in Yong-Un Han, *Love's Silence and Other Poems*, trans. Jaihiun Kim & Ronald B. Hatch (Vancouver, BC: Ronsdale

Press, 1999), pp. 13-18 and Beongcheon Yu, *Han Yong-Un and Yi Kwang-Su: Two Pioneers of Modern Korean Literature* (Detroit: Wayne State University Press, 1992), pp. 37-53. The definitive studies are Im Chung-Bin, *Han Yong-Un Iltaegi [The Life of Han Yong-Un]* (Seoul: Chongumsa, 1974) and Paek Chol et al., eds., *Han Yong-Un Chonjip [The Complete Works of Han Yong-Un]* (Seoul: Singu Munhwasa, 1973).

2. Yom Mu-woong, "The Life and Thought of Han Yong-woon" in International Culture Foundation, eds., *Buddhist Culture in Korea [Korean Culture Series 3]* (Seoul: Si-sa-yong-o-sa Publishers, 1982), p. 99. According to Yom many of the details of Han's early life are unclear and scholars are divided on which version of events is most accurate. For example, the chronologies of Yom and Jaihiun Kim and Ronald B. Hatch are somewhat different concerning Han's involvement in the Tonghak rebellion and the dates of such events as the trip to Vladivostok.

3. The definitive biography of Merton is Michael Mott, *The Seven Mountains of Thomas Merton* (Boston: Houghton Mifflin, 1984). A more popular biography is Monica Furlong, *Merton: A Biography* (London: Collins, 1980). A biography which sets Merton's life against the sociopolitical events of the time is William H. Shannon, *Silent Lamp: The Thomas Merton Story* (New York: Crossroad, 1992).

4. For an extensive discussion of Han's views on religious faith and socio-political action see Kim Yong-Bock, "Messianic Buddhism and Christianity in Korea" in *Perspectives on Christianity in Korea and Japan: The Gospel and Culture in East Asia*, eds. Mark R. Mullins & Richard Fox Young (Lewiston, NY: Edwin Mellen Press, 1995), pp. 81-94.

5. Cited in Yu, *Han Yong-Un and Yi Kwang-Su: Two Pioneers of Modern Korean Literature*, p. 41.

6 Han Yong-Un, "On Revitalizing Korean Buddhism" in *Sourcebook of Korean Civilization, Vol. II: From the Seventeenth Century to the Modern Period*, ed. Peter H. Lee et al. (New York: Columbia University Press, 1996), p. 497.

7. "On Revitalizing Korean Buddhism," pp. 499-500.

8. Yom Mu-Woong, "The Life and Thought of Han Yong-Woon" in *Buddhist Culture in Korea*, p. 103.

9. "The Life and Thought of Han Yong-Woon," p. 103.

10. See Kim Yong-Bock, "Messianic Buddhism and Christianity in Korea" in *Perspectives on Christianity in Korea and Japan*, p. 87.

11. Jaihiun Kim & Ronald B. Hatch, "Chronology of the Life and Work of Yong-Un Han" in *Love's Silence and Other Poems*, p. 14.

12. Thomas Merton, *Conjectures of a Guilty Bystander* (Garden City, NY: Doubleday, 1966), pp. 140-141.

13. See for example, the following works by Merton on war and peace: *Breakthrough to Peace* (New York: New Directions, 1962); *Seeds of Destruction* (New York: Farrar, Straus & Giroux, 1964); *Faith and Violence: Christian Teaching and Christian Practice* (Notre Dame, IN: University of Notre Dame Press, 1968); *Gandhi on Non-Violence: Selected Texts from Mohandas K. Gandhi's 'Non-Violence in Peace and War'* (New York: New Directions, 1965); and *Original Child Bomb: Points for Meditation to be Scratched on the Walls of a Cave* (New York: New Directions, 1962).

14. See Thomas Merton, *Contemplation in a World of Action* (Garden City, NY: Doubleday, 1971). See also Daniel J. Adams, *Thomas Merton's Shared Contemplation: A Protestant Perspective* [Cistercian Studies Series: No. 62] (Kalamazoo, MI: Cistercian Publications, 1979) for an in-depth study of Merton's views on contemplation and action.

15. James F. Andrews, "Was Merton a Critic of Renewal?" *National Catholic Reporter*, 6 (February 11, 1970), Lenten Supplement, 14.

16. Thomas Merton, *Disputed Questions* (New York: Mentor Omega Books, 1965), p. 104.

17. Thomas Merton, *Life and Holiness* (New York: Herder and Herder, 1963), p. x.

18. See the following books on interfaith relations by Merton: *The Asian Journal of Thomas Merton*, eds. Naomi Burton Stone, Br. Patrick Hart & James Laughlin (New York: New Directions, 1973); *Mystics and Zen Masters* (New York: Dell Books, 1969); *The Way of Chuang Tzu* (New York: New Directions, 1965); and *Zen and the Birds of Appetite* (New York: New Directions, 1968).

19. These exchanges are recorded in *Zen and the Birds of Appetite*.

20. Thomas Merton, *The Asian Journal of Thomas Merton*, pp. 233, 235-236. For a study of Merton's spiritual quest in relation to Asia see Alexander Lipski, *Thomas Merton and Asia: His Quest for Utopia* [Cistercian Studies Series: No. 74] (Kalamazoo, MI: Cistercian Publications, 1983).

21. Yu, *Han Yong-Un and Yi Kwang-Su: Two Pioneers of Modern Korean Literature*, p. 44.

22. Wanne J. Joe, *A Cultural History of Modern Korea*, ed. Hongkyu A. Choe (Elizabeth, NJ and Seoul: Hollym International, 2000), p. 808.

23. See *A Cultural History of Modern Korea*, pp. 808-812 for an extensive discussion of how the Declaration of Independence was written, signed, and presented to the public. The text of the document is included here as well.

24. *A Cultural History of Modern Korea*, p. 811.

25. Yu, *Han Yong-Un and Yi Kwang-Su: Two Pioneers of Modern Korean Literature*, p. 44. The reference to private meals refers to their imprisonment; they resolved to eat the food of the common prisoners.

26. These figures are given in Shin Yong-Ha, "Re-evaluation of the Samil Independence Movement" in *Main Currents of Korean Thought*, ed. Korean National Commission for UNESCO (Seoul: Si-sa-yong-o-sa Publishers, 1983), pp. 280, 285.

27. Thomas Merton, "Retreat, November, 1964: Spiritual Roots of Protest" in *Thomas Merton on Peace*, ed. Gordon C. Zahn (New York: McCall Publishing Co., 1971), pp. 259-260.

28. *Thomas Merton on Peace*, p. 259.

29. *Thomas Merton on Peace*, p. 259.

30. *Thomas Merton on Peace*, p. 260.

31. Gordon C. Zahn, "Original Child Monk: An Appreciation" in *Thomas Merton on Peace*, p. xiv. References here are to the cities in which the acts of protest took place.

32. Cited by Zahn in *Thomas Merton on Peace*, p. xiv.

33. When it became obvious that the Catholic Peace Fellowship did not approve of this kind of self-immolation, Merton rescinded his action.

34. In Kwon-Hwan cited in Yu, *Han Yong-Un and Yi Kwang-Su: Two Pioneers of Modern Korean Literature*, p. 72.

35. See Yu in *Han Yong-Un and Yi Kwang-Su* for an extensive discussion of Han's poetry on pp. 55-72.

36. *Han Yong-Un and Yi Kwang-Su*, p. 61.

37. See, for example, the following two books by Thomas Merton, *The Literary Essays of Thomas Merton*, ed. Brother Patrick Hart (New York: New Directions, 1981) consisting of essays published in literary journals, magazines, and newapapers and *Honorable Reader: Reflections on My Work*, ed. Robert E, Daggy (New York: Crossroad, 1989) made up of prefaces and introductions which Merton wrote for foreign translations of his works. *Monks Pond* (1968) has been published in a facsimile edition; see Robert E. Daggy, ed., *Monks Pond: Thomas Merton's Little Magazine* (Lexington, KY: University Press of Kentucky, 1989).

38. Thomas Merton, *My Argument with the Gestapo: A Macaronic Journal* (Garden City, NY: Doubleday, 1969).

39. Both books were published in New York by New Directions, *Cables to the Ace* in 1968 and *The Geography of Lograire* in 1969.

40. Patrick Hart, OCSO, "Thomas Merton's Literary Estate: What Is Left to Be Published?" *The Merton Seasonal: A Quarterly Review*, Vol. 25, No. 3 (Fall 2000), 18-19.

41. Yom, "The Life and Thought of Han Yong-Woon" in *Buddhist Culture in Korea*, p. 100.

42. Yu, *Han Yong-Un and Yi Kwang-Su: Two Pioneers of Modern Korean Literature*, p. 56.

43. Han Yong-Un, *Love's Silence and Other Poems*, p. 66.

44. Cited in Shannon, *Silent Lamp: The Thomas Merton Story*, p. 74; see also p. 73.

45. See *Silent Lamp*, pp. 200-201 for a brief description of this affair. Merton's own account is found in his journal *Learning to Love: Exploring Solitude and Freedom [The Journals of Thomas Merton: Volume Six, 1966-1967]*, ed. Christine M. Bochen (San Francisco: Harper San Francisco, 1997), especially pp. 35-176.

46. Merton, *Learning to Love*, p. 44.

47. See Anthony T. Padovano, "The Eight Conversions of Thomas Merton," *The Merton Seasonal: A Quarterly Review*, Vol. 25, No. 2 (Summer 2000), 13-14 where he suggests that Merton's love affair with M was in fact a conversion experience for him opening him up to the possibility of love and to an acceptance of the feminine in his life. See also Bonnie Bowman Thurston, " 'The Best Retreat I Ever Made': Merton and the Contemplative Prioresses," *The Thomas Merton Annual*, Vol. 14 (2001), 81-95.

48. Cited in Shannon, *Silent Lamp: The Thomas Merton Story*, p. 201. See also Thomas Merton, *Eighteen Poems* (New York: New Directions, 1985).

49. See Donald W. Mitchell & James Wiseman, OSB, eds., *The Gethsemani Encounter: A Dialogue on the Spirit Life by Buddhist and Christian Monastics* (New York: Continuum, 1998) for a complete account of this seminar.

50. Quoted in Yu, *Han Yong-Un and Yi Kwang-Su: Two Pioneers of Modern Korean Literature*, p. 52.

51. Thomas Merton, *The Last of the Fathers: Saint Bernard of Clairvaux and the Encyclical Letter, Doctor Mellifluus* (New York: Harcourt, Brace, 1954), p. 27.

Thomas Merton, Henri Nouwen, and the Living Gospel

Robert Ellsberg

This lecture was the Annual Thomas Merton / Henri Nouwen Lecture delivered at Corpus Christi Church in New York on January 28, 2006,

I'd like to begin by quoting one of my favorite authors, Jean-Pierre de Caussade, an eighteenth-century Jesuit, who wrote *Abandonment to Divine Providence*. He wrote these words, which suggested the title for my talk today:

> The Holy Spirit writes no more Gospels except in our hearts. All we do from moment to moment is live this new gospel of the Holy Spirit. We, if we are holy, are the paper; our sufferings and our actions are the ink. The workings of the Holy Spirit are his pen, and with it he writes a living gospel.[1]

Thomas Merton and Henri Nouwen are two figures who exemplified this teaching. They were of course both prolific writers. It was said of each of them that they never had an unpublished thought. And curiously, the outpouring of their published thoughts has scarcely been affected by their physical demise.

Thousands, perhaps millions of readers have profited from their writings. But what I would like to suggest is that in both cases, with Merton and Nouwen, we remember them not only for their written books, but for the text they wrote with their lives.

Of course they were both highly personal writers who deliberately held up their life experience as the material for spiritual reflection. But apart from their autobiographical writings, it is the actual *story* of their lives that represents what Caussade called "a living gospel"—a text written, as it were, with their own sufferings, their actions, their desires, and struggles.

For many years—if not my entire life—I have been preoccupied with the lives of holy people. This has resulted, among other things, in several books of my own, beginning with *All Saints*, in which I included both Merton and Nouwen among my list of "saints, prophets, and witnesses for our time."[2]

340

Sometimes, the people in our own lives are the last we would consider as examples of holiness. We know them all too well. We are aware of their weaknesses and idiosyncrasies. Brother Patrick Hart, Merton's former secretary at the Abbey of Gethsemani, told me that they had recently spent a whole year reading aloud from *All Saints* in the refectory. I said, "Did the monks have any trouble with the people I included as saints?" He said, "Well, there were some eyebrows raised about Thomas Merton."

Certainly, if there is anything I have tried to show in my writings on saints it is that holiness is not the same as genius, moral perfection, or even mental health. It is a quality that is expressed in the process of a life, in a person's total response, over a lifetime, to the divine voice that calls a person ever deeper into the heart of his or her vocation.

To tell their story is more than simply recounting their accomplishments or a list of their publications. It means reading their story in the light of the gospel—endeavoring to discern how their story relates to the story that God tells us through Jesus.

The story of Jesus, it is worth remembering, is not just a list of his teachings or glorious mysteries—whether walking on water or raising Lazarus. It is also a story of brokenness, abandonment, and sorrow. And if we ask, in the case of Jesus, *where is God in this story?* the answer has to be that God is there in the whole story.

The same is true for the saints, whether canonized or not. The story of Merton or Nouwen or any of God's faithful servants is not just a chronicle of their activities and accomplishments. It is a story that takes account of their restless search, their stumbling, their moments of doubt, their quirks and personal qualities. And if we ask, "Where is God in their story?" the answer is that God is part of the whole story.

And whether we realize it or not, the same is true for ourselves.

A friend of mine has served as a Eucharistic minister, bringing communion to the sick. One time she asked a man in the hospital whether he would like to receive communion and he answered, sadly, "I've been pretty far from God." To which she replied: "But I'm sure he hasn't been far from you." The expression on his face showed the immediate impact of those simple words.

But they could be directed to any of us. As we reflect on the living gospel, written in the lives of holy people, we become more adept at reading the signs of grace written in our own story—the signs that reveal God's presence in our own lives, drawing us, prodding us, toward our true home, even in the times when the thought of God was far from us.

In that light that I would like to reflect a bit on the living gospels of Thomas Merton and Henri Nouwen.

***

Let me start with Thomas Merton, whom I never knew in life. He died in 1968 when I was twelve. I didn't discover him until the next year, when I was thirteen. That's when I first discovered his edition of writings by Mahatma Gandhi. I can trace almost everything in my life to that encounter, including my decision, when I was nineteen, to drop out of college and join *The Catholic Worker* here in New York, and my decision five years later to become a Catholic. Like countless other readers, I was swept away by *The Seven Storey Mountain*, and afterward Merton became a constant friend and point of reference in my subsequent journey.

The Seven Storey Mountain, the autobiography Merton wrote in his early years as a Trappist monk, told a story—by turns funny and sad—of his search for his true identity and home, beginning with his orphaned childhood and his education in France, England, and eventually around the corner here at Columbia University, where he perfected his pose of cool sophistication, smoking, drinking all night in jazz clubs, and writing novels in the style of James Joyce. He regarded himself as a true man of his age, free of any moral laws beyond his own making, ready to "ransack and rob the world of all its pleasures and satisfactions." But increasingly his life struck him more as a story of pride and selfishness that brought nothing but unhappiness to himself and others. "What a strange thing!" he wrote, "In filling myself, I had emptied myself. In grasping things, I had lost everything. In devouring pleasures and joys, I had found distress and anguish and fear."[3]

Out of this anguish and confusion, Merton found himself drawn by the sense that there must be a deeper end and purpose to existence. All around him the world was tumbling toward war, the ultimate achievement of "Contemporary Civilization." Meanwhile he was reading Blake, St. Augustine, and medieval philosophy and beginning to suspect that "the only way to live was in a world that was charged with the presence and reality of God."[4]

It was a short leap from this insight to his reception in the Catholic church—here in this very church of Corpus Christi—and ultimately to the Abbey of Gethsemani in Kentucky. The Trappists had captured his heart from the first time he read about them in *The Catholic Encyclopedia*. "What wonderful happiness there was, then, in the world! There were still men on this miserably noisy, cruel earth, who tasted the marvelous joy of silence and solitude, who dwelt in forgotten mountain cells, in secluded monasteries, where the news and desires and appetites and conflicts of the world no longer reached them." When he later made a retreat at Gethsemani and there for the first time viewed the silent monks, dressed in their white habits and kneeling in prayer in the chapel, he felt that he had found his true home at last. "This is the center of all the vitality that is in America," he exclaimed.[5]

With the publication of Merton's autobiography, he was suddenly the most famous monk in America. The irony was not lost on him. He had become a Trappist in part to escape the claims of ego, the anxious desire to "be somebody." And yet his superiors felt his writing had something to offer the world and they ordered him to keep at it. And so he did. Yet for all the books he would go on to produce, in the public mind he was eternally fixed at the point where his memoir ended—as a young monk with his cowl pulled over his head, happily convinced that in joining an austere monastic community he had fled the modern world, never to return. It was difficult for readers to appreciate that this picture represented only the beginning of Merton's journey as a monk.

How many readers remember that *The Seven Storey Mountain* ends with a Latin motto: *sit finis libri; non finis quaerendi*—"here the book ends, but not the search"? At least this turned out to be true. Over the next twenty years Merton continued to search and grow more deeply into his vocation and his relationship with Christ. Eventually he reached the point where he would write, with some exasperation, "*The Seven Story Mountain* is the work of a man I never even heard of."[6]

One aspect of the book that he particularly came to regret was the attitude of pious scorn directed at "the world" and its unfortunate citizens. He had seemed to regard the monastery as a secluded haven set apart from "the news and desires and appetites and conflicts" that bedeviled ordinary humanity. Only with time did he realize that "the monastery is not an 'escape' from the world. On the contrary, by being in the monastery I take my true part in all the struggles and sufferings of the world." With this realization his writing assumed an increasingly compassionate and ecumenical tone.

In one of his published journals he described a moment of mystical awareness that marked a critical turning point in his life as a monk. It occurred during an errand into nearby Louisville, "at the corner of Fourth and Walnut, in the center of the shopping district."

> I was suddenly overwhelmed with the realization that I loved all those people, that they were mine and I theirs, that we could not be alien to one another even though we were total strangers. It was like waking from a dream of separateness, of spurious self-isolation in a special world, the world of renunciation and supposed holiness.[7]

Merton had discovered a sense of solidarity with the human race—not simply in shared sin, but also in grace. "There is no way of telling people that they are all walking around shining like the sun," he wrote. "There are no strangers! . . . [T]he gate of heaven is everywhere."[8]

No doubt many influences converged in this insight, enabling Merton to break through the limits of a certain narrow religious perspective. And yet it seems clear that this experience in Louisville was a crucial event, a moment in which everyday reality appeared "transfigured" in a way that permanently affected his vision.

For years Merton had devoted creative thought to the meaning of monastic and contemplative life. But from this point on he became increasingly concerned with making connections between the monastery and the wider world. Scorn and sarcasm gave way to compassion and friendship. This was reflected in his writing. Along with the more traditional spiritual books there appeared articles on war, racism, and other issues of the day. Long before such positions were commonplace in the church he was a prophetic voice for peace and nonviolence.

Ironically, this increasing engagement with the world and its problems was accompanied by an increasing attraction to an even more total life of contemplation. In 1965 he was given permission to move into a hermitage on the monastery grounds. There he continued to perfect the delicate balance between contemplative prayer and openness to the world that had become the distinctive feature of his spirituality.

Merton maintained a wide circle of friends. Many of them knew something of the tensions which at times characterized relations with his religious superiors. In the spirit of the 1960s some of them frankly questioned whether his vocation wasn't an anachronism and challenged him to "get with it." In fact, Merton's personal temptations were often in the direction of even greater solitude among the Carthusians or in some other remote setting. But in the end he always returned to the conviction that his best service to the world lay in faithfulness to his monastic vocation and that his spiritual home was at Gethsemani.

In his last year a more flexible abbot did permit Merton to venture forth. In 1968 he accepted an invitation to address an international conference of Christian monks in Bangkok. Merton was particularly excited about the prospect of exploring his deep interest in Eastern spirituality. In this respect, as his journals show, the trip marked a new breakthrough, another wider encounter with the 'gate of heaven' that is everywhere.

In Ceylon, in the presence of the enormous statues of the reclining Buddha at Polonnaruwa, he was "knocked over with a rush of relief and thankfulness at the *obvious* clarity of the figures..." He concluded:

I was suddenly, almost forcibly, jerked clean out of the habitual, half-tied vision of things, and an inner clearness, clarity, as if exploding from the rocks themselves, became evident and obvious...everything is emptiness and everything is compassion.[9]

On December 10 he delivered his talk in Bangkok and afterward retired to his room for a shower and nap. There he was later found dead, apparently electrocuted by the faulty wiring of a fan.

For all his restless searching, he had ended exactly as he had foreseen in the *The Seven Storey Mountain*. The book had concluded with a mysterious speech in the voice of God:

"I will give you what you desire. I will lead you into solitude. ... Everything that touches you shall burn you, and you will draw your hand away in pain, until you have withdrawn yourself from all things. Then you will be all alone.... That you may become the brother of God and learn to know the Christ of the burnt men."[10]

Thomas Merton will probably not be canonized, precisely because he lived out a model of holiness that isn't easily pigeonholed in a prefab Catholic mold. Just recently, the U.S. bishops decided not even to list Merton among a list of exemplary American Catholics to be included in a new catechism for young adults.

And yet I think he represented a type of holiness particularly suited and necessary to our times. Responding to God's call, he let go of his possessions, his ego, even a spurious kind of "supposed holiness"—until he came to rest in God's emptiness and compassion. It is a story of steadily "putting off the old person and putting on Christ"—the same process to which all of us are called— not for the sake of becoming a different person, but for the sake of becoming our true selves.

***

As I mentioned, I knew Merton only through his books. Henri Nouwen, on the other hand, is someone I knew very well over a period of twenty years, from my days at *The Catholic Worker* up to the time of his death.

By the time of his passing in 1996 Henri Nouwen had become one of the most popular and influential spiritual writers in the world. His popularity was only enhanced by his willingness to share his own struggles and brokenness. He did not present himself as a "spiritual master," but—like the title of one of his early books—as a "wounded healer." Those who knew him were aware of how deep his wounds ran. He was afflicted by an inordinate need for affection and affirmation; he was beset by anxieties about his identity and self-worth; there seemed to be a void within that could not be filled.

Nouwen had a great gift for friendship and wherever he went he sowed the seeds of community. But still something drove him from one place or project to another—from Holland to America, from Notre Dame to Yale, to a Trappist monastery, to the missions in Latin America, to the idea of serving as chaplain with a traveling circus troupe, to Harvard Divinity School. His lectures at Harvard attracted enormous crowds. But this only underlined his abiding sense of loneliness and isolation. Later he wrote with feeling about the temptations that Christ suffered in the desert: to be "relevant, powerful, and spectacular." Behind all this restlessness was an underlying effort to hear God's voice, to find his true home, and to know where he truly belonged.

At this point there came a great turning point in his life. Over the years Nouwen had visited a number of L'Arche communities in France and Canada. In these communities disabled people live together with able helpers. In 1986 he received a formal invitation from Daybreak, the L'Arche community in Toronto, to become their pastor. It was the first time in his life he had received such a formal call. With trepidation he accepted and Daybreak became his home for the last ten years of his life.

It was unlike anything he had ever known. Nouwen had written extensively about community, but he had never really known community life. A man of great intellectual gifts, he was physically clumsy and was challenged by such everyday tasks as parking a car or making a sandwich. On one of his first days in the house he appeared in the kitchen with a bag of laundry and said "What am I supposed to do with these?" You wash them, was the answer.

Like other members of L'Arche, Nouwen was assigned to care for one of the handicapped residents—in fact, one of the most severely handicapped adults in the community, a young man named Adam, who could not talk or move by himself. Nouwen spent hours each morning simply bathing, dressing, and feeding Adam. Some of his old admirers wondered whether Henri Nouwen was not wasting his talents in such menial duties. But to his surprise he found this an occasion for deep inner conversion. Adam was not impressed by Nouwen's books or his fame or his genius as a public speaker. But through this mute and helpless man, Nouwen began to know what it meant to be "beloved" of God.

This was not, however, the end of his struggles. After his first year at Daybreak Nouwen suffered a nervous breakdown—the culmination of long suppressed tensions. For months he could barely talk or leave his room. Now he was the helpless one, mutely crying out for some affirmation of his existence. As he later described it, "Everything came crashing down—my self-esteem, my energy to live and work, my sense of being loved, my hope for healing, my trust in God . . . everything."[11] It was an experience of total darkness, a "bottomless abyss." During these months of anguish, he often wondered if God was real or just a product of his imagination.

But later he wrote, "I now know that while I felt completely abandoned, God didn't leave me alone."[12] With the support of his friends and intensive counseling he was able to break through, and to emerge more whole, more at peace with himself. Above all he emerged with a deeper trust in what he called "the inner voice of love," a voice calling him "beyond the boundaries of my short life, to where Christ is all in all."[13]

In the summer of 1996 Nouwen was working hard, struggling to complete five books. To many friends he seemed happier and more relaxed than they had ever seen him—talking with great enthusiasm of his coming sixty-fifth birthday and plans for the future. Thus it came as a great shock when he suddenly died of a heart attack on September 21 while passing through Amsterdam on his way to work on a documentary in St. Petersburg.

There were numerous ironies at play in this death, the culmination of a "sabbatical" year from his work as chaplain to the L'Arche community. Among these was the fact that a man so much afflicted by a sense of homelessness throughout his life should die in his home town, surrounded in the end by his ninety-year-old father and his siblings. The subject of his planned documentary was his favorite painting: Rembrandt's "Return of the Prodigal Son."

But Nouwen's writings from the last years of his life make it clear how much he had contemplated and prepared for this particular homecoming. In one journal entry he wrote, "How much longer will I live? . . . Only one thing seems clear to me. Every day should be well lived. What a simple truth! Still, it is worth my attention. Did I offer peace today? Did I bring a smile to someone's face? Did I say words of healing? Did I let go of my anger and resentments? Did I forgive? Did I love? These are the real questions! I must trust that the little bit of love that I sow now will bear many fruits, here in this world and in the life to come."[14]

In the last months of his life, Nouwen was shaken by a particular death in the Daybreak community. It was Adam, the severely handicapped young man whom he had cared for during the first year after his arrival at Daybreak; Adam, who had helped him learn, so late in his own life, what it means to be "beloved of God." Finally, after a lifetime of illness and disability, Adam had succumbed to his ailments at the age of thirty-four. For the L'Arche community—which regards its handicapped members as its "core"—Adam's death was a devastating loss. Nouwen rushed back to Toronto from his sabbatical to share the grieving of Adam's family and friends.

Compared to, say, Henri Nouwen, Adam had accomplished nothing, not even the routine tasks that most people take for granted. He could not speak, or dress himself, or brush his own teeth. In the eyes of the world the question would not have been why such a man should die but why God had in the first place permitted him to live. And yet Nouwen saw in Adam's life and death a personal reenactment of the gospel story.

> Adam was—very simply, quietly, and unquietly—there! He was a person who, by his very life, announced the marvelous mystery of our God: I am precious, beloved, whole, and born of God. Adam bore silent witness to this mystery, which has nothing to do with whether or not he could speak, walk, or express himself . . . It has to do with his being. He was and is a beloved child of God. It is the same news that Jesus came to announce . . . Life is a gift. Each one of us is unique, known by name, and loved by the One who fashioned us.[15]

Jesus too had accomplished relatively little during his short public life. He too had died as a "failure" in the world's eyes. "Still," Nouwen wrote, "both Jesus and Adam are God's beloved sons—Jesus by nature, Adam by 'adoption'—and they lived their sonship among us as the only thing that they had to offer. That was their assigned mission. That is also my mission and yours. Believing it and living from it is true sanctity."[16]

Nouwen set out to write a book about Adam—it would be his last. And, as was the case with all of Nouwen's best writing, it was also about himself. He seemed to sense in the passing of this young man that he was being called to prepare for his own flight into the waiting arms of his Creator. It was as if, he wrote, Adam was saying, "Don't be afraid, Henri. Let my death help you to befriend yours. When you are no longer afraid of your own death, then you can live fully, freely, and joyfully."[17]

It was the voice he had heard before. "Many friends and family members have died during the past eight years and my own death is not so far away. But I have heard the inner voice of love, deeper and stronger than ever. I want to keep trusting in that voice, and be led by it beyond the boundaries of my short life, to where Christ is all in all."[18]

***

I first met Henri Nouwen in 1976 when I was managing editor of *The Catholic Worker* here in New York. At the age of twenty, I was not a terribly experienced editor—I was not an experienced anything, for that matter. I knew Henri was a writer of some repute, though I had never read any of his books. So I asked him if he would like to contribute something to the Worker newspaper and he graciously replied by sending me three essays on the subject of community. To be honest, I wasn't too impressed. They struck me as rather abstract. So I said, "Thanks, but do you have anything else?"

He was understandably miffed. "I've just given you three essays," he said. Realizing my gaffe, I hastened to tell him how pleased I would be to publish one of his fine essays, which I did. But he never offered us anything else, and honestly I didn't ask.

Many things happened over the following years, and our paths proceeded on strangely congruent tracks. Our relationship had its ups and downs.

But this early experience was still on his mind, ten years later, when I went to tell him that I had been offered the job as editor-in-chief of Orbis Books. "Well, if someone were to ask me if you would be a good person for this job, I would say, 'Intellectually, nobody better; a perfect fit.' . . . But I don't know whether you have the *human gifts* for that kind of work—being able to work with people, you know."

Our relationship was rather frayed at that point—a reflection in part of my resentment of his yawning neediness, and his frustration that I was not more available as a friend.

Nevertheless, I did become an editor, and Henri and I went on to work productively on several books. Undoubtedly, over time I had come to understand what Henri was talking about. Being an editor isn't just about knowing how to wield a red pencil. It is about relationships, and for Henri relationships were everything. As the years went on our mutual trust and affection grew and deepened.

Eventually he told me that during his sabbatical year he wanted to write a book about the Apostle's Creed. I responded eagerly, and went on to send him a pile of scholarly articles on the subject. He became discouraged. "Wow, this is a lot more complicated than I thought," he said. He wondered whether he could really pull it off. So it didn't come as a complete surprise when he called to say he wanted to change the focus of his book. I said, okay—what do you have in mind?

"Now hear me out," he said. "It will still be a book about the Creed, but I want to write the book as a biography of Adam."

Right, I said cautiously, using my best acquired human skills. I had heard him talk about Adam for years, and I had some idea of what his life and death must mean to Henri. But beyond that I didn't have the slightest idea what he was talking about.

A little time passed and Henri sent me his preliminary draft, and suddenly it became clear what he was doing. He intended to write Adam's story after the pattern of the gospels, beginning with his early years, or hidden life; his experience of the desert of institutional life; the public life and ministry that began when he arrived at L'Arche; his passion, death, and resurrection in the hearts of those who loved him.

At first it seemed peculiar to talk about the public mission of a mute and helpless man who could not perform the basic tasks of caring for himself. And yet Henri perceived that Adam, like Jesus, had a mission in his life. His mission was to bear witness to God's love and to make others aware—as he had for Henri himself— that we are all God's beloved. As was said of Jesus, "Everyone who touched him was healed." Similarly, "Each of us who touched Adam has been made whole somewhere."[19]

Over the next few months we worked closely on the book, exchanging drafts and comments. In August he delivered the final draft in person, coming to my home for dinner. It was the first time my wife had seen him in many years and afterward she remarked, as I had, that he seemed like a different person—as she put it, "so sane," though she might have used other words, like happy, whole, redeemed in some essential way.

I was terribly moved by the evening, and the next day I arranged to have a plaque made with the cover of his book *With Burning Hearts*. I sent it to him in Toronto along with a note, thanking him for his many years of friendship and all his many gifts.

A few weeks later came the news of his death. Everything was a blur. His family held a funeral Mass for him in Holland, and then, graciously, arranged for his body to be sent home for burial among his Daybreak community in Toronto. I flew up for the day and saw him there for the last time in his open casket—a plain pine box, decorated colorfully by the L'Arche residents.

I felt numb—unable to express any thoughts or feelings. But when I returned to work the next day there was a letter waiting for me in the morning mail, an envelope addressed in Henri's unmistakable hand. It was a letter he had written some weeks before: "Boy, oh, boy!" he said. "What a beautiful plaque! I don't know if I have any place worthy to hang it." He acknowledged his own gratefulness for our friendship and said how much he looked forward to all we would do together in the future.

It was the first sign that my relationship with Henri was not over. With the help of Sue Mosteller, Henri's literary executrix, we completed *Adam*. In a remarkable way, it was indeed an expression of Henri's "creed"—a culmination of all that he had learned in his years at L'Arche, and of the long journey that had ended there.

In concluding the book, Henri had written of Adam:

Is this when his resurrection began, in the midst of my grief? That is what happened to the mourning Mary of Magdala when she heard a familiar voice calling her by her name. That is what happened for the downcast disciples on the road to Emmaus when a stranger talked to them and their hearts burned within them. ... Mourning turns to dancing, grief turns to joy, despair turns to hope, and fear turns to love. Then hesitantly someone is saying, "He is risen, he is risen indeed."[20]

Over the years that I knew Henri, there were long stretches when I would have hesitated to include him in a calendar of saints. I had seen too much of the wounds—and not enough of the healer. But by the time he died it was easy for me to imagine him in that cloud of witnesses—not because he performed miracles or achieved some extra-human status, but because his life was so clearly a story marked by grace, conversion, and steady growth in the spiritual life. Through the broken pieces of his own complex humanity he managed to reveal an aspect of the divine image.

It is, once again, doubtful that he would be canonized. And yet he stands for me as a kind of paradigmatic saint—at least the type that interests me. He didn't entice me to want to be like him, but he made me more conscious of what it means to be God's beloved, and to see my own life in relation to the story of Jesus, another gospel in the making.

***

Looking back over my life it is possible to construe a narrative arc, in which Merton and Nouwen played central roles, leading from my early youth right up to the present moment. But at any particular moment it didn't necessarily seem that way. I did not realize when I first read Merton or met Dorothy Day or Henri Nouwen, "Ok, this is going to be the fundamental encounter of your life."

We go one step at a time, and occasionally those steps involve some dramatic gestures, such as when St. Francis kissed a leper. But as Dorothy Day said, "I have kissed a leper not once, but probably several times and I can't say I am any the better for it."[21]

One of my favorite religious films is, of all things, a Disney movie called "The Other Side of Heaven," about a young Mormon missionary in the South Pacific. After many trials and adventures he writes to his fiancée back home and sums up the lessons he has learned: "There is a thread that connects heaven and earth," he says. "If we find that thread everything is meaningful, even death. If we don't find it, nothing is meaningful, even life."

Sometimes I feel I have found that thread, only to lose it the very next moment in some fit of impatience or pique, whether at work or at home. It is a thread that runs through the lives of Thomas Merton and Henri Nouwen, as it does in each of our lives, whether we acknowledge that or not. It is a voice that calls us to be braver, more loving, more truthful, more holy. To the extent that we respond to that call, our lives become a parchment; our sufferings and our actions are the ink. The workings of the Holy Spirit are the pen, and with it God writes a living gospel.

Notes

1. Jean-Pierre de Causssade, *Abandonment to Divine Providence* (New York: Image, 1975), p. 45.

2. *All Saints: Daily Reflections on Saints, Prophets, and Witnesses for our Time* (New York: Crossroad, 1997).

3. Thomas Merton, *The Seven Storey Mountain* (Garden City: NY: Doubleday/Image, 1970), p. 203.

4. Merton, *Seven Storey Mountain,* p. 382.

5. Merton, *Seven Storey Mountain,* p. 393.

6. Thomas Merton, *The Sign of Jonas* (Garden City, NY: Doubleday/Image, 1956), p. 318.

7. Thomas Merton, *Conjectures of a Guilty Bystander* (Garden City, NY: Doubleday/Image, 1968), p. 156.

8. Merton, *Conjectures*, pp. 157-58.

9. Thomas Merton, *The Asian Journal* (New York: New Directions, 1973), p. 233, p. 235.

10. Merton, *Seven Storey Mountain*, pp. 510-12. Italics in original.

11. Henri Nouwen, *The Inner Voice of Love* (New York: Doubleday, 1996), p. xiii.

12. Nouwen, *The Inner Voice*, p. 118.

13. Nouwen, *The Inner Voice*, p. 118.

14. Henri Nouwen, *Sabbatical Journey* (New York: Crossroad, 1998), p. 61.

15. Henri Nouwen, *Adam: God's Beloved* (Maryknoll, NY: Orbis Books, 1997), pp. 36-37.

16. Nouwen, *Adam*, p. 37.

17. Nouwen, *Adam*, p. 102.

18. Henri Nouwen, *The Inner Voice of Love* (New York: Doubleday, 1996), p. 118.

19. Nouwen, *Adam*, p. 127.

20. Nouwen, *Adam*, p. 120.

21. Dorothy Day, *Selected Writings* (Maryknoll, NY: Orbis Books: 1992), p. 110.

Interview with James Finley:
Cultivating a Contemplative Lifestyle

Conducted and Transcribed by Glenn Crider

June 11, 2006

Crider: First, I would like to ask about your family background and how it influenced you as a child and teenager. Also, how influential was the Church for you while growing up?

Finley: I was born and grew up in Akron, Ohio. I was the oldest of six children. My father worked in rubber factories and then for the Post Office. The Church was very influential in my life. My father was a violent alcoholic. My mother was a devout Catholic. Through her I learned to find solace in faith, which became a primary influence in my life as a refuge from the abuse.

Crider: Was there a particular point when you first thought about a religious vocation?

Finley: In my ninth grade religion class, the instructor told us about Thomas Merton. I read Merton's *The Sign of Jonas*.[1] In fact, I read it over and over again, which led me to write the Vocation Director at Gethsemani. At fourteen, I became aware of an interior awareness or self-sense of God's oneness and then learned to rest in that. This then led to my entering the community a week after I graduated from high school in 1961.

Crider: Your experience at age fourteen was, I assume, unique considering your background. You mention the tangible experience of God. That is not acknowledged or even accepted in all Christian churches. On the other hand, I grew up in a Pentecostal church where direct experience of God was regularly sought after and celebrated.

Finley: Yes. Both the Pentecostal and the monastic traditions of the Christian faith emphasize the experience of God. But the emphasis is different. In the Pentecostal tradition the emphasis is on a felt sense of God's presence and the Holy Spirit being experienced in a flow of strong emotions. The monastic tradition also stresses the felt sense of God's presence. But the emphasis is more on contemplation as a silent, non-dual experience of God beyond both feelings and thoughts about God. There is a distinction between how the two traditions express that. But I do think they are traditions of this experience and the emphasis [is] on the actual experience.

Crider: You first heard of Merton while in the ninth grade. When did you hear about Gethsemani itself?

Finley: They were simultaneous because a religious instructor at the Catholic high school I was attending talked about Thomas Merton and *The Seven Storey Mountain*,[2] which was very popular at the time.

Crider: What year was that?

Finley: 1958. And I entered Gethsemani in 1961.

Crider: So you went there right after high school?

Finley: Yes. I went immediately. In fact, I think I went the day after graduation.

Crider: What were your first memories of Gethsemani?

Finley: I arrived in the afternoon on a Greyhound bus from New Haven. Then someone drove me out to the monastery. I then went up to the loft of the Church. This was when the visitors were in the loft in the back of the Church. The monks chanting vespers was the first experience that stands out to me. Although I had heard LP records of chants, I had never been in the presence of chanting like that. That was my first experience, and it was very moving. Along with that, during my initial stay there when I was being interviewed about being admitted to the community, it was the chanting combined with the silence that really affected me.

Crider: What was your religious name?

Finley: Br. Mary Finbar. St. Finbar was Bishop of County Cork in Ireland and also a hermit. I guess the idea was that your religious name was given in part due to your own cultural-ethnic background. Coming from an Irish background, I was given the name Br. Finbar.

Crider: How long did you live at Gethsemani?

Finley: I was there for five and a half years. When I went there to be interviewed and accepted, I went back home. Then I came back and entered formally in July (1961). So I was there from July 1961 to January 1967.

Crider: When did you first meet Merton?

Finley: I first met Merton as a novice under his direction. When I first entered, Gethsemani was divided up between the brothers and the choir. And each had their own novitiate. So the brothers lead lives of silence, prayer and manual labor. The choir monks lead lives of study, silence, prayer and manual labor. At the time in the tradition, the choir went on to ordination into the priesthood. When I entered, I entered in the brothers. Then after about a year, I changed over from the brothers to the choir. Since Thomas Merton was Novice Master of choir novices, I came under his direction. That is when I met him. Shortly after that, the two novitiates were merged anyway, and he became Novice Master of all the novices.

Crider: Do you remember the year?

Finley: That was 1962.

Crider: What kind of relationship did you have with Merton? What was it like?

Finley: Having come from all my childhood abuse, it was a kind of healing relationship. He was a safe "father-figure" for me. So I think that played a big part with my relationship with him. Secondly, I think he was a voice of common sense. He accepted me and gave me a lot of slack and kind of gave me permission to find my own way. He was honest with me, and that helped me be honest with myself. It was a lot of that kind of common-sense feel to it. Lastly, I really saw him as embodying the mystical monastic tradition itself. I really felt that I was in the presence of somebody from whom this tradition lived. So he embodied the reality of the tradition.

Crider: So you were comfortable with him.

Finley: I was. At first I was not because of my issues with authority figures. I was actually very nervous around him. But he helped me work that through. Once I worked through that, we could settle down and really start talking about prayer, meditation, silence and all of that. I felt very comfortable with him then.

Crider: I have spoken with a few others who knew Merton, and they all say he was very easy to talk to and to be with. Perhaps his common sense somehow allowed him to relate well with nearly all whom he came across. And he seemed to have a profound effect on those persons.

Finley: Yes. It was true for me. The thing about him is that he seemed so transparently present. He was authentically present. I think when we are in the presence of someone who is so present, we intuit that. It affects us.

Crider: At that time, he was very well known, even famous, yet he was able to connect to people in a real, authentic way.

Finley: Yes. He was at the peak of his powers then—the early 1960s. He was beginning to develop his own style with the Buddhist-Christian dialogue. B. Griffith and Thich Nhat Hanh had been to visit him. He was really at the height of his powers.

Crider: How often did you meet with him?

Finley: We were scheduled to meet him individually about twice a month. It was posted each day on a little board in the novitiate hallway. I think two a day would go in.

Crider: So he would meet with novices individually. How long were these meetings?

Finley: My impression was that it really varied. If you did not have much to say, the session ended quickly. But if you opened up and got into it, he would pursue that.

Crider: Are there other experiences with Merton that stand out for you?

Finley: Not really. I think that the deepest of all of it is that he encouraged me to be radically faithful to this inner path. He encouraged me not to compromise that.

Crider: Aside from Merton, what else do you remember about Gethsemani and how life there influenced you?

Finley: I saw it as everything about the life was designed to foster this awareness of God's presence. So the symbols of the life, the pace of the life, the reading—all of it was ordered toward that one end of following this contemplative path. That is how I saw it—as an atmospheric, all-enveloping path. The biggest of all for me was the silence. Having been so completely silent day-in and day-out had a profound effect.

Crider: Do you have any favorite memories about Gethsemani?

Finley: There were many pleasant memories that were simply part of the day-by-day patterns of just being there. For me, the most powerful memories were those of my own experiences, those moments where I truly felt a sense of oneness with God. But they came in the midst of the day-by-day ordinary rhythms of the life itself rather than something that happened externally.

Crider: The realization that routines inspire insight is, I think, key to developing a contemplative life.

If you could or would change anything about your years at Gethsemani, what would it be?

Finley: I think when I went in I was naïve. I kind of assumed that it was not possible to be hurt in the monastery in any way. I discovered though that monks are just people, and things happen in monasteries just like things happen throughout the rest of the world. So I wish, in hindsight, that I had had a more realistic sense of the humanness of monasteries. I will leave it at that.

Crider: Will you say a word about the significance or importance of monasticism?

Finley: I think monasticism bears witness to the human person's openness to transcendence. It is at the very heart of what it means to be human. That is the most important thing for me. Furthermore, monasticism makes it possible to pursue the realization of that openness. It is possible to devote your life to the path of awakening to that transcendence. It is open to all of us.

Crider: Do you distinguish monasticism as a better or more conducive route to transcendence?

Finley: Yes and no. I think at one level—at the psychological level—it is more conducive. It allows a quiet pacing of your schedule; living in silence, being surrounded by sacred symbols, and so on. All of these things are conducive to mindfulness and introspection and being vulnerable to God's presence. In that sense, monasticism is more conducive to opening one to transcendence because it is designed to do just that. That is the reason it exists. That is the genius of the life because everything about the life points in that direction.

I think at a deeper level, monasticism is not necessarily a better way to God. At a deeper level, we grow where we are planted.

Some people find that their present situations are most conducive.

Crider: Thinking about what draws one to monastic life, I wonder how that attraction develops.

Finley: I think there are many reasons—both healthy and un-
healthy—people are drawn to monastic life. Part of the admis-
sions screening process includes discernment and then considering the validity of what draws them. In a healthy way, it is important to recognize that the monastery is a place that fosters one's
desire to realize oneness with God. And they feel God personally
calling them to that. I also think that sometimes people have a
mystical experience or awakening, and they automatically assume
they should go to a monastery to foster that. If they go along and
sort it out, they discover they can be faithful to that [mystical ex-
perience] in other contexts.

Crider: You have mentioned psychology already. When did you
decide to study psychology?

Finley: When I left the monastery, I had not thought of studying
psychology. I got an undergraduate degree in English literature
and education as well as a master's degree in education. I taught
religion in the Catholic schools of the Cleveland diocese in Cleveland, Ohio. I co-authored a series of high school religion text books
with a colleague. It was also during that time that I then wrote
Merton's Palace of Nowhere.[3] That book came out in 1978. When it
came out, I began to receive invitations from around the country
to lead retreats on Thomas Merton and contemplative spirituality.
In 1979, about a year after the book came out, I was invited to
Seattle, Washington to give a retreat. The person leading the retreat, John Finch, a psychologist, asked me if I had ever considered integrating the work I was doing in spirituality with psychology. I said I had not thought of doing that. He said if I would
be willing to write a theoretical dissertation integrating contemplative spirituality with psychology, he would see to it that I had a
full scholarship for Ph.D. in psychology. So, to make a long story
short, I came back to my home in South Bend, Indiana and decided to do that. I left South Bend and came out to Pasadena,
California to the Graduate School of Psychology at Fuller Theological Seminary. I spent five years doing full time doctoral work
and then became a psychologist.

Crider: It sounds like your career in psychology snuck-up on you, or came unexpectedly.

Finley: It did. When I think about what was going on in my home when I was growing up—the violence and so on—it just amazes me that I ended up at Gethsemani. Likewise, after leaving, it amazed me that this guy comes and hands me this opportunity. So they both kind of snuck-up on me.

Crider: Given your experience in both monasticism and professional psychology, what can you say about the relationship between monastic writing and writings by those interested in spiritual direction and contemplation?

Finley: My basic understanding is that the writing of monastics tends to be writings in contemplative spiritual direction. It has this pragmatic quality of helping the person discern the path of self-transformation and spiritual awakening. So that is the quality to it. The writings of those interested in spiritual direction are in the same venue of helping people discern the path, but they tend not to be so specifically contemplative in nature. They are more broadly based on how to discern God's will in their present situation, or how to discern what is the most loving or Christ-like thing to do. But I think both monastic writings and more broadly based writings in spiritual direction are guidance on the spiritual path. But the writings of monastics, for understandable reasons, tend to be more specifically coming out of and focused toward those who have a more overtly contemplative emphasis in their journey.

Crider: When did you consider writing yourself?

Finley: I wrote at the monastery. I kept journals all the time. I never thought of being a writer, however. But writing was always a kind of meditative practice to try to put words to inner experiences.

Crider: Judging from the success and popularity of *Merton's Palace of Nowhere*, your writing appears to be quite a talent and gift.

Finley: Yes, I think it is a gift. Like any writer, I guess you keep working on it over time. But I really think the popularity of that book is due to a combination of factors. One, its popularity is due to a great extent that it was about Thomas Merton. He was especially popular then, which was not long after his death. So the book came out during a wave of growing interest in Merton. Secondly, I think the book put its finger on a very rich theme in Merton's writing: this whole question of the true self. For example, what is the self that transcends the ego? So it is the combination of Merton being an extremely popular religious figure and a theme in his writings. I tried to do that in a way that would be practical for people and, for example, help them gain insight into their own identity and so forth.

Crider: Do you continue to read Merton?

Finely: I do. I read him on and off, but in snippets. I will pull a book down and read a few paragraphs. I find that reading him instantaneously reinstates a sense of connection.

Crider: Regarding Cistercian monasteries, do you visit them often since you left?

Finley: I would like to more than I do. I was last at Gethsemani about ten years ago. I was supposed to give a retreat at Nazareth [...] last year but that did not work out. I just do not have much opportunity to visit those monasteries much. I give retreats around the country. But in terms of visiting a monastery for some time, I just do not have that opportunity often.

Crider: You have talked some about giving retreats, will you say more about what you do now?

Finley: I am a clinical psychologist in private practice in Santa Monica, California. My wife is also a therapist. We are in practice together. I work a lot with adult survivors of abuse and emotional deprivation from childhood. There are people who want their spirituality to be a resource in therapy. So I do that kind of in-depth therapy work three days a week—Mondays, Tuesdays and Wednesdays. Then Thursdays, Fridays and Saturdays, I write. And about one weekend a month, I give a retreat either locally or somewhere else in the United States or Canada.

Crider: Do you view your work as a ministry or related to a ministry?

Finley: I experience it as a ministry. In other words, what interests me about in-depth therapy is that it offers a safe place in which one can slow down and start to listen to oneself in the presence of another person who will not invade or abandon them. That process of slowing down and listening tends to evoke a more interior contemplative experience of their own presence. I think that process is in itself at the very heart of healing. Once a person discovers this experiential access to the mystery of their own presence, which is a very deep way of experiencing God's presence, then that gives them a base from which they can understand and look at whatever psychological issues they are struggling with. Low self-esteem, addiction, whatever it might be. I consider my work as therapist to be a ministry in that sense. I also see retreats as an opportunity for people to get together and experience kinship. There you have a collective desire to follow this interior path, to give talks on Merton or Meister Eckhart or John of the Cross or just the tradition. It is the same with writing too. I experience it all as a ministry.

Crider: Within therapy, do you find that a particular orientation serves you better than another?

Finley: I tend to work with people on a psychodynamic, existential, transpersonal continuum. What I mean by that is that my emphasis is on the existential. I try to help a person understand how they contribute to their own difficulties. As they start to understand that and how hard it is to stop doing that, in order to get to the root, they more or less have to go back to their childlike origins where those patterns formed as dysfunctional survival strategies. That is the psychodynamic part. Then I find that when two people sit like that, in that kind of vulnerable openness, they discover they are sitting on holy ground together. That is the transpersonal and contemplative part. That is how I express my theoretical orientation.

Crider: Psychodynamic therapy cuts to the root of behavior, in my opinion. It definitely helps a person better understand why he or she thinks and behaves in certain ways. It can be a truly transformative process.

To change the focus somewhat, a less talked about relationship is that between contemplation and marriage. It seems that most contemplative and spiritual writings focus on the individual. What do you think about the role of contemplation within a marriage?

Finley: First of all, for many reasons, people's experience of marriage does not tend to be conducive to contemplation. In other words, because of the day-by-day life and demands of marriage and children and so forth, a lot of people do not become aware of the potential of contemplation within marriage. But for those who

begin to become aware of this, they often see that there is something about marriage that is essentially contemplative. At the heart
of marriage is intimacy. At the heart of intimacy is two people
realizing that they are one. And they are one in some unexplain-
able way. They are one in a way that they cannot define or pin
down. That experience of oneness is itself a contemplative experience. This oneness has a certain boundless quality. Some couples
experience oneness with each other in the way they experience
God's oneness with them. Therefore, ideally speaking, marriage
is a path for contemplative awareness. For those who are aware
of this together, marriage can then be a contemplative way of life.
I am fortunate that way. This is my second marriage. My present
wife lived alone for many years kind of seeking this interior path
and so on. We are kind of hermits together. That is the basis of
our marriage.

Crider: Building on these comments, what do you think "ordinary" (non-monastic) people can do to cultivate a contemplative
lifestyle?

Finley: First, I think it is very hard to say this in the abstract. It is
easiest for me when I sit and talk with the person who is actually
asking me the questions. I usually start by asking them questions
about themselves so it becomes concrete in their own lives. It tends
to become more meaningful that way. But basically I would invite
people to slow down, to start becoming more aware of what is
already going on and to start to appreciate the depth of their day-
by-day life. It is a sheer miracle to be alive. It is a miracle that we
exist at all, that our hearts beat and that we breathe. This taps into
the sacredness of ordinary things. Becoming quietly reflective and
open allows one to grow in this awareness. Learning to do the
most loving thing in the moment is key. What can I do for myself
or this other person? How can I keep growing in this awareness
and presence of my life? That is the tone of what I tend to tell
people about the contemplative lifestyle.

Crider: So a first step is to become aware of what is already there,
of what is so easy to overlook?

Finley: That is right. Let us say you are asking me that question
now. You ask me and I then ask, "What prompts you to ask that
question?" You would answer. Then I would say, "Give me an
example." You would give an example, and within just a few min-

utes you are becoming more present to yourself. You are stopping to check in and to ask, "How am I going to answer that?" That very process of slowing down to check in with your self is already the beginning of a more interior, meditative awareness.

Crider: Why do you think a contemplative lifestyle is important for today's culture?

Finley: Without some sense of contemplation, I think we are lost. Thich Nhat Hanh says if we are not practicing mindfulness, our house is abandoned. Contemplation is the experiential access to the ground of our own being and its inherent holiness. When we are not grounded in some way in that, we are kind of spinning out. We are not rooted into what it means to be alive. That, I think, is its importance.

Crider: What about contemporary culture and how it may or may not make a contemplative lifestyle possible?

Finley: In a lot of obvious ways, there are many forces in contemporary society that make it challenging for anyone to be contemplative. Merton spoke a lot about that. Much of what he talked about is as true today as when he wrote, such as, the momentum of things, the externalization of our lives, our insensitivity to ourselves and to one another. But at the same time, I have found that the underlying genuineness of people is always there. Although it does not readily appear, when you take a closer look there are ways people try to find their way to a sacred place.

Crider: And, again, it is a matter of becoming aware of this possibility of living a more authentic life.

Finley: Exactly. That is the value of writings like Thomas Merton's. When people read Merton, it renews and deepens their awareness of this dimension in their lives. The fact that he spoke in such a straight-from-the-shoulder way, with such direct clarity so the words go straight to your heart, is what is so inviting about him. He gives people a way of accessing themselves.

Crider: Your book *The Contemplative Heart*[4] is also invitational in this way.

Finley: It is a series of essays on how to live a more contemplative way of life in the midst of the world. They are poetic essays on ways people can awaken this more interior awareness and how to cultivate it. So it is essentially a series of poetic essays on the cultivation of contemplative mindfulness and contemplative living. In hindsight, the writing style of the book, the long sentences do not make it as immediately accessible to a lot of people. My book *Christian Meditation: Experiencing the Presence of God*[5] and the book I am writing now show a shift in this style of writing. I have been more inspired by people like Josef Pieper and Merton's own writings where its shorter, more accessible style helps access that same depth of life.

Crider: Were your years at Gethsemani a significant influence on your writings?

Finley: It was very influential. I do not know how to put words to it exactly. While at the monastery, in my own limited way I broke through into a direct realization of God's oneness with us and with life itself. It changed me forever. The writing I have done since, tries to put words to that experience or to speak out of that space or to say things that might help others find their own way to that. It was the original place from which I broke through into the place I am writing out of.

Crider: So your time at Gethsemani provided a basic foundation for writing.

Finley: Yes. It did. But it also provided the basic foundation for my life. After I left the monastery my primary concern was how to continue living "out here" within the contemplative way of life which I was introduced to at the monastery. Because my writings come out of my life, they often come out of that particular space.

Crider: How did you decide to leave Gethsemani?

Finley: Some things happened at the monastery that opened up memories of the abuse I experienced at home, which I had never really processed or looked at. I just buried them inside of me, ran away from home and went to the monastery. I started having flashbacks of the abuse and became depressed. I realized that I could not run from that. It was inside of me and I had to deal with it. For different reasons, I felt that I could not deal with it inside the monastery. So I needed to come out here to face things on my own. I talked to Fr. John Eudes Bamberger about it as well as Dom James who was Abbot at the time. I went up to Merton's hermitage too. I got permission to see him. I did not tell him the details but gave him the jist of what was going on. And he agreed.

Crider: How helpful was Merton's advice or agreement that you should leave?

Finley: It was very helpful. I think he was telling me that at the deepest level, it does not really matter where you seek this path because it is really everywhere. So you need to take care of your unfinished business and trust that when you get to the bottom of all of that you will providentially be where you are meant to be. He gave me confidence in that and in my decision. He also thought I should become a hermit after I sorted that out. I had had permission to stay so many hours a day in an abandoned sheep barn. I helped him take care of his hermitage and I was in the novitiate under his direction. So he allowed me to stay so many hours a day in that sheep barn. Had I stayed, I probably would have gone in that direction. He saw me very drawn that way. As we talked, he gave me the address of someone who had a community of hermits somewhere in Nova Scotia. When I first left I thought that is what I would do, but I did not.

Crider: So did you spend more time with Merton than the others did?

Finley: Yes and no. As far as one-on-one time, I had no more than anyone else. During the two year novitiate I stayed longer after temporary vows just so I could still have access to him. Because of the role that he played in my life and because I was so drawn to this way of solitude, by helping him clean his hermitage and get fire wood and so on, I was perhaps more in his proximity than others. But I did not feel the need to talk to him after I left the novitiate except for the time I went to talk about leaving and then the night before I left.

Crider: What year did you leave?

Finley: January, 1967.

Crider: Do you have any final comments?

Finley: I think we have covered the bases well. I would like to comment on how *Merton's Palace of Nowhere* came to be written as a book. Right after Merton died, the Editor of the *National Catholic Reporter* came to Gethsemani and interviewed Fr. Flavian Burns (who was Abbot at the time) about Merton. In their discussion, Fr. Flavian mentioned to him Merton's idea of the True Self, the transcendent self beyond ego. This person was very taken by that and suggested to Fr. Flavian that if he put together an anthology of

Merton's passages on the True Self, it would make a good book. Fr. Flavian was not inclined to do that so he wrote to me and asked if I would be interested. So I put together what I thought would be a collection of Merton's quotes on the True Self. Then all these Merton books began coming out. And The Merton Legacy Trust said they were not inclined to approve of any more collections of Merton's quotes. They were concerned that the market would be glutted with all these Merton diaries and cook books and so on. Since I had the quotes already gathered, I decided to write a book using the quotes as the centerpiece. That is how it came to be written.

Crider: How long did it take to write?

Finley: It took about five years. Then it was published by Ave Maria Press in 1978.

Notes

1. Thomas Merton, *The Sign of Jonas* (New York: Harcourt Brace, 1953).

2. Thomas Merton, *The Seven Storey Mountain* (New York: Harcourt Brace, 1948).

3. James Finley, *Merton's Palace of Nowhere* (Notre Dame, IN: Ave Maria Press, 1978).

4. James Finley, *The Contemplative Heart* (Notre Dame, IN: Sorin Books, 2000).

5. James Finley, *Christian Meditation: Experiencing the Presence of God* (San Francisco: HarperSanFrancisco, 2004).

Return to Sources, Holy Insecurity and Life in a Tiny House: 2005 Bibliographic Essay

Gray Matthews

If for some reason it were necessary for you to drink a pint of water taken out of the Mississippi River and you could choose where it was to be drawn out of the river—would you take a pint from the source of the river in Minnesota or from the estuary at New Orleans?[1]

It seems to me that one of the most basic experiences of anyone who gets down into any kind of depth is the breakthrough realization that I am....This is the place where God's reality is going to break through. I become aware of my own reality, and then God's reality turns out to be the ground of mine. The door is there. And now they're telling us this is impossible. Do you have difficulty with this?[2]

Thomas Merton raised questions. The two questions above framed by Merton were formed a decade apart, but are not unrelated. The first question concerns the place where one should draw needed water; the second question concerns difficulties in the realization of being. One refers to Tradition; the other to the present moment. Each question implies hazards regarding the nature of creative response and freedom of choice. Merton's own answers to these two separate questions are short but not so simple: (1) Minnesota, and (2) Yes. If we put these two questions together in creative tension with one another, without force, we see their interconnection: Do you have any difficulties with others telling you it is impossible to realize and tap into the source of your fluid being? Or to put this question in the way it is being asked by many, many people these days: Are you finding it increasingly difficult to experience the depths of God's love and real presence in a hostile, shallow world being gutted daily by pervasive deception, terror and violence? This question is an old one, but is weighing heavily upon the minds of many in these reckless days of a new century. Merton scholars, particularly, are shadowed by this question.

Most of the works I have been asked to review have already
been reviewed effectively and in detail elsewhere; thus this essay
aims to do something other than rewind reviews: I want to reflect
on the moment in which these works were formed and which they
address. We are still in that moment, a moment in which a number of questions and writings have been forged together. The year
2005 occurred within that moment, too. The moment is a dark
one. Consequently, before I examine individual works, I would
like to take some time to explore more generally a set of significant questions prompted by the remarkable thematic harmony of
Merton publications in 2005. I ask for the reader's patience as
well as assistance in what I hope will be a mutual reflection concerning this significant moment we share.

Contemplation in a Dark Moment

After my initial reading of publications by and about Thomas
Merton in 2005, I was moved to reflect on how these diverse works
formed a psalmody, as if they were bound together as a deeply
concerned book of prayers in which contemplation and daily life
struggle together. Indeed, reviewing these works reminded me
particularly of those Psalms expressing anguish and distress and
cries of "how long, O Lord?" only to realize our only help is in
God Alone. In such a context of diverse works, Merton appears to
serve as a kind of cantor guiding our collective song about the
state of the world and the state of our souls. Why do we return to
Merton's writings again and again? Perhaps it is because of how
well Merton understood that the contemplative life in our time is

> modified by the sins of our age. They bring down upon us a
> cloud of darkness far more terrible than the innocent night of
> unknowing. It is the dark night of the soul which has de-
> scended on the whole world. Contemplation in the age of
> Auschwitz and Dachau, Solovky and Karaganda is something
> darker and more fearsome than contemplation in the age of
> the Church Fathers.[3]

The dark night continues late into our hour: September 11, evil,
genocide, ethnic cleansing, Rwanda, Darfur, Abu Grahib, torture,
terrorism, War on Terror, pre-emptive war, homeland security,
weapons of mass destruction, militarization of space, human traf-
ficking, global warming, desertification, natural disasters, and on

and on. Merton's nagging question continues to haunt us today: "Can contemplation still find a place in the world of technology and conflict which is ours? Does it belong only to the past?"[4] Merton answered with his life, arguing firmly that contemplation must be possible if we are to remain human because "the direct and pure experience of reality in its ultimate root is man's deepest need."[5] Thomas Merton continues to provoke us: Do we have difficulty with this?

Today, however, our difficulty appears to be less with those who are *telling us* it is impossible to realize our deepest, ultimate need as much as it is with the fact that forces appear to be actively *working* against us. Fortunately, there were many encouraging voices raised in 2005 that wished to speak to those difficulties, whose interests in Merton were prompted by a deeper, holy longing for God's presence and reality in the midst of an accelerated draining of compassion, truth, meaning, health, peace and justice from the world in which we live. Examples of such concern by Merton scholars in 2005 can be gleaned from conference, book or paper titles such as: "Across the Rim of Chaos," "Discerning Peace in Fearful Times," "Dark Before Dawn," "Destined for Evil? The Twentieth Century Responses."

Merton represents for many writers not only someone who wrestled with the real world but someone who won more matches than he lost. Although Merton repeatedly said he had no answers, only questions, many realize he was seemingly able to see his way clear through a dark world, and that a return to Merton's writings could possibly help more of us find a way to see through our own dark times. In essence, writings about Merton in 2005 were steeped in a concern with the question of **what would Merton say *now*?** Implicitly, they addressed and answered (either directly or indirectly) a second significant question: **Why read Merton today?**

One way to address questions is to turn them around. Anne Lamott took such an approach when she confronted the task of explaining to readers why still another book on genocide should be read.

So why look through another book of Africans barely surviving? Well, why read another poem? Why take another strenuous hike? Why visit a friend, who despite your tender presence, is going to die anyway? Because that's why we're here, to find out about life, to experience our humanity more deeply.

We're here to pay attention, bear witness, and find our way to an authentic relationship with spirit. We're here to grieve and cheer for one another and crack open our hearts, even though that often hurts terribly.[6]

So, why read Merton today? Because we're here to pay attention, bear witness, and find our way to an authentic relationship with spirit, and Merton helps us realize these things.

This essay, I hope, will turn some of these questions around so that we can better address them, or at least stir up some new ones. I must emphasize the fact that these questions and their significance were raised *for* me—not by me—as I began examining Merton scholarship in 2005. I may have missed some works, and I apologize to the authors and readers affected by my unintended neglect or oversight. The bulk of what I did read, however, was thematically bound by a concern for the relevance of Merton's teachings in what is now commonly referred by some as a post-9/11 world. This new designation for the world, of course, is a uniquely American culture-bound label and subject to legitimate criticism, for it is rife with implications for the reality of all beings sharing the same home we call earth. Many people have difficulties with what is being said about reality these days. Orientations to reality are a "dime a dozen," of course, yet they are apparently esteemed valuable enough to kill and die for. Merton, however, sought to *experience* reality without the use of orientations; thus many people yearn to discover how Merton realized so much without the aid of contemporary orientations.

What *would* Merton say today? This is a significant question to consider for several reasons. For one, the question reflects an urgent need to know, not merely curiosity, and seems to carry an assumption that Merton would be correct in whatever he said. Second, the question reveals both our perception that Merton read his times well, yet that such a reading was not, after all, bound to his culture and time only. Third, in asking that question we are acknowledging our own inability to read our own times for ourselves; we need help, in other words. Fourth, the question suggests, too, that there have been perhaps too few insightful, contemplative voices in the past 40 years of action, action, action. Fifth, it raises more questions *about what* Merton would see and address. Finally, the question is significant to consider because it is a real question.

I will certainly not attempt to put words into Merton's mouth, but my hunch is that he would continue to speak as one who was in-formed by Tradition and unconformed to the ways of a world in flight from God. Fundamentally, perhaps, the issue is not what Merton *said*, but rather what Merton *saw* and *heard*, and whether we can learn from him how to regain our own sense of vision and hearing in a culture of visual and aural noise. I recall Fr. Carlos Rodriguez, a monk at Gethsemani, making a similar point to a group of Merton scholars on retreat there in 2002: "We know what Merton said and did, but we need to better understand *how* he did it so that *we* can learn how to do it, too." Yes, this is what we must *realize*, and realize *for ourselves*, today. And here we come to one more significant question to address (along with Why read Merton today? and What would Merton say?): How can we realize what Merton realized? Or to put this into a more pressing form: Can we realize in the ways Merton realized? To really see the import of this question, I think it is useful to revisit Martin Buber's distinction between a realization and an orientation. From this vantage point, it may be possible as well as helpful to consider Buber's concept of realization in relation to Merton's practice of contemplation.

Orientations and Realizations

A few years before Martin Buber penned his classic work, *I and Thou*, he published a fascinating but too often overlooked work in 1913 entitled *Daniel: Dialogues on Realization*, in which he explored the differences between realization and orientation. This philosophical work is arranged in five fictional one-on-one dialogues in which Daniel converses with five different interlocutors (The Woman, Ulrich, Reinold, Leonhard, and Lukas). The themes or philosophical problems of each dialogue are, in successive order: Direction, reality, meaning, polarity and unity. Each conversation is also held in a different time and location: first, in the Mountains, then above the City, in the Garden, after the Theater, and by the Sea. Daniel provides advice in each dialogue; for example, in closing his conversation with Reinold, Daniel advises him to:

Live upright and attentive, opened and devoted in the peace of your becoming, Reinold, and love danger. You have no security in the world, but you have direction and meaning, and

God, who wants to be realized, the risking God, is near you at all times.[7]

The chief concern in all of Buber's advice offered via the character of Daniel is *to realize*. The alternative to realization is not its opposite, but rather its complement: Orientation. Buber presents these as two modes of being in the world, two different paths we tread to find our way in the world. Orientation offers a sure guide, yet a false security—the security of a sleepwalker. Realization, on the other hand, is a deepening awareness and experience of God's reality through one's very person; to realize is to discover partially the essential knowledge for conquering "separateness" from God in order to celebrate "an ever-new mystery" in realizing: "To live so as to realize God in all things. For God wills to be realized, and reality is God's reality, and there is no reality except through the man who realizes himself and all being."[8]

To realize is to experience a phenomenon without filters or litmus tests, relating one's experience to nothing other than the experience itself. To work from an orientation, however, is to impose a grid or structure onto an experience before, during and after the experience. In other words, for example, when one realizes where one is, one does not need a map for orientation. Daniel explains to Reinold that "orientation installs all happening in formulas, rules, connections which are useful in its province but remain cut off from a freer existence and unfruitful; realization relates each event to nothing other than its own content and just thereby shapes it into a sign of the eternal."[9] The eminent scholar and translator of Buber's work, Maurice Friedman, explains that "Buber's philosophy of realization does not mean a lofty divorce from the limitations of existence but a real progress in bringing the stubborn stuff of life into the circle of lived and meaningful experience. In our age, however, this task is far more difficult than before, for in our age orientation predominates as at no earlier time."[10]

The difficult task of realizing was close to Merton's own vocation as a monk, a task he found formidable in a managerial age of new and improved orientations to everything under the sun. Merton knew something, however, about what Daniel called "holy insecurity." In his memorable conclusion to *The Seven Storey Mountain*, Merton intimates that God's call to solitude is a call to holy insecurity: *"I will give you what you desire. I will lead you into soli-*

tude. I will lead you by the way that you cannot possibly understand, because I want it to be the quickest way."[11]   Similarly, Daniel exhorts:

Descend into the abyss! Realize it! Know its nature, the thousand-named, nameless polarity of all being, between piece and piece of the world, between thing and thing, between image and being, between the world and you, in the very heart of yourself, at all places, with its swinging tensions and its streaming reciprocity. Know the sign of the primal being in it. And know that here is your task: To create unity out of you and all duality, to establish unity in the world; not unity of the mixture, such as the secure ones invent, but fulfilled unity out of tension and stream, such as will serve the polar earth—the realized countenance of God illuminated out of tension and stream. But know too that this is the endless task, and that here no "once-for-all" is of value. You must descend ever anew into the transforming abyss, risk your soul ever anew, ever anew vowed to the holy insecurity.[12]

Forever restless with orientations Merton's descended into the abyss and realized it; he craved reality, not its outline. He knew his desire to experience God would never be fully realized this side of heaven, but he was undeterred by *that realization* even to the last day of his physical life. In his final public address shortly before his death, Merton tried to articulate a realization beyond orientation in this way: "What is essential in the monastic life is not embedded in buildings, is not embedded in clothing, is not necessarily embedded even in a rule. It is somewhere along the line of something deeper than a rule. It is concerned with this business of total inner transformation. All other things serve that end."[13] Earlier in the same address, Merton suggested that everyone "remember this for the future: 'From now on, everybody stands on his own feet,'" explaining that "we can no longer rely on being supported by structures that may be destroyed at any moment by a political power or a political force. You cannot rely on structures. The time for relying on structures has disappeared."[14]

Buber's philosophical reflections about orientation versus realization are immensely relevant to this particular annual review of publications about Merton, for the writings under review share a collective desire to learn how Merton practiced genuine contemplation—how he came to realize God and life under the sun—and not merely to utilize Merton as some type of orienting device. Orientation is not evil, of course; it just takes a long, long time to get where you are going. Many spiritual teachers have reminded us that one can see in an instant, although it may take a lifetime to open one's eyes. In a world of increasingly dizzying confusion, fragmentation and dispiritedness, it is tempting to close our eyes or desperately grab hold of anything resembling a set of guidelines, instructions, or directions for navigating one's way through the labyrinth. Fortunately, there is an alternative to sleepwalking, and this is what most of us declare we are striving to realize for ourselves, for all of us. Contemplation, therefore, is all about realization, and not orientation. Merton was clear about this: "The only way to get rid of misconceptions about contemplation is to experience it. One who does not actually know, in his own life, the nature of this breakthrough and this awakening to a new level of reality cannot help being misled by most of the things that are said about it."[15] He added: "Contemplation does not arrive at reality after a process of deduction, but by an intuitive awakening in which our free and personal reality becomes fully alive to its own existential depths, which open out into the mystery of God."[16]

Return to the Sources

In moving to consider some of the specific Merton publications in 2005, it is clear to me that we must begin with Merton himself, which means we must begin with *Cassian and the Fathers*. Because Merton always beckons us to return to the sources, there has been much excitement among Merton scholars regarding the anticipated publication of Merton's lecture outlines and teaching notes prepared for his conferences with novices. The first volume in the series (more volumes are forthcoming), *Cassian and the Fathers: Initiation into the Monastic Tradition*, was edited by Patrick F. O'Connell.[17] O'Connell's excellent and substantial introduction captures the brilliant value of Merton's notes, which lies "in the light it casts on Merton himself as teacher, novice master and monk. These notes provide a privileged standpoint for observing Merton functioning as an integral and important member of his monastic community. It is quite evident…that Merton took his duties as instructor of the young men in his charge very seriously."[18] Indeed, Merton's "notes" could easily be conceived as rough essays.

Part I centers on monastic spirituality and the early Fathers, while Part II focuses lecture material on Cassian—over 200 dense pages of "notes" in all.

One becomes a novice in reading *Cassian*, and keenly aware of one's hunger for solid teachings. Merton's advisory anthem, Return to the Sources, rings throughout: "[T]radition and spirituality are all the more pure and genuine in proportion as they are in contact with the original sources and retain the same content," adding the reminder that "Monastic spirituality is especially traditional and depends much on return to sources—to Scripture, Liturgy, Fathers of the Church. More than other religious the monk is a man who is nourished at the early sources."[19] Merton counsels his novices, and his readers, that return involves renewal, but not necessarily a complete revival of old ways by some detailed imitation. Instead, such return "means living in our time and solving the problems of our time in the way and with the spirit in which they lived in a different time and solved different problems."[20] Discernment is key for Merton, for he cautions us to see the aberrations as well as the genuine marks of Tradition in the early sources.

Merton views Cassian to be "*the* great monastic writer—the Master of the spiritual life par excellence for monks—the source for all in the West. He is a "*classic*" and "every monk should know him thoroughly."[21] Cassian's teachings on humility, purity of heart and discretion, and how to deal with the problems of pride, distractions, *acedia* and anger, are never treated by Merton as outdated spiritual practices; more than simply relevant, Merton presents Cassian as an able teacher for those of us living in a post-Christian era. As Bernard McGinn argues in his introduction to a volume of sermons by Isaac of Stella, we can approach classic texts for their relevance to us today, or we can approach them in ways that "allow them to measure us rather than to fit them into the confines of our own horizons, however generous we may judge these to be. We can turn to the past not only to mine it for our purposes, but also to be undermined."[22]

Merton was undermined by Cassian in the 1950s, yet Merton did not leave him there, let alone on a fourth-century island of ideas. Evidence of Cassian's influence on Merton's own journey through the political, economic and social matrix of the 1960s can be found in that final public address in Bangkok in which he tries to identify the essence of monastic life in the world today: "I am just saying, in other words, what Cassian said in the first lecture on *puritas cordis*, purity of heart, that every monastic observance tends toward that."[23] A few lines later, Merton reveals one way he has adapted Cassian: "The monk belongs to the world, but the world belongs to him insofar as he has dedicated himself totally to liberation from it in order to liberate it."[24]   As he records in these lecture notes on Cassian, "true peace is rooted in renunciation of our own will. This is the peace we must seek and follow with all our heart, not the other," referring to the "false peace" of "remaining undisturbed in our own will."[25]

Merton urges us to imitate Cassian and the Desert Fathers, but not in all their attitudes or actions; instead of using them as a mere orientation, we must realize their teachings by doing two things: (1) Discriminate and (2) Adapt, "as did St. Benedict himself, who consciously and deliberately, wrote a *Rule* which some of the Desert Fathers would have condemned as soft."[26] Merton locates vital teachings in Cassian for us as we continue to navigate through these dark early days of the twenty-first century. I would like to enlarge these two themes from Merton's notes on Cassian—discrimination and adaptation—in dividing my review of 2005 publications about Merton into two categories: (1) Those seeking to find in Merton, Cassian and other models of imitation (e.g. Desert Fathers) a source for training in the spiritual practices of discrimination, discretion and discernment in trying to see and understand the postmodern world from a sapiential perspective; and (2) those seeking to act upon and communicate those teachings through a variety of creative ways in adapting a wise, contemplative response to a world of anxiety and folly. In other words, (1) how does Merton help us see our world, and (2) how does he help us respond authentically.

Discernment and Wisdom

The Thomas Merton Society of Great Britain and Ireland hosted their fifth General Conference in 2004; papers from that conference in Birmingham were published in 2005 in a volume bearing the conference theme as title: *Across the Rim of Chaos*.[27] The title comes from a line in Merton's prayer for peace that was read before the U.S. Congress in 1962. The editor of this probing set of papers, Angus Stuart, frames the main concern of this collection as being a question of the response of faith in a world of greed, lucrative disasters and powerlessness in the midst of worldwide violence. Stuart accurately relays Merton's perspective in acknowledging that the challenges facing humanity today have as much to do with the inner world of the spirit as the outer world. The publication of *Across the Rim of Chaos* followed on the heels of Merton's *Peace in the Post-Christian Era* (2004), proving that Merton's 1960s contemplative criticism is still very much relevant and needed.[28]

The main addresses at this British conference reflect, in part, what was discussed earlier in this essay regarding Buber's treatment of "holy insecurity" in *Daniel*. For instance, Diana Francis in "War, Peace and Faithfulness" argues, "Sometimes the call to faithfulness can seem very daunting. Despair is a serious temptation. But here the 'faith' in faithfulness can help."[29] Tina Beattie follows this with her paper on "Vision in Obscurity: Discerning Peace in Fearful Times." Fernando Beltrán Llavador's paper, "Unbinding Prometheus: Thomas Merton and the 'Patient Architecture of Peace,'" focuses even more on the collective need to understand our dark moment: "The more one sees today's world events the more one agrees with Merton's diagnosis of the sickness of our age, namely, our belief in false gods who, 'in order to exist at all, have to dominate (man), feed on him and ruin him,'" and concludes "We need a joint spiritual and ethical alternative to power politics, a conscious collective effort to ground political action in genuine religious practice, that is, mercy or *charitas*, not *hubris* or pride. In the crystal clear words of *Pacem in Terris*: 'there is nothing human about a society welded together by force.'"[30] He suggests, in reference to Merton's introduction to the Vietnamese edition of *No Man Is an Island*, that we insert "Iraq" or "Rwanda" for "Vietnam" and we would see what Merton would say about today's atrocities.

Other articles dealing with related themes are presented with the same sustained focus on Merton's aid to us in reading the world, covering such problems as: the war on terror and crisis of language, faith and courage versus terror and fear, sane language in an insane world, mystery of hospitality, Merton's views on Alfred Delp, Martin Luther King, Jr., poetry as a creative social critique and the role of the artist in a time of crisis. The dogged point running throughout these fine articles is: Never give up. We are exhorted to stay firm in the faith, be prophetic and speak truth to power. Merton serves as an inspiring critic who offered a positive agenda for action rooted in contemplation of the mystery of truth. Merton is not merely a borrowed voice here, and one never senses that these authors are basically trying to convince themselves or make us feel better. They have learned from Merton well. Not a sentimental snake-charmer in the bunch.

A more difficult book to read, however, because of its intense focus, is *Destined for Evil? The Twentieth-Century Responses*.[31]   The book is a collection of previously published as well as new essays by such thinkers as Carl Jung, Hermann Hesse, Hannah Arendt, Camus, Tolstoy and Solzhenitsyn, Rabbi Michael Lerner, Daniel Berrigan, Gil Bailie, Nicholas Wolterstorf, including three Merton scholars—John Collins, Thomas Del Prete and Jonathan Montaldo—who present Merton's views on the ancient struggle with evil in ourselves and society.

The traditional Augustinian view of evil sees it as the absence of being (nothingness), whereas this book suggests it may be less a deprivation of being and more of a case of obstacles or obstructions to certain goods (e.g. obstacles to health, love, happiness). In his introduction to this work, editor Predrag Cicovacki elaborates, saying "such obstacles can be external or internal, natural or unnatural, intentional or non-intentional, individual or institutional. Whatever their origin and scope, they make it difficult, sometimes impossible, to continue with our lives in the way we intend, either by preserving the status quo, or by advancing our current role."[32] Cicovacki's statement seems to support Merton's question presented at the beginning of this review essay: *Do you have difficulty with this?* Clearly, the question and problem of evil transcends time and culture. The Merton scholars addressing this question effectively convey Merton's approach.

John P. Collins's article, "We are Prodigals in a Distant Land: An Essay on Thomas Merton," builds largely from Merton's perspective in *New Seeds of Contemplation*.[33]   Collins focuses on Merton's distinction between the true and false self, noting that it is out of the false self that we project division into the world. Hatred is a symptom of division, as is scapegoating and war. Humility is needed to return to our true selves. Collins discusses why the misunderstanding and distortion of God's creation leads to "despair" and "sadness" and evil.

Thomas Del Prete's article is titled "Rediscovering Paradise: Thomas Merton on the Self and the Problem of Evil."[34] Del Prete emphasizes freedom in following up on Collins' presentation of the true self. "We are free from evil in proportion as we are free from our dependence on something outside ourselves, or some assertion of ourselves, or some visible sign of our power as a way of affirming or convincing ourselves of the value of our existence," writes Del Prete; thus to be a person "is to be free from the cares of the illusory self."[35] Del Prete, in adopting a personalist perspective, treats paradise as another way of referring to our whole self.

The third Merton scholar included in this studied response to evil in the world is Jonathan Montaldo, whose entry is titled "Exposing the Deceitful Heart: A Monk's Public 'Inner Work.'"[36] Montaldo argues that "since God is at core hidden and transcendent, desiring God's presence is in the same genre of never to be completed human tasks as is ridding one's experience of evil. Whoever takes up either of these projects without being grounded in humility will have begun in delusion to reach an end in dismay" (p. 213). Both Del Prete and Montaldo object to the label "spiritual master" applied to Merton as if he were not completely human. Montaldo reasons in this way: "Anyone who takes up serious inner work in order to discover the truth about herself and her predicament, anyone who struggles to accept that she shares these same painful predicaments with all her neighbors, anyone who strives for a modicum of human integrity, will always find her experience as having an edge of being in exile from any supposedly settled questions (traditionally defended by corporate entities for whom settled questions preserve their own power), especially when she learns through experience that these settled questions systemically continue to reproduce evil effects."[37]

Montaldo's essay reminds me of Merton's "distrust of all obligatory answers," a viewpoint shared and promoted by practically all of the published works on Merton in 2005.[38] The Merton scholars addressing the question of evil, in particular, effectively illumined the sense of holy insecurity that Merton felt was essential if we are to detach ourselves from our destructive powers: "The great problem of our time," Merton said, "is not to formulate clear answers to neat theoretical questions but to tackle the self-destructive alienation of man in a society dedicated in theory to human values and in practice to the pursuit of power for its own sake."[39]

There were other noted Merton scholars writing independently of conferences and invited essays who attempted to identify Merton's value and place as a contemplative critic in our postmodern world. The most common single adjective used appeared to be that of "prophet," seeing Merton as a prophetic voice that still resounds with truthfulness in our times. Two of these are former abbots, John Eudes Bamberger and Basil Pennington, who knew Merton personally, a fact that richly enhances their insightfulness. Three other writers presented significant portraits of Merton as more than merely relevant to our times: Robert Inchausti, Philip Sheldrake and A.M. Allchin.

Bamberger's *Thomas Merton: Prophet of Renewal* deserves a fuller appraisal and interpretation than I can supply here.[40] In the context of this review, though, his work underscores the major themes and questions considered in this essay. Montaldo writes the Foreword and paints a picture of Merton as a monk who lived questions through the questions of his life and times:

> He was a monk who consciously sought to live out of and through his always deeper questions as to how to be a monk of his times and [to] summon all the personal integrity he could muster to seek God just as he truly was, paying a conscious price of demolishing any holy legend he was creating by his books. He truly sought God by going into monastic exile from easy answers.[41]

Bamberger's central thesis is that Merton was enabled to contribute to the renewal of society because he returned to the sources of his own monastic tradition and helped nurture renewal in his own order and the Church at large. "One of the functions of the Cistercian life," that Merton came to understand exceedingly well, was to keep "interior reality alive and to be a sign of its presence in our time and in our Western society."[42] Bamberger explains, "Merton understood that there is a great deal of will-to-power in the Western concept of outward, versus inner, work. The love of action and domination that have so long characterized the West all too frequently represent a substitute of this spiritual transformation in view of arriving at perfect love, in total illumination of the spirit."[43]

Basil Pennington's book, *I Have Seen What I Was Looking For*, was published in the same year of his death, 2005. This work is mainly a compilation of lengthy passages from Merton's writings, working as an introductory reader. Pennington's choices of long quotations are not necessarily expected or conventional. Some of Merton's major works are not featured strongly (such as *New Seeds of Contemplation*), but Pennington does relay a shrewd collection of letters and poetry that are often neglected in other overviews of Merton's work. Pennington supplies short introductions to each of his thematic sections and offers a short but intriguing introductory "Welcome" essay. In that opening piece, Pennington makes an eloquent case for Merton as a prophet who "listened with an exquisitely fine and developed listening and heard the voice of a new world, a voice that spoke of promise and inspired hope. And he had a fine and developed ability to give that voice a new voice in the written word. That is why we want to listen to Thomas Merton."[44]

In a slightly different vein, author Robert Inchausti places Merton in the company of "outlaws, revolutionaries and other Christians in disguise" in his new book entitled *Subversive Orthodoxy*.[45] Inchausti paints a picture of Merton as prophet-critic and praises his work in the nineteen-sixties in particular for bringing "social criticism out of its ideological cold war dichotomies by shifting terms away from the rhetorical battle between progressives and conservatives into the quest for a single unified expression of what it might mean to live life in accord with conscience."[46]

Philip Sheldrake's essay, "Thomas Merton's Contribution to 20th Century Spirituality: An Appraisal," makes a strong case for considering Merton as one who achieved paradigmatic status as a "spiritual classic"—classic as a person, a guide, and not merely a text. Sheldrake argues "For me, as for the great monastic scholar Dom Jean Leclercq, Merton's importance and continued popularity is linked to the fact that he both symbolized *and* addressed a time of critical transition in the West."[47] Sheldrake is doing something here that has long been needed: Rescuing Merton from being confined to the 1940s, 1950s and 1960s. For Sheldrake, as well as for this reviewer, Merton "is far from isolated in the long tradition of Western mysticism."[48] In this respect, Sheldrake considers Evelyn Underhill and John Ruusbroec as mystics whose life and works transcended their own respective cultural moments in time.

A.M. Allchin, writing in the same issue of *The Merton Journal* as Sheldrake, reflects on what Merton might be like today at age ninety (Merton was born in 1915). Representing, perhaps, the collective sentiment of all Merton scholars in 2005, Allchin's short reflection is a powerful one that envisions:

Here again is Merton for the 21st century, the Merton who has already got beyond September 11th, 2001, and here it is moving to observe that, on September 11th in 1960, Merton was meditating deeply on the life of prayer of the Staretz Silouan (St. Silouan of Athos) on the words spoken to him by the Lord: 'keep your mind in hell and do not despair.' I, for a long time thought that was the word of the Lord for the 20th century. I now have the feeling that is the word of the Lord for our own troubled time in which Merton's voice needs to be heard more clearly than ever.[49]

Before concluding this selection of works regarding Merton as a seer, prophet and contemplative critic, mention should be made of his inclusion in a British volume about Christian and Muslim dialogue: *Listening to Islam: With Thomas Merton, Sayyid Qutb, Kenneth Cragg and Ziauddin Sardar: Praise, Reason and Reflection*, by John Watson.[50] Watson uses September 11th as a springboard to consider the necessity to listen to Muslims. He describes four ecumenical voices in promoting such listening, beginning with Merton whom he considers a "courageous thinker" and one who was committed to the possibility of mutual understanding, but one who likely had not captured the essentials of Islam. Yet, even with this qualification, Merton is mentioned first as one who continues to inspire needed dialogue in a post- 9/11 world.

In sum, I have grouped the above articles and commentaries according to a central dynamic: The writers' interest in Merton's assistance regarding our need for contemplative voice and insight in our times. These works present Merton as a model, but not in the diluted sense of celebrity role models; rather, Merton as presented is one we should learn from in order to practice spiritual discernment in our dark times. The concern with what Merton would say today reflects more, perhaps, a collective need to discover our own voices. Merton did not discover his voice because he was a product of his era—he discovered it because he returned to the sources of not only his vocation as a monk, or the sources of his faith tradition, but rather because he returned to the Source of his very being. He went all the way down, again and again, to obtain the vital realizations of what it means to be alive in a deadening culture that cannot help but block our vision of the mystery and union of life.

Adaptation and Creativity

Although Rowan Williams does not refer to Merton in his *Grace and Necessity: Reflections on Art and Love*, which was also published in 2005, he does make some points that I think are helpful in further framing this section of my review-essay.[51] In this work, Williams discusses an "aesthetic of transcendence" with which he encourages Christians to engage culture. He argues "the artist's work is inescapably a claim about reality," yet one's perception must always be incomplete because "telling the truth about what is before us is not a matter of exhaustively defining the effects of certain phenomena on the receptors of brain and sense."[52] Holy insecurity, it would seem, applies as much to artistic expression as it does to the prophetic life.

I will now move to review selected works from 2005 that consider Merton as an artist able to communicate prophetically and creatively in a culture of noise. Merton's studies of Cassian led him to determine that if our first cautious step in returning to the sources is discretion, the second step—adaptation—is certainly more creative and tricky. There was much attention paid to Merton as an artist in 2005, understandably given his creative adaptation to the times in which he lived and our burning need to do the same.

Two of Merton's own essays on art appeared in the 2005 *Merton Annual* and set the stage for the rest of this review. Both are short articles, previously published in the 1950s, but their reappearance here, in these days of concern with a creative response to a fearful world, help reconnect hope and creative expression. In the first essay, "The Monk and Sacred Art," Merton finds the term "prophet" to be more concrete than "contemplative" and describes the monk as one who sees "what others do not see. They see the inner meaning of things. They see God in the darkness of faith."[53] Merton blends prophet and contemplative but also distinguishes them by describing the contemplative as one who sees essences while the prophet is one who sees persons and things. The relationship between the two is important to Merton, for the monk is both a *seer* and a *maker*, which means that "as a *seer* and a *maker* the monk is attuned to what is."[54]

In the second essay, "Art and Worship," Merton elaborates further on these relationships between seer and maker, promoting the realization of sacred art representing "the hidden things of

God" in all beings.[55]   To see such sacred art, one must see both essence and person or thing. This is necessary for inner and outer harmony, as Merton argues:

> ... man cannot be complete if he is only a scientist and a technician: he must also be an artist and a contemplative. Unless these elements in his life reach a proper balance, his society and culture will be out of harmony with the spiritual needs of his inner life. Hence art has a vitally important place to play not only in keeping man civilized but also in helping him to "save his soul," that is to say, to live as a Child of God.

Here, Merton promotes the idea of "eikons" not as reproductions but in terms of "creating something new, an *eikon*, an image which embodies the inner truth of things as they exist in the mystery of God."[56]

Poems are very much like icons, and Lynn Szabo has provided a tremendous service to Merton readers by recasting a substantial amount of Merton's poetry into a more focused spotlight: *In the Dark Before Dawn: New Selected Poems of Thomas Merton*.[57] Kathleen Norris supplies a wonderful preface to this important work and explains why Merton's poems need to be rediscovered today: "What may be most valuable for the contemporary reader is the way Merton's poems offer evidence that ecstasy, and specifically religious ecstasy, is still possible in this world, and still meaningful."[58] Szabo provides a splendid service to readers of Merton's poetry by her positioning the evidence of ecstasy and the reader into closer proximity. She accomplishes this with two masterful strokes: First, with her introduction, and second by grouping the poetry according to well-chosen thematic schemes.

In her introduction, Szabo captures the thrust of Merton's creative struggle in adapting to a world in which language has been gutted of its soulful roots: "His anxiety about the existential dilemma created by the debasement of language in modern American culture led him through and away from conventional paradigms for poetry and ultimately towards an antipoetry that sought to engage and rout the powerful tensions which erupt when the limitations of language distort and disrupt its possibility for meaning."[59] She describes silence and solitude as the conditions for the "beautiful terror" in Merton's creativity, "that is the paradoxical force at the center of Merton's poetics. From them emanate the hiddenness, complexity, and mystery that are the categories for many of his poems" as he "remained all his life a marginal man observing and reconfiguring for his readers what it means to be authentic" in our world today.[60]

Szabo's choice and use of themes to arrange Merton's poems is especially to be commended for the way in which the themes themselves assist us with recognizing the seasons of Merton's creative relation to changing times, both in his life and in the world around him. These themes not only help situate his poetry in time, but illuminate the nature of Merton's growing concern and responsiveness to the times. Thus, with this arrangement, the reader is enabled to consider the necessary relationship between the interior life and the exterior life. Such links were essential to Merton and his work, and Szabo is surely correct in arguing "Thomas Merton's single most important gift to his readers was his prophetic vocation to perceive and distinguish in his art the fundamental unity in the cosmos."[61]

The title of the collection is taken from a line in Merton's poem, "Elegy for a Trappist," which Szabo interprets as reflecting Merton's love of predawn hours. In the context of more brooding thought about our times as dark times, the title might suggest a strong ray of Merton's hope, as well. Merton's anti-poetry and social criticism was rooted in hope that we may come to see through the opaqueness of a false world. I am confident it is the hope of Szabo that this new selection of Merton's poetry will lead many new readers to that predawn light.

Joshua Harrod's Master's thesis, "Thomas Merton's Antipoetry of Resistance," is a short but trenchant examination of Merton's antipoetry in light of his writings on the social and political issues of his day.[62] Poetry, as art in general, is argued to be necessary for survival and not merely enjoyed as a luxury. Harrod writes with concern about the loss of communication and the power of the prophetic voice, and exhorts readers to become active participants in the unveiling of abusive language as evil obstacles to life itself. In short, Harrod is declaring "we are overdue for another strong dose of antipoetry."[63]

Many other writers in 2005 expressed concern about the role of art and language today in the midst of so much frantic expression and destructive communication. In fact, Volume 18 of *The Merton Annual* is filled with reflections on the creative and spiritual life today. Editor Victor A. Kramer notes "While this volume was not planned as a tribute to Merton as artist, the many pieces gathered here conjoin to reflect both his formation as artist and his monastic development which parallel movements within Catholic artistic circles during the years Merton lived the Cistercian life (1941-1968)."[64]   All of the articles in this gathering are superb, which makes it impossible to even replay the highlights here. I do think it is significant to point out that the same concerns in the papers collected in *Across the Rim of Chaos*, papers dealing with the problems of language and dialogue in today's time, mirror the concerns of the articles in this volume of *The Merton Annual*. Taken together, one senses an underground river of deep contemplative communication values coursing in our world today, preparing to transcend the deserted surface of social life today. A mammoth yet inspired task of creative spiritual expression. Anyone interested in this spiritual flowing current should wade into the 2005 *Merton Annual* for further inspiration.

Ron Dart published an interesting study on *Thomas Merton and the Beats of the North Cascades* in 2005, favorably connecting Merton with beat poets (namely Rexroth, Snyder, Kerouac and Whalen) as poets of resistance in their promotion of a cultural revolt against the modern urban rat race.[65]   This brief book combines a study of the poets with Dart's own desire to participate in a spiritual counterculture that seeks "something saner, deeper, more human and humane in a world dominated by rationalism, empiricism, technology and a frantic work ethic."[66]   Dart uses the metaphor of "lookout," drawn in part from Kenneth Rexroth's living in actual lookout stations in the North Cascade mountains for a time, as a creative observer and critic on the margins of society, seeking "to reverse a stubborn and obstinate way of knowing and being" in the world.[67]   Dart adds that Merton and the beats sought an older way instead, one that "could purify and clean, renovate and rebuild the home of the soul."[68]   Dart is following Merton here in desiring to create something new—through the art of living—that is connected to a Tradition of Life where seer and maker are in creative harmony and peace.

Place matters—from where one views the world as well as where one influences that world, matters deeply. In what might be seen as a departure from critical works under current review, I think a clear case can be made for considering the collaboration of Harry Hinkle, Monica Weis and Jonathan Montaldo on the beautiful work, *Thomas Merton's Gethsemani: Landscapes of Paradise*, as exploration and celebration of sacred art.[69] Br. Patrick Hart's preface elucidates the unique contributions of the book's three creative voices: Weis's "engaging essay essentially relies on Merton's best writings on nature, drawn mainly from his journals"; Hinkle's "splendid photographs, so reminiscent of Merton's own photography, complement the text"; and Montaldo's insightful introduction "sets the tone for an authentic experience of walking in the steps of Father Louis."[70]

This book, much like what Szabo did for Merton's poetry, can help the reader connect the interior and exterior of Merton's life as well as reflect upon one's own personal interconnections. One cannot separate the two, interior and exterior, nor separate the links between Gethsemani and the rest of the world. I think this book will be enjoyed even more thoroughly, perhaps, if one has been fortunate enough to have visited Gethsemani, walked in the woods for themselves, sat on the porch of Merton's hermitage. Like Blake's grain of sand, Merton was able to find the whole world in a place called Gethsemani. Merton was not born there—he was reborn there. In a wilderness, in an ordinary landscape where paradise is so often unseen, Merton learned to employ the arts of transforming a house into a home.

Of course, some of Merton's most significant lessons in the arts of homemaking occurred many years before. As Paul Pearson reminds us, "Thomas Merton's artistic worldview was no doubt inherited from his parents, Owen and Ruth Merton."[71] Thus it is fitting to end this bibliographic review with an assessment of the publication of *Tom's Book* by Ruth Merton.[72] The book is dedicated "to Granny with Tom's best love, 1916." I had not anticipated this brief book becoming the anchor for my wandering review, but reading it had quite a meditative effect on my synthetic interpretation of everything else I read from 2005. The book simply describes a two-year-old Thomas Merton from a Mom's point of view. Attention to Tom's vocabulary and level of awareness is highlighted. On an unnumbered page titled "November 1, 1916," Ruth writes: "When we go out he seems conscious of everything. Sometimes he puts up his arms and cries out 'Oh Sun! Oh joli!'"[73]

What was most striking, indeed inspiring, was discovering a short poem written by Ruth Merton. The poem was not included in Ruth's version, but is, thankfully, shared with us by the editor, Sheila Milton. Milton states that "Ruth was deeply concerned about the many ways art affects a person's life," and in addition to painting, Ruth was very much interested in interior design. One of her "theories" was presented in an article entitled "The Tiny House," which was published in the *American Cookery* the same month and year that she died, October 1921. Ruth drew the illustrations and concluded the article with a short poem entitled "To Make a Tiny House," which I represent here in full:

To Make a Tiny House

Oh, Little House, if thou a home would'st be
Teach me thy lore, be all in all to me.
Show me the way to find the charm
That lies in every humble rite and daily task within thy walls.
Then not alone for thee, but for the universe itself,
Shall I have lived and gloried my home.

This poem expresses everything Merton scholars and readers have been looking to him for, and here it is his mother—perhaps as it should be—who has passed down the wisdom we need to transform our lives on earth, to turn a house into a home.

Time and space do not permit lengthy commentary, but I would like to use this poem as a means to summarize this bibliographic essay. Ruth's poem can help identify the main themes of this essay, which began with the theme of Merton *answering the questions of life with his life*. His basic approach was to *return to the sources*, a second theme, from which he sought to use *discretion* in *adapting* their wisdom to the times and needs of his own day (third and fourth themes). Merton's approach requires that one be both a *seer and a maker*, a contemplative artist in dialogue with reality (fifth theme). These themes were used for reflecting on Merton publications in 2005, and Ruth's poem serves to illuminate each with lemon-scented freshness!

The opening line of Ruth's poem reflects her desire to make a home out of a house. The house, itself, is tiny, which reflects the values of simplicity and humility. Humility is also necessary to be able to learn the "lore" needed if she is to do such creative work. The Little House itself is her teacher; the capitalization of Little House symbolizes, perhaps, that more than a small structure is being considered. For us, especially given overpopulation and globalism, has not the earth become our Little House? Note that Ruth asks the house to be "all in all to me" and then moves to a pair of extraordinary lines one would expect to find in Hopkins or

Blake: "Show me the way to find the charm / That lies in every humble rite and daily task within thy walls." Ruth is open to the mystery that is in all things, an understanding that her son would later come to express as the "invisible fecundity" in all things, "a dimmed light, a meek namelessness, a hidden wholeness."[74] Is this not what we are all looking for? Is it not our inability to learn this wisdom that breeds destruction in / of our Little House? Ultimately, is not our ability to actually see these things, our capacity to learn the "lore" and "find the charm" that gives us hope and reason to shine as witnesses of God's love in this dark moment of human history? At the end of her poem, Ruth turns to reflect on the meaning of a glorious life. She says it is not for the house alone, but that one must live in this way for the sake of the whole universe. The interconnectedness of all beings with the cosmos *can be honored* if we are humble, open, and able to realize the sacred art of being alive in the most magnificent sense possible. In short, Ruth is talking about the sacred art of love. There is no higher art. Ah, this is my new favorite poem!

In closing this brief survey of 2005 publications concerning our creative response to the world, I would like to borrow one more writer's words to re-present the import of this vital theme and its reflection in Ruth's poem. Poet Kathleen Raine argues "to recreate a common language for the communication of knowledge of spiritual realities, and of the invisible order of the psyche, is the problem now for any serious artist or poet, as it should be for educators."[75] She adds, "this rediscovery, re-learning, is a long hard task—a lifelong task for those who undertake it; yet the most rewarding of all tasks, since it is a work of self-discovery which is at the same time a universal knowledge." If this is our lifelong task, how could we dare mistake the dark for the end? As Australian poet Francis Webb writes, "The tiny not the immense / Will teach our groping eyes."[76]

Conclusion

In conclusion, while I am still thinking of Ruth Merton's poem, "To Make a Tiny House," I think of the difficulties involved in such work today. I think of the evil that threatens to destroy anything and everything that is creative and constructive. But I realize, too, that there is a mystical charm in holy insecurity, in which true wisdom is communicated in such concrete and real ways that this world panics in its desire for it, for it has not learned to see what it cannot express, nor learned how to express what it cannot see in the dark. Ruth Merton understood the lore needed to make a tiny house. John of the Cross understood how to enter the dark night "unseen, my house being now all stilled."[77] And Thomas Merton realized how to live without orientations by returning to the Source of holy insecurity in this tiny house of a world, where

> No blade of grass is not counted,
> No blade of grass forgotten on this hill.
> Twelve flowers make a token garden.
> There is no path to the summit—
> No path drawn
> To Grace's house.[78]

In the end, perhaps the lesson of 2005, to paraphrase Meister Eckhart, is this: If you're looking for ways to Grace's house, that's just what you'll find—ways—and not Grace's house.[79]

Notes

1. Thomas Merton, *Cassian and the Fathers: Initiation into the Monastic Tradition*, ed. Patrick F. O'Connell, (Kalamazoo, MI: Cistercian, 2005), p. 5.

2. Thomas, Merton, "Presence, Silence, Communication," *The Springs of Contemplation* (Notre Dame, IN: Ave Maria, 1992), p. 25.

3. Thomas Merton, *The Inner Experience: Notes on Contemplation*, ed. William H. Shannon (San Francisco: HarperSanFrancisco, 2003), p. 121.

4. Thomas Merton, "The Contemplative Life in the Modern World," *Faith and Violence* (Notre Dame, IN: Notre Dame University Press, 1968), p. 215.

5. Merton, *Faith and Violence*, p. 215.

6. Anne Lamott, "A Note on the Photographs," *War and Faith in Sudan*, ed. Gabriel Meyer; Photographs by James Nicholls (Grand Rapids, MI: Eerdmans, 2005), pp. xxi-xxii.

7. Martin Buber, *Daniel: Dialogues on Realization*, trans. Maurice Friedman (New York: McGraw Hill, 1964), p. 98.

8. Buber, *Daniel*, p. 95.

9. Buber, *Daniel*, p. 94.

10. Maurice Friedman, Translator's Introduction, *Daniel*, p. 22.

11. Thomas Merton, *The Seven Storey Mountain*, (New York: Harcourt Brace, 1948), p. 422.

12. Buber, *Daniel*, pp. 98-99.

13. Thomas Merton, *Asian Journal* (New York: New Directions, 1973), p. 340.

14. Merton, *Asian Journal*, p. 338.

15. Thomas Merton, *New Seeds of Contemplation* (New York: New Directions, 1961), p. 6.

16. Thomas Merton, *New Seeds of Contemplation*, p. 9.

17. Thomas Merton, *Cassian and the Fathers* (see note 1).

18. O'Connell, Introduction, *Cassian and the Fathers*, p. xxiii.

19. Merton, *Cassian*, pp. 5-6.

20. Merton, *Cassian*, p. 6.

21. Merton, *Cassian*, p. 99.

22. Isaac of Stella, *Sermons on the Christian Year, Vol. I*, ed. Bernard McGinn (Kalamazoo, MI: Cistercian Publications, 1979), p. x. I recently asked Prof. McGinn, after a lecture he delivered on the relationship between monasticism and mysticism (a relationship he framed with ample quotes from Merton), on this particular line about mining versus his seeming preference for being undermined. He instantly replied with a broad smile: "That's my credo!"

23. Merton, *Asian Journal*, p. 340.

24. Merton, *Asian Journal*, p. 341.

25. Merton, *Cassian*, pp. 209-10.

26. Merton, *Cassian*, p. 101.

27. Angus Stuart, ed., *Across the Rim of Chaos: Thomas Merton's Prophetic Vision* (Stratton-on-the-Fosse, Radstock: Thomas Merton Society of Great Britain and Ireland, 2005).

28. Jim Forest, in his "Foreword" to Merton's *Peace in the Post-Christian Era*, ed. Patricia A. Burton (Maryknoll, NY: Orbis, 2004), wondered also about what Merton would say today; Forest assumed Merton would probably update some portions of the work; "But many paragraphs, even chapters, would remain unaltered. He would remind us once again that Christ waves no flags and that Christianity belongs to no political power bloc" (p. xxii).

29. Diana Francis, "War, Peace, Faithfulness," *Across the Rim of Chaos*, p. 11.

30. Fernando Beltrán Llavador, *Across the Rim of Chaos*, pp. 33, 41.

31. Predrag Cicovacki, ed., *Destined for Evil? The Twentieth-Century Responses* (Rochester, NY: Univ. of Rochester Press, 2005).

32. Cicovacki, *Destined for Evil?*, pp. 8-9.

33. John P. Collins's, "We are Prodigals in a Distant Land: An Essay on Thomas Merton," *Destined for Evil? The Twentieth-Century Responses*, pp. 197-203.

34. Thomas Del Prete, "Rediscovering Paradise: Thomas Merton on the Self and the Problem of Evil," *Destined for Evil? The Twentieth-Century Responses*, pp. 205-212.

35. Del Prete, *Destined for Evil?* pp. 206, 208.

36. Jonathan Montaldo, "Exposing the Deceitful Heart: A Monk's Public 'Inner Work,'" *Destined for Evil? The Twentieth-Century Response*, pp. 213-230.

37. Montaldo, *Destined for Evil?*, p. 218.

38. Thomas Merton, *Contemplation in A World of Action* (Notre Dame, IN: University of Notre Dame, 1998), p. 150.

39. Thomas Merton, *Contemplation in A World of Action*, p. 150.

40. John Eudes Bamberger, *Prophet of Renewal* (Kalamazoo, MI: Cistercian, 2005).

41. Jonathan Montaldo, Foreword, *Thomas Merton: Prophet of Renewal*. p. ix.

42. Bamberger, *Thomas Merton: Prophet of Renewal*, p. 121.

43. Bamberger, *Thomas Merton: Prophet of Renewal*, p. 121.

44. Pennington, *I Have Seen What I Was Looking For*, p. 16.

45. Robert Inchausti, *Subversive Orthodoxy: Outlaws, Revolutionaries and Other Christians in Disguise* (Grand Rapids, MI: Brazos, 2005).

46. Inchausti, *Subversive Orthodoxy*, p, 96.

47. Philip Sheldrake, "Thomas Merton's Contribution to 20th Century Spirituality: An appraisal," *The Merton Journal*, 12.1 (Eastertide, 2005), p. 32.

48. Sheldrake, *The Merton Journal*, p. 38.

49. A. M. Allchin, "Merton at Ninety," *The Merton Journal*, 12.1 (Eastertide, 2005), p. 4.

50. John Watson, *Listening to Islam: With Thomas Merton, Sayyid Qutb, Kenneth Cragg and Ziauddin Sardar: Praise, Reason and Reflection* (Brightland, Portland, UK: Sussex Academic Press, 2005).

51. Rowan Williams, *Grace and Necessity; Reflections on Art and Love* (Harrisburg, PA: Morehouse, 2005). Williams did, however, refer to Merton in another 2005 publication; see his article "The Courage not to Abstain from Speaking: Monasticism, Culture and the Modern World in the Public Interventions of a Disturbing Monk," *The Merton Journal*, 12.1 (Eastertide, 2005), pp. 8-18.

52. Williams, *Grace and Necessity*, pp. 16, 135.

53. Thomas Merton, "The Monk and Sacred Art," *The Merton Annual*, Vol. 18 (Louisville, KY: Fons Vitae, 2005), p. 16.

54. Merton, *The Merton Annual*, p. 17.

55. Thomas Merton, "Art and Worship," *The Merton Annual*, Vol. 18, p. 21.

56. Merton, *The Merton Annual*, pp. 19, 20.

57. Thomas Merton, *In the Dark Before Dawn: New Selected Poems of Thomas Merton*, ed. Lynn R. Szabo (New York: New Directions, 2005).

58. Kathleen Norris, Preface, *In The Dark Before Dawn*, p. xvii.

59. Szabo, *In the Dark Before Dawn*, p. xxvii.

60. Szabo, *In the Dark Before Dawn*, pp. xxx, xxxi.

61. Szabo, *In the Dark Before Dawn*, p. xxiii.

62 Joshua M. Harrod, *Thomas Merton's Antipoetry of Resistance* [Master's Thesis] (Radford University, 2005).

63. Harrod, *Thomas Merton's Antipoetry of Resistance*, p. 3.

64. Victor A. Kramer, "Monastic Awareness, Liturgy and Art: The Benedictine Tradition in Relation to Merton's Growing Artistic Interests," *The Merton Annual*, Vol. 18, p. 7.

65. Ron Dart, *Thomas Merton and the Beats of the North Cascades* (North Vancouver, BC: Prospect Press, 2005).

66. Dart, *Thomas Merton and the Beats of the North Cascades*, p. 41.

67. Dart, *Thomas Merton and the Beats of the North Cascades*, p. v.

68. Dart, *Thomas Merton and the Beats of the North Cascades*, p. v.

69. Monica Weis, *Thomas Merton's Gethsemani: Landscapes of Paradise*, Photographs by Harry L. Hinkle (Lexington, KY: University Press of Kentucky, 2005).

70. Patrick Hart, Preface, *Thomas Merton's Gethsemani: Landscapes of Paradise*, p. vii.

71. Paul Pearson, "A Monk with the Spiritual Equipment of an Artist: The Art of Thomas Merton," *The Merton Annual*, Vol. 18, p. 237.

72. Ruth Merton, *Tom's Book*, ed. Sheila Milton (Monterey, KY: Larkspur Press, 2005).

73. Ruth Merton, *Tom's Book*, (*joli* is French for "pretty").

74. Thomas Merton, "Hagia Sophia," *In the Dark Before Dawn*, p. 65.

75. Kathleen Raine, *The Inner Journey of the Poet* (New York: George Braziller, 1982), p. 13.

76. Francis Webb, from his poem "Five Days Old" quoted by Michael Griffith in "Thomas Merton on William Blake: 'To Look Through Matter into Eternity,'" *The Merton Annual*, Vol. 18, p. 122.

77. John of the Cross, "The Dark Night," *The Collected Works of St. John of the Cross*, trans. Kieran Kavanaugh and Otilio Rodriguez (Washington, DC: ICS Publications, 1991), p. 50.

78. Thomas Merton, "Grace's House," *In the Dark Before Dawn*, p. 93.

79. The exact quote from Meister Eckhart reads: "Whoever is seeking God by ways is finding ways and losing God, who in ways is hidden. But whoever seeks for God without ways will find him as he is in himself, and that man will live with the Son, and he is life itself." From

Sermon 5b in *Meister Eckhart: The Essential Sermons, Commentaries, Treatises, and Defense*, trans. Edmund Colledge and Bernard McGinn (New York: Paulist, 1981), pp. 183-184.

Reviews[*]

INCHAUSTI, Robert, ed., *The Pocket Thomas Merton* (London & Boston: New Seeds Books, 2005), pp. 217. ISBN 1-59030-273-7 (paperback). $6.95.

It is always strangely refreshing to be reminded of the truth at the heart of a well-worn cliché. Robert Inchausti's carefully selected collection from Thomas Merton's vast writings in *The Pocket Thomas Merton* reminds the reader that great things really do come in small packages. But yet that cliché remains a bit pedantic, especially in the context of Merton's often cliché-busting spirit. I found this little book (an abridgement of Inchausti's *Seeds* [Shambhala, 2002]) instead to be like gazing out of a small window onto a majestic mountain landscape. The frame through which one looks is

*Editor's Note:
These fifteen reviews divide into four categories. The first group consists of three texts by Thomas Merton:
1) *The Pocket Thomas Merton*;
2) *Cassian and the Fathers: Initiation into the Monastic Tradition*;
3) *Original Child Bomb* [A film inspired by Merton's poem].
The second category consists of texts about Merton:
1) *Thomas Merton: An Introduction*;
2) *Love Burning in the Soul: The Story of the Christian Mystics, from Saint Paul to Thomas Merton*;
3) *Thomas Merton's Gethsemani: Landscapes of Paradise*.
The third category emphasizes the importance of community as a conduit of faith development:
1) *Fully Human, Fully Divine: An Interactive Christology*;
2) *In the Heart of the Temple: My Spiritual Vision for Today's World*;
3) *The Way We Were: A Story of Conversion and Renewal*;
4) *Creating the Beloved Community*.
The final group focuses on spiritual direction and culture:
1) *The Inner Room: A Journey into Lay Monasticism*;
2) *With Open Heart: Spiritual Direction in the Alphonsian Tradition*;
3) *Humble and Awake: Coping with our Comatose Culture*;
4) *Engaging Benedict: What the Rule Can Teach Us Today*;
5) *Benedictine Daily Prayer: A Short Breviary*.
[GC]

decidedly small and limited but the view it provides is spectacular. My attention, though, to size here is not a critique, for the
brevity of the collection has its limitations, but I do not imagine it
was designed to satisfy entirely the reader's search or exhaust the
vast quantity of Merton's thought.

Just the same, I want to stay with the "great things in small
packages" theme as a guiding motif for this review because this
deceptively small book does present itself well for multiple types
of equally edifying usage. First, it certainly can serve as a solid
introduction to Thomas Merton for any reader who comes to it
unfamiliar with his work. It can also serve well to break down
many of the misunderstandings about Merton that seem to be currently rampant and seen in such things as the U.S. bishops' concern over whether or not to include Merton in an upcoming catechism geared for young people. Inchausti selects well from the
vast possibilities and gives the reader a glimpse into the heart of
Merton that breaks open the depths of the monk's intriguing
thought as it reveals his basic faithfulness and prophetic voice.
This editor also does well in providing clear references to the source
of each passage and lists, at the back of the book, the full titles so
the reader can easily find where to go for more in-depth searching, if he or she wishes to follow more fully a particular thread of
Merton's thought.

Secondly, this collection would serve well as a re-introduction
into Merton's writing. If someone, perhaps, encountered Merton
previously but never was able to read more of this challenging
spiritual writer's works, Inchausti provides the perfect re-entry
text. The selections in the text quickly engage the mind and heart.
And with the ample material provided, the reader is more likely
to find it difficult choosing a direction to go in, rather than not
finding enough to spark his or her interests. But that too is a tribute to the wealth and quality of Merton's work. One is rarely if
ever left, having to search for a thread to follow enthusiastically.
But even though this little book does both provide a quality entrée
into Merton for the first-timer and an enticing re-entry for the returning searcher, I believe it perhaps best serves as a book of prayer.

Staying true to the Benedictine-Cistercian monasticism that so
shaped Thomas Merton, Inchausti, in paying tribute to Merton as
a master of the paragraph, creates a text that lends itself beautifully to the practice of "Lectio Divina." Whether that was a consideration of this editor as he shaped the text I do not know but

this was how I primarily engage it. Praying with and through Merton is perhaps the best path into the heart of this writing monk as it also leads one along, through the Word to the heart of God. The editor indicates in his introduction that Merton is at his best as a writer in how he crafts paragraphs. He therefore chooses quotations that go often no more than two or three paragraphs and the majority of selections are single paragraphs in length. This certainly does highlight Merton's mastery of the paragraph but it also makes the text ideal for a slow read in the context of prayer and reflection. To pray with Merton is to get to the heart of his work and to see that all which underlies his insight, critique, and commitment is a profound love of God. The structure of this book lends itself quite well to prayer and I would highly recommend it for that purpose.

No matter, though, how the reader chooses to engage this collection, Merton's wisdom is revealed here as still so very necessary and what he offers still so very pertinent for the life of the individual seeker and the life of the world. Amid our culture's ever-increasing realization of groundlessness and impermanence which fuels the basic human temptation to grasp and cling, rigidify and codify, Merton's still unrealized "contemplative counterculture" (p. ix), as Inchausti so eloquently puts it in his introduction, needs to be cultivated more than ever. To pick up this collection of Merton's thought and to encounter him for the first time, or to come to know him all over again, or to simply pray with him, can help us all realize the vision which offers us "an interior life free from rigid philosophical categories, narrow political agendas and trite religious truisms" (p. ix). This small book expertly tackles the big task of moving us toward an authenticity of self that can help the world to continue to slough off its own falseness and illusion, if we will heed Merton's voice. So in the end we are reminded by Merton not to simply stay in our small-framed points of view but to remember the great vastness of life is not meant to be simply looked at but fully and freely lived in.

Jeff Cooper, C.S.C.

MERTON, Thomas, *Cassian and the Fathers: Initiation into the Monastic Tradition*. Edited with an Introduction by Patrick F. O'Connell. Monastic Wisdom Series 1 (Kalamazoo, Michigan: Cistercian Publications, 2005), pp. lxvi + 304. ISBN 0-87907-100-1 (cloth). $39.95; ISBN 0-87907-001-3 (paperback). $29.95.

Thomas Merton's *Cassian and the Fathers* inaugurates the new Monastic Wisdom Series published by Cistercian Publications. Patrick F. O'Connell has expertly edited and annotated these lecture notes prepared by Merton for a two part course given to novices on multiple occasions from around 1955 to 1962. The first part is called the "Prologue to Cassian" and consists of a review of ascetic and monastic spirituality from the apostolic fathers onward, with the emphasis on the fourth century. The second part is the "Lectures on Cassian." Here Merton begins by summarizing Cassian's life and teaching and then examines key sections of both the *Institutes* and *Conferences*. O'Connell's ample Introduction of fifty-one pages explains the context of these lectures delivered in Merton's official capacity as Master of Novices and discusses Merton's engagement with, and indebtedness to, Cassian and other early monastic figures. The Introduction also describes the three major and one minor witnesses to the text of *Cassian and the Fathers*, and in Appendix A (pp. 260–280) O'Connell has supplied abundant textual notes. He is to be commended for his meticulous attention to detail in the editing of this text.

Scholars and others interested in the thought and personality of Merton will find in this book a hitherto largely inaccessible aspect of the man which complements and at times contrasts with the "public" Merton found in his works written for publication, the "interpersonal" Merton revealed in his letters, and the "intimate" Merton unveiled in his recently-published journals. This work thus constitutes a unique perspective for those engaged in the retrieval of Merton's ideas and in the reconstruction of his monastic and personal identity. Yet as this book is the initial volume of the new Monastic Wisdom Series, in this review I would like to answer the following question, as suggested by the subtitle: would it be any good for initiating monastic novices or others into the monastic tradition? A reply to this question requires looking at each of the two parts of the course in some detail.

The "Prologue to Cassian" is largely derived from Pierre Pourrat's 1927 *Christian Spirituality*[1] and unpublished notes written by the Novice Master of Scourmont in Belgium, Fr. François Mahieu (later Dom Francis Acharya of Kurisumala Ashram in India), particularly in the earlier sections which summarize pre-fourth-century spirituality. There are four topics covered in these early sections: martyrdom and virginity in the first and second century, aberrant movements, Clement of Alexandria, and Origen. Merton's presentation of martyrdom and virginity as the spirituality of early Christians (pp. 7–16) is a decent introduction to the key principles, but is liable to give the impression that Christian thought on martyrdom and virginity was monolithic in the early centuries—which it was not. In the next section (pp. 16–19) Merton briefly deals with four "aberrations": Encratism, Montanism, Neoplatonism, and Gnosticism. Insofar as his terse descriptions are meant to highlight the errors of exaggerated asceticism they are successful, but they would not be acceptable today as scholars since the 1950s have done much to foster our understanding of these movements. In his discussion of Clement and Origen (pp. 20–29), Merton departs from Pourrat and relies more on Mahieu and on his own reading. As a result, these two sections are more satisfying. While one may quibble with certain details, such as Merton's understanding of the catechetical school of Alexandria (pp. 23–24), here he gives a pretty good summary of the works and the key points of the spiritual doctrine of these two Alexandrians.

Once he turns to the monastic figures of the fourth century, Merton depends more on his own reading of the primary texts and secondary scholarship. He deals with Antony (pp. 31–39), Pachomius (pp. 39–45), Basil (pp. 45–51), Gregory of Nazianzus (pp. 51–52), Gregory of Nyssa (pp. 52–60), Palestinian monasticism, including Jerome (pp. 60–69), Mesopotamian and Syrian monasticism (pp. 69–71), the desert fathers of Nitria and Scete and their apophthegmata (pp. 71–88), and Evagrius Ponticus (pp. 88–96). As a whole, these sections are better than the preceding as Merton's own greater engagement with these topics and thinkers is more evident.

His treatment of Antony's doctrine depends solely on the *Life of Antony*, an approach that would be questionable today given the numerous other ancient sources which preserve sayings and teachings of Antony, and given especially the widespread acceptance of the authenticity of Antony's seven letters preserved in Coptic. The section on Antony is more successful as an introduction to the *Life*—surely the seminal and single most important monastic text—than it is to the historical Antony.

Armand Veilleux's three volume translation of the Pachomian corpus,[2] of course, was not available to Merton for his discussion of Pachomius, so he is limited to using Jerome's Latin translation of the Pachomian rules. Still, his presentation is judicious: Merton avoids the pitfall found in earlier scholarship which saw the strictness of the Pachomian organization as amounting to a rigid system of military efficiency. Nonetheless, one detects here, perhaps, Merton's own bias influencing his treatment, in that he frequently compares Pachomian coenobitism to eremiticism, a concern not found in the sources.

In his survey of Basil's life and doctrine, while one could fault Merton for his facile characterizations of Basil (e.g. he is an "active, ascetic, organizing, administrating" saint rather than an "interior and contemplative" saint [p. 48]), he provides a summary of Basil's ascetical theology and his notion of coenobitism. Gregory of Nazianzus is mentioned almost in passing without any mention of his doctrine, seemingly because Merton must have considered him a "contemplative." Gregory of Nyssa, whom Merton calls "a *great contemplative theologian*" (p. 53), receives a far more extensive treatment. Here Merton shows himself familiar with recent critical scholarship, and his excitement over and personal engagement with Gregory is evident. All this contributes to making this section one of the best in this part of the course. Merton summarizes the key themes found in more than a half-dozen works by Gregory, stressing that his theology is drawn from his mystical experience.

The next section, on Palestinian monasticism, is less satisfying. Here Merton merely summarizes Jerome's *Life of Hilarion* and gives five very brief notices on other Palestinian monks from the fourth through seventh centuries without any discussion of their monastic significance or teaching. He then turns to Jerome and spends more time on giving an account of his life and controversies than his monastic doctrine, which is limited to comments on two excerpts from one of his monastic letters. While Merton fails to demonstrate that there was anything distinctive or even significant about Palestinian monasticism, his discussion of Jerome would be a good introduction to the complex saint if one were encountering him for the first time. Merton's treatment of Mesopotamian and Syrian monasticism is hardly more satisfying. Though it is little more than a list of names, stylites are discussed sympatheti-cally and not simply dismissed as bizarre. Nonetheless, Merton ultimately views both Palestinian and Syrian monasticism as de-fective for their extremism, betraying an implicit comparison to the "norms" of the desert fathers or Benedictine monasticism that does not obtain historically.

In the next section, Merton's favoritism towards the desert fa-thers of Nitria and Scete and their apophthegmata is apparent throughout, as evidenced once again by his engagement with criti-cal scholarship on them. He discusses the sources for the spiritu-ality of the desert fathers and the signal importance of the apophthegmata, and then proceeds to give an insightful thematic survey of their teaching. This results in the production of one of the best sections of this course. Indeed, the abiding interest in the desert fathers today is due in no small part to Merton's enthusi-asm for them. His treatment of Macarius is dominated by a dis-cussion of the authenticity of the pseudo-Macarian writings, on which subject he is conversant with the best scholarship of his day, and by a description of Messalianism, a "heresy" supposedly con-tained in the pseudo-Macarian writings. While Merton was evi-dently charged by this academic debate, one would question whether his summary of it is appropriate for an introduction to the monastic tradition, especially since not much is said that per-tains to *living* the monastic life.

In the final section of the "Prologue to Cassian," on Evagrius Ponticus, Merton again displays critical engagement with some of the best monastic scholarship of his day. Though this section also suffers from too much summarization of academic debates of ques-tionable relevance to monastic formation, it is salvaged by an ex-cellent account of the Evagrian doctrine of prayer.

Despite some good discussions, in the opinion of this reviewer the "Prologue to Cassian" would be on the whole an unsatisfying treatment of early Christian monasticism if it were to be used to-day as introduction to the monastic tradition. Though Merton was surely a pioneer in the retrieval of early monasticism, his presen-tation of the material is too reflective of the state of scholarship in his day and his own biases to be a reliable guide for those first encountering the monastic tradition. For example, he implicitly accepts the traditional view of monastic origins in which Antony is the first monk ever; influenced by his anchoritism, Pachomius initiates the coenobitic life; from these two men and in these two distinct forms all Christian monasticism spreads throughout Egypt, the East, and the West. In reality the development of monasticism in the third and fourth centuries was far more complex. The simple fact is that today we have much better understanding of early Christian monasticism for the period covered by Merton here, and much better surveys of it that would better serve the interested reader.[3] O'Connell informs us that Merton abandoned this course after 1962 in favor of another course entitled "Pre-Benedictine Monasticism," which covered much of the same material, but with more focus on Syrian and Palestinian monasticism (p. lxii). Perhaps this switch indicates Merton's own dissatisfaction with the course. Fortunately, plans are underway for the publication of "Pre-Benedictine Monasticism" in the Monastic Wisdom Series.

We turn now to the "Lectures on Cassian." Here Merton abandons Pourrat and Mahieu and relies upon his own reading of Cassian, though he used Owen Chadwick for historical background.[4] He begins with an account of Cassian's importance due to his influence not only on the monastic founders of the West such as St. Benedict, but also on medieval saints such as Sts. Thomas and Dominic. He then addresses the accuracy of the charge often made against Cassian, that he is a "semi-Pelagian." Merton adeptly handles the theological point at issue, demonstrating that it is erroneous to label Cassian a "semi-Pelagian." In the course of this he provides a summary of the basic teaching of *Conference* 13. Merton's choice to start here was a good one, I think, especially since his audience, even if they knew nothing else about Cassian, may have heard the heresy associated with his name. This enables Merton to launch into Cassian's teaching without lingering suspicion of his orthodoxy on the part of the audience.

Merton's first discussion of the monastic doctrine of Cassian comes in the course of his treatment of Cassian's life. After a brief description of Cassian's monastic residence in Bethlehem, he narrates his sojourn in Egypt by following the chronology presented by Cassian himself in the *Conferences*. This affords Merton the opportunity to summarize the contents of each conference as he tracks Cassian's progress through Egypt. For *Conferences* 3, 4, 11, 12, 14, 15, 18, 21, 22, and 23 Merton gives longer summaries, often filled with his own insight and observations and listing the key points of the conference. Shorter summaries are also given for *Conferences* 6, 7, 17, and 20. Worthy of particular mention are Merton's discussion of perfection (*Conference* 11); his insightful summary of "the three kinds of monks" (*Conference* 18) in which he describes more generally his understanding of the nature of the monastic vocation (pp. 119–20); and his critical presentation of Cassian's teaching on "wanting good but doing evil" (*Conference* 23) in which he speaks on the necessity of humility. Hence, in the course of this narrative, Merton has managed to provide a basic orientation for reading fourteen of Cassian's twenty-four conferences.

Merton next turns to a brief account of the Origenist controversy, which precipitated Cassian's departure from Egypt. Here Merton is far too unnuanced in his presentation of the very complex issue of Origenism. Some statements are wrong, such as the implication that Athanasius was an Origenist (p. 133). Fortunately, the interested reader has more recent and more satisfying accounts to supplant this one.[5] Merton then recounts Cassian's progress from Egypt to Constantinople and then to Marseilles, where he founded a monastery. This travelogue gives Merton the opportunity to speak briefly of John Chrysostom, Martin of Tours, Lérinian monasticism, and Caesarius of Arles, all but the first important for situating Cassian's monastic project in Gaul. In writing for Gallic monks, Cassian made "the great synthesis of monastic doctrine and adapt[ed] the Eastern tradition to the West" (p. 139).

The narrative of Cassian's life completed, Merton next turns to a detailed survey of the *Institutes* and *Conferences* 1, 2, 4, 9, 10, and 16. Though these sections seem to consist largely of summaries of the text under discussion, they are much more than that. They are astute distillations of Cassian's monastic doctrine. Furthermore, Merton continually tries to relate the monastic practices and teachings described by Cassian to the disciplines of his own monastery, modifying Cassian if necessary. In addition, he frequently uses the text of Cassian to discourse on his own perceptive viewpoints gained from reading Cassian, at times in dialogue with other monastic fathers, such as in his discussion of the crucial importance of obedience for any monk (pp. 148–49), of the tendency for monks to avoid true self-generosity (p. 171), and of how sadness can be sinful (pp. 179–80). In his treatment of the "eight principal vices" (*Institutes* 5-12) Merton often calls attention to Cassian's psychological acumen, thereby relating the categories of Cassian's ancient "therapy of the soul" to those of the modern science of psychology. Especially in his discussion of acedia, vainglory, and pride (*Institutes* 10-12) Merton weds his own psychological insight to Cassian's in a particularly fruitful way.

Yet it is in the final section of the course, in his discussion of *Conferences* 1, 2, 4, 9, 10, and 16 (pp. 203–59), that Merton is at his best. Though at times he devolves into mere summary, more often he distills Cassian's monastic wisdom found in these most important conferences through the lens of his own experience. Of particular excellence is his discussion of the proximate and ultimate goals of the monastic life (*Conference* 1) and his treatment of Cassian's teaching on monastic prayer (*Conferences* 9 and 10). This close reading and insightful presentation of Cassian in a way well-suited for modern-day audiences results in a new expression of classical monastic wisdom.

All in all, Merton's interpretations and explanations of Cassian constitute a "bridge" between the fifth-century monastic father and his present-day heirs and readers. Merton makes the sometimes obscure and verbose Cassian intelligible and applicable to modern-day sensibilities and concerns. Merton is no mere epitomizer of Cassian but rather his exegete and spokesman for men and women of today. In Merton, one hears the voice of the great synthesizer of monastic doctrine speaking to a contemporary audience and addressing their concerns.

For these reasons, I think that the "Lectures on Cassian" would be an excellent companion to reading Cassian himself if it were to be used today as introduction to the monastic tradition. There is really nothing like Merton's commentary on Cassian to help orient first-time readers through the massive works of Cassian.[6] Though today we have the excellent translations of Cassian by Boniface Ramsey, his introductions and annotations offer the reader little help when confronted with over 1000 pages of Cassian in translation.[7] Hence Merton could here supply a real need, for he treats of twenty-one of Cassian's twenty-four conferences, whether providing a short summary or discussing it at length. Merton would thus be a reliable guide for approaching Cassian.

Accordingly, Merton's *Cassian and the Fathers* is an excellent choice to inaugurate Cistercian Publications new Monastic Wisdom Series, just as his *The Climate of Monastic Prayer* was for the inauguration of the same publisher's Cistercian Studies Series back in 1969.[8] Though I have expressed my reservations about the "Prologue to Cassian," I would heartily recommend the "Lectures on Cassian" to anyone interested in drinking from this great fifth-century source of monastic wisdom.

Notes

1. Pierre Pourrat, *Christian Spirituality, Vol. I: From the Time of Our Lord till the Dawn of the Middle Ages* Translated by W. H. Mitchell and S. P. Jacques (1927; Westminster, Maryland: Newman, 1953).
2. *Pachomian Koinonia*, 3 vols. Translated by Armand Veilleux. Cistercian Studies Series 45-47 (Kalamazoo, Michigan: Cistercian Publications, 1980-82).
3. For example: William Harmless, S.J., *Desert Christians: An Introduction to the Literature of Early Monasticism* (Oxford: Oxford University Press, 2004). O'Connell lists other items in Appendix C.
4. Owen Chadwick, *John Cassian: A Study in Primitive Monasticism* (Cambridge: University Press, 1950; 2nd ed. 1968). Merton obviously used the first edition.
5. For example: Elizabeth A. Clark, *The Origenist Controversy: the Cultural Construction of an Early Christian Debate* (Princeton, New Jersey: Princeton University Press, 1992).
6. The only comparable thing is Adalbert de Vogüé, "Understanding Cassian: A Survey of the Conferences," *Cistercian Studies Quarterly* 19.2 (1982): 101–21, which attempts to help orient the reader by explaining the structure of the conferences. Vogüé does not deal with Cassian's teaching as Merton does.
7. John Cassian, *The Conferences.* Translated by Boniface Ramsey. Ancient Christian Writers 57 (New York/Mahwah: Paulist, 1997) and John Cassian, *The Institutes.* Translated by Boniface Ramsey. Ancient Christian Writers 58 (New York/Mahwah: Newman, 2000).
8. Thomas Merton, *The Climate of Monastic Prayer.* Cistercian Studies Series 1 (Spencer, Mass.: Cistercian Publications, 1969).

Mark DelCogliano

BECKER, Holly (Producer) and SCHONEGEVEL, Carey (Director), *Original Child Bomb* (Santa Barbara, CA: Unquiet Projects, 2004. DVD available for purchase at www.originalchildbomb.com $25.00.

Perhaps the greatest testament to the urgency, necessity, and achievement of this remarkable film adaptation of Merton's 1962 poem comes from the audience who most needs to see it: the young people of today. After viewing the film several times myself, I decided—in light of the current nuclear crisis in North Korea—to screen it for my sophomore world literature class. I was horrified to discover that only about one third of the class was aware of this crisis, and further shocked to learn that only about half of the students could name the two Japanese cities destroyed by atomic bombs in 1945. So we watched the film, and the written comments I received about it were both stirring and affirming. "Of all the movies I've ever watched in all of my school years, this one has affected me the most," wrote one student. "This movie has made an impact on my life and I was truly moved . . . I had only read about Hiroshima and Nagasaki in high school, and was hardly fazed. I had no idea of the destruction and horrific genocide the bombs caused," wrote another. Capturing perfectly the essence of all the comments I received, a student who was literally moved to tears in the classroom wrote of her reaction to the film, "Heartbreaking. Repulsive. May God have mercy on us all."

Many of my students are now reading for themselves Merton's poem, so the film certainly succeeds in inspiring interest in Merton's work. But to consider the film only as an adaptation of, or homage to, Merton's poem is unfair. The poetic image, as my students are learning, is different from the cinematic image, and while the message of both poem and film is the same, the film merits consideration of its own.

The film is comprised primarily of carefully edited archival footage, much of it now declassified and exhibited here for the first time. The film opens with shots from 1940s Hiroshima. Children are playing, people are walking the streets—smiling, shopping, working, simply going about the routine of daily life. There is a startling low angle shot of a little girl, a cut to a plane in the sky, and as Sergei Eisenstein expressed in his early theory of film montage, the juxtaposition of innocence and power is shocking. These are real people, the audience thinks, and that is a real plane, yet how the two collide with one another seems horrifyingly unreal. When the bomb makes impact, then, instead of seeing a literal image of its destruction, we see a starkly terrifying animation sequence that imagines what still is almost impossible to imagine.

Throughout, the film utilizes this rhythm of contrasts, what Eisenstein called oppositions. Beyond the effective and frequent juxtaposition of live action and animation, black and white footage alternates with color; newsreel footage of the bombings and Cold War nuclear tests is contrasted with reaction from contemporary students; and throughout we see and hear from American children and Japanese children, the young and the old, those scarred emotionally and those maimed physically. An occasional cold voiceover recites passages from the poem, and haunting whispers murmur as we watch past and present footage of modern Japan and New York, images of nuclear testing and Ground Zero. Typical documentary techniques of interviews and voiceovers are used sparingly and effectively. I don't think I will ever forget the pronouncement of President Truman, that the victory achieved by the dropping of the atomic bombs represents "the greatest achievement of organized science in history."

Perhaps the greatest effect of this constant shifting of perspectives is that it underscores the universality and enduring implications of those horrible days in August 1945. The film makes clear that rather than being a past threat, the possibility of nuclear holocaust is even more real today. The film only conveys the statistics that really matter; beyond the obligatory death tolls of the atomic bombings and the horrifying numbers of people who later died from radiation effects, the film makes clear the fact that there still exist 22,000 nuclear warheads, with more likely in production.

I'll not summarize here all the sequences in the film; to do so would detract from your own first encounter with it. I do want to address, however, a few techniques that emphasize the resonance of past events upon the present. In one effective sequence, for example, we meet a young Japanese boy who explains that when he first learned about the atomic bombings in the sixth grade, "it hurt [his] heart a little." This is a young man who, like many young Japanese, has adopted the dress, the music, the strut of American youth culture. Ironically, this child of a conquered and defeated nation has become as aloof as his conqueror. Yet the film depicts him, in color, walking against the black and white backdrop of the ruins of Hiroshima and Nagasaki, while we listen to the voices of survivors on the soundtrack. Whether he realizes it or not, the boy is a product of the past. This footage contrasts with that of American high school students who express a full range of opinions about their feelings about the bombings, and their sentiments range from compassion to rage, from shock to a disturbing sense of inevitability, even perhaps ambivalence. In his poem, Merton certainly wanted to address not only the horror of the children who died, but also the tragedy of all the children who might die in similar attacks. It is chilling to see and hear them represented here.

This childlike presence is beautifully achieved in the film by the voice of a girl who recites an alphabet in which, for example, D stands for "destruction" and N stands for "nuclear." And the film is meant to appeal to youth; its ambient soundtrack is immediately recognizable to a young audience who know and admire much of the music and musicians who contributed to the film. Indeed, much of the film's pacing and editing is very similar to contemporary music videos. Finally, that the film is fully aware of itself as a film is demonstrated by the frequent use of onscreen text and literal stops, reversals, and fast forwards. This approach achieves a jerky, edgy effect that is relevant to today's new digital media, but it also echoes the tone and rhythm of the Merton poem.

At one point in *Original Child Bomb*, we hear from a Japanese woman who recounts the story of her young daughter who survived the bombing only to die a few months later of a seizure caused by radiation effects. The mother remembers her grief, and says "but I suppose you cannot undo the past." Merton certainly hoped to redeem the past with his poem, and this film adaptation has the same aim. A terrible beauty was indeed born in August 1945, and though the human capacity for hope, compassion, and empathy was not destroyed by the bombs, it certainly needs constant nurturing from generation to generation.

Original Child Bomb is essential viewing for anyone who wants to be reminded of the responsibility we have to teach today's young people the lessons of past failures. Though the film does contain some graphic, even shocking images, it is certainly appropriate for high school and college audiences, and is highly recommended for classroom use. When the film concluded, my class literally left the room in stunned silence. But silence, as Merton knew so well, can be a remarkable catalyst for action.

David King

SHANNON, William H., *Thomas Merton: An Introduction* (Cincinnati, OH: St. Anthony Messenger Press, 2005), pp. xiv-199. ISBN 0-86716-710-6 (paperback). $16.95.

As expected from William Shannon, this is an excellent book. It is a revision of his *Something of a Rebel* (1997), which I have not read, and now will not need to. In the introduction, Shannon makes it clear that although he has changed this title, he is not backing away from its idea of Merton as in some sense a rebel. And in what sense? In his refusal "to be content with the *status quo* when it no longer nourished the human spirit" (p. 2), and in his ongoing work of making his faith and his monastic tradition truly his own in response to conventionality in all its forms.

For Shannon, the pivotal moment in Merton's life was his baptism in Corpus Christi Church in New York on November 16, 1938. Rather than give simply a chronological outline of Merton's life, he begins with an account of the summer of 1939 which Merton and his closest friends spent in Olean, New York, writing the Great American Novel and generally enjoying life, a time when the freshness of his baptismal experience was still with Merton, and before he found his monastic vocation.

From that summer in Olean, Shannon harks back to Merton's birth in France, his sojourns in various countries before and after the death of, first, his mother, and then his father, and his time at Cambridge and Columbia; and he looks forward to Merton's time of teaching at St. Bonaventure College and his 27 years as a monk of Gethsemani. He identifies two miracles of these monastic years (this is what Merton needs for canonization, right?): first, that Merton stayed at Gethsemani in the face of every temptation and provocation; and second, given the constraints of the monastic timetable, "the staggering amount of writing … that leaped out from his old banged-up typewriter" (p. 33). In outlining Merton's monastic years, he includes all the major elements—his years of preparation for profession and ordination, his years of teaching and pastoral responsibility as master of scholastics and master of novices, and the hermitage years. The one omission that I found curious in this section was the lack of any reference to the time of emotional or psychic breakdown (if that is the right word) between early fall of 1949 and December 1950 which Merton describes in *The Sign of Jonas*, a time which in my own view is very important for our understanding of the shift from the earlier Merton to later Merton.

The second chapter begins provocatively with its very title: "Is Merton for today, or is he passé?" The answer is predictable, but the question is still important. Acknowledging that Merton's popularity had begun to wane before his death, he asserts that since his death in 1968 his popularity has only increased, attributing this to the genuineness which comes so strongly through his writing, his ability to articulate the human condition, his respect for and interest in the people he encountered, his bursting of the bounds of the cultural limitation typical of monks, Americans and Catholics in his time, and his astonishing capacity (something to which I can personally attest) to act as spiritual-director-at-a-distance for thousands upon thousands.

All this adds up to Merton's role as public intellectual, or "American prophet," as Robert Inchausti calls him. Given the brevity of this chapter, however, Shannon might well have included in it the section of the next chapter in which he sets forth a paradigm of views of Merton based on responses to *The Seven Storey Mountain*. One group, small and shrinking I cannot doubt, sees Merton as still the apostle of *contemptus mundi*, and thus faithful to the original insights of the autobiography. A second group sees him as having betrayed the monastic vision of the *Mountain* either by becoming a secular humanist, a position with which Shannon firmly disagrees, or as having betrayed its Christian vision by his explorations of psychoanalysis, Eastern religion and Communism, with David Cooper as emblematic of the first sub-group, and Alice von Hildebrand as representative of the second. The third group, to which Shannon himself belongs, and in which I would also locate myself, sees Merton as having moved beyond the narrowness and rigidity of his autobiography to a pluralistic and integrative worldview. As Shannon concludes, if Merton's autobiography "continues to appeal to a whole new generation of readers, this is not because of, but in spite of, its theological stance. For today's readers the magnanimity of the writer somehow transcends the narrowness of his theology" (p. 62).

In the rest of this chapter, Shannon deals with the eight major themes of Merton's writings, which he lists as interiority, prayer, God, human identity, community/person and collectivity/individual, freedom as the expression of one's inner truth, and Zen. Each of these is manifestly essential for a broad understanding of Merton; and Shannon's summaries of them are balanced and helpful.

Then comes a very practical chapter: how to read Merton, given his massive and unsystematic corpus. He shares with the reader Merton's own classification of his major writings, including the famous graph (p. 126); and he acknowledges frankly that Merton could write badly as well as eloquently. Beside this he affirms that Merton's writing continued to improve as time went on, simply because he continued to write, and, I would add, to write in dialogical response to his constructive critics. Where then to start? Shannon opts for the *SSM* as the book with which to begin, and he expands on his choice with a very interesting commentary on the titles of its chapters. After the *SSM*, he lists *The Sign of Jonas, No Man Is An Island, New Seeds of Contemplation, Conjectures of a Guilty*

Bystander, Zen and the Birds of Appetite and the *Asian Journal* as first-order choices. Beyond these, of course, lie the vast reaches of the published letters and journals, which offer to the careful student a source of information and perspective which can richly contextualize the reading of the major works.

I am regularly asked to advise beginning readers of Thomas Merton on how to start and continue their initial acquaintance with this ever-searching monk, writer and pilgrim. For the foreseeable future, this book will be my suggested starting-place, given the depth of its scholarship in limited compass, its accessible and balanced treatment of man and writings, and its practicality. I have already suggested, in fact, to the Thomas Merton Society of Canada, that at future public events we keep a supply of this book on hand for immediate response to this kind of inquiry. Once again our gratitude goes to William Shannon for a uniquely useful contribution to our knowledge and understanding of Thomas Merton.

Donald Grayston

HARPUR, James, *Love Burning in the Soul: The Story of the Christian Mystics, from Saint Paul to Thomas Merton* (Boston: New Seeds, 2005), pp. xi + 241. ISBN 1-59030-112-9 (paperback). $16.95.

The subtitle of this historical survey of the Christian mystical tradition is a helpful indicator of the book's approach and its value – as well as of its interest to the reader of *The Merton Annual*. Harpur, a poet and literature professor from University College, Cork, takes a predominantly narrative approach to his subject: his "story of the Christian mystics" emphasizes the figures he considers the outstanding representatives of the Christian spiritual tradition from its beginnings through the twentieth century. Forty-nine figures are discussed, one of them, the influential neo-Platonist Plotinus, a non-Christian; most of the thirty-nine men and ten women are familiar names, though a few, like the Beguine Marguerite Porete (burned at the stake in Paris in 1310), have become prominent only relatively recently. (Actually the first figure discussed is Jesus himself, though including him as one of the "brackets" in the subtitle apparently seemed to author or publisher a bit presumptuous.) Each of the seventeen chronologically ordered chapters typically focuses on two or three mystical writers from a particular era (four for "The Rhineland Mystics" [ch. 8] and "The English Flowering" [ch. 10] and a perhaps excessive five [one a Spaniard!] for "French

Mystics and Quietism" [ch. 14]). But the subtitle is quite properly "story" not "stories": the author emphasizes the developments and continuities (as well as changes and even discontinuities) of the mystical tradition and the relationships and influences that connect his various subjects, rather than treating them in isolation from one another and their times.

Harpur states at the very beginning of his work that it is "not aimed at theologians or other specialists but at those who have little or no knowledge of the subject matter and who wish to dip their toes into the vast ocean of mysticism" (p. ix), and indeed readers who are already familiar with the field will find little here that is new. This does not mean, however, that the treatment is hackneyed or superficial. The author has clearly done his homework, as his references to primary source materials and to multi-volume works such as Bernard McGinn's *The Presence of God* and the Crossroad *World Spirituality* volumes attest, and he has summarized the material in an attractive and incisive fashion. He presupposes no previous knowledge of the subject, providing in his Introduction helpful definitions of mysticism and contemplation, a brief analysis of the distinction between apophatic and cataphatic mysticism, an overview of the traditional three ways (purgation, illumination, union) and other helpful orientation notes. Each chapter, typically ten to twelve pages, begins with an overview of the main events of the period, both secular and religious, and often includes brief mention of other significant figures not to be discussed in detail (for instance Charles de Foucauld and Simone Weil in the final chapter). Then each of the mystics representing that era is considered according to a standard pattern: a brief paragraph relating him or her to the historical context, a presentation of biographical highlights, and a capsule summary of the mystic's teaching. None of the sketches runs more than about four pages, so the material is obviously compressed, but Harpur has generally done a fine job in getting to the heart of the teaching of each of the figures chosen. As he acknowledges, this is no more than dipping a toe in the ocean, but he does provide encouragement to his readers to wade, or plunge, in deeper after these initial contacts, and his extensive bibliography (pp. 235-41) provides ample resources for doing so (though an arrangement that grouped works according to periods or specific figures rather than simply alphabetically might have been more useful).

There are some built-in drawbacks to the approach the author has taken, which he acknowledges but doesn't completely overcome. His interest in symmetry and continuity leads him to give relatively the same amount of space and attention to historical periods with little inclination or sympathy toward mysticism, like the Enlightenment (ch. 15) and the nineteenth century (ch. 16), as to high points of the tradition like the fourth century, the Age of Augustine and Gregory of Nyssa (ch. 3) or the twelfth century of Bernard and Hildegarde (ch. 5) – though he does give multiple chapters to the geographically varied mysticism of the fourteenth century, which spans Germany (ch. 8), England (ch. 10), and Italy (ch. 11). There is also the problem that Orthodox mysticism (ch. 9) and Protestant mysticism (ch. 12) are restricted to single chapters – though in the latter case further Protestant figures appear in chapters 15 and 16. Perhaps the least satisfactory chapter is the penultimate one on "Romantics and Nature Mysticism," which bridges the period between the Enlightenment and the twentieth century by focusing on the English poets Blake and Wordsworth, an anomalous shift in genre evidently due to the perceived scarcity of writers of mystical prose during the period (comparable figures such as Crashaw or Traherne in the seventeenth century, or Jacopone da Todi and Dante at the beginning of the fourteenth, don't rate even a mention, though they are certainly closer to the main line of the Christian mystical tradition than the two Romantics); the discussions are interesting in themselves, and while Blake is clearly an heir of Jacob Boehme, discussed in chapter 12 – as well as being an (unmentioned) influence on Merton, to be considered in the following chapter – Wordsworth's "mysticism" and his Christianity were largely successive and mutually exclusive phases of his life, so he fits somewhat awkwardly within the overall development of the "story" Harpur is telling.

Merton's four and a half pages (he is paired with Pierre Teilhard de Chardin as exemplars of "The Modern Age") provide a competent introduction to his life and thought within the small compass allowed, relying exclusively on *The Seven Storey Mountain, New Seeds of Contemplation* and, somewhat surprisingly perhaps, *The Ascent to Truth* to sketch in his teaching on contemplation and the true and false self. While Merton's mature interest in social and political issues and in Eastern religious thought is mentioned, these aspects are left undeveloped; more attention is paid to his familiarity with Freud and Jung, in "a world in which psychology and the psychoanalytic movement have made their mark" (p. 209), not an area that would probably occur to most commentators limited to so brief a scope, but a way of relating Merton's interest in the self to that of his age. Harpur mentions that Merton "had at least two spiritual experiences that affected him profoundly" (p. 210), then identifies them as his sense of his dead father's presence while in Rome at age eighteen and his awareness of the divine presence in the Havana church during his 1940 visit – rather than the "Fourth and Walnut" and Polonnaruwa experiences, neither of which is touched on at all, that most readers at all familiar with Merton's life would probably expect. But his final paragraph on the spiritual journey, the passage through the wilderness and discovery of peace "in the heart of this darkness" (p. 213), ends the discussion, and the "story" proper, on an authentic Mertonian note.

Harpur concludes the book with a brief Epilogue that looks to the future, recognizing a decreasing interest in institutional Christianity in the West, due in large part, he suggests, to the Church's failure to satisfy people's "hunger for spiritual and mystical experience" (p. 216). He sees signs of hope in the development of various "grassroots initiatives" that have arisen to meet this need, including Taizé, interest in Celtic spirituality (about which he is somewhat ambivalent in so far as it has become faddish – an attitude similar to Merton's feelings about Zen in the '60s), Creation spirituality (about which he could perhaps be a bit more ambivalent), and various retreat movements, including some that might be unfamiliar to an American audience (Julian Gatherings and the Quiet Garden movement); somewhat surprisingly, perhaps, there is no mention of centering prayer and its organizational arm, Contemplative Outreach, or of the World Community for Christian Meditation, associated with the Benedictines John Main and Lawrence Freeman. Harpur concludes that the various movements he has mentioned "are positive signs that Christianity is capable of renewing itself spiritually and that its long contemplative tradition still has relevance today" (p. 219); he also cautions that mystical experience is not an end in itself, not an effort to attain "personal ecstasy in a cocoon of peacefulness" (p. 219), but rather a way of participating in the divine life of compassion and love— the "Love Burning in the Soul" of the book's title—that extends itself to all humanity and all creation. This sane, balanced perspective, which characterizes the entire book, makes it an effective and attractive primer for those being introduced, or discover-

ing for themselves, the rich Christian mystical/contemplative tradition.

Patrick F. O'Connell

WEIS, Monica, *Thomas Merton's Gethsemani: Landscapes of Paradise*,
photographs by Harry L. Hinkle (Lexington, KY: The University
Press of Kentucky, 2005), pp. 157. ISBN 0-8131-2347-8 (hardcover).
$29.95.

One cannot read far into Merton's writings, from books to poems to journals, before being introduced to the natural landscapes
of Gethsemani; its "green ice and its dead trees and silences" (p.
78). Commentary on deer, day, sky, heat, poison ivy and weather
are typical first lines of many of his journal entries. And yet, with
all so many books about Merton's spirituality, only one recent volume, Kathleen Deignan's *When the Trees Say Nothing: Thomas
Merton's Writings on Nature*,[1] has addressed this significant source
for Merton's prayer life. The current volume fills this gap.

In *Thomas Merton's Gethsemani: Landscapes of Paradise*, a Merton
scholar and a Kentucky photographer have joined forces to produce a visual paradise, a "beautiful book with many windows"
(p. 1) says Jonathan Montaldo in the book's "Introduction." Patrick
Hart's "Foreword" suggests this elegant volume calls us to our
own pilgrimage through the Kentucky landscape that formed and
fed Merton's spiritual life. Merton lived on the margins of the
worlds here; it was his desert as well as his desert island. In these
woods, ice storms and visits from wildlife, Merton refined his ecological and sacramental vision, where each creature is "God coming to us" (p. 97). This book invites us to walk in the actual steps
of Father Louis. Prose and pictures intertwine, with Merton's own
voice and photographs peeking through those of Weis and Hinkle.
Here amidst the knobs, mists and woods of central Kentucky, Weis
and Hinkle beckon us to participate in the peace of this place.

The Introduction and five chapters are orchestrated to mimic
the trajectory of Merton's life at Gethsemani. Merton first arrived
at the abbey after dark in April, 1941, and already saw the landscape unfolding as soul music. Hinkle offers a photograph of a
starry night, one Merton might have seen that first night on the
"pale ribbon of road" that led to Trappist, Kentucky. Hinkle's photographs locate Merton's favorite haunts and hideouts. His photographs, each beautifully showcased with plenty of white space

on good paper, deliver us right into the middle of what Merton saw, and like him, we are called "to see with the heart" (p. 88).

Subsequent chapters follow Merton, or Father Louis as he was known, to the rusting red trailer and tool shed he used as early hermitages. Weis weaves her narrative into Merton's, to demonstrate that through nature "he understood 'something essential' about himself" (p. 88). As she harvested journal entries as departure points, we delight in the "Om" of the bullfrog, the woods that "cultivate me with their silences" (p. 86), and the *point vierge* between night dark and dawn, the pure nothingness that "attuned his heart to the cosmos" (p. 95). We encounter a few of Merton's favorite things: ponds, trees, weather, seasons, times of the day, and animals. Merton loved ponds, Weis says (Merton even named his poetry magazine *Monks Pond*) (p. 82). He loved to pray while walking under the trees, and described open-air prayer as "saturating the woods with psalms" (p. 86). Singled out by Hinkle's lens is one tall cedar tree next to the enclosure wall in shadows and light. These first landscapes move to photographs of those man-made: the east monastery wall (p. 24), the shops building and woodshed, scriptorium, a fence near the dairy barn. Hinkle, in the style of Merton, photographed landscapes and buildings, but also such ordinary things as "buckets, benches ... fence posts, [and] firewood" (p. xi).

The book's emphasis falls on Merton's final and most famous hermitage. Evocative photographs capture the stillness of the place, a place congenial to the solitude that Merton craved. Like Merton's own life, Weis and Hinkle move toward a conclusion to emphasize the conscious ecology of the smallest things: a bird, stones, a cup, a pair of jeans. Here we best see Merton's *one-pointed* unity of nature in God.

Before I opened the cover to discover Hinkle's fine photographs and Weis's gentle prose I held the book on my lap a good long while. I recalled my many trips to these same landscapes – the broad plains and grand vistas of monastery land, a Christmas Eve ice storm, a shivering white horse across a fence line, the steamy mist of July mornings after Lauds, sitting out an electric storm in a dark chapel, emerald moss encountered on the north side of a tree on the way to Brother René's prayer hut. Each of these deepens the miracle of Daily Office, the monk's chanting, the silence and sense of goodness that is found inside and outside the abbey walls. I longed to encounter not only Merton's Gethsemani in this volume, but my own Gethsemani, an invisible shimmer of God pulsing though field, flower, storm, mist, and moss.

Let's face it: it is easy enough to *not* go outside at Gethsemani— an expanse of dining room windows allows us to feast on the landscape in the comfort of heat and air conditioning, coffee cup, kitchen snacks, and favorite book in hand. The Vigil of the Hours keeps us busy, along with daily rosary and Chapel Talks, with naps and meals sandwiched in between. But it is in those in-between times that the *place* itself rises up and calls us outside, like medicine for the soul.

Thanks to Jonathan Montaldo's Introduction, it doesn't take but a few pages to consider this almost a poetic and artistic guidebook; like Merton, we too find these landscapes a source of prayer. Weis immerses us in geography on both sides of the road: the abbey itself, Dom Frederic's Lake, McGuinty's Hollow, and Saint Malachy's Field. Now the knobs that I look at from the retreatants' garden have names: Cross Knob, and Vineyard Knob.

A delicious extra is that the book's end papers offer a map of these very places. True to Patrick Hart's Foreword, I yearned to visit these far reaches of the territory, and so I paid another visit to Gethsemani. At the Gift Shop I asked if it was possible to walk the trails shown in the back of the book: not only was it possible, the clerk offered an even better map. I was delighted. I set off, grabbed a walking stick by the gate of the enclosure wall, and with water bottle and map in hand, I headed out on to encounter Merton's and possibly my own "Landscapes of Paradise."

Two hours later, past Dom Frederic's Lake and St. Enoch's stone house, I found myself in the middle of a field of wild yarrow and daisies, vaguely lost. If I turned back I could find my way to the Statues, if I forged ahead, perhaps I could intersect the path to Hanekamp's …. or, I could just … *stand* in this place. The late afternoon sun shone fat and golden in a Kentucky sky. A family of tiny blue butterflies lazed by. Monastery bells rang in the distance. Paradise. "It is a strange awakening to find the sky inside of you," Merton wrote about Gethsemani (p. 121). For a moment I was sure I heard Father Louis laughing.

Note

---

1. Kathleen Deignan, ed., and John Giulani, *When the Trees Say Nothing: Thomas Merton's Writings on Nature* (Notre Dame, IN: Sorin Books, 2003).

Cynthia Ann Hizer

CASEY, Michael, *Fully Human, Fully Divine: An Interactive Christology* (Liguori, MO: Ligouri / Triumph, 2004), pp. 352. ISBN 0-7648-1149-5 (paperback). $19.95.

As a Benedictine-engaged person whose work is in developing formational education programs for secular environments, I am continually reminded that "a little goes a long way" concerning works examining Christianity from a contemplative perspective. Casey, an accomplished writer and Cistercian monastic knows this also and prefaces his 300-plus page Marcan-centered study with the admonition, "This book needs to be read slowly. I would not consider it excessive if a reading of it stretched out over most of a year" (p. viii). This statement is in no way intended as a forewarning of content with a pronounced academic tone or structural awkwardness waiting to entangle; the book is not difficult to read. Instead, Casey offers us a sincere invitation to embark upon a challenging and extended exploration of our life and who we are as Christians.

As in all journeys taken with others, we learn much about others and ourselves through the relationship of being in a developing story together. Herein resides the technique referenced in the book's subtitle. The pedagogical interactivity provided for us comes about as Casey assimilates our story today, with our relational triumphs, challenges and failures, into juxtaposition with the divine and human interactivity present in the life and person of Jesus Christ. The approach works in a wonderful way and the text would serve well in support of a small group study or personal devotion.

John W. Smith

CHITTISTER, Joan, *In the Heart of the Temple: My Spiritual Vision for Today's World* (New York: BlueBridge, 2004), pp. 158. ISBN 0-9742405-1-6 (paperback). $14.95.

CHITTISTER, Joan, *The Way We Were: A Story of Conversion and Renewal* (New York: Orbis Books, 2005), pp. 255. ISBN 0-57075-577-9 (hardcover). $20.00.

This first volume under review is a collection of Joan Chittister's own essays. Joan's fans will recognize most of her favorite topics addressed in this small volume: Simplicity, Work, Sabbath, Contemplation, Prayer, Empowerment, Prophecy, Wholeness—translate, "women's gift to the human equation"—Equality, Ministry, Vision, Discipleship, Conversion . . . .

In her brief introduction, she asks the "what about" and "what to make of" questions that she addresses in the essays. For example, "What do we make of work in a society driven by profit margins, exploitation, and workaholism?" and "What does vision have to do with the discipleship of equals and with conversion?"

In Chittister's popular style, she reminds us of our rootedness in the people who have been mentors and models (Benedict, Thomas Merton, Mahatma Gandhi, Eshun) as she presents stories from religious traditions (the Bible, the Talmud, Sufi and Buddhist spiritualities). Consistently, she points out cross-fertilization among the above using the language of each within the concepts and language of the others. Her worldview is consistently global and ecological with a challenge to meet life from a contemplative stance.

In the light of Chittister's giving voice to the issues of justice-seeking and peace-making, I wonder if sociologists or many of the world's women, for that matter, would concur with her statement, "Only in the most backward, most legalistic, most primitive of cultures are women made invisible, made useless, made less than fully human, less than fully spiritual" (p. 149). Is she saying that any culture that has not turned this around, is backward, legalistic, primitive? In Minnesota alone (my home state) from January 2003 to May 2004, "30,000 women were victims of domestic violence; 10,000 more were sexually assaulted."[1] It's too close to home for me to agree with Chittister's conclusion here regarding the many levels of abuse that women regularly endure in cultures around the world.

As *In the Heart of the Temple* looks forward, *The Way We Were: A Story of Conversion and Renewal*, looks back to her community's 150 years of presence, mission and ministry in the new frontier of America.

The photos on the dust-jacket drew me into my own past, my memories, but not the nostalgia that some trade for the open and honest account of the painful changes that brought about conversion and renewal both in our monasteries and convents as well as in the Church after Vatican II, especially in the United States.

Any community originating as Mount St. Benedict Monastery in Erie, Pennsylvania did will identify with the various cohorts Joan writes about. Speaking of garb, Joan says (p. 132), "Clearly, dehumanization had set in where witness was supposed to have been. But it was who we were, and the very thought of having to come out from behind all of that to become, well, nothing, brought the whole purpose of the life into question."

The author became the prioress in 1978 when her community she writes, "was ripe . . . . The years of renewal had taken their toll, both in energy and in relationships . . . ." Joan, who speaks here about exercising her authority through the shared authority of the community, moved into the process of revitalization which, she says, ". . . sets out to channel old energy, now dissipated, into new directions" (p. 210). The new directions meant conversion of heart and a commitment to gospel living in the daily which is what Benedictines are called to by the ancient but ever new Rule of Benedict.

Note

1. *Minneapolis Star Tribune*, March 10, 2005.

Theresa Schumacher, O.S.B.

DEKAR, Paul R., *Creating the Beloved Community* (Telford, PA: Cascadia Publishing House, 2005), pp. 325. ISBN 1-931038-30-9 (paperback). $23.95.

It has become commonplace that communities need stories and history to build the bonds that give purpose and even permanence. The history of a nation binds together citizens, as religious history does the faithful. The same holds for the peace community. In fact, one might argue that, since it is such a minority whose views are so countercultural, the peace community needs such a narrative much more than these others. In most places those who work for peace are so few that they can fall under the illusion that the peace movement is just the group of people they know—and similar small groups dotted around the country and the world. Individualist and fragmented, the illusion can even be discouraging and isolating.

Creating the Beloved Community is an antidote to the sense of isolation. A history of the Fellowship of Reconciliation from its founding in the early Twentieth century, Dekar's book gives a vision of the sweep of this important part of the peace movement. FOR was started by Christians who understood the gospel as incompatible with war. As it has broadened its religious base and refined the conceptual basis for its opposition to war, the organization has had an amazing impact in its pursuit of peace. It is a story that incorporates generations of peacemakers and traverses several eras in the development of war and of peacemaking. The reader gains the sense of a movement that transcends individuals and their placement in time. We need such books as a counter to the history that is composed of princes and their wars. Against the story of "breaking things and killing people" we need the story of mending things and saving people.

Covering roughly a hundred years, the book has a non-linear, somewhat recurring structure. The first half is organized around six major themes in the FOR statements of purpose (pp. 24-25). The first, "abolishing war by refusing to participate in war or to sanction military preparations," covers the way in which FOR started as a movement of pacifist Christians before the outbreak of World War I. The history moves forward as FOR affiliates with Jewish, Buddhist, Muslim, and various Christian fellowships, while developing its opposition to war into the nonviolent direct action of Gandhi and King. Then, the story goes back to the beginning to tell how FOR worked to "build a just social order in which the resources of human ingenuity and wisdom are used for the benefit of all and in which no one will oppress or exploit others." The obvious relation between these two themes is that the second addresses the social problems that are frequently the causes of war. A peace movement cannot just oppose war; it must try to remedy its causes.

Naturally, this structure gives the story a recurrent character. We start anew each time. While some of the characters occur again, there are also a lot of new actors, with different talents and different goals, relevant to the different themes. The variation, in fact, leads to conflict in ideas about the direction of FOR; some people depart and others come on board. The effect is to give a broad view of the movement as a variety of activities and achievements. Still, Dekar preserves a sense of consistency to the facets of this history.

The second half of the book turns to organizations that have been associated with FOR. While FOR grew to tens of thousands during the Vietnam war, for most of its history it has been much smaller. Like most such peace groups, it has worked with allies. These have included the Historic Peace Churches, local groups of FOR, denominational groups, and the Jewish, Buddhist, and Muslim peace fellowships. Here we find a rich history of activities and accomplishments that goes beyond the history of the first half. For instance, in the aftermath of World War II, FOR worked with the Historic Peace Churches, Friends, Mennonites, and Church of the Brethren, to promote peace studies programs (pp. 172-178). In addition, even as it became less explicitly Christian in its ideology, FOR encouraged such denominational groups as the Baptist Peace Fellowship, Catholic Peace Fellowship, Methodist Peace Fellowship, and Presbyterian Peace Fellowship. These groups are able to mine the non-violent genius of the gospels for sustenance as well as move their own churches closer to the path of peace.

As valuable as this sort of endeavor is, it has built-in limitations. Like the history of a college or university, it cannot easily develop the larger context—especially the criticism of opponents. As a consequence, there is always a triumphalist tone to these kinds of stories. Perhaps that kind of emphasis is appropriate to a project that rightly wants us to know the good that FOR has accomplished. Still, at points one has the sense that there is a grittier background story that would add a useful context. A second criticism springs from another strength of the book. In the section about denominational fellowships, Dekar tells the fascinating story of Thomas Merton's role in convoking Catholic peace activists and others, including members of FOR, during the Vietnam war (pp. 205-207). The story leaves rather vague the relation between the Catholic Peace Fellowship and two other important groups, Pax Christi USA and the Catholic Worker movement. The result is that it is hard to tell where FOR leaves off and the others begin. This story is emblematic of those passages where the emphasis on the role of FOR leads to a distorted sense of its place in the larger peace movement.

These criticisms should not be taken to detract from the overall achievements of this book. *Creating the Beloved Community* gives us solid insight into a history that is remarkable in its witness to the power of peaceful non-violence.

Richard D. Parry

PLAISS, Mark, *The Inner Room: A Journey into Lay Monasticism* (Cincinnati, OH: St. Anthony Messenger Press, 2003), pp. 127. ISBN 0-86716-481-6 (paperback). $9.95.

In reviewing a book like this, one does not so much critique it as engage it. That is what I am going to do. I am writing this review at my monastery "home," my spiritual community, the Abbey of Our Lady of the Redwoods at Whitethorn, CA. My family makes the 160-mile round trip every other Sunday for Eucharistic celebration, knowing that we are called by God to be here. Sometimes, we spend three-day weekends working, praying, laughing, conversing, and being silent with the sisters and brother here, deepening our fellowship and faith together as part of the Cistercian charism. My wife and I can articulate some of the reasons for our spiritual home being a monastery when persons query us, but the truest and simplest response is what Mark Plaiss says, we are *called* to this *vocation* of *lay monasticism*.

For us, being Christian is *being* this way of living the faith. Our children know no other expression of Christian faith; on those three-day weekends, they were helping to paint the monastery kitchen at ages 8 and 10, working in the garden each summer, and praying the offices (not the early ones!). The Cistercian charism shapes them whether they are consciously aware of it or not. The flavor of the monastic mass is their sense of Christian worship, and it is particularly Cistercian. One short humorous example: In 2003-04, our family had the wonderful rich experience of spending a year at the Ecumenical Institute at the Benedictine community of St. John's University and Abbey in Collegeville, MN. The Benedictine brothers welcomed us into daily prayers and into the life of their community, and we quickly felt very much connected. Even so, I will never forget my son's comment (then age 15), after attending the first Sunday Eucharist celebration in the magnificent church, with the monastic schola singing, and the fine homily by a monk priest. As we arrived back at our apartment on campus, my son said "Well, mass here was nice, but different. Being raised Cistercian, it just felt so *busy!*" *Being raised Cistercian*...he had no idea how profoundly unique his utterance was in the history of Christianity.

Mark Plaiss' book is a description of this reality of lay monasticism. It is an engaging account of his life story of discerning this vocation while also being a reflection on the ambiguous nature of this vocation in general. The book is composed of short essays. Essays 1-5 relate events and stories of his life coalescing toward a monastic spirituality. Essay 6-8 are flashbacks to his earlier formative days being raised as a Methodist, then Baptist, Protestant. Essays 9-17 are a mixture of glimpses into the experiences of praying the offices on retreat and contemplative reflections on faith, prayer, and the place of the cell and work in the monastic life. It makes for an odd assortment, but it works overall, giving the reader an encounter with the author and an introduction to the experience of retreat at a Cistercian monastery. Appendices include a schedule of Offices and Psalm Schedule at New Melleray Abbey.

Essays 2 and 18 frame the book by examining the lay monastic vocation from two distinct points: the perplexing experience of finding oneself called to a vocation that has no or little precedent, and the resultant need to identify key elements that must structure the lay monastic life so that it does not become self-enclosed, given it is unlikely to have communal structure for vocation formation (though this is increasingly changing as the oblate/associate movements grow).

Essay 2 first appeared in 1999 as an essay entitled "Lay Monasticism" in *Cistercian Studies Quarterly*, Vol 34.3. I recall the deep rush of gratitude and affirmation and my identification with the emotions, ambiguity, and deep certitude that Plaiss describes there—it spoke my experience so clearly, and it continues to represent the experience of a large, now identified group of lay monastics associated with Cistercian and Benedictine monasteries. Up to that point (as far as I know), nobody had so clearly articulated in publication the *experience* of being called to this largely "hidden vocation," hidden only because it didn't fit either the parish life or the cenobitic life of a cloistered monastery. I think that essay, now chapter 2 in this book, remains a landmark piece, for it did not posit a *possibility*, it described with confidence a present *reality*, making clear that the existence of this vocation was undeniable—both exciting and perplexing to monastics on both sides of the cloister walls. What on earth is the Holy Spirit doing?

Here are some selections from that essay that speak the bewilderment and yet deep emerging conviction in understanding one is being called to a way of life whose primary model is found in a cloister:

> The lay monastic is a layperson called by God to transform his or her life into one continuous prayer by using the tools nor-

mally associated with monasticism...The vocation is largely invisible, thereby rendering it incapable of promotion or recruitment. The parish priest may issue an appeal for Eucharistic Ministers, but he is unlikely to issue a similar appeal for lay monastics...Because the vocation is hidden, a person receiving the call to it is often perplexed...Consequently, the person stumbles through one door after another trying to follow the voice that calls....

The search often leads to a monastery. There the person discovers the rhythm of life that speaks to the soul: prayer, work, silence. This discovery is often accompanied by deep spiritual rumblings, a sense of being overshadowed...What the person has uncovered is a vocation. The person has followed the voice, and the voice is monastic.

Now the person is thoroughly confused. Perhaps he or she is married, has children and is paying off a mortgage. How can all that be reconciled with this apparent call to monasticism?... (Plaiss, pp. 5-6).

This is a challenge both for the lay monastics, who want more contact with monasteries, and for monasteries who have a clear structure for cenobitic monk vocations, but are a bit squeamish when the spirituality of their charism is suddenly being claimed, or given, to the larger world.[1] This larger expression of monastic charism requires a redefinition of monastic identity, and birth pangs are always painful and promising. As Plaiss says in Appendix 3, "Monasteries Without Walls,"

It is too early to come to any sort of conclusion about the nature of the relationship between the monks on either side of the [monastery] wall. In my conversations with some members [of monasteries] I find some are wary of the associates and skeptical of what is called monasticism outside the walls; others there embrace it. All of this is too new. Time is needed to digest it and mull it over. I do suggest, though, that we are perhaps on the cusp of a new age in which the boundaries of the monastery will expand... (Plaiss, p. 126).

Essay 18 speaks to the issue of vocational formation for lay monastics. One of the key differences between the canonical monk and the lay monastic is the availability of a system of training and guidance in formation in community. Plaiss discusses six key elements that the lay monastic must incorporate into his or her life in a disciplined manner: Humility in recognition that this charism is a gift from God, and thus continued discernment of it through the study of Scripture; cultivating prayer practices so that life becomes a continuous prayer, including some hours of the Office, adapted as necessary given the demands of jobs, family, etc.; practicing *lectio divina*, and meditation; seeking a competent spiritual director; seeking out brother and sister monastics, most easily found in an oblate association; and finally, studying the *Rule of St. Benedict* and applying its principles in one's life setting.[2] The question remains, however—in what ways will monasteries adapt to provide a structure for this needed guidance of formation? Plaiss shows how one Cistercian monastery, New Melleray Abbey in Dubuque, Iowa, has responded with a Monastic Center where lay monastics live for extended stays, in close association with the resident monks, directly involved in the community life of the monastery.[3]

This book does not deal with some important questions. Is the phrase "lay monasticism" an oxymoron? The term "monasticism" has a long usage of application to a celibate, cloistered vocation. Yet the call to conversion of life totally toward God is the *Christian* vocation, and the Benedictine rhythm of life toward that conversion is being claimed as a rightful inheritance by Christians beyond the cloister walls. But for centuries, the very structure of the monastery has remained the symbol of the stability and clarity of that conversion. It should not easily be changed, nor the words that describe it. Likewise, the phrase "*lay* monasticism" is problematic when used to identify non-cloistered, non-celibate persons; monasticism began and remains a lay movement, even though now it is thoroughly formalized into orders and structures. Other persons speak of "the secular monk," using secular as meaning "in the world." But "monk" has implied a celibate, cloistered lifestyle, and that is not the case here. Family life is the central sacramental presence for most lay monastics. Perhaps "monastic spirituality" will become the identifying label, and we will speak of "associates" who are connected formally or informally to monasteries whose walls become less solid, but still remain clear boundaries. Neither associates nor monks want or assume the cenobitic vocation will or should fade away. The monastery as the school of conversion of manners is mother to them all.

But really, this book does not need to address these issues. These matters are all under prayerful reflection and discussion within a myriad of settings, from lay associate organizations to papal addresses.[4] This book is spiritual autobiography, but it is more than that. It is a witness to the Spirit of God moving in our midst. It is a challenge and an opportunity for the traditional structure of monastic communities; how can they embrace the world coming to their doorsteps to be trained, and in turn be blessed by the richness of their charism being manifest in new ways beyond their walls? How can the associates bring new vitality and support, and new expression to the monastic community? How can the monks and associates together find the right balance in this relationship that deepens the communion of God among them and into the world? Trust God. Seek discernment together. Tonight (April 22, 2006), as I sat in the darkness of Vigils, the reading reverberated through the monastic church, "I am the Lord...I am doing a new thing. Can you not perceive it?" (Isaiah 43:8-11, 19-19b).

> ...Lay monasticism exists. The lay monastic may be married or single, man or woman, parent or not. The call to the vocation comes from God and is a means of union with God.
>
> The monastery is a school where the lay monastic learns by both instruction and example the life of monasticism. That monastic life is, in turn, lived in the world, becoming a quiet, hidden, continuous prayer to God. (Plaiss, p. 9)

Notes

1. This claiming or giving of the charism to the larger world, and its manifestation as lay monasticism, is similar to the clarifying experience of Jesus in his encounter with the Gentile women (Mark 7:24-30) and to Peter's visionary experience of God's expansive intent (Acts 10). Michael Casey, in commenting on the former, says "Jesus appreciates the woman's feisty rejoinder and is won over by her boldness. She has held a mirror up to him and, as it were, for the first time he has seen himself and his mission more clearly. She has perceived in him more than a parochial savior; it was from her that Jesus began to consider the universality of the Good News." (Michael Casey, *Fully Human Fully Divine: An Interactive Christology*, [Liguori, MO: Liguori/Triumph, 2004], p. 145.) In simi-

lar fashion, perhaps lay monastics are holding up a mirror to cloistered monastics today.

2. In the past decade or so, there has been a plenitude of books on applying the principles and sensibilities of the Rule of St. Benedict to everyday life outside the monastery. To name just a very few on my shelf or that came up on a topical search ("Rule of Saint Benedict" on Amazon.com): Joan Chittister, *The Rule of Benedict: Insights for the Ages* (Crossroad Classic, 1992), and *Wisdom Distilled From the Daily: Living the Rule of St. Benedict Today* (HarperSanFrancisco, 1991); Esther de Waal, *Seeking God: The Way of St. Benedict*, 2nd edition (Collegeville: Liturgical Press, 2001); Hugh Feiss, *Essential Monastic Wisdom: Writings on the Contemplative Life* (HarperSan Francisco,1999); Father Daniel Homan and Lonni Collins Pratt, *Radical Hospitality: Benedict's Way of Love* (Brewster, MA: Paraclete Press, 2002); David Robinson, *The Family Cloister: Benedictine Wisdom for the Home* (Crossroad, 2000); Laura Swan, *Engaging Benedict: What the Rule Can Teach Us Today* (Christian Classics, 2005); Benet Tvedten, *How to Be a Monastic and Not Leave Your Day Job: An Invitation to Oblate Life* (Brewster MA: Paraclete Press, 2006) and Paul Wilkes, *Beyond the Walls: Monastic Wisdom for Everyday Life* (New York: Doubleday/Random House, 1999). These are listed to show variety only, not necessarily to imply endorsement.

3. For more information on the Monastic Center at New Melleray Abbey, see www.newmelleray.org, click on "Guests" and then on "The Monastic Center." Other contact information for the Abbey: New Melleray Abbey, 6632 Melleray Circle, Peosta, IA 52068; Phone: 563.588.2319; e-mail: frsteve@newmelleray.org

4. For example, on the International Lay Cistercians website, www.cistercianfamily.org under "Resources," one finds three sections of documents entitled "Documents Related to the O.C.S.O., "Homilies and Presentations from Monks and Nuns," and "Documents from Lay Associates," all of which reflect on lay monasticism in some form or fashion.

Harry Wells

BILLY, Dennis, C.Ss.R. *With Open Heart: Spiritual Direction in the Alphonsian Tradition* (Liguori, MO: Liguori Publications, 2003). pp. 128. ISBN 0764810901 (paperback). $18.95.

Spiritual direction is a ministry that combines artistry, grace and specific skills. In the Catholic tradition, discussions about spiritual direction often turn to the work of Ignatius of Loyola and his *Spiritual Exercises,* and for many, this particular approach has become a *totum pro parte*. Fr. Dennis Billy's book, *With Open Heart: Spiritual Direction in the Alphonsian Tradition*, successfully persuades the reader to consider the value of different traditions. The general acceptance of varied approaches to spiritual direction makes it easier, with Billy's encouragement, to specifically consider the Alphonsian approach, one with which many may not be familiar. The practice of spiritual direction in the tradition of Alphonsus de Liguori is one in which prayer is emphasized and re-enforced by the very structure of the spiritual direction session.

In his first chapter, "Spiritual Direction, Toward a Communion of Traditions," Billy, an American Redemptorist of the Baltimore Province, affirms the broad nature of spiritual direction. "When understood under the general heading of the 'care for and cure of souls,' spiritual direction encompasses virtually every aspect of the Church's pastoral ministry" (p. 1). Spiritual direction can be described as anything that assists someone's movement toward God. Billy further asserts that the specific helping relationship between director and directee "displays unique characteristics in its own right and emerges as a highly specialized ministry" (p. 1).

Borrowing from Tilden Edwards' *Spiritual Friend* (New York: Paulist Press, 1980) Billy offers the history of Christian spiritual direction as "a single river branching off into three streams: the Roman Catholic, the Protestant, and the Orthodox" (p. 3). The "gems" to be found in the Protestant branch are preaching, bible study, pastoral counseling, and small group prayer. The Catholic branch offers liturgy, confession, retreats and the liturgical life cycle. The Orthodox branch offers a mystical depth and the consistent emphasis on unceasing prayer (p. 4).

The narrowing of the historical discussion of spiritual direction to a Christian perspective is reasonable here since Billy's main goal is to explore the Catholic tradition, most especially the uniquely Catholic approach of Alphonsus. He arrives at his goal in rapid fashion. After acknowledging various religious orders and their contributions to spiritual direction (the Benedictine's *lectio divina* and liturgy; the Carthusian's "way of knowing"; the Franciscan's holy simplicity; the Dominican's teaching on virtues; the Carmelite's mysticism and Dark Night; and the Jesuit's Spiritual Exercises) (p. 6), Billy turns to his order, the Redemptorist, and its focus on conversion, prayer and confession as foundational for the practice of spiritual direction, but not until he stresses the point that spiritual direction in the Catholic tradition is "one of diversity in the midst of an underlying unity" (p. 7). He quotes Bernard of Clairvaux, who, in discussing his relationship to other religious orders stated, "I belong to one of them by observance, but to all of them by charity" (p. 7). Billy applies the sentiment to spiritual direction and avoids the temptation to be competitive or suspicious of another's orientation.

Some detail on the person of Alphonsus (1696-1787) and his own diverse influences is given in the chapter entitled, "Saint Alphonsus: Spiritual Master." Notably, Alphonsus regarded himself a missionary. "The major projects of his life—his missionary preaching, his writing, the work of founding the Redemptorist Congregation, and his life of prayer—were all motivated by his profound desire to share the Good News of plentiful redemption in Christ with others, especially the poor and most abandoned" (p. 17). He patterned his life and work on the person of Jesus and his spirituality is, therefore, a Gospel Spirituality.

Alphonsus was well read in the Scriptures, the writings of the Church Fathers as well as other spiritual masters. Among his influences were Teresa of Avila (1515-1582), Ignatius of Loyola (1491-1556) and Francis de Sales (1567-1622) (p. 21). Because of his openness to diverse spiritualities Alphonsus developed an eclectic, pragmatic style, keeping that which worked and developing an approach that was accessible to most. Emerging from this creative eclecticism was an approach to spiritual direction which was highly directive, rooted in prayer and closely attached to the practice of confession.

The incorporation of confession as part of spiritual development is worth underscoring as an integral part of the spiritual journey, but should not be mistaken for it. While Billy includes a discussion about the ministry of lay spiritual direction in his final chapter, entitled "Some Practical Concerns," the clerical emphasis remains and should be understood as a particular strength of the Redemptorist tradition.

Alphonsus traveled to the places where the poor were forgotten, finding himself in the tiny mountain villages and back roads of southern Italy. His development of a simple formula (what he preferred to call "manner") was in keeping with an effort to teach a practical method of prayer to as many people as he could. It speaks of his belief that prayer is essential in a relationship with God. For him, "Mental prayer is to the health of the soul as breathing is to the health of the body" (p. 58). Prayer, for Alphonsus, was the means of salvation (p. 18). Indeed, prayer was the hallmark of all his teaching on the spiritual life, eventually earning him the title of "Doctor of Prayer" (p. 19).

Billy's main thrust in this brief work on spiritual direction is contained in his comparison of Alphonsus's teaching on prayer to the structure of a typical spiritual direction session. Alphonsus understood prayer as "a familiar conversation (and) between the soul and God" (p. 47). Although God was the initiator of this intimate conversation and sufficient grace to pray was given to all by God, people still need instruction in the basics regarding the practice of prayer (p. 48). To this end, Alphonsus offered techniques for helping a person foster such an intimate conversation. Those techniques, culled from the master spiritual writers before him, were outlined by Alphonsus to include three movements in prayer: (1) the *preparation*, (2) the *body of the prayer* itself, and (3) the *conclusion*.

The *preparation movement* uses time to ready the body and mind for the action of God. The *prayer time movement* includes meditation (cognitive reflection), attention to affections (heartfelt responses to God), petitions (requests for graces) and resolutions (practical applications). The *conclusion movement* ends the prayer time by thanking God and by making a firm commitment to the resolutions made earlier (pp. 48-53). These same movements in prayer are offered by Billy as an ideal order and structure for a typical spiritual direction session. "The great benefit of a model of spiritual direction based on the dynamics of the Alphonsian approach to mental prayer is that the various elements of a person's intimate conversation with God are transposed onto the direction process itself" (p. 73).

Alphonsus's approach to mental prayer involves the whole person and so too does Billy's attempt to parallel this teaching on prayer to spiritual direction. The author wants the reader to understand that the process of spiritual direction must take into account the humanness of the person. While this statement is not new, using an Alphonsian approach that parallels his concept of prayer is a useful tool for keeping this notion in the forefront of the spiritual direction process: "Alphonsus's guidelines for mental prayer can be taken as a metaphor for the spiritual direction process itself" (p. 67). By projecting the Alphonsian method of mental prayer onto the plane of spiritual direction the author hopes to contribute to the rediscovery of this important form of prayer and its ability to consider the human person in relationship to The Divine (p. 67).

The maturing of the total self through reflection and expression is a crucial aspect of the spiritual direction process and an important aspect of the human journey to God. One may recall Thomas Merton's comments regarding spiritual direction, "The spiritual director is concerned with the *whole person*, for the spiritual life is not just the life of the mind, or of the affections, or of the 'summit of the soul'—it is the life of the whole person".[1] Since God is always dealing with the whole person, the enterprise of spiritual direction must, out of necessity deal with all aspects of the person.

This book can be a useful resource for stimulating discussion among seasoned spiritual directors, students of spiritual direction and those personally engaged in the process of spiritual direction. By using a flexible, pragmatic model of spiritual direction based on a manner of prayer that engages the whole person, Billy draws an important parallel between Redemptorist spirituality and the field of spiritual direction. He presents Redemptorist spiritual direction as one which values the importance of a contemplative lifestyle and emphasizes prayer as the most basic aspect of a relationship with God.

While there may be difficulties in distilling an eighteenth-century founder's thoughts on prayer into a modest volume, the application of theses concepts to a modern approach to spiritual direction is well worth the undertaking. Drawing from my own experience in spiritual direction, both personal and professional, I find it difficult to disagree with the author that "The whole purpose of spiritual direction, after all, is not unlike the goal of mental prayer itself: to help a person draw closer to God" (p. 78). Dennis Billy successfully directs the reader's attention to a useful understanding of spiritual direction in light of Alphonsian prayer.

Notes

1. Thomas Merton, *Spiritual Direction and Meditation* (Collegeville, MN: Liturgical Press, 1960), p. 14.

Mark A. Dannenfelser

CASEY, Thomas G., *Humble and Awake: Coping with Our Comatose Culture* (Springfield, IL: Templegate Publishers, 2004), pp. 206. ISBN 0-87243-265-3 (paperback) $12.95.

Irish Jesuit Fr. Thomas Casey brings a valuable perspective to North American readers of his compelling book: that of a "Westerner" not from the United States. Woven throughout the narrative is a profound awareness of the sex-abuse crisis in the Catholic Church, the events of September 11, 2001 and the conflict in Iraq, yet his "comatose culture" and our resultant comatose souls are not bound by nationality. This is a work of critical observation, of paradox, and of complex connections that remains rooted in hope. That hope is intimately tied to humility, an essential component of awakening.

The Latin word for humility, *humilitas*, derives from the root word for earth, *humus*, and Casey knows that humility is all about being grounded in our imperfect humanity. He succeeds in rescuing the word from a popular understanding of unworthiness and aligns it more with self-abnegation in service of the other, and also with abiding happiness. A counter-cultural and puzzling stance! To illuminate this paradox, Casey calls upon Mary the mother of Jesus, John the Baptist, apostles and saints, Dostoevsky's *The Brothers Karamazov*, John the Evangelist, the donkey of Passion Sunday, an eagle and the lowly earthworm. Each insight from these vastly different perspectives offers a glimpse of understanding. The author relies particularly on the Gospel of John for biblical references, and concludes that Jesus does not require perfection, but rather desires only our faithful connection, the branches to the vine. A realized humility can only be relational, embracing God, others, ultimately all of creation.

Any true recognition of humility must acknowledge our fundamental brokenness, and attempts to awaken are undermined in both obvious and subtle ways. The constant barrage of the media (with mostly bad news), "entertainers" like Jerry Springer, eager to comfort the masses with proof that others are in far more dire straits, and particularly our own fears can, and do, paralyze us. This is our comatose culture: a significant number of people unaware of the call to goodness and wholeness and in danger of slipping slowly past a point of potential response. Casey asserts that the very fact of our dissatisfaction with this "sorry state of affairs" is a sign that we are ready to awaken, ready to hear the call to wake up to life and beyond, to love and to loving service.

The chapter aptly titled "Signs of Wakefulness" is filled with wisdom and connections to prophets of past and present. First and foremost, wakefulness is about *being aware*, living each moment to the fullest in all life's circumstances. Jesus is clear throughout the gospels that we need not worry about the future. This is echoed today by Buddhist monk Thich Nhat Hanh who counsels an attentiveness to the present he calls the "miracle of mindfulness." Wakefulness is about *searching*, about *admitting* we cannot do it on our own, about *letting go and letting God*; the kind of freeing surrender explained and modeled so well by Ignatius of Loyola. Wakefulness is about *gratitude*, about *knowing oneself honestly*, about *loving service* and not loveless domination, so strikingly portrayed during Jesus' time of temptation in the desert. Finally and closest to my heart, wakefulness is about *joy*, the joy that comes from and is so far beyond mere happiness. Each of these is necessary for an openly loving, humble yet astutely aware worldview that allows the "other" a place at the table, exemplified by the work of liberation theologian Gustavo Gutierrez and others.

Several pages are devoted to a treatise on prayer as a vital part of awareness. The author again calls upon diverse sources from the account of the Fall in Genesis to contemporary Jewish and secular writers, popular movies (particularly *The Matrix*), and Mary's journey to Elizabeth, all reaffirming that God meets us exactly where we are. The challenge here is to see prayer as complementary to loving service, in community as well as time apart.

Casey devotes an entire chapter at the end of the book to his thesis that we are in a "Holy Week" period of history, an archetypal pattern of unease and conflict that calls us to seek God's voice through the signs of the times, particularly through the least likely among us. The reader is prepared for this detailed summation by perhaps the most imaginative and insightful parts of the entire book: an earlier chapter comparing John and Judas and the gripping chapter entitled "The Face That Wakes Us Up." These three constitute a passionate retelling and analysis of the events leading up to, and including, Jesus' last week on earth, making this book supremely appropriate and desirable as Lenten reading. I cannot remember a time when I was so deeply moved—to prayer, to tangible grief not only for Jesus and the disciples, but for the state of the world, to contemplation and action—yet never losing sight of hope and the endless possibilities for grace.

Casey's use of diverse resources: philosophy, the wisdom of other faiths, secular history, contemporary media, Hebrew and Christian Scriptures, fairy tales, donkeys, eagles and worms offers a broad perspective, enlightening his theses with richness and depth of understanding. His willingness to be thus informed proves his own wakefulness and awareness of our global culture, and heightens the reader's everyday awareness of the myriad connections surrounding us–the signs of our own times.

Cathy Crosby

SWAN, Laura, *Engaging Benedict: What the Rule Can Teach Us Today* (Notre Dame: Ave Maria Press, 2005). pp. 192 with Glossary of Terms and Selected Bibliography. ISBN: 0-87061-232-8 (paperback). $12.95.

Introduction:

Engaging Benedict is not an exhaustive commentary but rather a questioning dialogue with sections of the RB which can stir anger, that one can ignore rather than confront, or that touch upon some controversial current issues (p. 10). Swan relies on proven commentaries of foremost Benedictine scholars—Kardong, de Vogüé, Bockmann, Forman—for textual analyses, and her referencing them actually serves the secondary purpose of providing an overview of the critical literature and consensus. But she goes beyond their more focused spiritual dimension by drawing on leading contemporary writers in the social sciences, authorities in pastoral care, and in psychology.

A major thrust of Swan's examination is her questioning of the Rule as a woman monastic. She refers correctly to religious feminism as "an interpretive tool," a tool that can help us discover ways in which the Good News may have been inadvertently compromised. This is not a feminist statement but rather a contemporary reading through an important alternative lens. As such it challenges all readers.

Insights into Chapter Seven of the RB:

In ten chapters Swan considers the monastic tradition, Benedict's definition of the authentic monastic, prayer, obedience, the observance of Lent, hospitality, the prophetic dimension, and justice. The center of the volume, however, consists of two chapters devoted to humility, one of the aspects of the Rule that can be, and indeed has been most open to abuse (p. 72), "Contemporary Considerations" and "Benedict's Ladder of Humility Re-considered." Consideration of this "center" will serve to catch the method and tenor of the book as a whole.

Swan draws on psychological insights and theories of faith development, specifically those of Robert Kegen, and suggests that the ladder Benedict uses to describe the journey toward humility is better described as a helix, and considers the basic problem addressed—and corrected—by this concept, namely, the sense of self and the relationship to power. Drawing on Vogüé and Kardong in her pondering of the First Step of Humility, she interprets "Fear of God" as pregnant with love, mindfulness grounded in awe, astonishment, and exultation in the Divine Presence (p. 86). By probing etymology and the Hebrew language she stresses Benedict's call to experience ourselves as constantly observed by God, a call to spiritual awakening, to awareness of finding our true selves.

At this point she touches on one of her basic thrusts—the self-knowledge encouraged and especially crucial for women whose identity can have been mis-presented by the RB, the Church, and society. Thus her consideration of the Second Step ("delight not in satisfying our desires out of love of our own way") specifically addresses the situation of women who "often behave in self-sacrificial ways because they believe they are less important, less valuable, less essential than men" (p. 89), suggesting that one needs to discover one's center and one's own authentic voice.

Self-denigration damages the inner journey and separates us from God. In Step Two she hears Benedict inviting followers to let go "of all that possesses us and hinders our ability to hear and respond to God"—attitudes, motives, emotional ties, and thoughts that have held us back from a deepened relationship with God and ourselves (p. 90). She suggests that knowing our desires is not necessarily "self-will." Instead, one should discern how one's own desires relate to God's will and thus "trust that the God who creates us with these passions and desires intends to fulfill them" (p. 91).

Swan's reconsideration of the Ladder interprets the twelve rungs specifically, informing the RB's often dour phrasing with luminous invitations to joyful growth and inner work. An instance of an interpretation illustrative both of her healthy re-viewing and her concern with aspects of the RB which have been unsuitable for women monastics occurs in her commentary on one of the dourest passages of the Rule, the Seventh Step of Humility ("we believe. . . that we are lower and less honorable than all the rest, thus declaring . . . I am a worm . . ." [RB7:51-54] where Swan credits Benedict with developing a most affirmative *worm theology* (pp. 98-99), pointing out how deeply dependent our ecosystem is on worms who work with what is available and who turn what is "useless" into the soil that sustains life. "We can complain about what we must work with or we can resurrect our allotted 'garbage' into the sustenance of life. Flawed families, imperfect colleagues, fellow monastics with an abundance of foibles all become the realm of our worm-activity" (p. 98).

Male and Female Alike Take Heed:

Although Swan directs attention to women, the two specific issues she addresses in a woman's journey toward humility are germane to anyone: the sense of self and the relationship to power (p. 74). Humility is about being really real, and thus deeply aware of the Wholly Otherness of God, a journey from that public persona we may have built up in our early adult years toward that true self made in the image and likeness of Christ (p. 72).

Many persons, male and female, are hampered by a false self. So when Swan writes that the journey toward humility is about discovering and accepting the person created in the Divine image, and therefore about embracing one's value and importance before God (p. 75), or that the journey requires that one first discover who she is as distinct from the person patriarchy told her she is, the teaching applies equally to both women and men.

Since her study is steeped in the concern, so basic to the RB, of learning to discern between false and true self, that quintessential Mertonian concern, it is surprising that Swan never mentions Thomas Merton at all, either in her text or in her suggestions for further study. But the omission might well be seen as evidence for his pervasive influence on contemporary spiritual writing, having formed and informed many of her major sources.

The "Tool" of "Living *Lectio*":

In addition to the lens of religious feminism, Swan provides her reader with an additional "tool," one which requires the sort of intense dedication to a task implied by the term—"living *lectio.*" She recognizes that the "stuff" of our lives—daily events, unsettling news, troubling texts—can serve, in fact do serve to communicate God's words to us. Swan continually concludes her reflections on aspects of the Rule by challenging her reader to ponder such "texts." For example, after considering Benedict's instructions on praying the psalms, she asks us to risk facing our own anger, pain, confusion and curses through them.

How do we let these psalm texts speak our own stories, unpacking our true feelings and the ways God might be present in the rawness of our lives? How might we risk exploring new images of God based on our honest feelings and God's possible responses to us? (p. 43).

Conclusion:

Swan's consideration of the Rule would serve well as a study guide for groups trying to incorporate Benedictine teaching into their lives. Her copious questions are so intense and demanding that the support and input of fellow travelers would help to confront and wrestle with them. At times the text seems intended primarily for vowed monastics, as when she writes of the experience of her specific monastic community, or describes in intense paragraphs Benedict's "true monastic." Gradually, however, it becomes clear that this "true monastic" (who in fact is the goal toward whom we are all still journeying) is simply that person who longs for the kind of God-orientation, God-awareness, and God-relationship which is "merely" Christian. Laura Swan's volume can help us to engage Benedict's guidance in this undertaking.

Dewey Weiss Kramer

JOHNSON, Maxwell E., Compiler and Editor, *Benedictine Daily Prayer: A Short Breviary* (Collegeville: Liturgical Press, 2005). ISBN 139780-8146-2833-1, pp. 2,266 with index (plus additional unpaginated end papers with prayers, etc). $50.00 with simulated leather cover.

This book's title page implies the love which went into its conception and composition "…Edited by Maxwell E. Johnson, oblate at Saint John's Abbey and the monks of Saint John's Abbey." It is a beautiful book made primarily for persons who are either Benedictine Oblates or friends of Benedictine monasteries. Someone ought to do a similar project with Cistercians in mind.

This prayer book is designed to assist someone who is close to the Benedictine way of life to engage in daily prayer. It would, however, be of great value to any Christian even if there were no Benedictine connection. Its "Introduction" states:

> Any who have participated frequently in the Monastic Liturgy of the Hours at Saint John's Abbey, Collegeville, Minnesota, will find much in this book quite familiar, and, in some ways, *Benedictine Daily Prayer* is itself *a* version of *Saint John's Abbey Prayer* (p. xii).

This "Introduction" is fascinating for several complex reasons: 1) it is slightly defensive; 2) it provides a lot of information about Benedictine rhythms; 3) it provides the rationale for such a book—and makes it clear why there is such a strong relationship between this book and the Prayer of Saint John's Abbey:

> In the interests of space, however, while the Gospel readings for all three years of the Roman Catholic Sunday lectionary are included, only one [of the] patristic readings is provided for each Sunday, which means, of course, that it will not always correspond directly to all three Gospel texts. Also in the interests of space, the readings are often printed in an abridged form, though the complete reference is given for those who may wish to read the whole passage from a Bible. [And] customarily … at Saint John's Abbey on the evening before Sundays, solemnities, and certain feasts, one could easily replace First Vespers with the Office of Vigils on those days with the inclusion of the litany, the Our Father, and the prayer following the *Te Deum* or *Te Decet Laus* (p. xiii).

The arrangement of the full book is structured as follows: Introduction; An Aid to Praying *Benedictine Daily Prayer*; Monastic Calendar; Sunday and Weekday Readings; The Ordinary of the Liturgy of the Hours; The Weekly Psalter; Supplemental Psalms and Canticles for Vigils and Lauds; Festival Psalter; Common for Feasts of the Blessed Virgin Mary; Common for Feasts of Apostles; Common for Feasts of Martyrs; Common for Feasts of Holy Men and Women; Office of the Dead; Proper of Seasons: Advent; Christmas; Lent; Triduum; Easter; Pentecost; Proper of the Saints; and an Appendix: A Selection of Benedictine Prayers; Acknowledgements; along with an Index.

The translation chosen for the Psalms is the one currently used by the monks at St. John's, *The Psalms: An Inclusive Language Ver-*

sion Based on the Grail Translation from the Hebrew. This immediately does raise some contemporary questions of taste and/or appropriateness because while most men will perhaps not pay much attention to the wording, this language and its choices of pronouns could be problematic, especially for female readers.

The readings for each season are excellently chosen. For example, the Pentecost Sunday choice is from the treatise *Against Heresies* by St. Irenaeus:

> *"The mission of the Spirit"*…. Luke tells us that after the ascension the Spirit descended on the disciples with power to enliven all nations and to make the new covenant known to them. Jesus had promised to send a Paraclete who would unite us to God. For, as the dry grain cannot become one dough or one bread without moisture, neither can we many become one in Christ without heavenly water. Our bodies enter into unity through the bath of immortality, and our souls through the Spirit (pp. 325-326).

To study the index is very informative: It stands as a separate compendium of the history of holy worship in the Church. Look only at pp. 2,254-2,256, the "A" and "B" entry readings only which include the following writers, some with multiple entries: Aelred of Rievaulx (2); Ambrose (8); Andrew of Crete (3); Anselm (4); Athanasius (5); Augustine (26); Basil the Great (3); Bede (4); Benedict (8); Bernard (7); Bonaventure (2). One could wish, since the book was done for contemporary usage, that there would be more contemporaneous readings however. We have 26 entries for St. Augustine and 8 by St. Benedict. Thomas Merton rates one.

Several distinct topics of interest are handled in the "Introduction." Among them are the following: 1) Justification for this type of book (p. vii); 2) Explanation about the Benedictine Liturgical tradition (p. x); 3) Some relationships to St. John's (Minnesota) Worship; 4) Ecumenical connections (p. xv); and 5) "An Aid to Praying" this compilation (p. xvii). One could quibble about the supporting materials. More important for any user of this handsome book is the fact that it is wonderfully printed, a pleasure to hold and remains (relatively) compact at its hefty 2,266 pages. It can still fit into a briefcase or suitcase.

This handsome book was designed by Joachim Rhoades O.S.B. and printed in Belgium. It is beautifully printed. It is a pleasure to hold in your hand. No other book has been so beautifully produced for the purposes for which this successful "Breviary" exists. It should be welcomed by Oblates, friends of Benedictines—such as all members of Cistercian Lay Groups too. For what this book is, it is a bargain and an inspiration.

Anthony Feuerstein

Contributors

Daniel J. Adams is Professor of Theology at Hanil University in Jeonbuk, Korea. His book *Thomas Merton's Shared Contemplation: A Protestant Perspective* was published by Cistercian Publications.

John Eudes Bamberger, O.C.S.O., former Abbot of The Abbey of the Genesee, New York, has taken up residence in Ascension Hermitage on the abbey property. As a hermit he continues to participate in some community exercises including work and liturgy.

John Collins is a professor of Graduate Studies with the International Education Program Inc. He was Director of the Teacher Certification Program at the College of the Holy Cross where he organized the 35th Merton Anniversary Conference in 2003. He has delivered Merton papers at ITMS Conferences in 2001 and 2005 and has published articles in *The Merton Annual* and *The Merton Seasonal*.

Jeffrey Cooper, C.S.C. is a member of the Congregation of Holy Cross and is pursuing a Ph.D. in Christian Spirituality at the Graduate Theological Union in Berkeley, CA.

Glenn Crider, Production Manager and editorial contributor for *The Merton Annual*, served as co-chair of the Atlanta Chapter of The International Thomas Merton Society, 2001 to 2003. He holds an M.A. in psychology and a Master of Divinity from Candler School of Theology, Emory University.

Catherine Crosby, a former Montessori Department Chair, now heads *Pax Christi* Atlanta while serving as a spiritual director, retreat presenter, parish Religious Education coordinator, and twenty-five year catechist.

Mark A. Dannenfelser teaches for the Department of Theology at Spring Hill College, Atlanta. He is Director of Religious Education of Adults at Our Lady of the Assumption Church. He has a private psychotherapy practice in Atlanta, offering counseling and spiritual direction.

John Dear is a Jesuit priest, author, lecturer, activist and the former executive director of the Fellowship of Reconciliation. He has traveled the war zones of the world; organized demonstrations against war and nuclear weapons; and been arrested 75 times for acts of nonviolent civil disobedience. His books include *Living Peace, The Questions of Jesus, Peace Behind Bars, The Sound of Listening, You Will Be My Witnesses, Jesus the Rebel, The God of Peace* and *Disarming the Heart*. He lives in New Mexico, and coordinates a *Pax Christi* New Mexico campaign to disarm Los Alamos. For information, see: www.johndear.org

Paul R. Dekar is Niswonger Professor of Evangelism and Mission at Memphis Theological Seminary where he has taught a course on Merton since 1997. Recipient of a Shannon Fellowship in 2002, Dekar continues research, teaching and writing on Merton and technology. Recent publications include *Creating the Beloved Community* (2005), reviewed in this volume, and *Holy Boldness* (2004).

Mark DelCogliano is a Ph.D. student in the Graduate Division of Religion at Emory University, where he studies Patristics. His interests include ancient philosophy, the development of Christian theology, and early Christian monasticism. He has published articles as well as book reviews and translations, in *Cistercian Studies Quarterly, The American Benedictine Review,* and *The Journal of Early Christian Studies.*

Robert Ellsberg is Publisher and Editor-in-Chief of Orbis Books. A former managing editor of *The Catholic Worker,* he edited anthologies by Dorothy Day, Flannery O'Connor, Thich Nhat Hanh, and Gandhi. His books include *All Saints* and *The Saints' Guide to Happiness,* both of which include reflections on Merton. At Orbis he has overseen the publication of several Merton projects, including *Cold War Letters, Peace in the Post-Christian Era, Seeking Paradise,* and *Thomas Merton: Essential Writings.*

Anthony Feuerstein has written reviews as well as a bibliographical note for *The Merton Annual.*

James Finley, author of *Merton's Palace of Nowhere* (1978), is a clinical psychologist in private practice with his wife in Santa

Monica, CA. He leads silent weekend retreats throughout the United States and Canada. His most recent publication is *Christian Meditation: Experiencing the Presence of God* (2005). Dr. Finley was a member of the community at Gethsemani from 1961 to 1967.

Donald Grayston retired in 2004 from teaching Religious Studies at Simon Fraser University in Vancouver, British Columbia, and from his Anglican parish there in 2005. He is past president of the Thomas Merton Society of Canada and vice-president of the International Thomas Merton Society.

James Harford, an engineering graduate of Yale University, was for many years executive director of the American Institute of Aeronautics and Astronautics. On retirement he studied Russian, went to the Soviet Union to interview space veterans, and wrote a prize-winning book about the program's hero, Sergei Pavlovich Korolev. [KOROLEV *How One Man Masterminded the Soviet Drive to Beat America to the Moon*]. His book, *Merton and Friends: A Joint Biography of Thomas Merton, Robert Lax and Edward Rice* was published by Continuum International in 2006.

Fred Herron is a member of the Department of Theology and Religious Studies, St. John's University, Staten Island, chairperson of the Department of Religious Studies at Fontbonne Hall Academy, Brooklyn, New York and Director of Adult Faith Formation, St. Clare's Parish, Staten Island. His most recent book is *No Abiding Place: Thomas Merton and the Search for God* (University Press of America, 2005) reviewed in this volume.

Cynthia Hizer holds a Master of Divinity from Candler School of Theology, Emory University in Atlanta, Georgia. She is a candidate for ordination in the Episcopal Church and is presently seeking a Master of Sacred Theology and Anglican Certificate at General Episcopal Seminary, New York.

Judith Hunter is a retired attorney with a background in intellectual history. One of her many interests is the point where intellectual dissent and the Roman Catholic Church intersect.

David King is an Associate Professor of English and Film Studies at Kennesaw State University in Atlanta. He has a long association with *The Merton Annual*, as both editorial assistant and contributor. He teaches Merton in a variety of courses, as evidenced by the title of his *Merton Annual* 16 article "Merton's New Novices: *The Seven Storey Mountain* and Monasticism in a Freshman Seminar."

Dewey W. Kramer was a founding editor of *The Merton Annual* and has made frequent contributions over the years. She is author of *Open to the Spirit*, a history of The Abbey of the Holy Spirit (1986, revised 1996). In 2003-2004 she was a Research Scholar at the Institute for Ecumenical and Cultural Research of St. John's University, in Minnesota where she worked on the relationship between the Illuminations, Text and Music of Hildegard of Bingen.

Victor A. Kramer began study concerning Merton in 1972 and has remained active as a Merton scholar since then. He edited Merton's journal *Turning Toward the World: The Pivotal Years, 1960-1963* (1996). Presently he teaches for Spring Hill College (Mobile, Alabama) in its M.A. Extension Program in Atlanta. He has completed a two-year Certificate Program for Spiritual Direction in 2006.

Lucien Miller, Professor Emeritus of Comparative Literature, University of Massachusetts, Amherst, has specialized in East-West literary relations and Chinese language and literature. His studies and translations of Chinese fiction and minority folk literature include *South of the Clouds: Yunnan Tales, The Masks of Fiction in the Dream of the Red Chamber, Exiles at Home: Stories by Ch'en Ying-chen*, and Bai minority folktales. His studies of oral folk literature are based upon fieldwork conducted in China and India. Teaching specialties include Buddhism in America, Travel Literature, Thomas Merton and the Monastic Tradition.

Patrick F. O'Connell teaches English and Theology at Gannon University, Erie, PA. A founding member and former president of the International Thomas Merton Society, he serves as editor of *The Merton Seasonal*. He is co-author of *The Thomas Merton Encyclopedia* (2002), and editor of *The Vision of*

Thomas Merton (2003), *Cassian and the Fathers* (2005), and *Pre-Benedictine Monasticism* (2006), the first two volumes of Merton's novitiate conferences.

Richard Parry is Professor Emeritus of Philosophy at Agnes Scott College, Atlanta, Georgia. Parry's area of research is ancient Greek philosophy, in particular Plato's moral theory. In his book, *Craft of Justice* (SUNY, 1996), Parry defends the claim that Plato conceived of the virtues along the lines of craft, a position that has important contemporary implications.

Joseph Quinn Raab is Assistant Professor of Religious Studies and Theology at Siena Heights University in Adrian, Michigan where he lives with his wife Jane and their three children. Dr. Raab also teaches courses in Christology and Ecclesiology for the Saint Meinrad School of Theology.

Theresa Schumacher, O.S.B., is a Sister at St. Benedict's Monastery, St. Joseph, Minnesota. She is presently President of the American Benedictine Academy. She served as Novice Formation Director. Her work has included liturgical studies, campus ministry and spiritual direction.

John Winston Smith is the founder and director of Anchorhold, an ecumenical ministry providing formational education and spiritual guidance. Smith served as a local pastor in the United Methodist Church for eleven years before making a profession of vows to religious life and focusing on ministry outside the traditional church structure. He is a graduate of the Ministry Studies Program at Shorter College, received his Master of Theological Studies from Emory University, and is presently in doctoral studies at Columbia Theological Seminary.

Thomas Francis Smith, O.C.S.O., is a monk at the Monastery of the Holy Spirit, Conyers, Georgia. As author, speaker and retreat director, he has served in many capacities within his monastery.

Michael Sobocinski is Director of Residential Services at Alaska Children's Services in Anchorage, Alaska. His professional activities involve the care and treatment of children and youth who have experienced severe relational trauma, clinical training. He has been a regular contributor to recent ITMS Conferences, where he has given presentations on the interface between clinical practice, the psychology of the self, issues of justice, and spirituality.

Monica Weis, S.S.J., is Professor of English and Director of the Master of Arts in Liberal Studies program at Nazareth College, Rochester, New York. She is a frequent presenter at ITMS General Meetings and has published in *The Merton Seasonal* and *The Merton Annual*. Her most recent book, with photographer Harry L. Hinkle, *Thomas Merton's Gethsemani: Landscapes of Paradise* (UPK, 2005), is reviewed in this volume.

Harry Wells is Associate Dean of the College of Arts, Humanities, and Social Sciences and Professor of Religious Studies at Humboldt State University. His research interest is inter-religious dialogue, specifically Buddhist-Christian Dialogue. A recent publication "Beyond the Usual Alternatives in Buddhist-Christian Dialogue: A Trinitarian Pluralist Approach" is in *Journal for Buddhist-Christians Studies*. Forthcoming are "The Fourfold Maras: Evil and the Removal of Obstacles in Buddhist Thought" and "Self and Salvation: Buddhist Perspectives on Enlightenment" in *Human Fault and Cosmic Fault Lines: Southeast Asian Concepts of Evil* (Mercer University Press, 2006).

John Wu, Jr. has frequently attended meetings of the International Thomas Merton Society. He also visited Thomas Merton at Gethsemani in the mid-1960s and has previously contributed to *The Merton Annual*.

Index

Murti, T.R.V. 287
Mussolini, Benito 235
Muste, A.J. 326
My Argument with the Gestapo
    222, 331
My Twenty Years With the Chinese
    303
Mycenaean 211
Mystics and Zen Masters 156

N

Nagasaki 31, 168
Nash, Roderick
    *Wilderness and the American
    Mind* 137
National Catholic Reporter 367
National Guard 33
National Security Agency 36
Nativity Kerygma 278
NATO 241
Natural Law 300
Nazareth 362
Nazi Germany 277
neo-Thomist 304
Nepal 260
The New Man 154
The New Yorker 129
New Directions 236
New Haven 356
New Jersey 144, 304
New Mexico 32, 33, 35
New Orleans 369
New Seeds of Contemplation 96,
    103, 105, 131, 149, 173, 272,
    331, 380, 382
New Testament 258
New World 115
New York 236
New York City 136, 299, 313, 314,
    318, 340, 342, 350
Nhat Hanh 331. *See also* Thich
    Nhat Hahn

St. Nicolas-aux-Bois 269
Ningpo 289
No Man is an Island 109, 379
Nobel peace prize 34
Noonan, John 61
Norris, Kathleen 386
North America 137, 166
North Atlantic Treaty Organiza-
    tion. *See* NATO
North Cascade mountains 388
North Vietnam 245
northern India 315, 322
Nouwen, Henri 10, 340, 342, 346,
    347, 349, 350, 353
    Adam 352
    With Burning Hearts 351
Nova Scotia 367
Novice Master 357
Nugent, Robert 122

O

Oakham 242
O'Connell, Patrick F. 11, 39, 41,
    178
O'Connell, Patrick F., ed.
    Cassian and the Fathers 376, 377
O'Connor, Flannery
    Wise Blood 28
Oedipus 214
Ohio 355, 360
Okamura, Mihoko 288
Orbis Books 32, 350
Order of the Cistercians of the
    Strict Observance 318
Orient Express 194, 197
Original Child Bomb 121
Oseam Hermitage 315
Oshun 116. *See* Yoruba Orisishas:
    Oshun
Ottaviani, Alfred 55, 238, 239
Our Lady of the Angels 267
Owen, Wilfred 222
Ox-searching Hall 333

512